"In the 21st century, corporate survival will depend on how well vast amounts of data are mined. Berry and Linoff lead the reader down an enlightened path of best practices."

—*Dr. Jim Goodnight, President and Co-Founder SAS Institute Inc.*

"Data mining will be essential for understanding customer behavior on the Web and for helping the websites of the world create their personalized responses. In a sense, data mining recently 'got the order' to become one of the key ingredients of e-commerce. Now all of us need to understand and use data mining. In *Mastering Data Mining*, Berry and Linoff show the industry how to think about data mining: start with natural activities of data mining, show their obvious and compelling value, and then only talk about the component tools at the very end. This is a great book, and it will be in my stack of four or five essential resources for my professional work."

—*Ralph Kimball, Author of* The Data Warehouse Lifecycle Toolkit

"This book does two really important things. It addresses data mining at a practical level and it bridges the gap between the business world and the world of data mining. All too often data miners have forgotten that if at the end of the day they do not show business relevance to the work they are doing, then they are building pie in the sky. Berry and Linoff do not make this most fundamental of mistakes. If you have any interest in the topic at all, this book is a must."

—*Bill Inmon, Author of* Building the Data Warehouse, Second Edition

Mastering Data Mining
The Art and Science of Customer Relationship Management

Michael J. A. Berry

Gordon Linoff

Wiley Computer Publishing

John Wiley & Sons, Inc.

NEW YORK · CHICHESTER · WEINHEIM · BRISBANE · SINGAPORE · TORONTO

Publisher: Robert Ipsen
Editor: Robert M. Elliott
Managing Editor: Brian Snapp
Associate New Media Editor: Mike Sosa
Text Design & Composition: Benchmark Productions, Inc.

Designations used by companies to distinguish their products are often claimed as trademarks. In all instances where John Wiley & Sons, Inc., is aware of a claim, the product names appear in initial capital or ALL CAPITAL LETTERS. Readers, however, should contact the appropriate companies for more complete information regarding trademarks and registration.

This book is printed on acid-free paper. ∞

This publication is designed to provide accurate and authoritative information in regard to the subject matter covered. It is sold with the understanding that the publisher is not engaged in professional services. If professional advice or other expert assistance is required, the services of a competent professional person should be sought.

Library of Congress Cataloging-in-Publication Data:

ISBN 0471-33123-6

Printed in the United States of America.

10 9 8 7 6 5 4 3 2 1

CONTENTS

ACKNOWLEDGMENTS

In writing this book, we had all kinds of help from all kinds of people. We would like to single out a few of them for special thanks.

Our editor, Bob Elliott, first suggested a book of case studies and helped shape the final product.

Ronny Kohavi of Blue Martini and Ralph Kimball of Ralph Kimball Associates reviewed the manuscript for technical accuracy in their respective fields of expertise. Had we followed more of their advice, this book would have fewer errors.

In addition to our own work, this book builds on the work of other capable data miners including Alan Parker and Geoff Parker of Apower Solutions, Anne Milley of SAS Institute, and Bob Evans of R.R. Donnelley & Sons. We also benefited from many discussions with knowledgeable colleagues including Dorian Pyle, Herb Edelstein, Bill Inmon, and Erik Thomsen. Our understanding of the role of data mining in society has benefited from conversations with Esther Dyson and Nolan Bowie, among others.

We are indebted to several vendors of data mining tools who provided us with software, training, and access to designers and developers. We would like to thank Cliff Brunk, Brad Fiery, Peter Maysek, Marc Ondrechen, Lorna Lusic, Manuel Hoffman, Aydin Senkut, and Mario Schkolnick of SGI for making sure we had what we needed to use MineSet successfully for many of the projects described in this book. At SAS Institute we want to acknowledge Will Potts who taught us much of what we know about neural networks as well as Herbert Kirk, Anne Milley, Austin Tripensee, Padraic Neville, Mark Brown, Rich Rovner, and Bruce Brown who all helped us to become successful users of Enterprise Miner. Charlie Berger of Thinking Machines provided us with information and access to Darwin software. Debra Daily and Ken Elliott of SPSS provided us with information and access to Clementine software. Ken Ono and Eric Apps of Angoss provided information and access to Knowledge Studio software. Cliff Lasser, Craig Stanfill, Marie Campbell, Sheryl Handler and Paul Bay of Ab Initio provided information and access to their dataflow software. Beth Maerz, Brett McTammany, Susan Ellis and Tatyana Kofman of Tessera Enterprise Systems provided us with information on the Rapid Modeling Environment. Rob Utzschneider, Paul Guerin, and Katherine Engelke of Torrent Systems provided information on Orchestrate. Peter Adams, David Sabel, and Matt Grosso provided information on e-commerce and their company, Primary Knowledge. Several of our projects took place at the DSS Lab of DST/Condor where we would like to acknowledge Erik Thomsen, George Spofford, and Barry Grushkin.

And, of course, we would like to thank our clients without whose fascinating business problems there would be nothing to write about. Over the last several years we have been privileged to work with many exciting corporations including NCC, Wells Fargo, Banco Velox, Huntington Bank, American Express, Customer Analytics, Cogit Corporation, Blue Martini, SK Telecom, MCI/WorldCom, SkyTel, BellSouth, Vermont Country Stores, WAM!Net, Liberty Mutual, and John Hancock—not to mention a number that prefer not to be.

Finally, we offer special thanks to the following individuals:

Abhay Mehta
Al Fan
Anjana Pursnani
Anne M. Grim
Anthony Cote
Ben Swanson
Bill Walsh
Brian Guscott
Clark Abrahams
Dave Trevorrow
David Anderson
Ed Zyszkowski
Elly Pieper
Eric Williams
Erin McCarthy
Evangelos Simoudis
Greg James
Injung Hwang
Jason Mallen
Jim Bell
Jim Stitzlein

Joan Forrester
Judy Barden
Larry Shaw
Lounette Dyer
Mary Bohannon
Mayank Prakash
Mike Wade
Miles Adams
Rebekah Peterson
Ruy Cardoso
Sabine Shea
Sandra Batra
Sheridan Young
Steve Mohan
Sue Osterfeld
Su Yoon
Ted Browne
Thulasiram Kesavan
Vandy Johnson
Youngho Oh

Michael and I have been very impressed by the response to our first book, *Data Mining Techniques for Marketing, Sales, and Customer Support* (John Wiley & Sons, 1997) and the positive feedback that we received from many readers. We succeeded in our intention to write a comprehensive and comprehensible introduction to data mining.

Since writing *Data Mining Techniques*, much as changed. We have now founded our own company, Data Miners, so we can focus exclusively on data mining. Data Miners is dedicated to a vision of data mining that puts as much emphasis on *understanding* as it does on model results, and as much emphasis on *process* as it does on technology.

For those readers who have not had the experience, leaving the regularity of a paycheck to work independently is, shall I say, a fascinating and sometimes traumatic experience. It has given us the opportunity to learn first-hand about business and the business problems facing our clients; about different approaches to allocating budgets and choosing vendors; and so on. It has also given us the opportunity to partner with the leading data mining vendors, and to work with some of the top people in the field.

As our families and friends have asked us on more than one occasion, why would we take time out to work on a second book? The answer is simply that *Mastering Data Mining* needed to be written. The field of data mining has been changing rapidly over the past few years, and we want to address the needs of practitioners, on both the business and the technical sides.

To see how quickly the data mining market is evolving, we have only to look to the business pages. During the time it took to write this book, we witnessed a number of mergers and acquisitions that spoke eloquently of the burgeoning role for data mining in customer relationship management and e-commerce:

- The world's largest privately held software company, SAS Institute, had its most successful product introduction ever—a data mining package. We used to joke that "statistics is everything in the SAS library and data mining is everything else." By that definition, data mining has now ceased to exist!
- The closest competitor to SAS in the analytical software market, SPSS, acquired a leading data mining package, further legitimizing what just a few years ago was on the fringes or respectability.

- DoubleClick,, the largest seller of advertising on the World Wide Web bought Abacus, a company that specializes in using catalog data to build predictive models.

The signs are easy to read—whatever the problem, data mining is becoming part of the solution. Done well, data mining can indeed solve many problems, but doing it well requires understanding the entire process. This understanding comes from both successes and failures of earlier projects. Each project is a learning experience. In this book, we take you through many of our own projects in order to share the lessons we have learned.

Mastering Data Mining addresses data mining in context. Part One looks at the business context. These four chapters answer questions such as: Why is data mining important? What is a successful approach to data mining? The last chapter in this set looks at customers and customer relationship management. Although data mining is applied through a myriad of fields, it is in the area of customer relationship management that it garners the most press.

Part Two of the book looks at data mining from a technical perspective. One chapter reviews data mining techniques (covered in much more detail in our earlier book). Another looks at data, and a third on good modeling practices. This chapter, in particular, is very important—it embodies many of the lessons that we have learned through the years.

Part Three is the most important—and the longest—part of the book. These are case studies in data mining. Although all the case studies are in business, they range over many facets, from the exploration of hundreds of gigabytes of data, to predicting the next banner ad to display to a Web banking customer, to improving the printing process. All the case studies discuss the relevant business problems, as well as showing the technical approach, the data used, the results (where possible), and lessons learned.

The final chapter looks at data mining in the broadest context—that of society. Data mining has underscored some of our fears of "big brother" and other threats to privacy. Michael and I tend to look at the benefits that data mining offers. However, it is important to understand the issue of privacy, particularly in the context of analyzing data.

Throughout the book, we have stressed practical applications of data mining. We hope that this book helps you master the art.

Setting the Focus

Part One of this book introduces data mining in the context of customer relationship management (CRM) in companies with large numbers of customers. This does not mean that data mining is not useful in other fields! Data mining is used in the pharmaceuticals industry to aid in drug design and to analyze data generated by high-throughput testing of chemical precursors for new drugs. It is used in law enforcement to find suspicious patterns of international funds transfer. It is used by both public and private insurers to uncover potential cases of fraud. Even in the marketing context, data mining is not restricted to business-to-consumer relationships. On the World Wide Web, which offers many opportunities for data mining, business-to-business e-commerce transactions outweigh direct-to-consumer transactions, at least as measured by dollar amount.

Why then this focus on customer relationship management? There are three different (though not uncorrelated) answers:

1. We have done most of our data mining work in the service of improved marketing, sales, and customer support for large corporations with millions of customers or prospects. We naturally find it easier to write about data mining in the context of our own work, and by doing so we can share the kinds of insights and lessons that are learned only through direct experience.

2. Customer-relationship management and its servants, database marketing, customization, and individualization, have been responsible for the sudden surge of popular interest in what were once obscure and academic data mining techniques. These are the applications that have grabbed the attention of both the press and the investment community.

3. These are the data mining applications that touch each and every one of us directly. No matter what our profession, we are all consumers. Every time we make a telephone call, use a credit card, click through an ad, or show a supermarket loyalty card, we are providing fodder to data miners. This personal connection with the data being mined makes it easier to understand the goals of the data mining exercises we present. It also helps make sense of the data transformations that are required to get good results.

For all these reasons, most of the case studies in this book are somehow tied to analyzing customer behavior. The first chapter, *Data Mining in Context*, supplies a bit of historical background for the current explosion in both data and data mining and examines the current data mining environment from three viewpoints—business, technical, and societal.

The second chapter, *Why Master the Art?*, addresses the need for companies that are serious about organizing their business around their customers to develop a core competency in data mining and why it is not sufficient simply to purchase scores of prebuilt models or to rely on outside experts.

Chapter 3, *Data Mining Methodology: The Virtuous Cycle Revisited*, revisits the data mining methodology introduced in our earlier book and examines the assumptions that must hold true in order for data mining to be successful. This chapter describes in general terms the procedures that are described in detail during the course of the case studies.

Chapter 4, *Customers and Their Lifecycles*, introduces two kinds of customer lifecycles—the lifecycle that we all share as human beings and the lifecycle of a customer's relationship with a firm. This latter lifecycle determines the business goals that can be supported by data mining and the kinds of data available to be mined.

CHAPTER 1

Data Mining in Context

To say that the past century saw rapid change is both a cliché and an understatement. Although the rapid pace of change was felt in nearly every area, it is hard to find examples of anything, anywhere that has changed as fast as the quantity of stored information. This information explosion has created new opportunities and new headaches in every field, from manufacturing to medicine to marketing. To appreciate just how fast the world's store of information has grown in recent years, it is instructive to compare it against some of the standard benchmarks of the twentieth century.

In 1900, the world population (another area where growth has frequently been described as "explosive") was 1.6 billion. A hundred years later, the population topped 6 billion. So, the population explosion caused the number of people living on Earth to increase by a factor of 3.75 over the course of the century.

In 1906, the Stanley twins, Francis and Freelan, established a world land speed record of 122 miles per hour with their Stanley Steamer. The land speed record was, of course, the only one that counted; 15 miles per hour was a pretty good speed for a ship and airplanes had only been in the air for three years, so they were in no position to challenge the speed record. On their journey to the moon 63 years later, the Apollo astronauts traveled at nearly 25,000 miles per hour—223 times as fast.

The trip to the moon provides another yardstick. In 1900, the longest journey one could reasonably make was 25,000 miles—the distance required to circumnavigate the globe. The round trip distance to the moon is 19 times as far.

Impressive numbers all, but nothing compared to the growth in corporate data. At the beginning of the twentieth century, or even at its midpoint, no company had more than a few tens of megabytes of data lying around in company ledgers, order books, and file cabinets. Today, the largest corporate databases are measured in terabytes. For these organizations, corporate data has grown by a factor of 100,000. This comparison (like all the size comparisons in this book) is made on the basis of text and numbers alone. Video and audio recordings take up huge amounts of storage, and are very interesting in their own right, but the data mining techniques that we discuss cannot yet easily be applied to them.

WARNING

Comparing data sizes is a tricky business. This is especially true when we get away from structured data such as the records in a database and into areas like music or photography. How large is a picture? That depends on the method of encoding it, the resolution of the image, the amount of data compression, and so on. Even comparisons of structured, relational databases can be misleading. Should we count the space used for indexes? What about the disk required for scratch space? Vendors sometimes report the total disk capacity of the database server instead of the actual size of the database in order to come up with a more impressive number. The data size comparisons in this chapter are based on the actual space required to store uncompressed text with no illustrations or indexes.

How large are today's databases? A comparison is instructive: From the time, over five thousand years ago, when some Sumerian took a reed to a clay table to scratch out the world's oldest known shopping list, an awful lot has been written. The Library of Congress contains 17 million books (and millions more manuscripts, maps, works of art, etc.). If each of those books were the same size as this one—about a megabyte of text in MS Word format—then the world's largest compendium of human knowledge, if typed into a computer database, would consume about 17 terabytes of disk space. As it happens, 17 terabytes is also the size of the package-level detail database used to track shipments at UPS.

In other words, a single company has as much data on where and when its customers are shipping packages as is contained in all the books in the Library of Congress. It seems incredible, but it is a natural consequence of increasingly automated operations. When every bar-coded package is scanned several times in transit, it doesn't take long to build up a lot of records—especially when you ship millions of packages every day. The same is true of manufacturing processes that are run by statistical controls based on readings from thousands of sensors, or telephone systems that keep track of time, duration, and network routing for every call.

For the most part, this data is not being collected so that it can be analyzed or used for predictive modeling; it is being collected to improve the efficiency of underlying operations. Once collected, however, it represents a wealth of information that can be used to improve business decision-making in every area, including the one that is the primary focus of this book: customer relationship management.

As more and more commerce moves onto the Web, the volume of data collected and the need for analysis are both increasing dramatically. The volume increases because e-commerce Web sites can keep track of much more than orders: every link followed and every item viewed is noted in the log. The need for analysis increases because these slender electronic traces are all the e-business has to go on when trying to form lasting, profitable relationships with customers who may be anywhere on earth and are free to switch to another supplier at the click of a mouse. Turning millions of transaction records from Web log files, call detail databases, or point-of-sale devices into recognizable portraits of consumers or business-to-business customers requires art and science, mathematics and intuition.

Data miners—the people who apply this potent mixture of massive computing power, clever algorithms, business knowledge, and human intuition—do not ply their trade in a vacuum. This chapter attempts to put data mining in its proper context by showing how it relates to business processes, information technology, and the wider world.

What Is Data Mining?

In our earlier book, *Data Mining Techniques for Marketing, Sales and Customer Support* (1997, John Wiley & Sons), we gave the following definition:

> Data mining is the process of exploration and analysis, by automatic or semi-automatic means, of large quantities of data in order to discover meaningful patterns and rules.

Revisiting that definition a few years later, we find that, for the most part, it stands up pretty well. We like the emphasis on large quantities of data, since data volumes continue to increase. We like the notion that the patterns and rules to be found ought to be *meaningful*. If there is anything we regret, it is the phrase "by automatic or semi-automatic means." Not because it is untrue—without automation it would be impossible to mine the huge quantities of data being generated today—but because we feel there has come to be too much focus on the automatic techniques and not enough on the exploration and analysis. This has misled many people into believing that data mining is a product that can be bought rather than a discipline that must be mastered. In this book, although we discuss algorithms and techniques when necessary, we put the focus back where it belongs: the data mining *process*. But before we can discuss process, we need to establish a common understanding of what data mining is and how it can be used. For readers of our earlier book, this will be review.

What Can Data Mining Do?

The term data mining is often thrown around rather loosely. In this book, we use the term for a specific set of activities, all of which involve extracting meaningful new information from the data. The six activities are:

- Classification
- Estimation
- Prediction
- Affinity grouping or association rules
- Clustering
- Description and visualization

The first three tasks—classification, estimation, and prediction—are all examples of *directed* data mining. In directed data mining, the goal is to use the available data to build a model that describes one particular variable of interest in terms of the rest of the available data. The next three tasks are examples of *undirected* data mining. In undirected data mining, no variable is singled out as the target; the goal is to establish some relationship among all the variables.

Classification

Classification consists of examining the features of a newly presented object and assigning to it a predefined class. For our purposes, the objects to be classified are generally represented by records in a database. The act of classification consists of updating each record by filling in a field with a class code.

The classification task is characterized by a well-defined definition of the classes, and a training set consisting of preclassified examples. The task is to build a model that can be applied to unclassified data in order to classify it. Examples of classification tasks include:

- Assigning keywords to articles as they come in off the news wire.
- Classifying credit applicants as low, medium, or high risk.
- Determining which home telephone lines are used for Internet access.
- Assigning customers to predefined customer segments.

In all of these examples, there are a limited number of already-known classes and we expect to be able to assign any record into one or another of them.

Estimation

Classification deals with discrete outcomes: yes or no, debit card, mortgage, or car loan. Estimation deals with continuously valued outcomes. Given some input data, we use estimation to come up with a value for some unknown continuous variable such as income, height, or credit card balance.

In practice, estimation is often used to perform a classification task. A bank trying to decide to whom they should offer a home equity loan might run all its customers through a model that gives them each a score, such as a number between 0 and 1. This is actually an estimate of the probability that the person will respond positively to an offer. This approach has the great advantage that the individual records may now be rank ordered from most likely to least likely to respond. The classification task now comes down to establishing a threshold score. Anyone with a score greater than or equal to the threshold will receive the offer.

Other classification tasks can also be recast as estimation tasks. For instance, churn modeling—figuring out which customers are likely to stop being customers (*churn*)—may be viewed as classifying people as likely or unlikely to churn, or it may be viewed as estimating the length of time that a customer will stay.

Other examples of estimation tasks include:

- Estimating the number of children in a family.
- Estimating a family's total household income.
- Estimating the value of a piece of real estate.

Often, classification and estimation are used together, as when data mining is used to predict who is likely to respond to a credit card balance transfer offer and also to estimate the size of the balance to be transferred.

Prediction

Arguably, there should not be a separate heading for prediction. Any prediction can be thought of as classification or estimation. The difference is one of emphasis. When data mining is used to classify a phone line as primarily used for Internet access or a credit card transaction as fraudulent, we do not expect to be able to go back later to see if the classification was correct. Our classification may be correct or incorrect, but the uncertainty is due only to incomplete knowledge: out in the real world, the relevant actions have already taken place. The phone is or is not used primarily to dial the local ISP. The credit card transaction is or is not fraudulent. With enough effort, it is possible to check. Predictive tasks feel different because the records are classified according to some predicted future behavior or estimated future value. With prediction, the only way to check the accuracy of the classification is to wait and see.

Examples of prediction tasks include:

- Predicting the size of the balance that will be transferred if a credit card prospect accepts a balance transfer offer.
- Predicting which customers will leave within the next six months.
- Predicting which telephone subscribers will order a value-added service such as three-way calling or voice mail.

Any of the techniques used for classification and estimation can be adapted for use in prediction by using training examples where the value of the variable to be predicted is already known, along with historical data for those examples. The historical data is used to build a model that explains the current observed behavior. When this model is applied to current inputs, the result is a prediction of future behavior.

Affinity Grouping or Association Rules

The task of affinity grouping is to determine which things go together. The prototypical example is determining what things go together in a shopping cart at the supermarket. Retail chains can use affinity grouping to plan arrangement of items on store shelves or in a catalog so that items often purchased together will be seen together. Affinity grouping can also be used to identify cross-selling opportunities and to design attractive packages or groupings of products and services.

Clustering

Clustering is the task of segmenting a diverse group into a number of more similar subgroups or clusters. What distinguishes clustering from classification is that clustering does not rely on predefined classes.

In clustering, there are no predefined classes and no examples. The records are grouped together on the basis of self-similarity. It is up to the miner to determine what meaning, if any, to attach to the resulting clusters. A particular cluster of symptoms might indicate a particular disease. Dissimilar clusters of video and music purchases might indicate membership in different subcultures.

Clustering is often done as a prelude to some other form of data mining or modeling. For example, clustering might be the first step in a market segmentation effort. Instead of trying to come up with a one-size-fits-all rule for "what kind of promotion do customers respond to best," first divide the customer base into clusters or people with similar buying habits, and then ask what kind of promotion works best for each cluster.

Description and Visualization

Sometimes the purpose of data mining is simply to describe what is going on in a complicated database in a way that increases our understanding of the people, products, or processes that produced the data in the first place. A good enough description of a behavior will often suggest an explanation for it as well. At the very least, a good description suggests where to start looking for an explanation. The famous gender gap in American politics is an example of how a simple description, "women support Democrats in greater numbers than do men," can provoke large amounts of interest and further study on the part of journalists, sociologists, economists, and political scientists, not to mention candidates for public office.

Data visualization is one powerful form of descriptive data mining. It is not always easy to come up with meaningful visualizations, but the right picture really can be worth a thousand association rules since human beings are extremely practiced at extracting meaning from visual scenes.

The Business Context for Data Mining

Data mining—extracting meaningful patterns and rules from large quantities of information—is clearly useful in any field where there are large quantities of data and something worth learning. We would not be surprised to learn, for example, that military intelligence organizations use data mining techniques to process large quantities of satellite imagery in an attempt to classify things on the ground as tanks or tractors—targets or public relations disasters in the making.

In the business context, the same rule applies: Data mining is useful wherever there are large quantities of data and something worth learning. In business, there is an explicit definition of what it means for a thing to be worth learning. For a business, something is worth learning if the resulting knowledge is worth more money than it costs to discover. Actually, the definition is even stricter than that: Something is worth knowing if the return on the investment required to learn it is greater than the return from investing the same funds some other way.

In academia, knowledge is considered to have intrinsic value quite apart from any application. In the business context however, knowledge can be valuable in two ways: It can increase profit by *lowering cost*, or it can increase profit by *raising revenue*. Actually, there is a third way: it can increase the stock price by holding out the promise of *future* increased profit via either of these mechanisms.

Data Mining as a Research Tool

One way that data mining can lower costs is at the very beginning of the product lifecycle, during research and development. The pharmaceuticals industry provides a good example. This industry is characterized by very high R&D costs. Globally, the industry spends $13 billion a year on research and development of prescription drugs. At the risk of oversimplifying a very complex business, the drug development process is like a large funnel with millions of chemical compounds going in the wide end and only a few safe and useful drugs emerging at the narrow spout.

To make it through the funnel a potential drug must first be found to bind with the correct target molecule. Those that do are called *leads*. Next, the lead must be shown to have some desired effect in the test tube—those that show no effect are discarded. Next the lead must be shown to be capable of being absorbed by the body and surviving in the complex and hostile environment of a living organism—those that are not absorbed are discarded. Then the lead must be shown to be nontoxic and to have some useful effect in animal trials—those that are toxic or useless are discarded. Finally, the lead must go through a series of clinical trials to prove that it is safe and effective in humans. Very few candidate molecules make it through this whole process and become drugs—about one in ten thousand—at an average cost of $300 million.

There is certainly plenty of data on which predictions might be based. Modern pharmaceutical laboratories employ a technique called high-throughput screening (HTS) to select candidate drugs. Automated systems perform combinatorial chemistry to create a wide variety of organic molecules from a small set of known reagents. These molecules are then screened by exotic robots that manipulate special plates containing dozens of cavities that hold chemical solutions with the target receptor molecule. These robots can recognize when a molecule binds to the target receptor. Molecules that bind to the target receptor, but not to similar ones, are likely leads.

All this automated testing yields data that is perfect for data mining—many input variables and a simple yes/no output variable. The pharmaceutical companies use sophisticated prediction techniques to determine which chemicals are likely (or highly unlikely) to produce useful drugs. By focusing the research on the appropriate chemicals (or not doing the research on unlikely chemicals), these companies can save millions and millions of dollars.

An entire discipline of *bioinformatics* has grown up to mine and interpret the data being generated by high throughput screening and other frontiers of biology such as the mapping of the entire human genetic sequence.

Data Mining for Process Improvement

Another area where data mining can be profitably employed to save money is manufacturing. Many modern manufacturing processes from chip fabrication to brewing are controlled using statistical process control. Sensors keep track of pressure, temperature, speed, color, humidity, and whatever other variables are appropriate to a particular process. Computer programs watch over the output from these sensors and order slight adjustments to keep the readings within the proper bounds. But what *are* the proper bounds? There are so many complex interactions between the variables that even expert human operators often cannot be sure.

The consequence of a problem in the manufacturing process is often a ruined batch of product and a very costly shutdown and restart of the process. Once again, the data produced by automated manufacturing systems is perfect for data mining: huge volumes of input, consisting of precisely measured values for scores or hundreds of variables and a few simple outputs like "good" and "bad." In Chapter 14 there are two case studies of data mining in the commercial printing industry where millions of dollars were saved by using data mining techniques to generate process control rules.

Data Mining for Marketing

Many of the most successful applications of data mining are in the marketing arena, especially in the area known as database marketing. In this world, data mining is used in both the cost term and the revenue term of the profit equation. In database marketing, the database refers to a collection of data on prospective targets of a marketing campaign. Depending on the situation, this data may be detailed behavioral data on existing customers culled from operational systems such as order tracking systems, billing systems, point-of-sale systems, etc. Or it may be rudimentary information of the kind that, for a fee, is readily available on every U.S. household and, to a lesser extent, on households in other countries as well.

 Data mining can be used to cut marketing costs by eliminating calls and letters to people who are very unlikely to respond to an offer. For example, the AARP (formerly, the American Association of Retired People, now an allegedly meaningless acronym) saved millions of dollars by excluding the 10 percent of eligible households who were judged least likely to become members. On the revenue side, data mining can be used to spot the most valuable prospects, those likely to buy the highest insurance coverage amounts or the most expensive, high-margin automobiles. Since much of the authors' experience is in this area, this book is full of examples of data mining used to improve the targeting of marketing campaigns.

Data Mining for Customer Relationship Management

The phrase "customer relationship management" seems to be on the lips of every chief executive and management consultant these days. The term has come to embody much of what used to be called one-to-one marketing, along with ideas about sales force automation and customization. Good customer relationship management means presenting a single image of the company across all the many channels a customer may use to interact with the firm, and keeping a single image of the customer that is shared across the enterprise. Good customer relationship management requires understanding who customers are and what they like and don't like. It means anticipating their needs and addressing them proactively. It means recognizing when they are unhappy and doing something about it before they get fed up and go to a competitor.

Data mining plays a leading role in every facet of customer relationship management. Only through the application of data mining techniques can a large enterprise hope to turn the myriad records in its customer databases into some sort of coherent picture of its customers. In Chapter 2, we see how data mining allows a corporation to *learn* from all the observations of customer behavior that are stored in the customer information warehouse that serves as the corporate memory. In Chapter 4 we trace the customer lifecycle from before the prospect becomes a customer until after the customer has left, and show how data mining can be applied to improve customer relationship management at every point along the way.

The Technical Context for Data Mining

In the second part of this book, we will be looking at the technical context of data mining. This context has three main areas:

1. Algorithms and techniques
2. Data
3. Modeling practices

The field that has come to be called *data mining* has grown from several antecedents. On the academic side are machine learning and statistics. Machine learning has contributed important algorithms for recognizing patterns in data. Machine-learning researchers are on the bleeding edge, conjuring ideas about how to make computers think. Statistics is another important area that provides background for data mining. Statisticians offer mathematical rigor; not only do they understand the algorithms, they understand the best practices in modeling and experimental design.

The final thread is decision support. Over the past few decades, people have been gathering data into databases to make better informed decisions. Data mining is a natural extension of this effort.

Data Mining and Machine Learning

The machine learning people come from the computer science and artificial intelligence worlds. They have focused their efforts on getting computers to display intelligence. In particular, the machine learning community is interested in writing computer programs that are capable of learning by example. The first kind of learning manifests itself by a newfound ability to perform some task such as balancing a broom handle or recognizing written characters. In other cases the new learning is expressed as rules that have been induced from the examples. Neural networks have proved to be very successful at the first kind of learning and decision trees have proved to be very successful at the second.

The term data mining, in its present, nonpejorative sense, was first used by people who took the methods of the machine learning and began to apply them to fields outside of computer science and artificial intelligence (AI)—fields such as industrial process control and direct marketing. This search for practical applications was probably encouraged by the collapse of funding for artificial intelligence research in the early 1980s when the over-ambitious claims from the 1960s and 1970s (machine translation, natural language recognition) failed to materialize. The choice of the term *data mining* for the new, business-oriented applications of AI research shows how little overlap there was between this group and the statisticians, actuaries, and economists who had long been doing predictive modeling. For the latter group, the term "data mining" meant searching for data to support a particular point of view rather than letting the facts speak for themselves. The data miners were smart people getting good results, but they were not mathematicians.

Data Mining and Statistics

Statistics has been another important thread that has supported data mining. For centuries, people have used statistical techniques to understand the natural world. These have included predictive algorithms (which statisticians call *regression*), sampling methodologies, and experimental design. Now, they are applying these techniques to the business world.

For years, the work done by the machine learning researchers worked in practice but had a very limited foundation theoretically. The machine learning folks preferred anthropomorphic terminology and allusions to the biological sciences to rigorous mathematical proofs. Statisticians, who are by nature much more comfortable with numbers, were not impressed by this approach.

Data Mining and Decision Support

Decision support is a broad term for the entire information technology infrastructure that companies and other organizations use to make informed decisions. The term covers both relational and dimensional databases used for decision support. Decision support systems contrast with online transaction processing systems (OLTP). OLTP databases are designed to process large numbers of transactions very fast. In database terminology, a transaction is a complete action that must either finish successfully or appear not to have happened. For example, transferring money from your savings account to your checking account at an ATM machine is a single transaction. It would not be acceptable for this transaction to be interrupted in the middle after your savings account has been debited but before your checking account has been credited. OLTP databases are designed to ensure the sanctity of such transactions and to allow very efficient access to single records, such as one customer's account balance—or room reservation, or airline seat assignment, or last payment.

Decision support databases have very different requirements. In decision support, it is rarely useful to look at individual records. Decision support databases are designed to support complex queries such as "Which customers spent more than $100 at a restaurant more than 100 miles from home in two of the last three months?" To answer this question, you need to be able to translate each customer's address into geographic coordinates (using the centroid of the zip code is sufficient) and do the same for the restaurants before beginning to aggregate the charges.

It turns out that the design requirements for the two types of database are so incompatible that the same information must often be stored at least twice—once in an operational system that takes care of transactions and once in a decision support system where the historical record can be studied.

Data Warehouses

A special case of a decision support database is the *data warehouse*. A data warehouse is a large decision support database fed by many operational systems. Data warehouses are motivated by the need to view the entire enterprise from a single point of view instead of as a collection of narrowly defined "silos." On its way into the warehouse, data from the operational systems is cleaned and transformed so that database fields from disparate sources share the same definitions.

A data warehouse sounds like a great resource for data mining, and in some cases it is, but all too often the transformations applied to the incoming data destroy valuable information. Data warehouses are often *normalized*, so they have the property that any given item of information is stored exactly once. This is very efficient for storing large amounts of data. However, it often requires "killer queries" to access data of interest.

Of particular concern is aggregation and summarization. Although it is increasingly common for data warehouses to store atomic data, and indeed, some warehouses are now designed with data mining in mind, we still run across many data warehouses that contain only summaries of historical data. For instance, a data warehouse may store the monthly balances on a credit card, but may not include the individual transactions. In the past, data warehouses have been designed for reporting, not for mining. Data mining requires access to data at a detailed level because that is where the most interesting patterns are discovered. This is not to say that the inputs to data mining models cannot be summarized; they often are. It is just that the aggregations performed by the data miner may not have been anticipated by a warehouse designer.

Data warehouses often focus on the customer level—a useful and appropriate focus. However, the focus on customers often requires summarizing more detailed data, such as call records, line item detail, or individual banking transactions. Even if the detailed data is supposed to be available in the warehouse, accessing a normalized set of tables requires "killer queries" that never get run for practical reasons. When the data is organized in a "star schema" as advocated by Ralph Kimball in his excellent books on data warehouse design, the response time may be better. These star-schema databases are discussed in the following section.

OLAP, Data Marts, and Multidimensional Databases

Another common type of decision support database is the data mart designed for online analytical processing (OLAP). Data marts address a weakness of normalized data warehouses, which is that in their desire to represent a holistic view of an entire enterprise, they insist on centralizing the implementation, which may add months or years to the project.

OLAP databases for decision support offer improved speed and responsiveness by limiting themselves to a single view of the data. Typically, this point of view is that of the department that owns the database. OLAP databases are organized along the different *dimensions* of the business such as time, product type, and geography, allowing analysts to slice and dice data along them. This multidimensional structure is often called a *cube* (even when there are many more than three dimensions). Each dimension can, and usually does, have many levels of aggregation. In fact, a single dimension may have multiple hierarchies. So the geography dimension might be arranged into stores, cities, states, and countries, or into stores, sales regions, and countries, or both. Or the time dimensions may be organized into days, weeks, and years, or days, months, quarters, and years. An added complication is that the dimensions are not static. For example, many companies redraw their sales regions every time a new VP of sales comes along, if not more frequently. The structure chosen for a multidimensional database limits the kind of analysis we can perform. Often, a dimension of particular interest to us, the *customer dimension*, is entirely absent!

When a multidimensional database is stored in a relational database system, the arrangement of the tables—one central fact table with many dimensional tables surrounding it—is called a *star schema*, or dimensional model. Such an arrangement is especially appropriate for a database that serves the interests of a particular department such as finance or marketing since it is easier to get agreement as to what are the central facts to be tracked and what dimensions would be useful for tracking them within a single department than across a larger enterprise. These specialized decision support databases are often called *data marts*. Sometimes a data warehouse is made up of a collection of data marts.

In this approach to data warehouse design, dimensional models are the basis for a style of incremental design of an enterprise data warehouse that is inherently distributed. The main challenge for the data warehouse teams building these distributed data marts is to establish what are called conformed dimensions and conformed facts so that the separate data marts will work together. For more on this topic, see Ralph Kimball, et al.'s book, *The Data Warehouse Lifecycle Toolkit* (Wiley, 1998). We discuss OLAP and multi-dimensional databases in more detail in Chapter 6.

Decision Support Fusion

To the business user, the distinctions between online analytic processing, data mining, and data visualization seem pointless. To make better decisions, management needs answers to all kinds of questions. Today, some of those questions ("How have widget sales changed quarter over quarter by sales rep and widget type?") are answered using OLAP. Other questions ("How are sales varying by geography and widget type?") are best understood through visualization—in this case, perhaps a map with different countries shown in relief with height representing total sales and color representing product mix. Another family of questions ("Which customers should receive the 96-page holiday catalog, and which should receive the 120-page catalog?") are best addressed through data mining.

The VP of Marketing wants answers of all three types of question, and probably does not understand why the answers have to come from three different software systems, quite possibly running on different computers and accessing slightly different data. We believe that the future will bring tighter integration of various decision support technologies such as data mining, OLAP, data warehousing, and visualization. Already, there are signs: The OLAP Council, an industry group, has changed its name to the Decision Support Council. Some data mining packages (SGI's MineSet is a notable example) include sophisticated visualization tools. As this book was being written, Oracle, the leading relational database vendor, announced the acquisition of the data mining business unit from Thinking Machines and of its Darwin data mining package. All of these demonstrate convergence in the market.

Data Mining and Computer Technology

Data mining requires complex calculations to be applied to vast quantities of data. Only a few years ago much of the work described in this book would not have been technically feasible within reasonable cost constraints. The incredible advances in computing power, price/performance, and data input and output speeds have made large-scale data mining practical and profitable. For the most part, computing technology remains behind the scenes in this book, but in a few cases where large collections of transactions are involved (as in the analysis of telephone call detail records discussed in Chapter 12) the need for parallel processing becomes explicit.

The Societal Context for Data Mining

Data mining as a technical activity and a business activity takes place against the background of rapidly changing societies that are having to adapt to new circumstances brought about by the information revolution. Authoritarian governments that could once "protect" their citizens from outside points of view are finding it very hard to control the Internet. On a more personal level, the authors can determine the number of volumes in the Library of Congress while sitting at home—or search the world for a favorite out-of-print book or vinyl record album that we might never have found in years of searching second-hand stores, and bid on it in an electronic auction.

On the down side, things that once seemed personal and private such as our taste in magazines, the groceries we buy, and even the drugs we are prescribed, are finding their way into databases. Even information that has long been a matter of public record—our real estate tax assessments, car registrations, marriage licenses, and birth announcements—seem a bit more public when they can readily be retrieved from an electronic database rather than copied by hand from a dusty ledger.

Data Mining and Individual Predictions

We often speak of using data mining to "predict who is likely to respond to an offer" or to "predict who is likely to cancel a subscription." Since people often feel they don't know themselves what they are likely to do next month or next year, this supposed ability to predict individual behavior imbues data mining with an unjustified aura of near-magical power. The fact is that, to take a typical application of data mining to direct marketing, *95 percent of the people picked by data mining to be likely responders to an offer will not respond.* In other words, at the level of individual consumers, *data mining predictions are nearly always wrong.* If this is a crystal ball, it is a pretty cloudy one!

The reason that data mining is valuable, despite being so very inaccurate, is that although only 5 percent of the people predicted to respond actually do so, that may be a significantly higher number than would have responded if no data mining model had been used. The ability of data mining to identify a population within which we can expect a 5 percent response rate, instead of the 2.5 percent response rate we could achieve without data mining, makes it worthwhile from a business point of view.

Unfortunately, it is awkward, when talking or writing about data mining, to lard every sentence with words like "overall response in the population" so, as shorthand, we speak of "finding responders" or "identifying churners." It may be comforting to readers who have no idea what kind of car they will buy when the current one dies to know that we don't either!

Since data mining is often portrayed—even by its practitioners—as a means of using this sort of information to predict what individual consumers will do before they even know themselves, it is not surprising that it is sometimes controversial. Actually, as described in the sidebar, data mining is not very good at targeting individuals for anything, but since we data miners have been so caught up in the rhetoric of individualization and one-to-one marketing, we can hardly blame the public for thinking that it is.

In a world where there is suddenly more information more readily available than ever before, data mining is bound to play an increasing role in helping both consumers and businesses find the signal—whatever it is they are really looking for—in all that noise. Along the way, many issues around privacy, ownership of data, and proper use will have to be addressed much more fully than they are today. We explore some of these issues in the final chapter of this book. In the next chapter, we start our journey toward mastering data mining by asking and addressing the question "why bother?"

CHAPTER 2

Why Master the Art?

In its infancy, any technology requires a great deal of specialized knowledge and experience on the part of its users. The history of photography provides an apt metaphor for that of data mining, which is still in its infancy. This chapter develops this metaphor and uses it to describe four methods of putting data mining to work for your company.

The pinhole camera or *camera obscura* has been known since at least the time of Leonardo da Vinci. For hundreds of years the ephemeral images projected on the wall of a darkened room were little more than curiosities that could be viewed only in real time. It wasn't until the 1830s that Louis Daguerre developed a method of capturing these fleeting images in a lasting form.

The first photographers could not simply take pictures; they had to be chemists as well. The creation of a single daguerreotype required hours of work—first a copper plate was exposed to iodine to form a thin layer of light-sensitive silver iodide. The exposed plate was then held over hot mercury, whose highly toxic fumes combined with the silver nitrite to produce a positive image directly on the plate. The plate was then rinsed in salt water to fix the image. The resulting pictures were so lifelike and so remarkably detailed that many contemporary observers believed that the new process would replace painting and other traditional art forms. In fact, the new process was described as a "self-operating process of fine art."[1]

---

1. See *A History of Photography* by Robert Leggat (www.kbnet.co.uk/rleggat/photo/).

The daguerreotype was a huge commercial and artistic success, but like the current crop of data mining tools, it hardly deserved to be called self-operating. The technique could be mastered only by skilled professionals or truly dedicated amateurs. The next 50 years saw a series of important improvements to photographic technology including negatives that allowed multiple prints to be made from the same exposure and more reactive emulsions that brought exposure times down from minutes to seconds. But it took George Eastman's introduction of the Kodak camera in 1888 to put photography into the hands of casual users. The Kodak camera was simple and portable. When its flexible film was exposed, the user sent the entire camera off for processing at the Kodak factory where it would be reloaded and returned along with the developed negatives and prints. The advertising slogan for the Kodak camera anticipates the message from many of today's data mining software companies: "You press the button, we do the rest."

By the twentieth century, anyone wishing to make a record of a fishing expedition or important family gathering could point an inexpensive, mass-produced camera at the subject, focus the lens, cock the shutter, and take a snapshot. After exposing a roll of film, the amateur would send it out for developing and printing. Only at this point would his or her mistakes become apparent. The photographer might forget to advance the film and end up with double exposures or misjudge the light and get a picture that was under- or over-exposed. The shutter speed might be too slow and blur the image of a fidgety child. The aperture might be too wide leading to insufficient depth of field. All those ruined snapshots put evolutionary pressure on the camera.

Today, cameras have become so smart that we do not have to think very much to take decent pictures. The auto-focus mechanism picks some element in the scene and adjusts the lens so that it is in perfect focus. A microprocessor determines a suitable combination of shutter speed and aperture after automatically sensing the light conditions and the speed of the film. Once the picture has been snapped, the film is automatically advanced to the next frame. Or perhaps, there is no film at all and the image is stored directly to disk in JPEG format. In short, much of the expertise formerly required of the photographer has now been embedded in the camera.

There is no denying that all this progress has made it much harder for amateur photographers to completely ruin their vacation snapshots, but what relation do these albums and shoe boxes full of 4-by-6 glossies bear to the powerful images displayed in the photography galleries of an art museum? Clearly, there is a trade-off between quality and automation. This is no less true of data mining than it is of photography. Of course, you do not have to be an Annie Leibovitz or Richard Avedon to take perfectly adequate pictures, and you do not have to become a full-time professional data miner to extract useful information from data. Most people are content to rely on the photographic expertise embodied in their cameras for day-to-day situations, only calling in an expert for special occasions. That's fine so long as we recognize that learning to change the battery in a point-and-click camera is not the same as mastering the art of photography!

Mastering the art of photography means understanding composition, becoming familiar with the tricks of light and shadow, understanding the uses of different filters, films, and papers, and learning the countless other elements of the craft that allow a photographer to tell stories with a single picture that could never be captured in the proverbial thousand words. Mastering data mining means learning how to get data to tell a true and useful story. There are now many tools to assist in the process and even some that claim to automate it. But, as in photography, study, practice, and apprenticeship will be rewarded with better results.

Four Approaches to Data Mining

There are essentially four ways to bring data mining expertise to bear on a company's business problems and opportunities:

1. By purchasing scores (see later) from outside vendors that are related to your business problem; analogous to using an automatic Polaroid camera.
2. By purchasing software that embodies data mining expertise directed towards a particular application such as credit approval, fraud detection, or churn prevention; analogous to purchasing a fully automated camera.
3. By hiring outside consultants to perform predictive modeling for you for special projects; analogous to hiring a wedding photographer.
4. By mastering data mining skills within your own organization; analogous to building your own darkroom and becoming a skilled photographer yourself.

There are plusses and minuses to each approach and, depending on the circumstances, we may recommend any of the four, or some combination, to our clients. The clear bias of this book, however, is toward those who want to at least consider option four as a long-term goal. The balance of this chapter examines each of the four approaches and explains why companies that want to put customer relationship management at the center of their business strategy should make data mining one of their firm's core competencies.

Purchasing Scores

Scores are a powerful mechanism for reducing complex judgments based on hundreds or thousands of factors to a single number that can be used to assign grades, rank applicants, and even, in the case of IQ scores, attempt to quantify human intelligence. Most predictive models are designed to produce scores. You can always buy or build such a model and use it to score your own data, but in many industries, someone has already built the models and scored the population for you.

These days, when a customer fills in a loan application at a U.S. bank, the loan officer is likely to run an instant credit check. One of the pieces of information that is returned is a FICO score for the applicant. FICO stands for Fair, Isaac & Company, the firm that pioneered the use of credit scoring. When scoring systems came out, many banks were sure that their loan officers could do a better job of spotting a good credit risk. Test after test, however, showed that the scores did a better job than experienced loan officers. Actually, the tool that Fair Isaacs introduced was not a score, but a model in the form of a score card. To use a score card, the bank officer asks the applicant a standard series of questions and the score is calculated from the answers. In the instant system, since the credit bureaus already know (or think they know) the answers to the questions the applicant would be asked, they can deliver the score without asking the questions.

As the example shows, one advantage of purchasing scores instead of building models is that it is quick and easy. On the other hand, much information is lost when all the information you have about something is squashed into a single number. Imagine trying to settle an argument about who was smarter, Shakespeare or Newton, by stepping into a time machine and giving them standard IQ tests. Even if their scores came out equal, it wouldn't prove much. If, however, we could examine their answers to each question, we might actually gain some insight into their genius. The test, like the score card, is a model and the model reveals much more than the score alone.

Purchasing Software

Data mining expertise can be embodied in software in one of two ways. The software may embody an actual *model*, perhaps in the form of a set of decision rules or a fully-trained neural network that can be applied directly to a particular problem domain. Or, it may embody knowledge of the *process* of building models appropriate to a particular domain in the form of a model-creation template or wizard of some kind.

Purchasing Models

The attraction of the first approach is clear—why spend tens of thousands of dollars on training or consultants if the problem you are faced with has already been solved? Thousands of companies face the same decisions yours does: Who should receive the next mailing? Who should be granted credit? Who is at risk for attrition? If data mining can produce predictive models to answer these questions, what is the point of reinventing the wheel? Shouldn't it be possible simply to purchase the answer?

The answer is a qualified "yes." It is certainly possible to purchase and apply models developed elsewhere. The qualification is that these will work well only to the extent that your products, your customers, and your market conditions match those that were used to develop the models in the first place. One area where these conditions are likely to be met is retail lending within a particular national market. Vendors such as Fair, Isaac & Company have been very successful developing models to asses the credit worthiness of loan applicants. The inputs to these models are facts that can be obtained from the credit application or initial interview combined with information available from a credit bureau. The output is a credit score. Numerous controlled studies have shown that credit decisions based on a score card of this kind are better than those made by loan officers based on their own intuitions and "rules of thumb."

The credit score card is an example of deploying a static model embedded in an application. This approach allows for a complete separation of the model building and scoring environments. This separation makes it easy to deploy the model in whatever computing environment customers happen to have. On the other hand, since the model is cut off from the model development software that created it, it cannot easily be modified to meet changing conditions. Worse, the model will not reflect any peculiarities of the local market in which it is deployed. The embedded model need not be static, however. There are examples of self-modifying or learning models that continue to evolve in the field as they adapt to changing circumstances. The sidebar on fraud detection describes an application for detecting credit card fraud that continuously adapts itself to the changing purchasing patterns of the credit card holders.

Applications designed to meet the needs of a particular industry are often called *vertical applications* because they attempt to cover every layer from data handling at the bottom to report generation at the top for a particular industry. Vertical applications trade off generality for ease-of-use by incorporating knowledge of a particular industry in the form of business rules, customized graphical user interfaces, and industry-specific vocabulary. A general-purpose data mining tool, on the other hand, is *horizontal*—it provides a set of tools with broad applicability to many problems but does not take advantage of any domain-specific knowledge.

Neural Net Models for Credit Card Fraud Detection

HNC, a company based in San Diego, California, has made a very successful business around embedded neural network models for predicting fraud in the credit and debit card industry. HNC's neural network models evaluate a large percentage of all credit card transactions before the transaction is allowed to complete. HNC's models are now also deployed in the wireless industry to spot fraudulent calls and in the insurance industry to spot fraudulent claims. The company has also moved beyond fraud detection with vertical applications for predicting profitability, attrition, and bankruptcy.

HNC's flagship product, Falcon, addresses credit card fraud. Since large issuers may lose as much as $10 million per year to fraud, there is strong demand for the product. According to the company, it is used by 16 of the top card issuing banks in the world.

Locating the few transactions among thousands that represent potential fraud losses is a difficult problem. Part of the difficulty is that false positives—transactions that are flagged as potentially fraudulent but turn out to be innocent—can be nearly as costly as false negatives because cardholders tend to get very annoyed when their legitimate transactions do not go through. Falcon works by modeling each cardholder's behavior and then comparing the current transaction with that customer's historical spending pattern. If the current transaction falls too far outside the customer's historical patterns, the software will flag it before it is allowed to complete.

In 1998, Falcon monitored over 250 million payment card accounts worldwide.

Will a Vertical Application Work for You?

When evaluating a vertical application with embedded data mining models, try to find out as much as possible about the assumptions under which the application was built and compare those assumptions to your own situation. Some questions you might ask include the following:

- Was the application developed under similar assumptions about competition? If not, response rates and retention rates are likely to follow very different patterns. For example, in a recently deregulated market for airline service, cable television, or telephone service, models that work for the incumbent former monopoly will not be germane to the new upstart providers and vice versa.

- Was the application developed with similar assumptions about pricing practices to those that apply in your market? For example, in the United States, cellular subscribers pay for both incoming and outgoing calls. This leads to very different calling patterns than one would expect to see in a market where only the outgoing calls are charged.

Specialized Software for Churn Management

Churn is the word used in the wireless industry for customers canceling their service, usually because they have replaced it with service from a competitor. Churn is a major concern for service providers in competitive markets. Not surprisingly, churn management for wireless telephone service providers is a vertical application for data mining that has attracted attention from a number of vendors. One of these, **Lightbridge of Waltham, MA**, sells a product called **Churn Prophet**. The product continually rescores the customer population for likelihood to churn using a model that is itself continually retrained as the determinants of churn change over time. Lightbridge's original product was also an embedded predictive model—an expert system for approving or rejecting applications for service based on predicted credit risk.

- Was the application developed in a similar regulatory environment? Auto insurance models built in Massachusetts will not be valid in New Jersey. Both states require any company writing insurance to cover pretty much anyone who comes through the door, but the specifics of what coverage must be offered and how rates are set are quite different.

- What assumptions does the application make about the number of customers to be scored? The number of products to be kept track of? The amount of historical data available? An application that works well for ten thousand customers may be completely unable to cope with ten million.

If you can determine that the application you are considering was developed using assumptions about the customers, products, transaction volumes, market conditions, and regulatory environment that match your own, there is a good chance that it will perform well for your company. If not, it is best to consider a more general-purpose solution even though it will require more effort to implement.

Purchasing Model-Building Software

Another way to embody data mining expertise in software is to supply model-building templates and wizards to guide novice model builders through the process of creating models based on their own data. Such tools automate the process of creating candidate models and selecting the ones that perform best, once the proper input and output variables have been identified. This approach solves one problem—the problem of using models that do not reflect local conditions—but it leaves other problems untouched. The biggest difficulty with this approach is that it is impossible to automate the most important parts of the data mining process—understanding the business

Integrating Data Mining with Customer Relationship Management Tools

One of the most popular vertical applications for embedded data mining is customer relationship management. Two companies with different approaches to this market are Quadstone and Customer Analytics. Quadstone, of Edinburgh, Scotland, sells a customer data analysis package called Decisionhouse that does many of the things that general-purpose data mining packages do (and does them quite well—Decisionhouse took third place in the 1998 KDD Cup, an annual data mining competition), but the user interface and reporting are geared to marketing people rather than quantitative analysts (see Figure 2.1). One of the clearest indications of the way Decisionhouse is positioned is its pricing structure. Users pay for the software based on the number of rows in their customer database.

A number of the more established campaign management software companies are also finding ways to integrate predictive models with their software. One example is Exchange Applications of Boston, MA. Their ValEx product can call models produced by SAS Enterprise Miner and other data mining tools as part of the query that defines a campaign segment.

A rather different approach is being tried by Customer Analytics of Burlington, MA. Customer Analytics integrates predictive models into its customer relationship management package for the financial services industry, but they don't expect the clients to develop the models themselves. Instead, the company uses its own library of predictive modeling templates to produce a corresponding library of predictive models for each customer. Each customer's models are based on their own data. The models are deployed as part of the application where they are used to score customers for propensity to purchase mutual funds, certificates of deposit, and other financial products as well as for loyalty and other indicators of customer value.

problem, preparing the data for modeling, creating derived variables to reveal latent information, and extracting actionable information from the results. As we will see in later chapters, there are all too many ways to create meaningless or nonsensical models—it is not only the problem of "garbage in, garbage out," although that maxim certainly holds. There are also problems, such as inadvertently exposing the model to future information, that can be quite difficult to spot and can lead to models that look good when built, but fail to live up to expectations when deployed.

On the other hand, there is certainly something to be said for taking some of the drudgery out of building predictive models. Though the ability of software products to create valid and useful models at the touch of a button has been

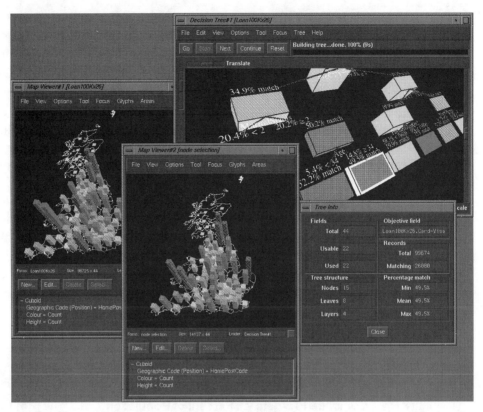

Figure 2.1 Screenshot from Quadstone Decisionhouse.

grossly oversold, an intelligent user interface with built-in knowledge of the problem domain can greatly simplify the process. One way that a problem-specific user interface can help is by making use of the normal vocabulary or jargon of the industry in question. To a professional data miner, any binary classification problem looks pretty much the same. The question might be whether or not to approve a credit application, whether or not to pay an insurance claim, or whether or not to place a particular name on an outbound tele-marketing call list, but the model takes the same basic form. The users, however, have different words for the inputs and outputs to these models, and addressing them in terms of "loss ratios" or "responders" as appropriate can make them feel more comfortable.

For example, the popular Model 1 product from Unica Technologies contains four modules, each of which addresses a particular direct marketing challenge. The four modules are called Response Modeler, Cross Seller, Customer Valuator, and Customer Segmenter. Each module is really just a graphical user interface layer over the same core routines along with a preconfigured approach to the particular problem. So, for example, the response modeler could actually be used for any binary outcome classification task for which there are training examples as long as the user is happy to refer to one class as "responders" and the other as "nonresponders."

One of the data mining tasks that Model One attempts to automate is experimenting with different data mining algorithms to see which one will get the best results for a particular data set. The tool generates a large number of models and displays the cumulative response charts for each on a single graph so that it is easy to pick out the best one. The graphs are updated dynamically as new models are built and tested with the current best model highlighted. This gives the user a pleasing sense that progress is being made. A similar automated search for models is provided by the Model Seeker wizard that is part of the Darwin product from Oracle (see Figure 2.2).

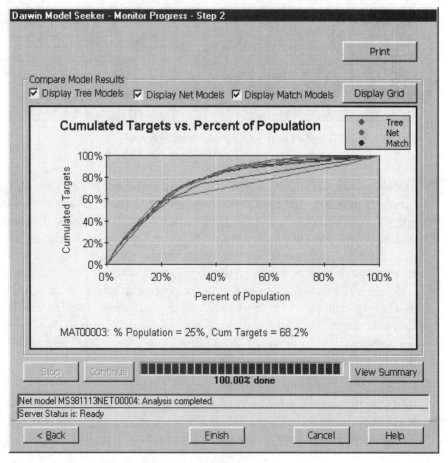

Figure 2.2   Darwin's Model Seeker wizard.

What Tools Can and Cannot Automate

Even the most modern, fully-automated camera can automate only what happens in the time between the moment the photographer's finger presses the button and the moment, a fraction of a second later, when the shutter closes with the new image captured on film. Although certainly helpful, this is a very small part of what goes into creating a satisfactory photograph. The camera has no control over the choice of subject matter, the composition of the shot, the lens, the type of film loaded, the lighting of the scene, the vantage point from which the picture is taken, or the lens filter used. Nor does it have any control over what will happen during the multistep transformation from film to negative and negative to print.

Even the decisions that the camera *does* make on its own, such as shutter speed, aperture, focal point, and whether to use a flash will be correct only if the assumptions used to program the camera match the intentions of the photographer. Consider how all of these automated decisions affect a typical sports action shot that a soccer mom might take at a local youth league match. To get the settings just right, the camera needs to understand the photographer's intentions:

- Does she want the whole team in focus, or just her own star player? This affects the aperture setting decision that will control the depth of field.

- Does she plan to pan with the motion of the player so that the fast-moving subject will be in focus against a blurred background, or does she want to freeze the action? This affects the shutter speed decision.

- Are there contrasting areas of dark and shadow in the scene? If so, does the photographer wish to reveal or conceal detail in the shadowed areas? This affects the decision to use flash.

The camera is programmed with some set of assumptions about the user's intentions. When all goes well, these assumptions are close enough to what the photographer had in mind so that the resulting pictures are satisfactory. When the assumptions are violated, the result is disappointment. A data mining tool or vertical application with embedded expertise has the same potential to please or disappoint depending on how well its assumptions match the actual requirements of the business. And, like the automatic camera, it can automate only the small portion of the data mining task that takes place between the time when the shot is set up—a modeling data set is assembled and ready to go—and the time when the model itself is built. It can do little about what comes before and after. As we will see in the next chapter, the actual building of models is only one stage in a continuous cycle of activities that make up the data mining process.

The automated tool does not address the activities that are analogous to setting up the shot, nor does it address the activities that are analogous to the work that goes on in the darkroom to enlarge, enhance, and reproduce the results. Among the activities *not* addressed by an automated tool are:

- Choosing a suitable business problem to be addressed by data mining.

- Identifying and collecting data that is likely to contain the information needed to answer the business question.

- Massaging and enhancing the data so that the information content is close to the surface where the data mining tool can make use of it.

- Transforming the database to be scored by the model so that the input variables needed by the model are available.

- Designing a plan of action based on the model and implementing it in the marketplace.

- Measuring the results of the actions and feeding them back into the database where they will be available for future mining.

The first three items are things that need to happen before any automated modeling can take place. The last three items are things that need to happen if the automatically created models are to be of lasting value. This does not mean that modeling wizards and the like are useless. Indeed, they can be very helpful. But, it is important to understand what they can and cannot do. The slogan "you press the button, we do the rest" is no more accurate for today's data mining tools than it was back when George Eastman used it to sell his cameras.

Hiring Outside Experts

If you are in the early stages of integrating data mining into your business processes, the judicious application of outside resources can be very valuable. Indeed, we have seen many cases where outside consulting has led to successful conclusions to projects that would almost certainly have failed without it. On the other hand, we have seen many organizations that are overly dependent on outside resources and are failing to get the full benefit of data mining because the data, the models, and even the insights generated by applying the latter to the former are in the hands of outsiders. The real question is not whether to use outside expertise, but how.

The answer will depend on many factors, including the answers to these questions:

1. Is the data mining activity meant to address a one-time problem or an on-going process?

2. What are the sources of the data to be analyzed?
3. How will the data mining results be employed?
4. What is the availability and skill level of your own analytic staff?

The answer to the first question determines how much emphasis you need to place on transferring data mining skills to your own organization. In Chapter 14 we will see an example of data mining used to solve a one-time problem in a manufacturing process. Here the transfer of information was mostly one-way—from the company with the problem to the data mining consultants who helped to fix it. More typically, data mining becomes part of an ongoing process such as customer relationship management. Under these circumstances, it is important not to get hooked forever on outside services. In Chapter 14 we will see two examples of companies using outside consulting to ease the introduction of data mining into their organizations.

The answer to the second question may determine whether you or the data vendor is more likely to have enough understanding of what the data actually means to make good use of it for data mining. If you are purchasing demographic overlays or other data with which you are not familiar, it is probably a good idea to purchase a small amount of consulting from the data vendor. We have worked with data from most of the major suppliers of household level data in the United States and we have found their data descriptions and documentation to be sorely lacking. We prefer not to speculate whether this is an intentional inducement to use their consulting services. Even when your own operational systems generate the data, if your organization has not used the data for analytic purposes in the past, it may be beneficial to bring in someone who is familiar with your industry and the ways that data similar to yours has been successfully exploited in the past.

Data mining results are useful only when they lead to some kind of action, which can range from small tweaks to a marketing campaign to a major corporate reorganization. The nature and scale of the intended actions will obviously have bearing on the nature and scale of the outside consulting you may require. It is well known that the prophet from another land may have more success in persuading management of the importance of a new approach to customer relationships or a new product bundling strategy than even the most knowledgeable insider.

Finding Outside Expertise

If you do decide to use outside expertise, there are three places you are likely to find it:

- From a data mining software vendor

- From a data mining center
- From a consulting company

Data Mining Software Vendors

If you have already selected your data mining software, the company that provided it is probably the first place you will look for help. All software providers have training classes in their products and many also have professional services groups that can help you with data mining projects. Be warned, however, that product knowledge and technical expertise do not always translate into good data mining results. A successful data mining project requires people that understand the business problem well enough to do a good job of translating it into a technical problem to be solved. Often, the data mining tool expert will not be good at listening to what the business people have to say and translating their domain knowledge into definitions for derived variables that reflect your organization's accumulated lore and wisdom.

Data Mining Centers

There are several data mining centers where you can take your own data and work side-by-side with data mining experts using software and hardware installed at the center. Many of these centers are collaborations between universities and private industry such as the Bologna data mining center in Italy, which was set up by IBM and a consortium of Italian universities, and the data mining centers at Carnegie Mellon and the University of Northern Arizona in the United States, both of which are collaborations with commercial companies. Other data mining centers are run by companies who supply hardware or software to the data mining market such as the Advanced Data Mining Center run by Compaq in Austin, Texas. The authors are associated with the Decision Support Laboratory in Cambridge, Massachusetts. This lab brings together researchers from various decision support subspecialties such as OLAP and data visualization with data mining research groups at Simon Fraser University in British Columbia and at the University of Massachusetts.

A pilot project in a data mining center can be a good way to wet your feet in the data mining waters without having to make an investment in hardware, software, and staff before your long-term data mining plans are finalized.

Consulting Companies

Data mining is undeniably a buzzword, which means that consulting companies large and small are anxious to help. Caveat emptor! Willingness and ability are not always strongly correlated. Be sure to ask the would-be consultants about their specific experience mining data in your industry, and be sure to call a couple of references. Also, remember what it is you are looking for in a consultant. Although it is a good idea to find a consulting group that is at least a little bit familiar with your industry so you won't have to waste a lot of time explaining every term and business practice, you are not really looking for an expert in your business. You are looking for someone who can understand enough about your business to build intelligent models describing it. The consultant's primary expertise should be in data mining. That is the new skill you are paying to bring in.

Developing In-House Expertise

Any business that is serious about converting corporate data into business intelligence should give serious thought to making data mining one of its core competencies by developing in-house expertise. This is especially true of companies that have many products and many customers. Companies in that situation are striving to achieve the goal of one-to-one marketing. One-to-one marketing means letting your customers teach you about themselves through their interactions with your firm, and *using what you learn to increase your profits by making their lives easier*. By making their lives easier, you increase the loyalty your customers feel towards your company and make it harder and harder for competitors to lure them away. Note that this loyalty is not based on any inherent superiority of your products and services (although good products and services certainly do contribute to customer loyalty!), but only on your ability to capitalize on the investment your customers have made in teaching you about themselves. This means that the ability to *learn* is central to the true one-to-one company, and data mining is central to the learning process. The ability to learn from experience is the in-house expertise you need to develop.

By taking control of the data mining process, a company can take full advantage of the fact that, by their actions, its customers are continually teaching it about themselves. Only when data mining is a core competency of the organization will it be possible to marry the business knowledge built up over the years with the insights available through data mining. People who understand both the data and the business it represents will build better models than people who understand only the data or only the business. Such people are more likely to be found on your own staff than on the staff of a general purpose data mining consultancy. Moreover, the model-building *process* is often as informative as the results delivered by the finished models so it makes sense to keep that process within your own organization.

You know more about your business and about your customers than any outside firm can hope to learn. By mastering data mining, you can exploit that fact to maximum advantage.

Learning and Loyalty

We have said that data mining allows a company to do a better job of learning about its customers, but why is that so essential? Web-based travel services provide a good example. You can browse to any number of Web sites that all offer the same services—airline reservations, hotel bookings, and car rentals. Initially, there is little reason to choose one over another. At least for frequent travelers, however, just typing in seven or eight frequent flyer numbers and a couple of credit card numbers with their expiration dates and billing addresses into a profile is painful enough that we might hesitate before using a competing travel service the next time. The second service could offer the same flights, hotel rooms, and cars, but only after asking a bunch of questions that we have already answered for the first one. Of course, in this example, the travel site has not done any active learning; all it has to do to be more attractive than a competitor is to recognize us when we return to the site (through a user name and password, a stored cookie, or both) and then remember the profile entered during the earlier visit. Sounds simple, but it is easy to find examples of customer interactions that don't do even that:

- cash machines that ask what language you'd like to use even though you've used the same card and answered the same question the same way a thousand times before
- catalog companies that still ask for your shipping address the twentieth time you place an order
- credit card companies that haven't figured out that you are never going to order the credit insurance they offer you in every bill
- long distance companies who haven't learned which prospects do not want frequent flyer miles for their telephone calls.

If the travel site really wants to hook us, it will learn by watching. Each time we return to the site, a few more blanks will be filled in with appropriate default values—the usual departure airport, the aisle seat, the nonsmoking hotel room, the four-door compact car, the preferred airline, the first-choice hotel chain, the nonrefundable ticket. A *really* clever system (more clever than any we have yet encountered) would even change some defaults dynamically as we filled in the

Lessons Learned

Although data mining tools have improved greatly over the last few years, it is still not possible to get good results from data mining without considerable

blanks based on things it has learned about the ways we behave differently at different destinations: "Oh, the destination is in Europe! That means he'll want a business class fare instead of coach and a standard transmission car instead of an automatic." If this seems far-fetched, it is only because most companies, even those that pride themselves on customer service, are not even coming close to their self-proclaimed goals for building relationships with each individual customer. Technology is not the problem; the continuously learning customer-focused organization can be constructed with readily available off-the-shelf software. What is missing is a clear vision of the one-to-one future and a real understanding of just how much the ability to learn is worth.

The one-to-one organization must be able to do three things, each of which is associated with a different technology:

1. First, it must be able to *notice* what its customers are up to. Online transaction processing systems are the eyes, ears, nose, fingers, and tongue of the corporation. Supermarket scanners, Web logs, ATMs, order processing systems, and telephone switches record customer behavior in minute detail. Hardly any interaction goes unnoticed.

2. Second, it must *remember* what it has noticed. That is the role of data warehousing. The data pouring out of the operational systems that actually touch the customer feed these decision support systems that provide the corporation with a memory. Without a memory, it is impossible to learn from the past. The same "lost" customers may come back every Christmas, but with only six months of history you'll never know it.

3. Finally, it must be able to *learn* from what it remembers. That is where data mining comes in. Data mining gives the corporation the ability to use what has happened in the past to predict what is likely to happen in the future: which products each customer is likely to find desirable; which customers are likely to cancel their subscriptions unless some action is taken to retain them; which policy holders are most likely to crack up their cars this year.

Thanks to the data they provide through their day-to-day interactions with your firm, you know more about customers than your competitors can ever hope to learn. To take full advantage of this knowledge, you need to master data mining.

expertise because the activities that can be automated by a tool form only a small part of the data mining process. Understanding the business problem, selecting relevant data, transforming data to bring the information content to the surface, and interpreting the results are all activities that have not yet been automated and are not likely to be any time soon.

In restricted domains, it is possible to embed some, but not all, of this human expertise in software. It is also possible (and often desirable) for an organization to bring in outside expertise in the form of consultants, or to send data to an outside modeling shop. For the very best results, however, it is important to achieve mastery of data mining within the enterprise where technical skills and understanding of the data can be married to a deep understanding of the business goals that are driving the process.

Data Mining Methodology: The Virtuous Cycle Revisited

The great American photographer Ansel Adams did not just step outside and "snap" pictures of sunsets in the West. Even though the images were captured by just pressing a button, he had to plan the photos and wait until just the right moment. One great irony of photography is that the most natural and unposed shots are often the most work, requiring a great deal of planning and preparation. The same is true in data mining. Being successful in data mining requires planning and understanding the business problem.

To continue the analogy, photography has a whole range of technical options for developing prints: one-hour photo labs, amateur darkrooms, professional darkrooms, and digital photography. Mastering photography requires understanding the development process as well as composition. The ultimate result is a combination of the aesthetic and the technical.

Similarly, mastering data mining requires combining the business and the technical. Data mining connects business needs to data; it is about understanding customers and prospects, understanding products and markets, understanding suppliers and partners, understanding processes—all by leveraging the data collected about them. A basic understanding of the technical side of data mining is critical for success, especially the process of transforming data into information.

Failure to follow the rules of photography can lead to fuzzy, poorly exposed pictures—even when using the best equipment. The same is true of data mining—failure to follow the rules of good model building will lead to inaccurate information and poor decisions.

The data mining methodology presented in this chapter is designed for those companies that want to build a core competency in data mining, although anyone who relies on data analysis can benefit from it. We originally introduced this methodology in *Data Mining Techniques* (John Wiley & Sons, 1997); here we have elaborated and condensed it to focus on its most important parts. Following the methodology leads to better models that support more informed decisions. This methodology is built around the virtuous cycle of data mining, which highlights the business aspects of data mining while recognizing the interplay between the business and technical. The discussion on the methodology begins, appropriately, with the two different styles of data mining.

PEOPLE ARE NECESSARY!

There is a fear that as computers become more and more powerful, they will eventually replace people in many different fields. With respect to data mining, the day is very far off! At the technical level, data mining is a set of tools and techniques that make people more productive. Automated algorithms can spot patterns. People will always be needed to know when the patterns are relevant, what problems need to be addressed, when the results are meaningful, and so on.

Two Styles of Data Mining

There are two styles of data mining. *Directed data mining* is a top-down approach, used when we know what we are looking for. This often takes the form of predictive modeling, where we know exactly what we want to predict. *Undirected data mining* is a bottom-up approach that lets the data speak for itself. Undirected data mining finds patterns in the data and leaves it up to the user to determine whether or not these patterns are important.

These two approaches are not mutually exclusive. Data mining efforts often include a combination of both. Even when building a predictive model, it is often useful to search for patterns in the data using undirected techniques. These can suggest new customer segments and new insights that can improve the directed modeling results.

Directed Data Mining

The top part of Figure 3.1 shows a model as a black box. What this means is that we do not care what the model is doing; we just want the most accurate result possible. This is the approach used when we know what we are looking for, when we can direct the data mining effort toward a particular goal.

A model takes one or more inputs and produces an output.

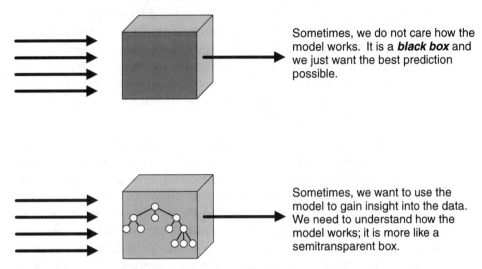

Sometimes, we do not care how the model works. It is a **black box** and we just want the best prediction possible.

Sometimes, we want to use the model to gain insight into the data. We need to understand how the model works; it is more like a semitransparent box.

Figure 3.1 Data mining uses both black-box models and semitransparent models.

Typically, we are using already known examples, such as prospects who already received an offer (and either did or did not respond), and we are applying information gleaned from them to unknown examples, such as prospects who have not yet been contacted. Such a model is called a *predictive model*, because it is making predictions about unknown examples. Predictive models answer questions such as:

- Who is likely to respond to our next offer, based on the history of previous marketing campaigns?
- What is the right medical treatment, based on past experience?
- Which machine is most likely to be the next one to fail?
- Which customers are likely to leave in the next six months?
- What transactions are likely to be fraudulent, based on known examples of fraud?

The predictive models use experience to assign scores (and confidence levels) to some relevant outcome in the future. One of the keys to success is having enough data *with the outcome already known* to train the model. Predictive models are never 100 percent accurate. They are helpful because making informed decisions in business should lead to better results.

In the past, predictive modeling has often been a very specialized function—the work of actuaries, corporate forecasters, and statisticians. Although their work is quite important, they have been relatively far removed from daily business concerns; they provide little assistance on the front line, for the typical brand manager, account manager, or product manager. These specialists speak their own language. Consider an example from the risk management group in one credit card company. They have a label for customers who earn high incomes, are unlikely to go bankrupt, and use the card infrequently. For most of the company, this segment represents the highest potential value. For the risk management group, they are simply "possible future write-off." Quite a difference in perception!

Nowadays, even amateurs can attempt to build predictive models on their desktops. Unfortunately, it is easier to build misleading models than predictive models. The goal in making predictions is to learn from the past, and to learn in such a way that the knowledge can be applied to the future. Perhaps the most important insight in this chapter is this: the best model is not the one with the highest lift when it is being built. It is the model that performs the best on unseen, future data. Although there is no 1-2-3 recipe for building perfect models, this chapter covers the fundamentals needed to build effective models, and we will see these lessons applied in the case studies.

Undirected Data Mining

Sometimes, though, predictive accuracy is not the only or even the primary goal. Undirected data mining is about discovering new patterns inside the data. These patterns provide insight, and this insight might even prove very informative.

We represent this form of data mining with *semitransparent* boxes. Unlike directed data mining, we want to know what is going on, we want to know how the model is coming up with an answer. In the case study on cellular churn, we see how to use a decision tree to discover an important segment of customers.

The case study is a good example, showing that undirected data mining and directed data mining are both valuable in many data mining efforts. Undirected data mining is often used during the data exploration steps. What is in the data? What does it look like? Are there any unusual patterns? What does the data suggest for customer segmentation? These types of questions are answered using tools that support clustering, visualization, and market basket analysis.

At the same time, some predictive modeling techniques, notably decision trees, explain the models they produce. These techniques sometimes provide important insights in addition to the predictions they make. Two things are happening. An example of directed data mining is that a decision tree makes predictions. An example of undirected data mining is that a person looks at a decision tree and possibly notices an interesting pattern.

Undirected data mining is necessarily interactive. Advanced algorithms can find patterns in the data, but only people can determine whether the patterns have any significance and what the patterns might mean.

The Virtuous Cycle of Data Mining

The virtuous cycle of data mining, depicted in Figure 3.2, highlights the fact that data mining does not exist in a vacuum. Data mining has a purpose. In the case studies, we will see data mining applied to many problems in many industries. Its most common applications are in marketing, specifically for customer relationship management; we see it applied to prospecting for new customers, retaining existing ones, and increasing customer value. We also see it applied to understanding customer behavior and optimizing manufacturing processes.

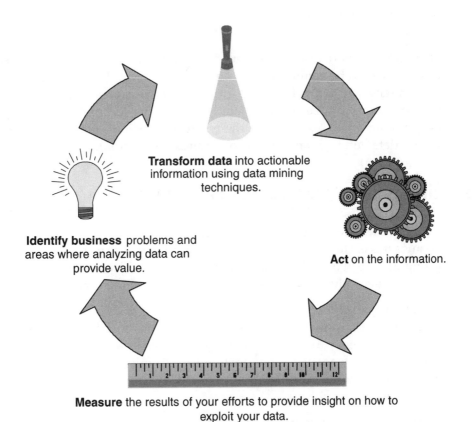

Transform data into actionable information using data mining techniques.

Identify business problems and areas where analyzing data can provide value.

Act on the information.

Measure the results of your efforts to provide insight on how to exploit your data.

Figure 3.2   The virtuous cycle of data mining leads to a learning organization.

Clearly, data mining has many applications. And, although they may have much in common, every application has its own unique characteristics. Industries differ from each other; within a single industry, different companies have different strategic plans and different approaches. All of this affects the approach to data mining.

The previous chapter outlined three ways that companies can incorporate data mining solutions into their business. Here, we focus primarily on the companies that want to build core competencies in data mining, because data analysis supports critical business processes.

The virtuous cycle is a high-level process, consisting of four major business processes:

- Identifying the business problem
- Transforming data into actionable results
- Acting on the results
- Measuring the results

There are no shortcuts—success in data mining requires all four processes. Results have to be communicated and, over time, we hope that expertise in data mining will grow. Expertise grows as organizations focus on the right business problems, learn about data and modeling techniques, and improve data mining processes based on the results of previous efforts. In short, successful data mining is an example of *organizational learning*.

Identifying the Right Business Problem

Defining the business problem is the trickiest part of successful data mining because it is exclusively a communication problem. The technical people analyzing data need to understand what the business really needs. Even the most advanced algorithms cannot figure out what is most important.

A necessary part of every data mining project is talking to the people who understand the business. These people are often referred to as *domain experts.* Sometimes there is a tendency to want to treat data analysis as a strictly technical exercise. Resist this tendency! Only domain experts fully understand what really needs to be done; and ultimately, they are likely to receive the credit or blame for bottom-line results.

While taking into account what the domain experts have to say, it is also important not to be constrained by their expertise. Important results often come from "thinking outside the box"—ignoring supposed wisdom by understanding what is really happening.

Working with the business people allows you to answer questions such as the following:

- Is the data mining effort really necessary?
- Is there a particular segment or subgroup that is most interesting?
- What are the relevant business rules?
- What do they know about the data? Are some data sources known to be invalid? Where should certain data come from?
- What do their intuition and experience say is important?

Answering these questions requires a combination of skills that includes being able to work with the domain experts as well as understanding the technology and data. There is no specific right or wrong way, because this is an interactive process between people. The next few sections begin with business scenarios (shown in italics) that should help shed light on the process.

Domain experts have a very good idea of what is going on. They can focus data mining efforts by answering questions such as:

What is really important to the business?

What information, that you cannot now get, would you be able to act on immediately?

Is data mining really necessary to solve this problem?

What important business rules are relevant in this case?

What does your experience and intuition add to the equation?

It is also important to keep the business people in the loop, so they are aware of new insights gleaned along the way and so the data mining remains focused on areas of value to the business.

Is the Data Mining Effort Necessary?

A Senior Vice President in the credit card group of a large bank has spent tens of thousands of dollars developing a response model. This predictive model is designed to identify the prospects who are most likely to respond to the bank's next offering. The VP is told that by using the model, she can save money: using only 20 percent of the prospect list will yield 70 percent of the responders. However, despite these findings, she replies that she wants every single responder—not just some of them. Getting every respon-der requires using the entire prospect list, since no model is perfect. In this case, data mining is not necessary.

Moral: She could have saved tens of thousands of dollars by not building predictive models in the first place.

Data mining is not always necessary. As this example shows, not every marketing campaign requires a response model. Sometimes, the purpose of the campaign is to communicate to everyone. Or, the communication might be particularly inexpensive, such as a billing insert or e-mail, so there may be less reason to focus only on responders.

Is There a Particular Segment or Subgroup That Is Most Interesting?

On the other side of the globe, another marketing group at a cellular telephone provider has specified that it wants a propensity-to-churn score for all existing customers. A propensity-to-churn score is a number ranging from 0 to 1, where 0 means that the model finds no indications of churn and 1 means that the model has the highest confi-dence of churn. The marketing group wants to do an intervention (marketing-speak for communicating to the customers in some way) on the 10,000 customers most likely to churn. However, the results are very disappointing. It turns out that they really want to retain their elite customers—and of the 10,000 on their list, fewer than a quar-ter were elites. The campaign was disappointing.

Moral: The campaign would have been more successful by focusing on the right cus-tomer segment when building the models.

Matching expectations is a key to successful data mining efforts. In this case, the need was for a list with only elite members, and the business people did not realize that modeling elites separately would produce better results. Mismatches of this type occur in many ways. For instance, a marketing campaign wants to focus on consumers, but the models return a mix of consumer and commercial customers; a model is built in one geography or on one customer segment and then applied somewhere else. And so on.

What Are the Relevant Business Rules?

In the cross-selling example in Chapter 10, we will see that a bank was putting together a marketing campaign to sell brokerage accounts to existing customers. The predictive models did a very good job of determining who would want a brokerage account; one of the key determinants was whether the customer had a private banking account. Alas, bank rules forbid including private bank customers in marketing campaigns.

Moral: The modeling effort needed to understand business rules to avoid a particular segment of customers.

What about the Data?

A large, converging telecommunications provider wants to use data mining to figure out who has fax machines. This requires starting with a list of known fax machines and determining who calls them and who does not call them. Where can they obtain this list?

A large retailer wants to analyze returns—merchandise returned by customers. Where can it get the data on returns and link them to the original purchaser and market basket? How are returns represented in the data?

Moral: Domain experts know where data resides and how it is stored. Using this information can save a lot of time in understanding the data.

The business people understand the business environment and business processes. Sometimes, they also have a very good understanding of what should be in the data—or what cannot possibly be. In some other cases, they have some important data that never makes it into data warehouses. This often includes information residing on their desktops, which may have important attributes about competitors, suppliers, particular products, and so on.

Of course, the IT group responsible for databases and applications also understands the data and may be the only group that recognizes obscure values in the data.

Verifying the Opinion of Domain Experts

Domain experts provide experience and intuition, but this can be a double-edged sword. Their intuition can be a source of valuable insight, allowing the data mining effort to focus on particular sources of data or suggesting ways to segment data for building multiple models (such as building a separate churn model for high-value customers and low-value customers).

Their experience can also be a source of gotchas. For instance, after extensive analysis, the data may reveal that call forwarding is always sold with call waiting. The business people already know that, because call forwarding is always bundled with call waiting. They also know what has worked in the past and what has not.

However, as far as possible, their intuition and experience should be verified by looking for patterns that support them. The purpose of data mining is to let the data speak; and data does not lie (although the data may be dirty). If they believe that the best customer is married with an age between 35 and 50, is this true in the data? If they believe that customers who purchased something in the last six months are most likely to make another purchase, is this true? If they believe that home equity customers have highly variable incomes (such as sales people), is this true? And so on.

Transforming Data into Actionable Results

The heart of data mining is transforming data into actionable results, and there will be much more to say about this topic throughout the book. Here, our goal is to give an outline of the major steps taken to build data mining models and to emphasize that this is an iterative process.

Figure 3.3 illustrates the basic steps taken to transform data into actionable results. Throughout this book, we will be delving into these topics in greater detail.

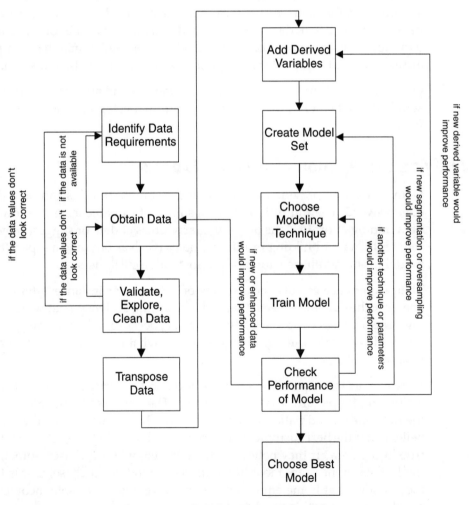

Figure 3.3 Building data mining models is an iterative process.

Identify and Obtain Data

The first step in the modeling process is identifying and obtaining the right data. Often, the right data is simply whatever data is available, reasonably clean, and accessible. In general, more data is better.

It is important to verify that the data meets the requirements for solving the business problem. For instance, if the business problem is to identify particular customers, then the data must contain information about each individual customer. There may be additional detail data—such as transaction-level information—but it must also be possible to tie this data back to individual customers.

In addition, we want the data to be as complete as possible when modeling. This can make it impractical to use survey data or other data available only for survey respondents. If the data from the survey proves valuable, then how will nonrespondents be scored? (In other situations, using survey data for data mining may prove very fruitful; just don't expect to apply the resulting model to nonrespondents without some extra work.)

The purpose of the data mining effort may be to identify customer segments, perhaps for the purpose of directing advertising or purchasing lists of prospective customers. In this case, the data needs to contain fields that are appropriate for purchasing advertising space and lists. This often includes fields supplied by outside list providers, location information, demographics, and so on.

When doing predictive modeling the data also needs to contain the desired outcome. One brick-and-mortar retailer was trying to set up a catalog for their identified customers (members). They were building a response model, based on three earlier catalog mailings; this model would determine who was likely to respond to the catalog based on previous responses to test catalogs in the past. They had the following data, as shown in Figure 3.4:

- Marketing data about all members
- Responses data to previous catalogs
- Tons of transaction-level detail about what members had purchased

The one thing they were missing was who had been sent the earlier catalogs! Knowing who has responded without knowing who had been contacted is almost useless. Without this information, the attempts at predicting response were doomed.

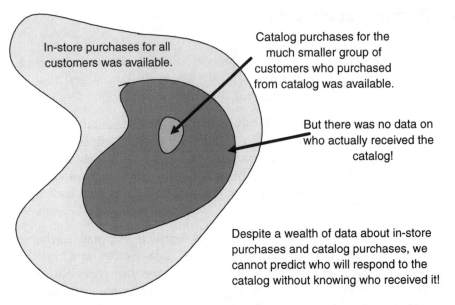

In-store purchases for all customers was available.

Catalog purchases for the much smaller group of customers who purchased from catalog was available.

But there was no data on who actually received the catalog!

Despite a wealth of data about in-store purchases and catalog purchases, we cannot predict who will respond to the catalog without knowing who received it!

Figure 3.4   Without the right historical data, data mining will yield disappointing results.

WARNING

Data from OLAP (online analytic processing) systems is not usually sufficient for data mining purposes. This data has already been summarized along important business dimensions, such as time, geography, and product lines. In doing so, the customer dimension is often not one of the underlying dimensions—the number of customers is often so large that a customer dimension would require a much larger amount of storage. So, data mining efforts centered on customers require additional sources of data.

Validate, Explore, and Clean the Data

The next step is to validate the data and to cleanse it. The outcome of the data mining effort depends critically on the data.

- Are the fields populated? Will missing data be a big problem?
- Are the field values legal? That is, are numerical fields within proper bounds and are code fields all valid?
- Are the field values reasonable?
- Are the distributions of individual fields explainable?

Data inaccuracies creep in from many different places. Usually, fields that are critical to the business are quite accurate. So, the amount of money billed each month is usually accurate as is the billing address. However, data that is not used (which is the vast majority of the fields) is often inaccurate. The business collects the data but no one ever really looks at it. Data mining, because it is hungry for lots and lots of data, is often the first business process that really uses most of the data fields.

OUR FAVORITE DATA QUALITY QUOTE

"The data is clean because it is automatically generated—no human ever touches it." The data in question contained information about file transfers on a distributed computer system. Data packets were often sent between systems. When we looked at the data, though, 20 percent of the transactions described files that arrived before they had even been sent! Evidence of spectacular network performance? Not really. Not only did people never touch the data, but they didn't set the clocks on the computers either.

Transpose the Data to the Right Granularity

Granularity refers to the level of the data that is being modeled. Data mining algorithms work on individual rows of data. So, all the data describing a customer (or whatever we are interested in) must be in a single row. The data needs to be summarized to the right level of granularity.

For instance, an automobile insurance company may keep track of every vehicle covered for every year of coverage. For each year, there might be information on the type of vehicle, the total number of claims, the total cost of claims, the estimated value of the car, and so on. However, a marketing application is unlikely to be interested in this data at the vehicle level. People buy insurance policies, and these policies often cover more than one car. So the data has to be transformed from the year-vehicle format to a summarized format by policy, as shown in Figure 3.5.

This is an insurance example, but the problem is omnipresent. Billing data is recorded by month, and all months of data need to be in the same record. Data on different products has to be combined for individual customers. Market basket data needs to be summarized to describe household behavior. Web clicks need to be summarized to describe a single visit. And so on and so on and so on.

This summarization is often a tricky process. Because of the complex data formats, the full power of a programming language is often needed for the summarization. For this reason, tools, such as SAS, SPSS, Ab Initio, and PERL, are often used.

Policy	Year	Car	Premium	Claims	Number of Claims
000 000 0001	1997	CAR01			
000 000 0001	1998	CAR01			
000 000 0001	1998	CAR02			
000 000 0001	1999	CAR01			
000 000 0001	1999	CAR02			
000 000 0002	1997	CAR01			
000 000 0002	1997	CAR02			
000 000 0002	1998	CAR01			
000 000 0002	1999	CAR01			
000 000 0002	1999	CAR02			
000 000 0003	1998	CAR01			
000 000 0003	1999	CAR01			
000 000 0004	1999	CAR01			

This is an example of car insurance data. Every year the insurance company keeps track of claims by policy number, year, and car on the policy.

Data mining algorithms typically require the data in the format of one policy per row when we want to make predictions about policies. All rows need to have the same number of columns.

This requires transposing the data and calculating new values for the columns.

Policy	Number of Years	Number of Car-Years	Number of Claims	Value of Claims	Total Premiums
000 000 0001	3	5			
000 000 0002	3	5			
000 000 0003	2	2			
000 000 0004	1	1			

Figure 3.5 An example of summarizing automobile insurance data.

Add Derived Variables

The next step in the process is adding derived variables. Derived variables have values based on combinations of other values inside the data. Some simple examples of derived variables are

- Total number of transactions and sum of dollar amount
- Number of months when new charges were equal to 0
- Growth in usage from beginning of the period to the end
- Ratio of usage attributed to international, long-distance, and local calls
- Ratio of weight to height squared (the obesity index)

These are all examples of derived variables coming from the data within a single row. Another type of derived variable gives information about that row relative to all the others. For instance:

- **The revenue decile for each customer.** This is determined by taking the total amount spent in a given period for all customers and assigning 1 for the customers in the top decile, 2 for the customers in the second decile, and so on.

- **The churn rate by type of wireless phone.** This is determined by taking the most recently available churn information and determining the rate for each type of handset.

- **Profitability by demographics.** This is determined by taking historical profitability information by age and gender.

- **Fraud by amount of transaction.** This is determined by determining the amount of fraud that has historically been identified for transactions of different sizes.

These variables are powerful because past behavior is often a strong predictor of future behavior. In the wireless industry, for instance, handset churn rates are an important part of every churn model. However, these historical variables are not enough. Obtaining better predictive results requires combining the historical information with other types of data.

This type of derived variable is often available through an OLAP system. In fact, these types of variables show that there are many synergies between OLAP and data mining. Sometimes you can get the data from an OLAP system; sometimes you want to calculate these historical variables directly from the data used for data mining.

Prepare the Model Set

The model set is the data that is used to actually build the data mining models. Once the data has been cleaned, transposed, and derived variables added, what more needs to be done?

There are a few things that we still have to take into account. If we are building a predictive model from historical data, then what is the frequency of the rarer outcomes in the model set? A good rule of thumb is that we want between 15 and 30 percent density of the rarer outcomes.

Consider fraud. The data may contain fewer than 1 percent cases of known fraud. Almost any model that we build on such a model set will be 99 percent accurate—by simply predicting no fraud. Very accurate and entirely useless.

There are several ways of handling such rare data. The most common is over-sampling, which we discuss in Chapter 7.

At this point, we also need to divide the model set into the training, test, and evaluation sets. Only some of the data is used to create the model initially; other data is held back to refine the model and to predict how well it works.

We may also decide to build different models on different segments of data. For instance, when building a cross-sell model, we may start by building a model for the propensity to buy each different product. In this case, we might create a separate model set for each product as a prelude to making a prediction about that product.

Choose the Modeling Technique and Train the Model

Once upon a time, training a neural network or building a decision tree was difficult, often requiring custom coding. Fortunately, data mining tools have eliminated most of the cumbersome details in building models, as well as providing much friendlier graphical environments in which to work. So, in a way, the actual building of models is the least time-consuming part of data mining, because it is now as simple as point and click.

At this point, we have entered the technical realm of building models. There are a variety of different data mining techniques to choose from; each technique has advantages and disadvantages, which are discussed in Chapter 5.

When time is available, multiple different models are often built on the same model set. The best algorithm and set of parameters is generally unknown in advance, and experimentation can determine what best fits the data in the model set.

The specifics of training a model depend, of course, on the algorithm chosen and on the tool being used. Some tools can generate lots of different models and will choose the best one automatically. Others are more interactive, requiring the user to determine which is the best.

Check Performance of the Models

The final step is to check the performance of different models on the data. Different data mining techniques have different ways of measuring results. To compare the results between different models, though, we want to see how well the model performs on unseen data. This hold-out set is the evaluation set (which is part of the model set).

Figure 3.6 shows a confusion matrix, both graphically and as a table. This tells us how many predictions made by a predictive model are correct and how many are incorrect. Which is the best model depends on the business problem.

Anticonfusion Matrix?

The name *confusion matrix* puts off a lot of people. In fact, on hearing the word confusion, the concept suddenly becomes difficult to understand. Perhaps a better name would be a prediction accuracy chart. Alas, the name has stuck. A confusion matrix is measuring whether a model is confused or not; that is, whether the model is making mistakes in its predictions. Far from leading to confusion, they help clarify the performance of models—eliminating a bit of confusion in understanding the models.

For a marketing response problem, we want to get as many potential responders as possible and we are not too concerned if a bunch of nonresponders are also in the data. That is, we do not care about false positives.

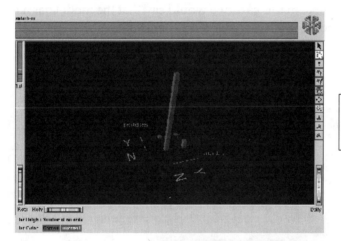

		Actual	
		Y	N
Predicted	Y	2%	4%
	N	12%	82%

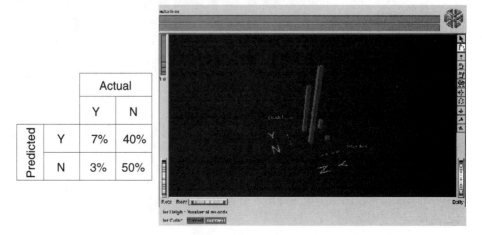

		Actual	
		Y	N
Predicted	Y	7%	40%
	N	3%	50%

Figure 3.6   Using confusion matrixes to see how well a model performs.

For a medical diagnostic test for cancer, the situation is quite different. We might use such a model as an initial screen. When there is an indication of cancer, the doctors would then run more elaborate tests. For this type of problem, we want to be sure that when the test says "no" it really means "no." In this case, we care a lot about false negatives—and we want as few as possible.

The lift chart or cumulative gains chart is another way of comparing the performance of different models. Figure 3.7 shows a cumulative gains chart for several different models. The greater the area between the line for the model and the diagonal line, the better the model.

What is the cumulative gains chart? The horizontal axes represent the ranking of the data according to the model. So, the 10 percent mark represents the 10 percent of the data that scores the highest with the model. The vertical axis shows the actual density of the outcome. If the top 20 percent of the data has 70 percent of the desired outcomes, then the model is doing well. It is far from the diagonal baseline. In this case, we would say that the model has a lift of 3.5; it is doing 3.5 times as well as we would expect.

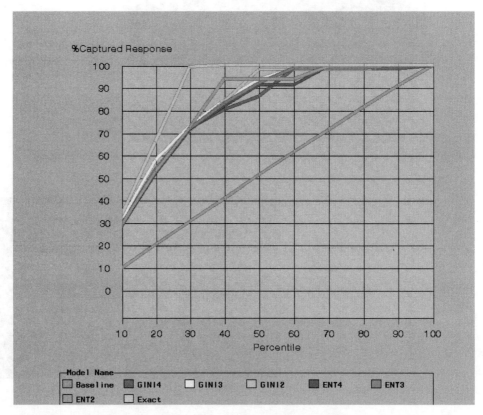

Figure 3.7 A comparison of different models using a cumulative gains chart.

Acting on the Results

Data mining serves no purpose if we never act on the results of the model. Acting on the results can take several different forms:

Insights. During the course of modeling, we may have learned new facts from the data. These may lead to insights about the business and about the customers. The insights need to be communicated!

One-time results. The results may be focused on a particular activity, such as a marketing campaign. In this case, the marketing campaign should be carried out, based on the propensities determined by the model.

Remembered results. The results may provide interesting information about customers, and this information should be accessible through a data mart or a data warehouse. Predicted customer profitability and best next offer are two examples that are often worthy of "publication" in a database.

Periodic predictions. The model may be used to score customers periodically, to determine the best next offer to make them or to determine whom to target for retention efforts.

Real-time scoring. The model itself may be incorporated into another system to provide real-time predictions. For instance, the profitability of a customer may be updated based on the results of online transactions, or a Web site may be customized based on a customer's predicted needs.

Fixing data. Sometimes the data mining effort uncovers data problems that significantly affect the performance of models. In these cases, sometimes the only actions are those that will result in cleaner, more complete data for future efforts.

The type of action can have an effect on the modeling. For instance, when using the scores that the model produces, there is always a time lag needed to deploy the results. This time lag is due more to the availability of recent data and to deployment scheduling than it is to the process of actually scoring the data. The time lag needs to be taken into account when building the models.

Deploying a model in real-time imposes requirements on how the results are scored and, perhaps, on the complexity of the data transformations permitted in the model. In these cases, we may want to export the model as code, such as C, C++, SAS code, C/SQL, or using database access languages.

Sometimes it is also valuable to incorporate a bit of experimental design into the process. For example, if we are predicting customer response to a product, we might actually have three different groups:

- A group of customers chosen based on the results of the data mining model, who get the marketing message

- A group of customers chosen at random, who get the marketing message
- A group of customers, chosen at random, who do not get the marketing message

What we hope is that the first group will have a high response rate, the second group will have a mediocre response rate, and the third will have a negligible response rate. In any case, we can test both the strength of the marketing message (the difference in response between the second and third groups) and the strength of the data mining (the difference between the first and second groups).

Even when data mining is used in a production environment, it is still valuable to have an additional, random group exposed to the marketing message. This helps future data mining efforts by bringing in an unbiased sample. For instance, if we predict that young couples between 25 and 35 with moderate incomes are most likely to purchase a home, then we might direct all marketing messages to them. Well, if we ever look at the data, we will find—lo and behold—that this group has a high response rate. This phenomenon is known as sample bias. By including a random group of people, not predicted to respond, we prepare ourselves for finding new patterns that may arise in the future.

Measuring the Model's Effectiveness

We have already discussed measuring the effectiveness of models on a hold-out set. This is for the purpose of evaluating the model. We also need to compare the results to what actually happened in the real world. This is particularly true when we are making predictions about future behavior.

Did the predicted behavior actually happen? That is, did the prospects accept the offer, did the customers purchase the new product or service, did they churn? The only way to really know is by comparing what actually happened to the prediction.

We have already discussed lift charts and confusion matrixes as methods of comparing the results of models. These are readily adapted to compare actual results to predicted results.

For a predictive model, actual results will usually be worse than predicted. The discrepancy arises because models perform less well the farther they get from the model set—the set of data used to create the model. Typically, the data set we are acting on is more recent than the data set used to create the model. The model captures patterns from the past and, over time, the patterns become less relevant. Figure 3.8 illustrates what typically happens on a monthly basis. Because the model set is older than the score set, we expect the results to degrade over time.

This model time chart shows that six months of historical data is being used to predict one month into the future.

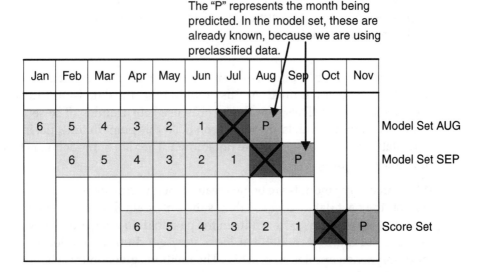

The "P" represents the month being predicted. In the model set, these are already known, because we are using preclassified data.

Jan	Feb	Mar	Apr	May	Jun	Jul	Aug	Sep	Oct	Nov	
6	5	4	3	2	1	✕	P				Model Set AUG
	6	5	4	3	2	1	✕	P			Model Set SEP
			6	5	4	3	2	1	✕	P	Score Set

Model performance usually degrades over time. We expect the model's predictions to be a bit less accurate on the score set than on the model set.

Figure 3.8   A model time chart shows that the score set is usually more recent than the model set.

What Makes Predictive Modeling Successful?

"Consistency is the hobgoblin of little minds," is a frequent misquote of Ralph Waldo Emerson (he actually wrote "A foolish consistency . . ."). Quite the opposite is true for predictive modeling. Predictions are only useful because they are consistent—and especially, because they are consistent over time. Otherwise, they would have no predictive value. With hard work and a bit of luck, our predictive models will not produce foolish consistencies.

Time Frames of Predictive Modeling

Although the inner workings of the data mining techniques are interesting, it is possible to approach predictive models without considering the details of the techniques. Models simply transform inputs into predictions, whether using statistical regressions, neural networks, decision trees, nearest neighbor approaches, or even some technique waiting to be invented in the future. There are really two things to do with predictive models, as shown in Figure 3.9:

- The models are created using data from the past to make predictions. This process is called *training* the model.

- The models are then run on another set of data to assign outcomes. This process is known as *scoring*, and often predicts future outcomes based on the most recent data.

There are two time frames associated with developing models. The first is when they are being trained. At this point in time, the data is historical *and the outcomes are known*. These are the records used for training. The second time frame is when the models are being scored. At this point in time, the input data is available, but the outcomes are not known. The role of modeling is to assign probable outcomes.

When predictive models are being created, their performance can be measured only on the past data—because that is the only data that is available. Often, it is possible to achieve good results in the past that do not generalize well in the future, resulting in a model that looks very good on the model set and fails miserably when applied in practice. The methods given in this chapter help to reduce the likelihood of developing poor models.

Fortunately, a good predictor of the future is the past, so predictive modeling has proven to be a good approach for many types of problems. However, the past is by no means perfect. To make effective use of predictive models, we need to understand not only how to build them but also when they work well and when they don't.

Modeling Shelf-Life

Looking at time frames also brings up two critical questions about models and their predictions:

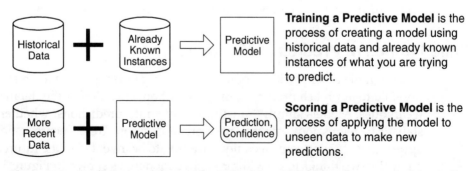

Training a Predictive Model is the process of creating a model using historical data and already known instances of what you are trying to predict.

Scoring a Predictive Model is the process of applying the model to unseen data to make new predictions.

Figure 3.9   Predictive models must be trained (created) before they are used (scored).

What is the shelf-life of a model? The things being modeled change over time, such as the business environment, technology, and customer base changes. This means that a model created five years ago, or last year, or last month, may no longer be valid. When this happens, you need to train a new model on more recent data.

What is the shelf-life of a prediction? Predictions also have a shelf-life. They are valid during a particular time frame. The classic example is predicting what will happen during a particular month (such as churn or making a purchase). And then using the prediction during a different month.

The whole process of predictive modeling is based on some key assumptions. These assumptions shed light on the process of building models.

Assumption 1: The Past Is a Good Predictor of the Future

Using predictive models assumes that the past is a good predictor of the future. If we know how patients reacted to a drug in the past, we can be confident that similar patients will have roughly similar reactions in the future. Or if certain customers who are going bankrupt have behaved in a certain way, then similar customers will behave in similar ways in the future. Or, customers who bought widgets last month are similar to customers who will buy widgets next month. And so on.

It is important to recognize that this is an assumption about the problem being addressed and about the business environment. It is usually a pretty reasonable assumption, too. However, there are some cases where the past may not be a particularly good predictor of the future, because it can be hard to capture significant external events in the data. For instance, retail sales decrease during cold weather and blizzards. Lumber sales go up after a hurricane. Mortgage lending increases when interest rates go down. Trying to predict retail sales, lumber, or response to mortgage campaigns may produce anomolous predictions. One year, South Florida may look like a strong market for lumber sales; another year South Carolina, and another Louisiana. This is a case where past sales may not directly predict future ones.

Such seasonal patterns appear in many places. Electricity usage during the summer is driven by heat waves. The Christmas season and back-to-school season drive many retail sales. A strike at a competitor or currency devaluation may totally change the market. All of these can significantly change the assumption that the past is a good predictor of the future. For retail sales, for instance, it is usually a good idea to have at least one year of data available for data mining.

More subtle reasons may prevent the past from being a good predictor of the future. Definitely last year's Christmas-time toy fad is unlikely to sell as well this year. Perhaps a more insidious danger is that data collected about customers during a booming economy may not have much predictive power in a less stable economy. During the very volatile world markets in 1998, several financial institutions went under for precisely this reason—the models they developed during years of relatively stable financial markets were not applicable in the more volatile markets.

External factors, to a greater or lesser degree, will always have an influence on the models being built. How do we know when the past—and especially the data we have about the past—is a good predictor of the future? Well, we can never know for sure. This is one major reason why it is critical to include domain experts in the modeling process. They understand the business and the market, and they often have insight about important factors that affect predictive models. It is also critical to include enough of the right data to make good decisions—especially when seasonal factors play a major role.

Assumption 2: The Data Is Available

The data is available. Such a simple statement, and yet there are so many challenges in practice. Data may not be available for any number of different reasons:

- The data may not be collected by the operational systems. This is rather common: the telephone switch does not record the fact that a customer turned off call waiting; the cash register does not record the employee who rang the sale; the customer service system is unable to capture the customer ID, and so on.
- Another department may own the data, so it is difficult to get.
- The data resides in a data warehouse or other database, but the database is too busy most of the time to prepare extracts.
- The data is owned by an outside vendor, who manages the operational or decision support systems.
- The data is in the wrong format or the keys do not match.
- And so on.

It is important to remember that the data used to build the model must also be available to apply the model. For example, it is tempting to use survey responses as inputs into predictive models. There are several issues with this, but the most basic is that the same inputs must be available for scoring as well. So, if the responses are useful, it might mean having to survey all customers in order to apply the model. Such a survey is prohibitively expensive. An alternative is to try to find an outside vendor who can supply the same information—but if you can buy the information, why do a survey? (Of course, analyzing survey data using data mining techniques can be very enlightening and valuable.)

A similar situation arises when a sample of the customer base is used to build a prototype data warehouse. This is one approach to building a data warehouse, and it has a nice, iterative feel. And, predictive models built using all the relatively clean and complete data from the prototype warehouse look really good—but they can't be scored for the larger customer base until the same data is available about all the customers. In this situation, it is often more valuable to build a less effective model using fewer attributes—but a model that can be scored for everyone.

Themes about data quality recur throughout the book, because data quality is the biggest issue facing data miners and other analysts. And ensuring that the right data is available is critical to building successful predictive models.

Assumption 3: The Data Contains What We Want to Predict

To apply the lessons of the past to the future, we need to be comparing apples to apples and oranges to oranges. Predictive modeling works best when the goal is to predict the same outcome over and over and over again. In areas such as predicting risk for life insurance or predicting credit worthiness for mortgages, modeling has proven quite effective.

Often, the business people phrase their needs very ambiguously. They say, "we are interested in people who do not pay their bills." Does that mean missing a payment for one month? For three months? For six months? For four of the last six months? Does nonpayment mean not making the minimum payment or making no payment at all? These decisions can have a big effect on the resulting models.

Sometimes, predictive modeling can be hard to apply at all. For instance, it may or may not help in trying to predict which customers are likely candidates for an entirely new product. In this case, the new product may be targeted at a new customer base—and all information collected about existing customers is unlikely to help. Or, the new product may be targeted at a specific segment, such as high-end customers.

Sometimes business users have unreasonable expectations from their data. For instance, when building a response model, it is important to know two things: who responded to the campaign and who received the campaign. For advertising campaigns, the second group is not known—we would have to know who saw the advertisement. Without this information, it is not possible to build an effective response model. We can, however, compare the responders to a random sample of the general population.

Lessons Learned

The virtuous cycle of data mining focuses on using data mining to derive business benefit. It consists of the following stages:

Identifying the right business problem. This stage uses the domain experts to identify important business problems and the data needed to resolve them. However, it is important to verify the assumptions made by the domain experts.

Transforming the data into actionable results. Building models is an iterative process that needs to focus on how the results will be used.

Acting on the results. The purpose of data mining is to act on the results, and this can happen in different ways. Sometimes, the results are insights into the business; sometimes results are used only once. At other times, they may be remembered and put into a data warehouse. Sometimes, the goal is to provide the capability for real-time scoring (particularly true in e-commerce). Disappointing results often show a need for richer and cleaner data.

Measuring results. The final stage is to measure the results of actions. These measurements feed the virtuous cycle by providing more questions and more data for additional data mining efforts.

Predictive modeling is the most common application of data mining. Its success rests on three assumptions. The first is that the past is a good predictor of the future. The second is that the data is available. And the third is that the data contains what we want to predict. Its success also requires taking into account the time frame of the model, and acting on the results before the model and predictions expire.

Customers and Their Lifecycles

B roadly speaking, there are different stages in the customer lifecycle. These stages describe the customer relationship and provide a framework for understanding the economic relationship between a consumer and a business. Either explicitly or implicitly, this framework drives much of the work of data mining and of marketing in general.

Combined with the customer relationship lifecycle is another lifecycle, one that we as individuals are more acutely aware of. Our own personal lifecycle is unique, consisting of many events, from our first kiss, to purchasing our first house, to retiring. Many important events are part of this lifecycle, which affect us and our economic relationships.

It is important to remember that all the data being collected shows only a shadow of what is really going on. An automated teller machine records when a particular customer withdrew a particular amount of money from a particular account. But the machine does not record any of the myriad of other details about the transaction—what the money is used for, whether the customer entered alone or with other people, drove to the ATM or walked, kept the receipt or dropped it on the floor, read the promotion on the receipt or not, waited for a free machine or did not wait at all. All the ATM records is the actual transaction—a mechanical description of a much richer event.

It is not practical, of course, to capture all the details of every transaction. And most customers would not appreciate the intrusion into their lives, in any case. The challenge is not to capture every detail, but to maximize the value of what is gathered. In delving into customers and their lifecycles, the place to being is by finding out who the customer is.

Who Is the Customer?

This is a tricky question. Chapter 6 addresses it from the technical perspective, but that is only one aspect of the problem. There are many different answers. The lesson from that chapter is simple. There are no shortcuts. However the customer is defined, it will take a lot of work to transform available data to the right level of granularity. No one answer is necessarily "right" from the technical perspective.

The real answer depends on the needs of the business, as it competes to acquire new customers, to keep old customers and to make existing customers more profitable. There are fundamentally two different types of customers, consumers and business, that we will discuss in more detail.

Consumers

To address the question "What is a consumer?" let's look at different aspects of consumer behavior. Even within the same household, the answer is not always the same. To give a simple example, consider a young couple with two children. The choice of which movie to see or which cable channels to subscribe to might involve the whole family. On the other hand, only the parents might make the choice of which car to buy. Only one person typically makes the choice of which credit card to use for any given purchase.

Marketing sometimes talks about economic marketing units. However, there is no single answer because consumers play multiple roles in economic transactions:

- The *action role* describes entity or entities responsible for a particular interaction, such as making a telephone call, paying a bill, purchasing a marketing basket, or opening an account. An action often corresponds to a particular service or transaction, and takes place at the account level.

- The *ownership role* describes entity or entities who own particular actions. By looking at ownership, a company can identify the individual responsible for a broad range of actions, even across different groups within a business.

- The *decision-making role* describes entity or entities who make and influence purchasing decisions and behavior. Often, this dimension refers to households.

These represent different roles that people play as consumers. In some cases, the same individual acts, owns, and makes all decisions. In other cases, these roles are shared among several individuals.

Let's dive in a bit and look at these roles in some familiar industries. For example, in a bank:

- Actions, such as depositing money or making a credit card payment, occur within product lines. So the action dimension occurs at the account level. Often, data mining is focused on the "cardholder" or on the "account." A single individual may have several relationships, but each one is treated as a different customer.

- Ownership is a legal definition for many types of accounts, and most often, corresponds to a single individual or couple. So the ownership dimension allows all the commonly owned accounts to be grouped together.

- Decision making typically occurs once within a household for any given decision. The household dimension gathers together all the accounts and transactions owned by individuals in the household.

This is a useful breakdown, even though it oversimplifies the real world. The sidebar tells the true story of a bank that rejected a credit application from the daughter of an important customer. Who is the customer here?

Understanding the dimension of customer behavior is important because it can also influence the business problem. Consider churn in the wireless industry. Does a customer churn when one telephone in the household is canceled? Does a customer churn when all telephones are canceled? Does a customer churn when a highly profitable monthly plan is downgraded to a basic plan?

There is no right answer to these questions. The answer depends on the definition of customer. Is the customer a telephone number, a household, or the owner of a particular service plan? Understanding customers is an ongoing process. It is always worthwhile, though, remembering the full complexity of the customer relationship, even when using accounts (or some other unit) as proxies for full customer relationships.

Business Customers

The relationship between business and consumers is pretty simple: The role of the customer is to purchase products and services, the role of the business is to market, sell, provide, and service. Relationships between businesses are much more complex.

Complex Customer Relationships

A student has just moved to another state and started college. She applies for a credit card, where she and her family have always banked, and the bank turns her down. From the bank's perspective, this is a reasonable decision, since college students are often a high-risk group. Little did they know that this would turn into a crisis at the highest levels.

The executive vice president of sales at a large regional bank in the United States related this story. In this case, the student happened to be the daughter of a large real estate developer. Her father's company was one of the bank's largest and most profitable customers. He was also a close friend of several members of the bank's Board of Directors.

The unhappy student told her father about the rejected credit application. The father told the board, the board asked the bank president what was going on. And the president demanded an explanation from the EVP. A simple business practice turned into a crisis.

Two things explained the credit rejection. First, when the young woman lived at home, she was considered part of her parent's household. However, when she left, she was no longer part of that household. The bank no longer knew the most important fact about her customer relationship. Second, the systems supporting the consumer and business sides of the bank did not talk to each other (and sometimes there are good reasons for keeping such information in separate places).

Who is the customer? In this case, the rather standard rejection of a single credit card application threatened a much more profitable relationship. Should the credit card group automatically approve applications from family members of important customers? Probably not. However, all the divisions of the bank should know who the important customers are so they can make more informed decisions.

Companies, for instance, often rely on distribution networks to sell their goods. This means that the makers of the product have little control over actual purchases. And, conversely, the people who sell the product don't care what customers buy—so long as they buy a lot. So, when a customer buys soda at a supermarket, the supermarket does not care if it is Pepsi or Coke. The supermarket wants to sell both of them, and usually makes a comparable margin on either. However, the manufacturers do care, and care a lot.

Data mining can help manufacturers learn about how their product is being used. In Chapter 13, we will see some good examples of this from the retail grocery industry. It is useful to realize that just obtaining the data in this case required cooperation among several companies. The grocery store used another company to process point-of-sale transactions, and all this data had to get back to the packaged goods manufacturer. Cooperation among businesses is a fact of life. Is one of these the "customer"? That is not important. Data mining and visualization can help producers understand what products are selling where, and predict what will be needed in the future, especially when they can obtain point-of-sales data from cooperative retailers.

This distribution network occurs in many different areas besides groceries:

- Pharmaceutical companies make drugs, but these are sold only when doctors prescribe them.
- Insurance companies offer policies, but these are often sold through agents.
- Financial service companies offer retirement plans, but first they have to sell to a company and then to the employees, because the employees can choose from only a fixed set of options.
- Vineyards sell wines, but these are available only at stores and restaurants that carry the wine.

These are all examples of indirection in the marketplace where intermediaries complicate the relationship with the customer. Pharmaceuticals, insurance companies, financial service companies, and vineyards are examples of companies that must work with their suppliers and distributors to reach consumers. The customer relationship is more complicated; it must take intermediaries into account as well.

Not all data mining questions are about consumers, however. What is the practice variation among physicians? And how do the variations affect outcomes of patients with certain conditions? Which insurance agents are finding the most profitable customers? And so on.

There is a distinction between business customers and consumers. Often, it makes sense to focus on each separately. Banks, telephone companies, insurance companies, and so on usually treat corporate accounts differently from consumer accounts.

One big difference between consumers and businesses is the presence of account management teams. At the corporate level, data mining must support the account managers. For consumers, dedicated account managers are too expensive (except for very, very profitable individuals, such as those who qualify for private banking). But business customers are much bigger, so they do rate personalized attention. The purpose of the data mining, of finding patterns, can be to help these people perform their jobs more effectively.

Figure 4.1 provides a very simple example from a project whose goal was to understand the behavior of business customers. This is an example of visualizing customer behavior; in this case, the chart shows how many "communication events" originate from a group of companies over a particular network.

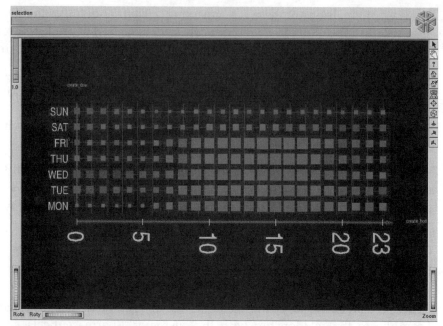

Figure 4.1 Communication events originating from a particular business by day of the week and hour of the day.

The size of the box shows the total number of events on that day of the week and hour of the day. The darker boxes indicate longer events, and brighter boxes indicate shorter events.

A picture such as this can be very useful. This one shows that most communication takes place during working hours, as expected. However, longer communications are taking place at other times, such as Wednesday mornings and on the weekends. Diving into the data a bit further reveals that the companies who are using the network late at night and early in the morning are, indeed, behaving differently from most of the customers. They actually constitute a very important segment. This example shows how visualization of usage patterns can reveal important insight into business customers.

Not all businesses are big businesses. There are many, many small businesses out there, which are often best treated as consumers. There are so many of them that the sales force is not organized into account teams. And, they have traditionally been willing to settle for more standardized products. These are the same characteristics that make data mining so powerful for understanding consumers.

Customer Segments

Customer segmentation refers to the process of dividing customers into mutually exclusive groups, presumably because customers within each group are more similar to each other than to others. Here are some examples of segments:

- Regular, gold, and platinum credit card holders
- Mass market versus corporate customers
- Customers with 12 months or more of history and more recent customers

Segments are useful because they allow business users to add domain-specific information into the data mining effort. The business people expect platinum cardholders to behave differently from gold cardholders, so they develop different marketing campaigns for each group and also build separate models for them. This separation often produces better models, because the data mining algorithms do not have to rediscover what is already known.

On the other hand, not all customer segmentations yield fruitful results. Often, the belief in separate segments has been driving the business in the past. However, there is no data to support these differences. As with all assumptions made about the data, it is important to validate assumptions made about customer segmentation. Are the churn rates different for platinum cardholders versus gold cardholders? Are average charges? And so on.

Of course, data mining algorithms, such as clustering, can help find segments. These data mining segments are different from segments known to the business, precisely because they are not driving the business. Or, they may be driving the business, but management cannot take advantage of what it does not know.

Visualization can be a powerful tool for spotting and understanding clusters. Figure 4.2 is a scatter graph that shows sales of products at a small group of pet stores over a period of a few weeks that uses an affinity card to track repeated visits by the same customer. In these pet stores, many products are associated with particular pet types, such as birds, cats, dogs, fish, and reptiles. Each axis of the graph corresponds to a purchase of an item associated with that pet. So the box at the intersection of "bird" and "reptile" shows the number of customers who purchased a bird item and a reptile item. The box at the intersection of "bird" and "bird" is the number of customers who purchased two bird items.

This visualization shows several interesting groups of customers. As expected, the largest groups are cat owners and dog owners. Then, there is a sizable group of customers who own both cats and dogs, and another that owns fish. Notice though, that fish owners do not tend to own other types of pets. And bird and reptile owners are not a significant portion of the business (at least by counts of individual items).

These observations lead to four important segments of customers. The most important are only-dog-owners and only-cat-owners. These are followed by only-fish-owners and cat-and-dog-owners. The rest can be lumped together as "other" since they are so small.

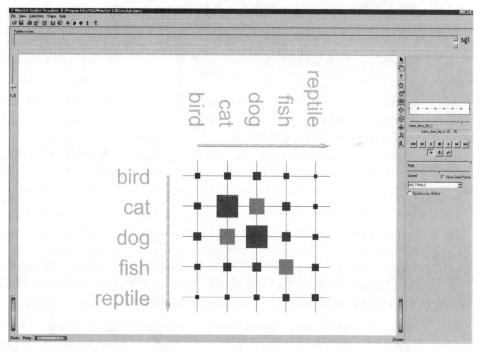

Figure 4.2 A scatter graph helps to understand and visualize clusters of customers.

The Customer Lifecycle

The customer lifecycle refers to the various stages of the relationship between a customer and a business. The customer lifecycle is important because it directly relates to long-term customer value.

As a place to start, it is often said that there are only three ways to increase the value of customers:

- Increase their usage (or purchases) on the products that customers already have.
- Sell them more or higher-margin products.
- Keep them for a longer period of time.

A valuable customer is not usually a static customer. The relationship evolves and changes over time. Understanding this relationship is a critical part of customer relationship management. And predicting important customer lifecycle events is the most common use of data mining. So, mastering data mining requires understanding customer relationships.

The customer experience refers to the details of customers' interactions with a company. How are new customers signed up? How do they register complaints? What forms must be filled out to open a new account? How does a customer upgrade their telephone? And so on, and so on. The answers to these questions and innumerable similar questions are highly specific to a particular business.

What is interesting is that the customer experience clumps into a few major stages that constitute the customer lifecycle. These are general stages, and it is possible that not every customer passes through every stage at the same rate, and the details of the stages depend on the business and the industry. However, these stages are very useful guidelines.

Why is the customer lifecycle important? For one thing, the customer lifecycle is a framework for understanding customer behavior. Data mining fits in at different points in the lifecycle, and understanding the lifecycle makes data mining more effective. In addition, certain lifecycle events are critical. Being able to predict these changes is very valuable indeed.

Stages of the Lifecycle

Figure 4.3 illustrates the major stages of the customer lifecycle:

- Prospects are people in the target market, but not customers yet. This is an important distinction—we don't want to sell renter's insurance to home-owners.

- Responders are people who have made a serious inquiry or signed up. The exact process for transforming responders into established customers depends on the industry.

- Established customers are using the product or service. When they first become established customers, they are new customers. In many cases, the early behavior of established customers is highly predictive of future behavior.

- Former customers have churned, voluntarily or involuntarily.

Basically, the customer lifecycle says that customers are initially interested (because they are in the target market). At some point they become customers. Their initial behavior may be very important. As ongoing customers, they may be high value, high potential, or low value. And eventually, they are no longer customers. Let's look at this lifecycle with respect to particular industries.

Consider a company that sells disability insurance. In the United States, their target market would be individuals under 65 years old (before retirement age), and of them, the company would generally want healthier, lower risk people.

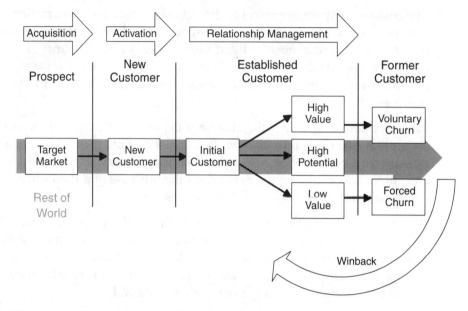

Figure 4.3 Customers evolve through different stages.

Someone becomes a responder by filling out insurance forms. Responders have to go through underwriting before they can become established customers. This process is invasive, often requiring medical exams, so many responders never become established customers.

Consider a credit card company. Their target market is usually people who need credit and who are able to pay it back. Someone becomes a responder by filling out a credit application. Responders become established customers when the credit application has been approved and the customer activates the card. And established customers may stop being customers in several ways. A *voluntary churner* tears up the card and sends it back. A *silent churner* simply stops using the card. And an *involuntary churner* stops making payments until the account is closed and the balance is written off.

The catalog industry usually targets people with a particular interest. Their responders are people who have asked for the catalog (rarely) or who have made an initial purchase. Their established customers are those who've purchased something somewhat recently, such as in the past 18 months. And they, too, are faced with voluntary churners, silent churners, and involuntary churners.

In the Web world, there are similar distinctions. A prospect is anyone in the world in the target market. They become responders by visiting the e-commerce Web site and registering. People who regularly make purchases are established customers. Established customers end their relationship as voluntary churners, silent churners, or involuntary churners.

Major Lifecycle Events

Throughout the customer lifecycle, there are important events, specific to the different stages in the lifecycle. Figure 4.4 shows typical lifecycle events. Each stage in the lifecycle offers opportunities for data mining and customer relationship management.

Prospects

Acquisition campaigns are marketing campaigns directed to the target market, seeking to interest prospects in a company's product or services. Acquisition campaigns have certain characteristics, notably, that there is a scarcity of data for the campaign. Since the target market consists of people who are not yet customers, there is no customer data about them.

Can data mining help? Of course. Data mining can profile people who have responded to previous, similar campaigns in order to focus the marketing effort on previous responders. An even better approach is to look for prospects who are similar to today's profitable customers—just bring in the right customers in the first place.

Often, prospecting campaigns use advertising and other broadcast media. Whatever the channel, it is often possible to use data mining profiles to find the best customer segments, and then to buy lists, advertising space, and so on, directed at the good profiles.

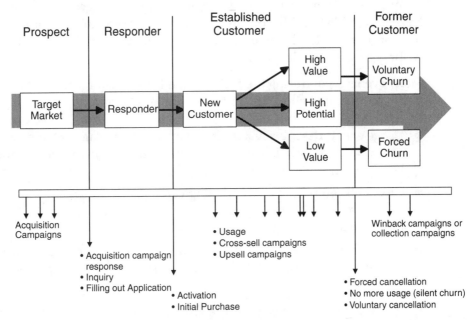

Figure 4.4 Events during the customer lifecycle are tied to the customer lifecycle stages.

Responders

Prospects become responders in several different ways:

- By signing up on a Web page
- By calling a toll-free number
- By filling out an application
- By returning a warranty card
- And so on

All of these change the anonymous prospect into a named person, someone who can be targeted and tracked over time. Although responders have not yet spent any money, they are the most likely people to do so—and to become established customers. In some cases, such as people who visit a Web site and make an initial purchase on the same visit, there may be little distinction between responders and established customers.

Data mining is often used to determine which prospects will become responders. Predictive models are also commonly used to determine which responders will become established customers.

Established Customers

Responders become established customers when the economic relationship has been established. This means that they have made an initial purchase, that their application has been approved, that they have made it through underwriting, or some similar action.

Many events occur during the cycle of established customers. The most important events fall into one of the following three categories:

- Usage events describe customer behavior. When usage is the major source of revenue, stimulating usage is a very important business imperative. Usage patterns also differentiate among different customer segments.
- Cross-sell campaigns are marketing campaigns encouraging customers to widen the relationship by purchasing services and products outside of their initial set.
- Up-sell campaigns are marketing campaigns that encourage customers to deepen the relationship by upgrading existing products and services.

Established customers are clearly a fruitful area for data mining. Customer usage events provide the best insight available into customer behavior patterns.

Predicting when events are likely to happen and determining which customers are likely to respond to cross-sell and up-sell campaigns are very valuable to the business.

The behavior of established customers is often buried in large amounts of detail records that record many of the details of every transaction. Using this data requires extracting features from this data, as discussed in Chapter 6.

Early purchase and usage patterns can be very valuable. In some businesses, initial behavior is a big predictor of future usage. Customers may be high-spenders or low-spenders; they may focus on a single product or many. These types of behavior are often apparent based on the first few purchases.

Former Customers

At some point, established customers cease being customers. There are two fundamentally different types of churn. The first is voluntary churn, which refers to established customers who no longer want to be customers. It is important to understand that voluntary churn can occur for many different reasons:

- The customer moves out of the geographic area served by the company.
- The customer has a change in lifestyle (such as retirement) and no longer needs the product or service.
- The customer has found a better offer from a competitor.
- The customer no longer sees the value in using the product.

On one project predicting churn in the credit card industry, the authors found a small cluster of churners. This cluster consisted of people who had held their card for the maximum amount of time (over 10 years) and had relatively few purchases. These people also had a high average age. On further examination, this cluster turned out to be people who had passed away. Not an important customer segment for churn prevention!

One of the big questions is, when will established customers churn? This is related to the lifetime value of the customer, because the longer someone is a customer, typically the higher his or her value.

The other type of churn is involuntary churn, where the established customer is no longer a good customer, usually because they have stopped paying their bills. It is critical to distinguish between voluntary churn and involuntary churn, it is very expensive to have customer retention campaigns focused on customers who are not going to pay their bills anyway.

A big question is which established customers are likely to churn involuntarily. The answer can be surprising. One project, for instance, found that people who had never made a late payment on their mortgage were more likely to default than those who were habitually tardy payers. Further analysis revealed that the on-time payers who defaulted had lost their jobs and so had no means to pay their bills. On the other hand, the habitually tardy people presumably had the means but simply did not put a high priority on paying on time.

All is not lost when an established customer becomes a former customer, though. Win-back campaigns are targeted at winning back former customers.

Data Appears at Different Times in the Lifecycle

The closer the relationship, the more data available. Figure 4.5 illustrates different types of data that appear in different stages.

Prospects usually have the smallest amount of data, especially because prospect lists are often purchased from outside service bureaus. At the extreme, advertising campaigns are usually targeted at specific demographic groups. However, nothing is known about who actually receives an advertising message until they respond to the campaign. On the Web, it is possible to determine all the different ads that a given browser has been exposed to—and to tie them together once someone makes a purchase using the same browser.

However, over time, the same prospect may receive multiple campaigns. Knowing the campaign history, and especially which campaign finally converted the prospect into an established customer can be very valuable information. For this

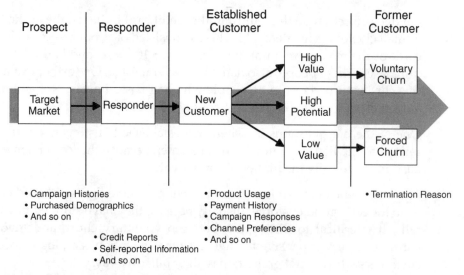

Figure 4.5 Data during the customer lifecycle.

reason, many companies want to keep track of prospects the same way that they keep track of their own customers. Some are investing in prospect data warehouses, while others use an outside bureau to keep track of their prospecting campaigns.

Often, when someone "applies" for a product or service, they leave a trail of information. This may be in the form of credit applications, customer surveys, medical forms, and so on. Capturing this information is valuable, although it is subject to some caveats.

When someone is signing up as a customer, they usually do not want to be bothered with filling out unnecessary forms. If the form is required, they may take short-cuts and not fill in fully accurate information. Or, credit checks may not be run on every potential customer. So the data gathered at this point is often incomplete and inaccurate.

It is the behavior data generated by established customers that is the most valuable. This data contains a wealth of information describing customers and their segments.

Response data refers to data about responses and nonresponses to campaigns. It is important to remember who is exposed to every marketing campaign, as well as remembering who responded.

The Customer's Lifecycle

In addition to the customer lifecycle, we must also consider the customer's life cycle. That is, every person has life events that affect his or her value as a customer. These life events may determine when someone becomes an established customer, when they churn, and what products they need. Some of these events are

- Changing jobs
- Having a first child
- Marrying
- Divorcing
- Retiring
- Moving
- Major illness

These events often provide opportunities for enhancing customer relationships. Unfortunately, people do not widely broadcast this type of information—it is personal and intimate.

In some cases, it is possible for companies to identify certain important changes. For instance, when people move, they often report a change of address. This suggests that a field such as address is important, not only for its current content, but to understand when the last move occurred.

When women (and even some men) marry or divorce, they often change their names. Banks can sometimes tell when people change jobs, by noting changes in direct deposit behavior. These are some examples of how companies can use data to derive some useful attributes of their customers. And companies that have their customer's ages can often "guesstimate" factors about lifecycle events.

Health maintenance organizations know about the health of their members, so they can ensure, for instance, that pregnant women are receiving adequate prenatal care. Insurance companies often know when people marry, because marriage often affects insurance policies (for instance, by combining automobile insurance on one policy).

Are there any other ways? Often companies resort to purchasing lists. For instance, people who subscribe to bridal magazines are likely to be planning a wedding. Or visitors to Web sites directed at children are likely to be children, their parents, or teachers.

None of this is foolproof—and for good reason. Data about people's private lives needs to be treated very respectfully. However, in managing the customer relationship, it is sometimes valuable to take into account factors about lifecycle events.

Targeting the Right Customers at the Right Time

The theory of customer relationship management can be summed up in one phrase: targeting the right offer to the right customer at the right time for the right price. As with the famous stock market advice to "buy low and sell high," this theory is more easily expounded than executed. And, it begs of the question of measuring how well customer relationships are being managed.

This section offers two perspectives on the value of customer relationship management. The first is the simplest. Focusing on customers saves money and increases profits. The second is optimizing the value of each customer. This leads to a discussion on conflict resolution, later in this chapter, for handling the situation where many marketing campaigns are targeted to the same customers.

Budget Optimization

This is a common scenario: *ACME Corporation, a (fictitious) mail order catalog specializing in equipment for capturing and blowing up fictional small animals, has a* *new product, "roadrunner bait." This product is targeted at their loyal audience of wily coyotes. They have $300,000 to spend on the campaign and want to spend it as effectively as possible.*

The first approach is to optimize the budget. The marketing campaign has to fit within a specific budget, so it makes sense to spend the money as wisely as possible by focusing on customers who are likely to respond. How do we know who is likely to respond? Here are three common methods:

- Randomly select customers for the mailing or guess who the target audience is.

- Perform an RFM (recency, frequency, monetary) analysis and target customers who have made many purchases in the recent past for a large amount of money.

- Build a data mining predictive model, based on past experience, to determine who is likely to respond to this offer.

- Use data exploration and undirected data mining to profile likely responders to the offer.

What these methods have in common is that they assign a score to each customer. Customers with a high score are included in the campaign; customers with a lower score are excluded. What is the right score threshold? To answer this, we need more information.

On a typical marketing campaign, ACME Corporation spends about $1 for each item mailed. This covers the cost of creating, printing, and mailing the collateral, and assumes a minimum of 20,000 envelopes.

So, ACME can afford to mail 300,000 customers for $300,000. As a simple check, 300,000 is greater than 20,000, so it meets the minimum level for a marketing campaign. Simple enough. Score all the customers and select the 300,000 highest scoring ones for the campaign.

Cumulative gains charts and lifts charts are popular ways of looking at data mining results, as in Figure 4.6. The purpose of lift is to generate the "wow!" factor: "Wow! Targeting only 20 percent of the customers, we can reach 50 percent of the people who would respond." This is usually considered a good thing.

However, lift charts themselves do not provide hard quantitative measures. In this example, each decile accounts for 100,000 customers, so the top three deciles account for 300,000 customers appropriate for the campaign. The lift chart shows that the first three deciles (300,000 customers) are predicted to contain 65 percent of the responders.

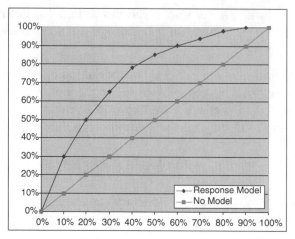

This chart shows the cumulative gains made by the response model. It says, for instance, that using the model, the customers with the top 10% of the scores account for 30% of known responders.

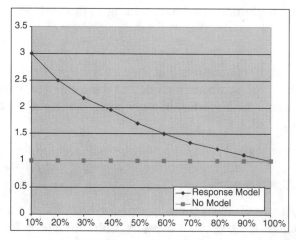

This chart shows the actual lift. It says that using the model, the top 10% of the scorers are 3 times more likely to respond than would be expected.

Figure 4.6 Two ways of depicting "lift" for the same model.

In this example, data mining has been used to optimize the campaign. By building a model that scores the propensity of the customers to want a particular product, we have managed to contact 65 percent of the responders instead of just 30 percent.

Campaign Optimization

Despite the "wow" factor, lift does not give a quantitative valuation of a model. The campaign has met its budget and the model has produced more responders than without the model. But, will the campaign yield a profit? This is the next step. A quantitative evaluation requires developing a net revenue model. And the net revenue model requires additional information:

On this marketing campaign, a typical responder is expected to order about $100 worth of products. Of the $100, $55 covers the costs of the product, shipping, and handling.

This is the information needed to develop a simple profit model. The two key items of information are

- The "cost" of mailing an offer is $1.
- The "net revenue" of a responder is $100–$55 = $45.

This is often expressed as a revenue matrix (see Table 4.1). This table says, for instance, that those customers who are predicted to respond to the campaign who actually do respond are worth $44. Why $44? This is their net revenue minus the cost of the marketing mailing. People who are predicted to respond, but don't, cost $1—the cost of sending them the mailing.

Notice that only the PREDICTED YES row of the cost matrix is used in this net revenue model. This makes sense. The people reached by the campaign are only those who are predicted to respond. There are no costs or net revenues associated with PREDICTED NO since they are not included in the campaign. In other words, the PREDICTED NOs are never used.

There are three other items of information needed to predict the profit. The first is the estimated response rate for the general population. Remember that lift tells us how much *better* a model performs. It does not say how many responders there are. So, a predicted lift of 3 could refer to a predicted 3% response rate, or a predicted 90% response rate—depending on whether response rate for the general population is 1% or 30%. For ACME Corporation, let's assume a response rate of 1%.

The second item of information is the overhead cost. This may refer to a fixed cost for a marketing campaign. Sometimes, the overhead is also used to incorporate a "minimum" campaign size constraint. Remember that ACME had a minimum campaign size of 20,000. Well, this corresponds to $20,000 of overhead, assuming that all 20,000 are nonresponders to the campaign.

Table 4.1 Cost Matrix for ACME Corporation Marketing Campaign

		ACTUAL	
PREDICTED		YES	NO
	YES	$44	–$1
	NO	$0	$0

The final item is the potential size of the mailing. This is needed to convert a number, such as 3% response rate to a dollar amount, such as $35,000. For ACME, we are going to look at different mailing sizes, assuming that there are one million potential recipients.

Table 4.2 shows the calculation of campaign profit based on these assumptions ($44 net profit per responder; $1 cost per non-responder; $20,000 overhead; 1 percent overall responses, one million customers). The first column is the decile. The next three columns are measures of the model's performance. GAINS is the proportion of the responders in that decile. Notice that it decreases from a high of 30% down to 0%. CUM is the cumulative gains, which is just the sum of all the gains up to that decile. The first decile has 30% of the responders and the second decile has 20% more. In total, they have 50%. The lift is how much better the model does up to that decile than a random model.

The GAINS, CUM, and LIFT numbers are all interchangeable. That is, given one of the columns, the other two can be calculated. The important columns are SIZE(YES) and SIZE(NO). These are, respectively, the predicted number of responders and nonresponders up to and including that decile. So, in the second decile, there are predicted to be 5,000 responders and 195,000 nonresponders, for a total size of 200,000. These are the numbers used to calculate the profit, based on the profit matrix shown earlier.

Notice that the profit starts at –$20,000, then reaches a maximum at the first decile, and then starts to decline thereafter. This is the typical shape of the

Table 4.2   Spreadsheet Showing Profit for Each Decile for a Given Model

DECILE	GAINS	CUM	LIFT	SIZE	SIZE(YES)	SIZE(NO)	PROFIT
0%	0.0%	0%	0.000	0	0	0	($20,000)
10%	30.0%	30%	3.000	100,000	3,000	97,000	$15,000
20%	20.0%	50%	2.500	200,000	5,000	195,000	$5,000
30%	15.0%	65%	2.167	300,000	6,500	293,500	($27,500)
40%	13.0%	78%	1.950	400,000	7,800	392,200	($69,000)
50%	7.0%	85%	1.700	500,000	8,500	491,500	($137,500)
60%	5.0%	90%	1.500	600,000	9,000	591,000	($215,000)
70%	4.0%	94%	1.343	700,000	9,400	690,600	($297,000)
80%	4.0%	98%	1.225	800,000	9,800	790,200	($379,000)
90%	2.0%	100%	1.111	900,000	10,000	890,000	($470,000)
100%	0.0%	100%	1.000	1,000,000	10,000	990,000	($570,000)

curve. Also, notice that a mailing to all customers would be unprofitable, but that a mailing to the first decile is profitable. Understanding the profit curve can turn around an unprofitable campaign. However, the profit curve is highly sensitive to the numbers used to generate it.

Figure 4.7 shows three different profit curves, with three different assumptions. The most profitable curve assigns a value of $100 to each responder, while holding the cost at $1. Notice that, under these conditions, a mailing to any of the deciles is profitable. However, the maximum profitability is attained at the fourth decile. The middle curve is the one described earlier, with a profit of $44 and a cost of $1. The bottom has a profit of $44 and a cost of $2. Under these assumptions, the mailing can never be profitable.

This figure also illustrates one of the problems with using predicted profitability to optimize campaigns: the answers are highly sensitive to assumptions in the data. Changing the expected response rate from 1% to 1.5% changes the maximum profit from $15,000 on decile 1 to $118,750 on decile 3—a very large difference for such a small change in a parameter. It is unlikely that the parameters used in the profit model will be known with a high degree of confidence. Therefore, the predicted profit should be used with care.

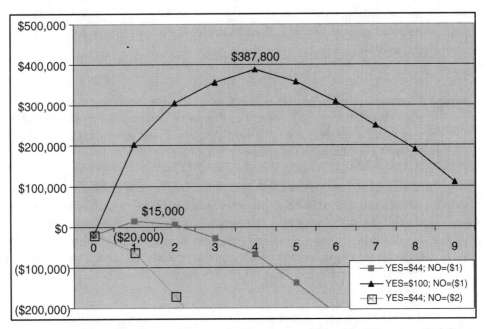

Figure 4.7   Three different profit curves for the same model, with different profitability assumptions.

Customer Optimization

Profit is a good measure for a single campaign. However, real life is more complicated:

As time goes by, ACME Corporation expands its range of products. From its humble beginnings trying to rid the world of roadrunners, it has now turned into a full-scale pest-control company, with different divisions devoted to different vermin, including roadrunners, of course, but also bunnies, baby birds, and ducks. They are now managing many more campaigns for their full range of pest control products.

The question is no longer maximizing the return on any given campaign. It is, instead, finding the right marketing message to send to each potential customer. That is, given a set of campaigns, they want to optimize the next campaign for each customer.

Figure 4.8 illustrates what happens with the profit optimization approach. A single campaign reaches only a minority of potential customers. As more and more campaigns are added, some customers are exposed to many different campaigns. This is usually considered a bad thing, because overloading people with marketing messages makes it very, very unlikely that they will respond to any of them. And many customers never participate in any campaign at all.

Do not overload customers with too many diverse marketing messages. Find the right message for each customer and focus on communicating that message. At the very least, customers will tune out all the messages. Worse, they may go to a competitor to cut down on the noise.

The campaigns are competing with each other for customers. And, many customers are not exposed to any message at all. Solving this requires turning our thinking inside out. The strategies so far have consisted of optimizing a single campaign—this is a product-oriented strategy. The solution is a customer-focused strategy. Instead of maximizing the value of each campaign, maximize the value of each customer. That is, for each customer or prospect, what is the best next message?

The best next message refers to any types of offer, including:

- Different types of promotional offers for new customers (free weekend long distance or airlines miles, for instance)

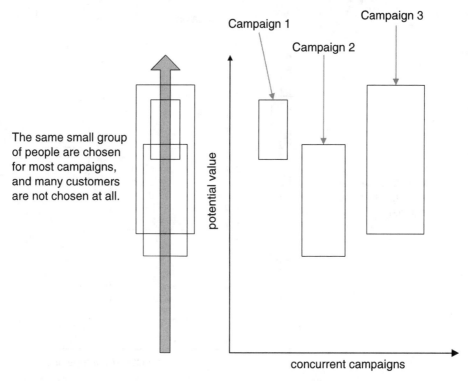

Figure 4.8 The same good customers (or prospects) tend to be chosen over and over for marketing campaigns.

- Choosing the right channel or channels for the message
- Retention programs focused at customers who are likely to leave
- Intervention programs, focused on customers who are likely to stop paying
- Prospecting offers, tailored to different customer needs
- Different product offers

Another way of thinking about this is by looking at all the possible messages and channels that can be directed at anyone—prospect, customer, former customer. Optimization is assigning each message to the right customer. Figure 4.9 offers a view of what happens.

Instead of having some customers receive many messages and many customers receive no messages, each customer receives the best message for him or her. What this means is that each customer is more likely to respond. Overall, there are more responders and presumably more revenue and profit as

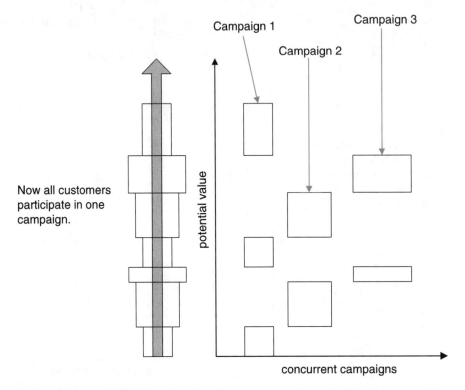

Figure 4.9 Maximize the value of each customer.

well. Now, every customer is getting a message and presumably this message is the most profitable message for that customer. This makes overall marketing more effective than merely optimizing for each campaign.

This approach is optimizing the customer. Customer optimization makes an assumption. Customers who are bombarded with multiple different messages are less likely to respond to any of them than customers who receive targeted offers. So, having a core group of customers who are part of many different campaigns may be self-defeating. Instead, it is often better to cycle through different messages, making one offer for a period of time (say, 1–3 months) and then moving on to another offer.

Optimizing the customer has another benefit. It allows the business to develop migration paths for their customers. A migration path is a sequence of events in the customer relationship that leads to long-term customer value. This can be as simple as recognizing that the college students of today are going to be a very profitable segment in the future—and so directing efforts at acquiring them. Or it can be more complicated, such as introducing new customers to sequences of messages over time that lead to more profitable behavior.

Conflict Resolution

The real world complicates the marketing process. Optimizing customer value works, but it highlights some of the organizational issues in marketing. That is, the organization and the business environment introduce constraints into the marketing process. Here are some questions that arise:

- *Who owns the customer?* Particular business units may feel that they "own" particular customers. This fact encourages those divisions to focus on their view of the customer relationship instead of the whole view. For instance, a credit card group at a bank may prefer to offer its customers gold cards instead of other banking services, even though additional banking services may be better for long-term customer value.

- *When was the customer last contacted?* Large companies that run hundreds or thousands of marketing campaigns per year often limit customer contact. Often, there are limits on the number of times that customers can be contacted within a given time period. Multiple campaigns may want to include the same person, but only one is allowed—hence the name, "conflict resolution."

- *Can the customer be contacted?* Some customers inform companies that they do not want to participate in marketing campaigns; others are on no-mail or no-telephone lists (maintained by the Direct Marketing Association (www.the-dma.org). And some high-end customers, such as private banking customers, are excluded from direct mail and telemarketing campaigns.

- *What products is the company trying to push?* Often, people are included in campaigns because the company is trying to push products. These imperatives can take precedence over campaigns that are more focused on customers.

- *How many people are targeted by the campaign?* There may be a floor or a ceiling for any given offer. Floors are often covered by budget constraints—such as having to send out at least 200,000 pieces of mail. Ceilings may be due to resources, such as the ability to contact 20,000 people per month from the call center. In other cases, the business plan may call for a target number of customers, and exceeding the target strains customer service.

- *How are channels being managed?* Scheduling issues, such as when direct mail can be printed and when an outbound telemarketing center is available, can influence how many customers are being contacted and which ones are the most appropriate.

Resolving these issues is part of optimizing the value of customers. Building the best data mining models is not the only goal; these need to be implemented in the most effective way possible.

Lessons Learned

This chapter has focused on the customer dimension, a critical dimension for successfully using data mining for marketing, sales, and customer support. Important points are as follows:

- The answer to the question "Who is the customer?" must be provided by the business. The answer should look at the different roles of the customer relationship, including the action role, the ownership role, and the decision-making role.

- Business relationships are usually different from consumer relationships, because they are more complex. Data mining can still provide insights into businesses. And small businesses should often be treated as consumers for marketing purposes.

- The customer lifecycle maps out the relationship between a consumer and a company. This relationship evolves over time, and includes different stages, such as prospect, responder, customer, and former customer, that heavily influence data mining.

- The customer's lifecycle is also important because it can drive important events. However, it is harder to find information about the customer's lifecycle, and it is very important to consider the privacy of individuals during the marketing process.

- Marketing campaigns are focused on customers. There are different ways to optimize campaigns. Focusing on the customer is the most effective, overall, but it requires cooperation among different departments.

In many cases, the purpose of data mining is to better serve customers. Mastering data mining requires understanding the full marketing process that communicates with them.

PART TWO

The Three Pillars of Data Mining

The next four chapters focus on the more technical aspects of data mining. Although the path is more technical, the goal remains the same: using patterns in data for business success. In some ways, the technical side is more challenging because it is so broad. It spans many disciplines, including statistics, machine learning, databases, and experimental design. Any of these could be the subject of an entire book—and many are. A single technique in Chapter 5, neural networks, is the subject of dozens of different books and hundreds of Ph.D. theses.

How can we hope to cover such a diverse field in just a few chapters? The answer is quite simple. We are looking at the big picture, which is how to extract business value from data, instead of trying to focus on each and every detail. This is not the place to learn how to implement neural networks, for instance, or the difference between training using backpropagation versus conjugate-gradient. Nor is it a comprehensive compendium of every type of decision tree. This is the place to learn how to apply these techniques to relevant real world problems.

Consider driving a car. It is not necessary (fortunately) to be an expert on internal combustion engines to be a good driver, or to be able to build a muffler from scratch, or to explain the role of each additive in gasoline. If a thorough understanding of all aspects of automobile manufacturing were necessary, there would be far fewer drivers on the road. Some understanding is useful—to handle an automobile on wet roads, or to diagnose what is going wrong when the car does not start. However, details are better left for the experts, and even the experts benefit from the perspective of the driver.

The situation is quite similar with data mining. For a long time, people did need to know many of the arcane details about data analysis to be successful. These people are statisticians. Now, the volumes of data and the business needs have grown enormously. There are not enough statisticians around to analyze all the data. Fortunately, the tools have become easier to use. And the methods (as discussed in the first part of the book) are better understood. The next few chapters contain mini-case studies and vignettes whose purpose is to illuminate the technical concepts. These are taken from our personal experiences in working with our clients. Their purpose is to act as streetlights, to help data miners stay on (or close to) a well-trodden path of best practices.

This introduction to Part Two provides an overview of the technical material in the next four chapters. The purpose is to lay out a map that will help to keep the focus on the bigger business problems rather than on the details of algorithms, data layouts, or experimental design.

The Three Pillars

The next three chapters discuss the three pillars of data mining: data mining techniques, data, and the modeling of data. The three pillars of data mining represent three core areas of competency that are needed to be successful in data mining. Practitioners need to have hands-on skills in these areas. On the other hand, managers and business users should understand enough about them to know when and where data mining can be effective.

Data Mining Techniques

The first pillar consists of the data mining techniques themselves. To some people, the data mining techniques seem a bit mysterious—are they evidence that computers can think like people? The answer, for better or worse, is that data mining techniques are no more mysterious than anything else a computer does, such as storing files or creating a spreadsheet (and both of these are admittedly a bit mysterious to us). The techniques are general approaches to solving problems, and there are usually many ways to approach the technique. Each of these ways is a different algorithm. The algorithms are like recipes with step-by-step instructions explaining what is happening.

Without requiring a background in mathematics or statistics, we try to go into enough detail to demystify the techniques, to convey how they actually work. It is important to have some understanding of their inner workings to know when to apply them, how to interpret the results, and whether or not they are working. In the chapter on techniques, our purpose is to explain the techniques with enough detail so you can

- Distinguish between different techniques, knowing their advantages and disadvantages
- Follow the techniques as they are used in the case studies
- Understand which technique is most appropriate for a given business problem
- Become familiar with important variations

The major techniques discussed here are the ones that are found in most comprehensive data mining tools: decision trees, neural networks, and clustering. These techniques are also available on a wide range of computing platforms, from individual desktops, to departmental servers, to the most powerful parallel computers. However, as desktops are becoming more powerful, it is often not necessary to purchase expensive hardware to run data mining algorithms. These techniques are the most commonly used techniques in the case studies. However, data mining has a broad reach, and we are not able to cover every algorithm used in the case studies in as much detail as we would like (without doubling the length of the book).

Each technique, in turn, has a myriad of different algorithms and implementations—almost every tool has some nuance that makes its implementation a little different from the next tool's. Although driving a Porsche 911 is different from driving a Honda Civic, it is easy enough to adapt to the differences—the steering wheel, the brake pedal, the gears are all sufficiently similar. Just as it is possible to learn how to drive a car, and generalize to any car, it is possible to learn how to use neural networks or decisions trees, and generalize to any tool.

It simply would not be possible to explain every possible variation in this book. And, in addition to boring most readers, the minor variations have much less effect on data mining results than other issues, such as preparing the data and building the right models.

Data

The second pillar of data mining consists of the data used in the process. Without data, there would be no data mining. Business would have to rely on hopefully intelligent guesswork (which is still often the case even when data is available). The power of data mining is leveraging the data that a company collects to make better informed business decisions.

Data mining has a very simplistic view of data that consists of a single table (or file or view) with well-defined columns. Most algorithms prefer that there be no missing data, and that the values all make sense—outliers can have a big impact on results. Data in the real world does not look like this; it comes from many different sources in many different formats, sometimes incomplete, always dirty. The process of bringing together all the disparate sources of data and extracting useful features from them is the biggest challenge in data mining.

The internal data that a company collects can be a competitive advantage, because competitors do not have access to it. The most voluminous source of data in many industries are the actual transactions recorded by individuals—each purchase made on a credit card, every web apge viewed, each line item recorded at a grocery store check out, every telephone call made. These are the richest source of information, and at the same time, the most challenging. To be useful for data mining, they must be summarized and yet, it does not work to store presummarized data because the same transactions can usefully be summarized in many different ways.

However, internal data is not the only source of data. Much data comes from external sources, such as:

- Demographics, psychographics, and webgraphics—information about individuals and households that bureaus glean from many different sources

- Data shared within an industry, such as credit reports, credit scores, and catalog subscriptions

- Summary data about geographic areas, store catchment areas, and so on

- Purchased external lists that meet some particular criteria

- Data shared from strategic business partners

The chapter on data covers how to work with data for data mining in the real world. Its purpose is to cover the important issues that arise with data and to act as a guide in planning and doing data mining. We do not intend for it to teach the particulars of specific data sources, such as "how to create dimensions on an OLAP cube" or "how to access data in SQL" or "how to do it in JDBC." We assume that these technical skills are available, in some form, to any company that wants to make data mining a core competency.

Modeling Skills

The third pillar of data mining consists of the set of modeling skills needed to build predictive models. The focus is on predictive models—directed data mining—instead of undirected data mining for two reasons. First, data mining is often about building predictive models. These models find patterns in data from the past to make predictions about unknown outcomes. Second, undirected data mining requires noticing patterns. It is much less susceptible to a repeatable methodology because it is about discovering new things; there is necessarily a human element. The predictive modeling process leads to many interesting insights, especially during the data exploration phase or while analyzing how models are working.

There is a methodology for building effective predictive models. This methodology is based on principles of experimental design, which is a way of saying that we need to understand all the factors that affect the model. A model that predicts churn in the wireless industry in the United States may not be appropriate in other countries. Or a propensity-to-buy model developed last year may not be appropriate this year, because the market has changed. Or the marketing collateral may change from one campaign to the next. The data miner needs to be aware of these factors to judge when and whether predictive models will be effective.

The models are built on preclassified data; that is, on data where the desired outcome (or some proxy for it) is already known. The process of building models involves holding back some of the data for validation and test purposes. This process is encapsulated in the creation of the model set. Another very important factor is time. Typically, models are built using data from the past, since this is the data that is available. However, we often want to make predictions about the future, using current data. So between the time that the model is developed and it is used, the time frame shifts.

Predictive data mining injects a bit of the scientific method into business processes. Of course, the purpose of most data mining is to improve business decisions, such as choosing the right customers for a particular marketing campaign. Data miners are not scientists. We do not have to create repeatable processes, defending every detail to our peers. On the other hand, we often do have to explain what we did to colleagues and have confidence in the ultimate results, so it is worthwhile paying attention to the details.

Putting It All Together in a Data Mining Environment

Pillars hold things up: It is fair to ask the question, "What rests on the three pillars of data mining?" Chapter 8 explores creating a data mining environment. Such an environment needs to take the best practices from working with data mining techniques, transforming data, and building models, and combine them with the business needs to deliver effective results.

As data mining becomes an increasingly important part of business, managers want to understand how best to take advantage of the new technology. Once, they merely wanted to know what data mining was. Then, they wanted to know if it was relevant to their business. Those days have past. Now, they want to know how to implement it successfully inside their organization (or whether they should outsource it).

The tools have matured, so success is more an organizational issue than a technical one. We have seen many organizations with top-notch technology, where lack of communication between different groups hinders the effectiveness of their efforts. However, better groups learn from their experiences and improve over time. American Express is a good example of a company where modeling plays a strategic role in their business, and related issues, such as customer privacy, are part of the core culture. As of this writing, the primary group responsible for modeling has hundreds of people and high corporate visibility. Few data mining groups will grow to this size, but it does point to the potential strategic importance of data mining.

Tool selection is one of the first big decisions facing data mining groups. Unfortunately, the process of tool selection often overshadows the fact that data mining software is one of the least important ingredients for effective customer relationship management. Different tools do have different strengths and are appropriate under different circumstances. However, we only very rarely have seen data mining efforts fail because of the choice of tool—and the software has been improving significantly over the past few years. Organizational commitment, access to data and data cleansing, and good modeling techniques are all far more important.

Another important consideration is that the data mining expertise does not exist in a vacuum. This is true from a technical perspective as well as an organizational one. The data used for data mining comes from many different systems. This makes data mining part of the enterprise-wide effort for data warehousing and business intelligence. Often, the results of data mining efforts feed back into other systems, such as campaign management or e-commerce systems. Managing technical interdependencies, while maintaining business relevance, is a challenge for effective data mining groups.

Data Mining Techniques
and Algorithms

Because data mining is viewed as a technical subject, people often get the notion that mastering data mining is largely a matter of studying advanced algorithms and learning the techniques for applying them. Having read this far, you know that this technical understanding is actually only one small component of the mastery you seek. It is, however, a very important one! Without at least a high-level understanding of the most important data mining algorithms, you will not be able to understand when one technique is called for and when another would be more suitable. You also need to understand what is going on inside a model in order to understand how best to prepare the model set used to build it and how to use various model parameters to improve results.

Fortunately, the level of understanding needed to make good use of data mining algorithms does not require detailed study of machine learning or statistics. Just as it is possible to take wonderful photographs without understanding exactly how exposure to light causes the photosensitive chemicals in the emulsion to change color, it is quite possible to make good use of data mining tools without understanding all the details of how they work. By the same token, just as a some understanding of the photographic process is essential to making good choices of film speed, aperture, and length of exposure, so a basic understanding of the principal data mining algorithms is essential for anyone wishing to master the art of data mining.

Techniques and Algorithms

In this book, we distinguish between data mining techniques and the algorithms used to implement them. We use the word *technique* to refer to a conceptual approach to extracting information from data. We use *algorithm* for the step-by-step details of a particular way of implementing a technique. So, for example, automatic cluster detection is a technique that can be implemented using self-organizing maps, simple *k*-means, Gaussian *k*-means, and a number of other algorithms.

This chapter introduces three important data mining algorithms and the techniques for applying them in real-world situations such as those described in the case studies in Part Three. Of course, the step-by-step mechanics described here are not usually visible to users of the data mining tools that automate them.

Different Goals Call for Different Techniques

Data mining can be prescriptive or descriptive. This distinction refers to the *goal* of the data mining exercise. The chief goal of a prescriptive data mining effort is to automate a decision-making process by creating a model capable of making a prediction, assigning a label, or estimating a value. Normally, the results in prescriptive data mining will be acted upon directly: Someone will or will not be offered credit or insurance or a chance to win a trip to Orlando, depending on the results of a model used for these purposes. Under this scenario, the most important measure of a model is its accuracy. For a direct mail response modeling application, the model that does the best job (however best is defined for the campaign in question) of ranking the prospects from most likely to least likely to respond is the best model—even if another model is easier to build or easier to understand.

Often, however, data mining is descriptive rather than prescriptive. The primary goal of descriptive data mining is to gain increased understanding of what is happening inside the data and thereby in the wider world that the data reflects. Descriptive data mining often results in actions, but these are not the sort of actions that can be automated directly from the results of the model. With descriptive data mining, the best model may not be the one that makes the most accurate predictions. Often, the insight gained through building the model is the most important part of the process. The actual scores from the model may never be used at all.

Prescriptive Versus Descriptive Data Mining: An Example

To appreciate the difference between prescriptive and descriptive data mining, consider two projects where data mining was employed to analyze response to a direct mail offer. The two projects have nearly identical inputs to work with—demographic, financial, and lifestyle data on the targets of a similar campaign in the past along with a flag indicating which of those candidates had responded. The goal of the first project is to produce a model that gives each new prospect, drawn from a similar population, a score based on the likelihood that he or she would respond to a similar offer in the future. This score will be used to select recipients for a direct mail solicitation. The second project has a different goal: to understand the principal drivers of response to past campaigns in order to improve future marketing efforts. At first glance, these goals may seem to be the essentially same. However, they are different, and their differences have a material effect on the data mining effort.

Because these projects are both examining prospective customers, the only internal data available are the names and addresses of people who had received similar offers in the past along with a flag indicating who had responded to the offer. As usual in such cases, the names and addresses were sent to a third-party data supplier for enrichment with demographic and lifestyle variables. The lifestyle variables (boat ownership, golf handicap, hobbies, and the like) are very sparse. Indeed, most people had null entries for most of the lifestyle fields.

Because of the sparsity of the data, it is difficult to make use of these variables to support the model building goals of the first project. Not only do the large number of missing values make it difficult for the data mining algorithms to discover meaningful rules on these sparse fields—any rules that might be generated would necessarily apply to only a very small fraction of future cases.

Data of this kind is extremely ill-suited to neural network modeling since, as we will see later in this chapter, the inputs to a neural network must be converted to a numeric representation with no missing values allowed. Decision trees are capable of treating a null value as simply one more value taken on by a categorical variable, but this sort of sparse data is problematic for them as well. Decision trees look at one variable at a time in order to find the ones with the most information content with which to create the tree. Any variable that has the same value (whether null or the square root of pi) for most records is unlikely to be chosen. Derived variables, such as a count of a person's non-null lifestyle variables help somewhat, but the final models still have little predictive power and are disappointing for determining who is likely to respond to the mailing.

In the second project, these same variables proved to be very useful. Although none of the lifestyle variables contain a non-null value very often, a few of them are very predictive of response in the rare cases where they are filled in. The first project is unable to make much use of the strong predictors because it has a significant constraint: It assumes that the data sample available for training are representative of the total population of potential customers. The second project looks at these results quite differently: If people with certain unusual interests or hobbies are more likely to respond to an offer, the right course of action is to find a new population from which to draw prospects. The second project built clusters that were rich in responders and compared these clusters with the general population variable by variable. Wherever a particular interest or hobby, however rare in the population, turned out to be significantly more common among responders, the company went in search of mailing lists from magazines and organizations associated with that pastime.

Different Data Types Call for Different Techniques

Chapter 6 covers data in all its wondrous variety and examines data transformation issues in great detail. For now, we simply note that most data mining algorithms are designed with specific kinds of predictions and specific types of input data in mind. If the goal of a data mining project is to estimate some kind of numeric quantity such as customer lifetime value or the load factor of a future flight, the data mining algorithm will need to produce numeric output. If the variables available for making the estimate are primarily categorical, we will want to stay away from algorithms that only work for numeric inputs. Of course, there are ways of assigning numerical values to categorical variables and any numeric variable can be transformed into an ordered categorical variable through binning. These transformations, along with many others, are discussed in the next chapter. Be warned, however, that type transformations of this sort can be difficult and they are certainly not without danger. They run the risk of destroying valuable information or adding spurious information that may lead to incorrect conclusions. That is why the types of both input and output variables should be taken into account when selecting a data mining algorithm.

Three Data Mining Techniques

The three data mining techniques described in this chapter are

- Automatic cluster detection
- Decision trees
- Neural networks

These three were chosen because they are implemented in a large number of commercial software applications and because, together, they cover a wide range of data mining situations.

As noted in Chapter 3, data mining tasks can be either directed or undirected. Most of the data mining projects discussed in this book (and most of the data mining projects going on out in the real world) are directed. In directed data mining the goal is to predict, estimate, classify, or characterize the behavior of some pre-identified target variable of variables in terms of a collection of input variables. Examples of directed data mining include classifying insurance claims, estimating loan balances, identifying prospects, and predicting attrition. Two of the data mining techniques described here, neural networks and decision trees, are used primarily for directed data mining. (Neural network and decision tree approaches to clustering, an undirected task, do exist, but the examples of their application in this book are all directed.)

In undirected data mining, there is no target variable to be predicted. Instead, the goal is to discover structure in the data set as a whole. Examples of undirected data mining include determining what products should be grouped together for a specialty catalog, finding groups of readers or listeners with similar tastes in books and music, and discovering natural customer segments for market analysis. One useful application of undirected data mining is to carve up a complex data set into a collection of simpler ones in order to give directed data mining techniques like neural networks and decision trees a better chance of finding explanations for the behavior of a target variable within each cluster. The undirected data mining technique described here is the most commonly implemented algorithm for automatic cluster detection.

Automatic Cluster Detection

There are many mathematical approaches to finding clusters in data, and whole text books are devoted to the subject. Some methods, called divisive methods, start by considering all records to be part of one big cluster. That cluster is then split into two or more smaller clusters, which are themselves split until eventually each record has a cluster all to itself. At each step in the process, some measure of the value of the splits is recorded so that the best set of clusters can be chosen at the end. Other methods, called agglomerative methods, start with each record occupying a separate cluster, and iteratively combine clusters until there is one big one containing all the records. There are also self-organizing maps, a specialized form of neural network that can be used for cluster detection.

K-means, the clustering algorithm discussed here, is available in a wide variety of commercial data mining tools and is more easily explained than most. It works best when the input data is primarily numeric. For an example of clustering, consider an analysis of supermarket shopping behavior based on loyalty card data. Simply take each customer and create a field for the total amount purchased in various departments in the supermarket over the course of some period of time—diary, meat, cereal, fresh produce, and so on. This data is all numeric, so *k*-means clustering can work with it quite easily. In fact, the automatic cluster detection algorithm will find clusters of customers with similar purchasing patterns. (And, lest you believe that analyzing supermarket transactions is this simple, rest assured that we have left out many onerous details of working with real grocery data.)

How K-Means Cluster Detection Works

This algorithm divides a data set into a predetermined number of clusters. That number is the "k" in the phrase *k* means. A mean is, of course, just what a statistician calls an average. In this case it refers to the average location of all of the members of a particular cluster. But what does it mean to say that cluster members have a location when they are records from a database?

The answer comes from geometry. To form clusters, each record is mapped to a point in "record space." The space has as many dimensions as there are fields in the records. The value of each field is interpreted as a distance from the origin along the corresponding axis of the space. In order for this geometric interpretation to be useful, the fields must all be converted into numbers and the numbers must be normalized so that a change in one dimension is comparable to a change in another.

Records are assigned to clusters through an iterative process that starts with clusters centered at essentially random locations in the record space and moves the cluster *centroids* (another name for the cluster means) around until each one is actually at the center of some cluster of records. This process is best illustrated through diagrams (see Figure 5.1). For ease of drawing, we show the process in two dimensions, but bear in mind that in practice the record space will have many more dimensions, because there will be a different dimension for each field in the records. Don't worry about drawing the clusters, there are other ways of understanding them.

In the first step, we select *k* data points to be the seeds, more or less arbitrarily. Each of the seeds is an embryonic cluster with only one element. In this example, *k* is 3. In the second step, we assign each record to the cluster whose centroid is nearest. In Figure 5.2 we have done the first two steps. Drawing the boundaries between the clusters is easy if you recall from high school geome-

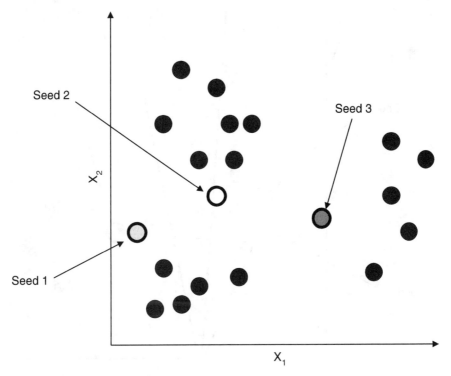

Figure 5.1   Initial cluster seeds.

try that given two points, X and Y, all points that are equidistant from X and Y fall along a line that is half way along the line segment that joins X and Y and perpendicular to it. In the illustration, the initial seeds are joined by dashed lines and the cluster boundaries constructed from them are solid lines. Of course, in three dimensions, these boundaries would be planes and in N dimensions they would be hyperplanes of dimension N–1.

As we continue to work through the k-means algorithm, pay particular attention to the fate of the point with the box drawn around it. On the basis of the initial seeds, it is assigned to the cluster controlled by seed number 2 because it is closer to that seed than to either of the others. It is on seed 3's side of the perpendicular separating seeds 1 and 3, on seed 2's side of the perpendicular separating seeds 2 and 3, and on the seed 2's side of the perpendicular separating seeds 1 and 3.

At this point, every point has been assigned to exactly one of the three clusters centered around the original seeds. The next step is to calculate the centroids of the new clusters. This is simply a matter of averaging the positions of each point in the cluster along each dimension. Remember that k-means clustering requires that the data values be numeric. Therefore, it is possible to calculate

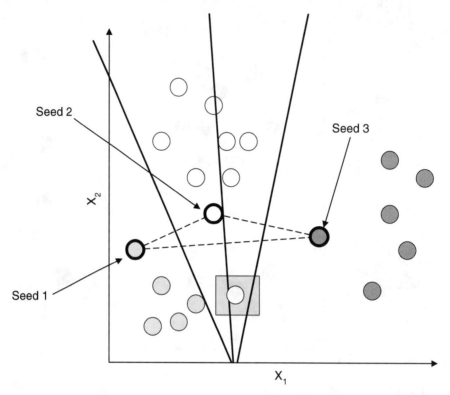

Figure 5.2 Initial cluster boundaries.

the average position just by taking the average of each field. If there are 200 records assigned to a cluster and we are clustering based on four fields from those records, then geometrically we have 200 points in a four-dimensional space. The location of each record is described by four fields, with the form (x_1,x_2,x_3,x_4). The value of x_i for the new centroid is the average of all 200 x_1s and similarly for x_2, x_3, and x_4.

In Figure 5.3, the new centroids are marked with crosses. The arrows show the motion from the position of the original seeds to the new centroids of the clusters. Once the new clusters have been found, each point is once again assigned to the cluster with the closest centroid. Figure 5.4 shows the new cluster boundaries—formed, as before, by drawing lines equidistant between each pair of centroids. Notice that the point with the box around it, which was originally assigned to cluster number 2, has now been assigned to a cluster number 1. The process of assigning points to cluster and then re-calculating centroids continues until the cluster boundaries stop changing. Happily, for most data sets, the cluster boundaries are set after a handful of iterations.

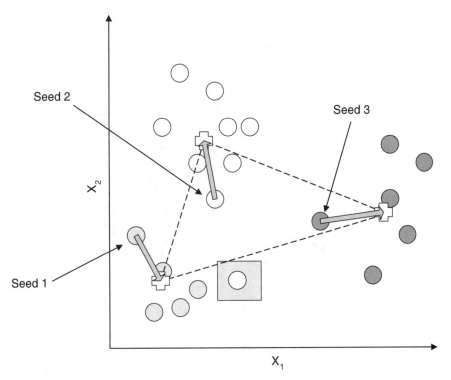

Figure 5.3   After one iteration.

Consequences of Choosing Clustering

The choice of automatic clustering as the data mining technique to apply to a problem has consequences for the kinds of questions that can be addressed and for the kinds of data preparation that will be required.

Because automatic cluster detection is an undirected technique, it can be applied without prior knowledge of the structure to be discovered. On the other hand, since the clusters that are automatically detected have no natural interpretation other than that, for a given mapping of records to a geometric coordinate system, some records are close to one another, it can be hard to put the results to practical use.

Choosing Weights and Measures

By choosing different distance measures, automatic clustering can be applied to almost any kind of data. For instance, there are measures of the distance between two passages of text that can be used to cluster newspaper articles into subject groups. Most clustering software, however, uses the Euclidean

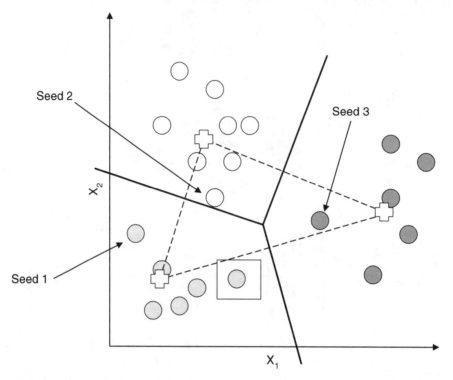

Figure 5.4   New cluster assignments.

distance formula we all once learned in school—the one where you take the square root of the sum of the squares of the displacements along each axis. That means that non-numeric variables must be transformed and scaled before they can take part in the clustering. Depending on how these transformations are done, the categorical variables may dominate the clustering or be completely ignored.

Choosing the Right Number of Clusters

In the k-means method, the original choice of a value for k determines the number of clusters that will be found. If this number does not match the natural structure of the data, the technique will not obtain good results. Unless there is some *a priori* reason to suspect the existence of a certain number of clusters, the miner will probably want to experiment with different values for k. Each set of clusters must then be evaluated. In general, the best set of clusters is the one that does the best job of keeping the distance between members of the same cluster small and the distance between members of adjacent clusters large. For descriptive data mining, though, the best set of clusters may be simply the one that shows some unexpected pattern in the data.

Some tools give automatic help with iterating over a list of values for k. One, SGI MineSet, has an interesting approach to automating the search for the right number of clusters. If the user supplies a range of clusters to search for, say 5 to 10, MineSet will first create five clusters according to the k-means algorithm sketched previously. It then looks at the clusters and orders them by their geometric size. Some clusters will be tightly packed around the centroid. Others will be much larger. MineSet takes the most dispersed of the original five clusters and splits it into two clusters. This process of re-clustering the most dispersed clusters is continued until the upper bound (ten, in this case) is reached. Along the way, the software keeps track of a measure of the overall fitness of the cluster groups and uses it to select the final collection of clusters.

Interpreting the Clusters

A strength of automatic cluster detection is that it is an undirected knowledge discovery technique. Every strength has a corresponding weakness. When you don't know what you are looking for, you may not recognize it when you find it! The clusters generated by the automated clustering algorithms (whether k-means or any other algorithm) are not guaranteed to have any practical value. Once the clusters have been created, it is up to you to interpret them. There are several approaches to understanding clusters. Three that we use frequently are

- Building a decision tree with the cluster label as the target variable and using it to derive rules explaining how to assign new records to the correct cluster.
- Using visualization to see how the clusters are affected by changes in the input variables.
- Examining the differences in the distributions of variables from cluster to cluster, one variable at a time.

When to Use Cluster Detection

Use cluster detection when you suspect that there are natural groupings that may represent groups of customers or products that have a lot in common with each other. These may turn out to be naturally occurring customer segments for which customized marketing approaches are justified.

More generally, clustering is often useful when there are many competing patterns in the data making it hard to spot any single pattern. Creating clusters of similar records reduces the complexity within clusters so that other data mining techniques are more likely to succeed.

Figure 5.5 shows a MineSet visualization of the results of a clustering done on supermarket shoppers, showing clusters of shoppers based on the time of day that they typically shop. This visualization chooses the three most important variables for showing the clusters—of course, all available variables are used to calculate the clusters, but the tool sorts them in order of their importance to the cluster definitions. These clusters differentiate strongly among customers who primarily shop in the morning, afternoon, and evening.

Figure 5.6 illustrates how a single variable affects the clusters. This image only shows a single variable and four of the eight clusters. In this case, the variable is the ratio of spending that takes place in the morning, and it varies from 0 to 1. In cluster 1, the average value is 0.153—meaning that most people in this cluster do less than 15 percent of their shopping in the morning. In cluster 2, on the other hand, the average value is 0.859—indicating that shoppers in this cluster make all but 15 percent of their purchases in the morning.

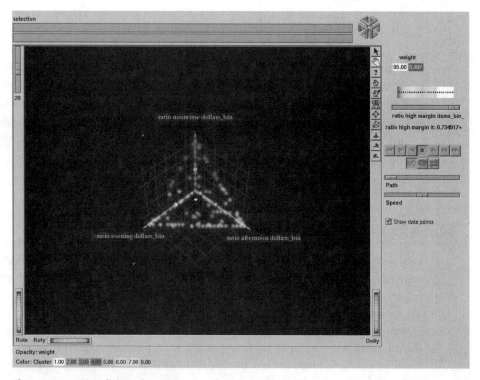

Figure 5.5 Visualizing clusters.

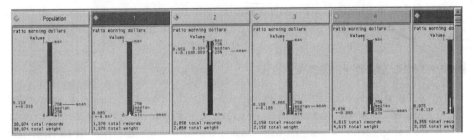

Figure 5.6 How one variable behaves across clusters.

Decision Trees

Decision trees are a wonderfully versatile tool for data mining. Decision trees seem to come in nearly as many varieties as actual trees in a tropical rain forest. And, like deciduous and coniferous trees, there are two main types of decision trees:

Classification trees label records and assign them to the proper class. Classification trees can also provide the confidence that the classification is correct. In this case, the classification tree reports the class probability, which is the confidence that a record is in a given class.

Regression trees estimate the value of a target variable that takes on numeric values. So, a regression tree might calculate the amount that a donor will contribute or the expected size of claims made by an insured person.

All of these trees have the same structure. When a tree model is applied to data, each record flows through the tree along a path determined by a series of tests such as "is field 3 greater than 27?" or "is field 4 red, green, or blue?" until the record reaches a leaf or terminal node of the tree. There it is given a class label based on the class of the records that reached that node in the training set or, in the case of regression trees, assigned a value based on the mean (or some other mathematical function) of the values that reached that leaf in the training set.

Various decision tree algorithms such as CHAID, C4.5/C5.0, CART, and many with less familiar acronyms, produce trees that differ from one another in the number of splits allowed at each level of the tree, how those splits are chosen when the tree is built, and how the tree growth is limited to prevent overfitting. Although these variations have led to many a doctoral thesis, for our purposes they are not very interesting. Today's data mining software tools typically allow the user to choose among several splitting criteria and pruning rules, and to control parameters such as minimum node size and maximum tree depth allowing one to approximate any of these algorithms.

How Decision Trees Work

The discussion on clustering described how the fields in a record can be viewed as the coordinates of that record in a multidimensional record space. That geometric way of thinking is useful when talking about decision trees as well. Each branch of a decision tree is a test on a single variable that cuts the space into two or more pieces. For concreteness and simplicity, consider a simple example where there are only two input variables, X and Y. These variables take on values from 0 to 100. Each split in the tree is constrained to be binary. That is to say, at every node in the tree, a record will go either left or right based on some test of either X or Y.

In Figure 5.7, a decision tree has been grown until every box is completely pure in the sense that it contains only one species of dinosaur. Such a tree is fine as a description of this particular arrangement of stegosauruses and tricer-

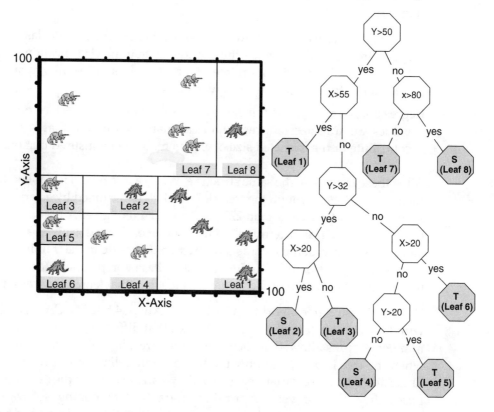

Figure 5.7   A decision tree cuts the space into boxes.

atopses, but is unlikely to do a good job of classifying another similar set of prehistoric reptiles.

WARNING

For some training sets, it is possible to build a decision tree that correctly classifies every single record. This is possible when the training set contains no examples of records whose input variables all have the same values, but whose target variables belong to different classes. Although such a tree provides a good description of the training data, it is unlikely to generalize to new data sets. That is why the test set is used to prune the tree once it has been grown using the training set.

Why? A tree that precisely describes the data from which it was derived is unlikely to generalize well to another sample drawn from the same population. This problem is known as *overfitting*, a topic we will return to frequently in this and other chapters. But ignoring that for the moment, how would we use this tree to classify an unknown dinosaur for which X=40 and Y=75? Starting at the root node, we go to the right because the Y-value is greater than 50. Then, since the X-value is not greater than 80, we classify the unknown dinosaur as a Triceratops. Equivalently, by looking at the box chart we can see that the point (40, 75) is clearly in a box containing only triceratopses.

How Decision Trees Are Built

Decision trees are built through a process known as recursive partitioning. Recursive partitioning is an iterative process of splitting the data up into partitions—and then splitting it up some more. Initially, all of the records in the training set—the preclassified records that are used to determine the structure of the tree—are together in one big box. The algorithm then tries breaking up the data, using every possible binary split on every field. So, if age takes on 72 values, from 18 to 90, then one split is everyone who is 18 and everyone older than 18. Another is everyone who is 18 or 19, and everyone who is 20 or older. And so on. The algorithm chooses the split that partitions the data into two parts that are purer than the original. This splitting or partitioning procedure is then applied to each of the new boxes. The process continues until no more useful splits can be found. So, the heart of the algorithm is the rule that determines the initial split.

Finding the Initial Split

The process starts with a training set consisting of preclassified records. Preclassified means that the target field, or dependent variable, has a known class. The goal is to build a tree that distinguishes among the classes. That is, the tree can be used to assign a class to the target field of a new record based on the values of the other fields or independent variables.

For simplicity, assume that there are only two target classes and that each split is a binary partitioning. The splitting criterion easily generalizes to multiple classes, and clearly any multiway partitioning can be achieved through repeated binary splits. We don't lose much by addressing the simpler case in order to make the explanation easier to follow.

The first task is to decide which of the independent fields makes the best splitter. The best split is defined as one that does the best job of separating the records into groups where a single class predominates. The measure used to evaluate a potential splitter is the reduction in *diversity* (which is just another way of saying "the increase in purity"). Because the concept of diversity (or conversely *purity*) is at the very heart of the decision tree methods, it is worth spending a little time on it.

There are several ways of calculating the index of diversity for a set of records. Even though it is intuitively obvious in Figure 5.8 that the group at the root is more diverse than either of the groups at the children nodes, how is this fact actually measured? Ecologists, concerned about the diversity of actual populations of plants and animals in the wild, have developed one measure, called Simpson's diversity index. To calculate this index, which in the data mining world is usually called the Gini index, imagine reaching out and touching a single member of the population and then letting it go before reaching out again. The diversity index is the probability that the second thing touched belongs to a different class than the first.

The root of the tree contains nine triceratopses and seven stegosauruses. The chance of touching a triceratops on the first try is 9 out of 16 or about 0.56, and the chance of touching a stegosaurus is 7 out of 16 or about 0.44. To calculate the chance of touching two different species in two attempts, consider first the chance of touching members of the same species. Then, the chance of touching members of two different species in two attempts is simply what is left over after taking away the probability of touching a member of the same species twice in a row. Since this is sampling with replacement, the probability of touching a member of any particular class the second time is the same as it was the first time. So, the chance of touching a triceratops twice in a row is 0.56×0.56, the chance of touching a stegosaurus twice in a row is 0.44×0.44, and the diversity index, the chance of touching a different kind of dinosaur each time, is what's left over or $1-(0.44^2+0.56^2) = 0.49$, which is close to the maximum possible diversity index of 0.5. The limiting value, 0.5 (or, generally, $1/n$ where n is the number of categories), is reached when each class has exactly the same number of members and therefore exactly the same probability of being picked.

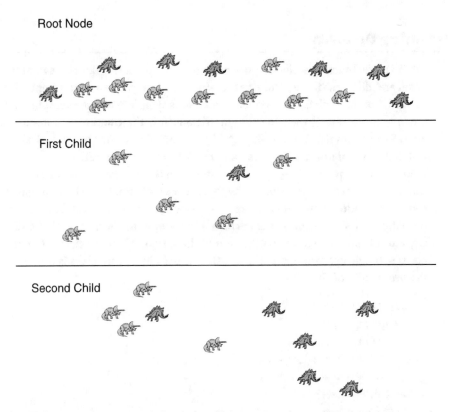

Figure 5.8 A diverse population is split into two subpopulations of greater purity.

The formula for the diversity index for binary targets is $2p_1(1-p_1)$ where p_1 is the probability of class one. (This formula is derived in the sidebar for those who are interested). Using this formula, after the first split, the first child has five triceratopses and only one stegosaurus, giving it a diversity value of 0.28. The second child has four triceratopses and six stegosauruses for an index of diversity of 0.48. The weighted average of the diversity at the children is $((0.28\times6)+(0.48\times10))/16$, which equals 0.41. The total reduction in diversity is the diversity at the root minus the weighted average of the diversity of the children. In this case, the split on X>50 has reduced the total diversity from 0.49 to 0.41.

To choose the best splitter at a node, the decision tree algorithm considers each input field in turn. In essence, each field is sorted. Then, every possible split is tried. The diversity measure is calculated for the two partitions, and the best split is the one with the largest decrease in diversity. This is repeated for all the fields. The winner is chosen as the splitter for that node.

Measuring Diversity

The diversity index described in the main text has been developed several times in several different fields, and has therefore been given several different names. To statistical biologists, it is the Simpson diversity index. To cryptographers, it is one minus the repeat rate. To econometricians, it is the Gini index, named after an Italian economist. The developers of the CART algorithm (Breiman et al. 1984) called it the Gini index, so that is what most software tools call it.

Whatever its name, its purpose is to measure the diversity of a population. It can be interpreted as the probability that any two elements of the population chosen at random with replacement will belong to different classes. Since the probability of any one class being chosen twice in a row is simply P_i^2, the diversity index is simply one minus the sum of the all the P_i^2. When there are only two classes, things get even simpler since the probability of one class is one minus the probability of the other:

```
1-(P₁²+P₂²)
1-(P₁²+(1-P₁)²)
1-(P₁²+(1-P₁)(1-P₁))
1+ -1(P₁²+(1-P₁)-P₁ +P₁²)
1+ -P₁² + -1 + P₁ + P₁ + -P₁²
2P₁-2P₁²
2P₁(1-P₁)
```

Growing the Full Tree

The initial split produces two nodes, each of which is then split in the same manner as the root node. First, if all the outcomes in the node are the same, then there is no sense in trying to split it. In this case, the node is labeled as a leaf node.

Otherwise, the decision tree algorithm examines all the input fields to find candidate splitters. If the field takes on only one value, it is eliminated from consideration since there is no way it can be used to create a split. A categorical field that has been used as a splitter higher up in the tree is likely to become single-valued fairly quickly. The best split for each of the remaining fields is determined. When no split can be found that significantly decreases the diversity of a given node, then it is a leaf node.

Eventually, only leaf nodes remain and the full decision tree has been grown. As we shall see, however, the full tree is generally not the tree that does the best job of classifying a new set of records.

There are several other popular diversity measures, some of which follow. All of their graphs have similar shapes going from 0 when the population is all one class to a maximum value when the two classes are equally represented. A high index of diversity indicates that the set contains an even distribution of classes, whereas a low index means that members of a single class predominate. The best splitter is the one that decreases the diversity of the record sets by the greatest amount. Three common diversity functions have simple formulas when there are only two outcomes:

```
min(P₁,P₂)
2P₁(1-P₁)          Gini index
P₁logP₁+P₂logP₂    Entropy
```

All of these functions have a maximum where the probabilities of the classes are equal and evaluate to zero when the set contains only a single class. Between the extremes of full diversity and complete uniformity, these functions have slightly different shapes. As a result, they produce slightly different rankings of the proposed splits. It has been shown that the Gini criterion tends to favor splits that isolate the largest target class in one branch of the tree, and the entropy criterion tends to favor balanced splits. The reason that software packages often allow the user to choose a splitting criterion is that there is no single best choice. The data miner must experiment to determine which one gives the best results for the data set in hand.

Pruning the Tree

Pruning is the process of removing leaves and branches to improve the performance of the decision tree. A pruned tree is, in fact, a subset of the full decision tree. The decision tree keeps growing as long as new splits can be found that improve the ability of the tree to separate the records of the training set into classes. If the training data were used for evaluation, any pruning of the tree would only increase the error rate. Does this imply that the full tree will also do the best job of classifying new data sets? Certainly not!

Tree building algorithms make their best split first, at the root node where there is a large population of records. Each subsequent split has a smaller and less representative population with which to work. Towards the end, idiosyncrasies of the training records at a particular node display patterns that are peculiar only to those records. The patterns are meaningless and harmful for prediction.

For example, say the decision tree is trying to predict height and it comes to a node containing one tall Dorian and several shorter people with other names. It can decrease diversity at the node by a new rule saying that "people named

Dorian are tall." This rule helps classify the training data, but if, in the wider universe, Dorian turns out to be a fairly rare name and, in any case, not particularly well-correlated with stature, the rule will be worse than useless. (Of course, in practice, we would not include irrelevant fields, such as name, in the model set. This example is for illustration.)

Look again at Figure 5.7. The first split on Y>50 seems to reflect some general rule about the dinosaur population. At the third level down in the tree, however, there is a split on Y>20 that only serves to separate two records. This split is much more suspicious. It probably makes a distinction that happens to be true in the training set, but seems unlikely to hold in general. By this depth in the tree, the model is overfitting the training set.

What can be done about overfitting? There are several approaches to this problem. They can be divided into pruning techniques and bonsai techniques. The bonsai techniques try to stunt the growth of the tree before it grows too deep. They work by applying various tests at each node in order to determine whether a further split is likely to be useful. The test may be as simple as requiring a minimum number of records that must be in a node or it may be more complicated, involving a statistical test for the significance of the proposed split. A potential problem with all of the bonsai methods is that they rely only on information in the training set and so are unreliable as a means of avoiding the memorization of training data that leads to overfitting. Experience shows, however, that simply setting a fairly large minimum node size tends to result in well-behaved trees. This is because when the nodes contain many records, they are more likely to be a representative sample.

Pruning methods, on the other hand, allow the initial decision tree to grow quite deep and then find ways to prune off the branches that fail to generalize. Actually, many pruning techniques share the drawback of only making use of information in the training set. One common approach is to find the classification error rate associated with various smaller and smaller subtrees of the initial tree. Of course, when these error rates are calculated on the same data used to create the tree, the error keeps dropping as the tree gets more complex, so a complexity term is added to the error in order to punish greater complexity. In this kind of pruning, a branch is kept only when the improvement in classification performance is large enough to outweigh the extra complexity.

This approach to pruning works reasonably well, but when data is plentiful (as is rarely the case in the academic environments where algorithms are developed, but is frequently true in the commercial world where they are applied), a better approach bases the pruning decision on the actual performance of the tree. The performance of the tree and all of its subtrees is measured on a separate set of preclassified data, called the test set. With a single test set, the algorithm can prune back to the subtree that minimizes the error on the test set. The graph in Figure 5.9 shows how this works. With multiple test sets, we can even more directly address the issue of model generality by selecting the subtree that performs most consistently across several test sets.

Consequences of Choosing Decision Trees

Now that you understand how decision trees are built, it is easy to see some of the consequences for the data miner. First, notice that since every split in a decision tree is a test on a single variable, decision trees can never discover rules that involve a relationship between variables. This puts a responsibility on the miner to add derived variables to express relationships that are likely to be important. For example, a loan database is likely to have fields for the initial amount of the loan and the remaining balance, but neither of these fields is likely to have much predictive value in isolation. The ratio of the outstanding balance to the initial amount carries much more helpful information, but a decision tree will never discover a single rule based on this ratio unless it is included as a separate variable.

Handling of Input Variables

In some situations, the way that decision trees handle numeric input variables can cause valuable information to be lost. When a split is chosen only the rank order of the observations comes into play. For the most part, this does not

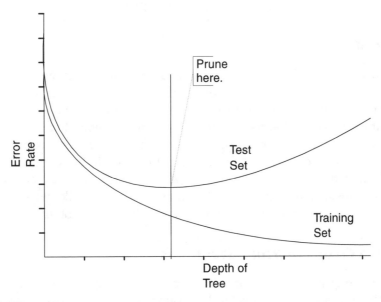

Figure 5.9   Error rate on training set and test set as tree complexity increases.

cause any problems, but under certain circumstances, information carried in the distribution of the values will be lost. Some decision tree algorithms first bin all numeric variables and then treat them as if they were categorical. This process can destroy information.

One advantage to the way decision trees treat numeric inputs is that they are not sensitive to differences of scale between the inputs, nor to outliers and skewed distributions. This means that data preparation is less of a burden with decision trees than it is with neural networks and k-means clustering, the other techniques examined in this chapter.

The handling of categorical variables can also cause problems. Depending on the particular algorithm employed, categorical variables may be split on every value taken on by the variable, leading to a very bushy tree that soon runs out of records on which to base further splits. Other algorithms find ways to group class labels into a small number of larger classes by combining classes that yield similar splits. Since the number of possible groupings grows very large, very fast as the number of classes grows, an exhaustive search of all combinations quickly becomes impractical. Software products use various shortcuts to pare down the space to be searched, but the clustering process can still be quite time consuming. Categorical target variables that take on many values are also problematic.

Decision trees are error-prone when the number of training examples per class gets small. This can happen rather quickly in a tree with many levels and/or many branches per node. They are very sensitive to the density of the outcomes, a topic discussed in more detail in Chapter 6.

Trees and Rules

Decision tree methods are often chosen for their ability to generate understandable rules. This ability can be overstated, however. It is certainly true that for any particular classified record, it is easy to simply trace the path from the root to the leaf where that record landed in order to generate the rule that led to the classification—and most decision tree tools have this capability. Many software products can output a tree as a list of rules in SQL, pseudocode, or pseudo-English. However, a large complex decision tree may contain hundreds or thousands of leaves. Such a tree is hardly more likely than a neural network to communicate anything intelligible about the problem as a whole.

Ability to Clearly Indicate Best Fields

Decision-tree building algorithms put the field that does the best job of splitting at the root node of the tree (and the same field may appear at other levels in the tree as well). It is not uncommon for decision trees to be used for no

When to Use Decision Trees

Decision-tree methods are a good choice when the data mining task is classification of records or prediction of outcomes. Use decision trees when your goal is to assign each record to one of a few broad categories. Decision trees are also a natural choice when your goal is to generate rules that can be easily understood, explained, and translated into SQL or a natural language.

other purpose than prioritizing the independent variables. That is, using a decision tree, it is possible to pick the most important variables for predicting a particular outcome because these variables are chosen for splitting high in the tree.

Another useful consequence of the way that important variables float to the top is that it becomes very easy to spot input variables that are doing *too* good a job of prediction because they encode knowledge of the outcome that is available in the training data, but would not be available in the field. We have seen many amusing examples of this, such as discovering that people with nonzero account numbers were the most likely to respond to an offer of credit—less than surprising since account numbers are assigned only after the application has been processed!

Neural Networks

Neural networks are at once the most widely known and the least understood of the major data mining techniques. Much of the confusion stems from over-reliance on the metaphor of the brain that gives the technique its name. The people who invented artificial neural networks were not statisticians or data analysts. They were machine learning researchers interested in mimicking the behavior of natural neural networks such as those found inside of fruit flies, earthworms, and human beings. The vocabulary these machine learning and artificial intelligence researchers used to describe their work—"perceptrons," "neurons," "learning," and the like—led to a romantic and anthropomorphic impression of neural networks among the general public and to deep distrust among statisticians and analysts. Depending on your own background, you may be either delighted or disappointed to learn that, whatever the original intentions of the early neural networkers, from a data mining perspective, neural networks are just another way of fitting a model to observed historical data in order to be able to make classifications or predictions.

To illustrate this point, and to introduce the various components of a neural network, it is worth noting that standard linear regression models and many other functions equally devoid of mystery can easily be drawn as neural network diagrams. Take for example, the function z= 3x+2y−1. There are two variable inputs, x and y. For any values of x and y, the function will return a value for z. It might be that this function is a model, based on many observed values of x, y, and z that is now being used to predict values for z given new, previously unobserved values of x and y. If so, it is a predictive model just as surely as anything created by a data mining software package. In fact, this particular predictive model is represented by the simple neural network in Figure 5.10.

In neural network terminology, this network has an *input layer* and an *output layer*. Each of the inputs x and y gets its own *unit*, or network node. In general, it is not the actual values of the input variables that are fed into the input layer, but some transformation of them. Each input unit is connected to the output unit with a *weight*. In this case, the weights are the coefficients 3 and 2. Inside the output unit, the input weights are combined using a *combination function* (typically summation, as in this case) and then passed to a *transfer function*, the result of which is the output of the network. Together, the combination function and the transfer function make up the unit's *activation function*. The value produced by the output node's activation function is usually some transformation of the actual desired output. In this case, the network outputs z+1 rather than z. Just as some function is applied to the input variables in order to generate suitable inputs to the neural network, some function of the network's output is required to translate it back to the actual range of the target variable.

The Hidden Layer

Most neural networks are not as simple as the one in Figure 5.10. There is usually one, but sometimes more than one, additional layer of units between the input layer and the output layer. These layers are called *hidden layers* and the units in them are *hidden units*. Figure 5.11 shows a neural network similar

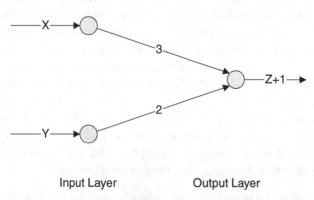

Input Layer   Output Layer

Figure 5.10 Neural network representation of z=3x+2y−1.

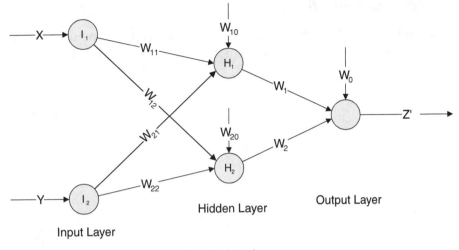

Figure 5.11   A neural network with a hidden layer.

to the one in Figure 5.10 but with a hidden layer. With the addition of the hidden layer, the function represented by the network is no longer a simple combination of its inputs. The output value is now calculated by feeding the weights coming from the two hidden units to the activation function of the output unit. The weights produced by the hidden units are themselves functions of the input units, each of which is connected to both units of the hidden layer. All this gets pretty complicated, pretty quickly, which is why no one ever actually writes out a neural network as an equation. The point is, though, it could be done!

The network illustrated here is a feed-forward network with a hidden layer. By feed-forward, we mean that data enters at the input nodes and exits at the output nodes without ever looping back on itself. Networks like this are also called *multilayer perceptrons*. If there is a "standard" neural network, it is the fully connected, feed-forward network with one hidden layer and a single-node output layer, but there are many, many variations. Often, there are multiple nodes in the output layer, each estimating the probability of a separate class of the target variable. Sometimes there is more than one hidden layer. Sometimes there are direct links from inputs to outputs that skip the hidden layer. There are neural network architectures that include loops and ones where the inputs arrive in waves, not all at the same time. In fact, we could write a whole book about neural networks—and many people have! When we speak of neural networks in this book, however, we are referring to fully connected, feed-forward, multilayer perceptrons.

Activation Functions

Inside each unit of a neural network, there is an activation function that consists of a combination function and a transfer function. The combination function is

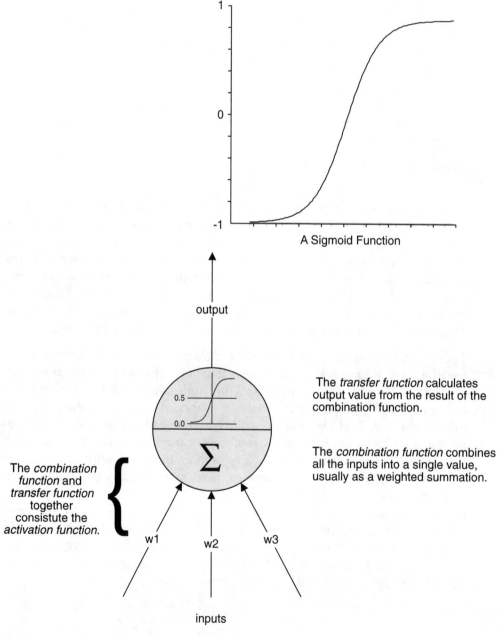

The *transfer function* calculates output value from the result of the combination function.

The *combination function* combines all the inputs into a single value, usually as a weighted summation.

The *combination function* and *transfer function* together consistute the *activation function*.

Figure 5.12   Sigmoidal transfer functions.

nearly always the weighted sum of the inputs. Transfer functions come in many more flavors. In Figure 5.12 we used a linear transfer function because the network was drawn to represent a linear function. More commonly, the transfer function is *sigmoidal* (S-shaped) or bell-shaped. The bell-shaped transfer functions are called *radial basis functions*. Common sigmoidal transfer functions are the arctangent, the hyperbolic tangent, and the logistic. The nice thing about these S-shaped and bell-shaped functions is that any curve, no matter how wavy, can be created by adding together enough S-shaped or bell-shaped curves. In fact, multilayer perceptrons with sigmoidal transfer functions and radial basis networks are both *universal approximators*, meaning that they can theoretically approximate any continuous function to any degree of accuracy. Of course, theory does not guarantee that we can actually find the right neural network to approximate any particular function in a finite amount of time, but it's nice to know. (Incidently, decision trees are not universal approximators.)

The sigmoidal transfer functions used in the classic multilayer perceptrons have several nice properties. The shape of the curve means that no matter how extreme the input values, the output value is always constrained to a known range (–1 to 1 for the hyperbolic tangent and the arctangent, 0 to 1 for the logistic). For moderate input values, the slope of the curve is nearly constant. Within this range, the sigmoid function is almost linear and exhibits almost-linear behavior. As the weights get larger, the response becomes less and less linear as it takes a larger and larger change in the input to cause a small change in the output. This behavior corresponds to a gradual movement from a linear model to a nonlinear model as the inputs become extreme.

Training Neural Networks

Training a neural network is the process of setting the weights on the inputs of each of the units in such a way that the network best approximates the underlying function, or put in data mining terms, does the best job of predicting the target variable. This is an optimization problem and there are whole textbooks dedicated to optimization, but in broad outline most software packages for building neural network models use some variation of the technique known as *backpropagation*.

Backpropagation

Training a backpropagation neural network has three steps:

1. The network gets a training instance and, using the existing weights in the network, it calculates the output or outputs for the instance.

Terminology Note

We use the term *backpropagation* to refer to any method of training a neural network that involves comparing the expected result for a given set of inputs to the output of the network during a training run, and feeding that difference back through the network to adjust the weights. By our definition, most of the neural networks in use today are trained using backpropagation. However, the original backpropagation networks popularized in the 1980s used an optimization method called *steepest descent* to correct the network weights. This turns out to be inefficient and is now generally replaced by other algorithms such as conjugate gradient or modified Newton. Some writers reserve the term "backpropagation networks" for the earlier, less efficient variety and coin new terms for each combination of error estimate and optimization method. We find that confusing, so to us, they are all backpropagation methods.

2. Backpropagation then calculates the error, by taking the difference between the calculated result and the expected (actual result).

3. The error is used to adjust the weights. We think of this as feeding the error back through the network.

Using the error measure to adjust the weights is the critical part of any backpropagation algorithm. In classic backpropagation, each unit is assigned a specific responsibility for the error. For instance, in the output layer, one unit is responsible for the whole error. This unit then assigns a responsibility for part of the error to each of its inputs, which come from units in the hidden layer, and so on, if there is more than one hidden layer. The specific mechanism is not important. Suffice it to say that it is a complicated mathematical procedure that requires taking partial derivatives of the transfer function. More recent techniques adjust all the weights at once, which is one of the things that makes them more efficient.

Given the error, how does a unit adjust its weights? It starts by measuring how sensitive its output is to each of its inputs. That is, it estimates whether changing the weight on each input would increase or decrease the error. The unit then adjusts each weight to reduce, but not eliminate, the error. The adjustments for each example in the training set slowly nudge the weights toward their optimal values. Remember, the goal is to generalize and identify patterns in the input, not to match the training set exactly. Adjusting the weights is like a leisurely walk instead of a mad-dash sprint. After being shown enough training examples, the weights on the network no longer change significantly and the error no longer decreases. This is the point where training stops; the network has learned the input.

One of the concerns with any neural network training technique is the risk of falling into something called a local optimum. This happens when the adjustments to the network weights suggested by whatever optimization method is in use no longer improve the performance of the network even though there is some other combination of weights—significantly different from those in the network—that yields a much better solution. This is analogous to trying to climb to the top of a mountain and finding that you have only climbed to the top of a nearby hill. There is a tension between finding the local best solution and the global best solution. Adjusting parameters such as the learning rate and momentum helps to find the best solution.

Consequences of Choosing Neural Networks

Neural networks can produce very good predictions, but they are neither easy to use nor easy to understand. The difficulties with ease of use stem mainly from the extensive data preparation required to get good results from a neural network model. The results are difficult to understand because a neural network is a complex nonlinear model that does not produce rules.

Data Preparation Issues

The inputs to a neural network must somehow be scaled to be in a particular range, usually between –1 and 1. This requires additional transforms and manipulations of the input data that require careful thought. Simply dividing everything by the largest magnitude is unlikely to get good results due to what might be termed the "Bill Gates problem." If we were to scale a variable containing net worth information by dividing all the values by Bill Gates' net worth, everyone else's net worth would be clumped together near zero while Bill's would be at one. The network would be unable to make use of "small" differences in net worth like one or two million dollars in order to make predictions. Something else—perhaps removing outliers or using log transformations—is required.

Categorical variables need to be converted to numerical variables in a manner that does not introduce spurious ordering. If states of the United States were given numbers in alphabetical order, then Alaska and Alabama would be close neighbors but Alabama and Mississippi would be far apart. You may think that the ordering doesn't matter, but there is no way to stop the neural network from trying to make use of it. Many categorical variables do have a natural order for a given data set and there are techniques for discovering it, but again, thought is required. Another approach to categorical variables is to create one binary flag variable for each value the variable might possibly take on. Unfortunately, this can lead to an explosion in the number of input nodes in the network and larger networks are slower to train and more likely to create unstable models.

Neural networks cannot deal with missing values. If records containing missing values are simply dropped, the training data will probably be skewed since the subset of records for which all fields are filled in is not likely to be representative of the population. Somehow, the missing values must be estimated, preferably while recording in another variable the fact that the field was missing. Predicting the best replacement for a missing value given the values of the filled-in fields is itself a data mining problem.

The requirement to pay so much attention to the input data is not entirely a bad thing. Since data quality is the number one issue in data mining, this additional attention can forestall problems later in the analysis.

Neural Networks Cannot Explain Results

This is the biggest drawback of neural networks in a business decision support context. For our clients, understanding what is going on is often as important, if not more important, than getting the best prediction. In situations where explaining rules may be critical, such as denying loan applications, neural networks are not a good choice. There are many situations, however, when the prediction itself matters far more than the explanation. The neural network models that can spot a potentially fraudulent credit card transaction before it has been completed are a good example. An analyst or data miner can study the historical data at leisure in order to come up with a good explanation of why the transaction was suspicious, but in the moments after the card is swiped, the most important thing is to make a quick and accurate prediction.

When to Use Neural Networks

Neural networks are a good choice for most classification and prediction tasks when the results of the model are more important than understanding how the model works. Neural networks actually represent complex mathematical equations, with lots of summations, exponential functions, and many parameters. These equations describe the neural network, but are quite opaque to human eyes. The equation is the rule of the network, and it is useless for our understanding.

Neural networks do not work well when there are many hundreds or thousands of input features. Large numbers of features make it more difficult for the network to find patterns and can result in long training phases that never converge to a good solution. Here, neural networks can work well with decision-tree methods. Decision trees are good at choosing the most important variables—and these can then be used for training a network.

Lessons Learned

This chapter has introduced three of the most common data mining techniques—clustering, decision trees, and neural networks—by describing the inner workings of at least one of the algorithms used to implement each one. We have seen that each technique is applicable to a wide range of situations, but that each has strengths and weaknesses that must be taken into account. The primary lesson that you should take away from this chapter is that no one data mining technique is right for all situations.

CHAPTER 6

Data, Data Everywhere...

"Data, data, everywhere nor any drop to drink." With apologies to Samuel Taylor Coleridge, this is often the situation we find ourselves in with respect to data. Like the thirsty sailors in *Rime of the Ancient Mariner*, available data satisfies our thirst for information as well as seawater satisfies our thirst for water. The thirst goes unquenched.

The proliferation of data is a feature of the modern world. Consider a seemingly simple transaction, a customer purchasing some items from a catalog. Such a transaction leaves a long list of transactions, an electronic trail, in multiple systems at different companies:

- The local telephone company knows when the telephone call was placed, who was called, how long the call lasted, and so on.
- The long distance company, handling the toll-free number, knows when the called was placed, who called, the duration, the route through the switching system, and so on.
- The catalog company knows items ordered, time and duration of call, promotion response, credit card used, inventory update, shipping method requested, and so on.
- The credit card processor knows transaction date, amount charged, approval code, vendor number, and so on.
- The credit card issuer has the billing record, interest rate, available credit update, and so on.

- The package carrier knows zip code, value of package, time stamp at truck, time stamp at sorting center, and so on.

Each company has the opportunity to learn from this simple interaction and to apply what they learn to improve their business and more profitably serve their customers. In a nutshell, this is the goal of data mining, and we see that it rests firmly on the foundation of data.

The electronic trail leads to some basic truths about data. Data comes in many forms, in many types, and on many systems. It is always dirty, incomplete, and sometimes incomprehensible. And yet, this is the raw material of data mining. If we compare data mining to searching for oil, then understanding the data is comparable to knowing where to drill for oil. The most powerful machinery is unlikely to find significant oil deposits beneath New York City or Boston, because they are not in an appropriate geography. Similarly, the most power-ful data mining techniques cannot find interesting patterns in data without adequately preparing it and knowing where to look.

This chapter undertakes an ambitious task, to cover the most important data issues that arise in data mining. These include choosing the right data, under-standing the structure of the data, adding derived variables, and working with dirty data. It also shows a practical example of work with data to derive important features from time series that describe customer behavior.

What Should Data Look Like?

To start the discussion on data, let's begin at the end: What should the data look like for data mining? All data mining algorithms use a very simple view of data, illustrated in Figure 6.1. This view of data, as a single table with rows and columns, is probably familiar to most readers. Alas, this single-table columnar format is not the way that data is created and stored in most environments—and for good reason. What is good for data mining is not optimal for most other purposes.

This simple view immediately brings up two questions. What are the rows? And, what are the columns? The answers to these questions are the most important step in preparing data for data mining.

The Rows

What is the process for determining what a row refers to? A row is the unit of action, and should be determined by understanding how the data mining results will be used. That is, data mining serves a purpose, in helping the busi-ness eventually take some action. A row is the unit of action. It is one instance

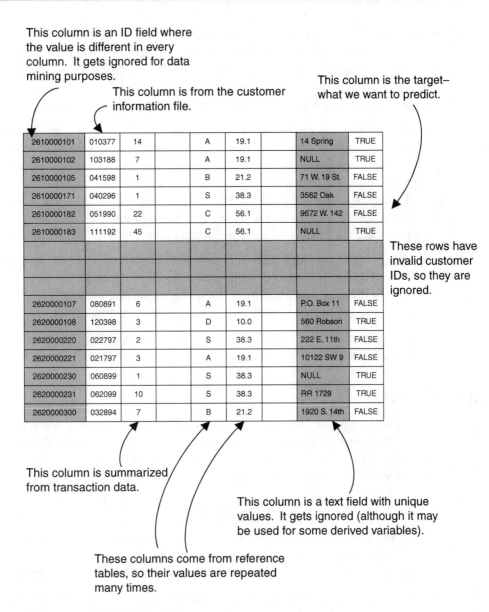

This column is an ID field where the value is different in every column. It gets ignored for data mining purposes.

This column is from the customer information file.

This column is the target—what we want to predict.

2610000101	010377	14		A	19.1		14 Spring	TRUE
2610000102	103188	7		A	19.1		NULL	TRUE
2610000105	041598	1		B	21.2		71 W. 19 St.	FALSE
2610000171	040296	1		S	38.3		3562 Oak	FALSE
2610000182	051990	22		C	56.1		9672 W. 142	FALSE
2610000183	111192	45		C	56.1		NULL	TRUE
2620000107	080891	6		A	19.1		P.O. Box 11	FALSE
2620000108	120398	3		D	10.0		560 Robson	TRUE
2620000220	022797	2		S	38.3		222 E. 11th	FALSE
2620000221	021797	3		A	19.1		10122 SW 9	FALSE
2620000230	060899	1		S	38.3		NULL	TRUE
2620000231	062099	10		S	38.3		RR 1729	TRUE
2620000300	032894	7		B	21.2		1920 S. 14th	FALSE

These rows have invalid customer IDs, so they are ignored.

This column is summarized from transaction data.

This column is a text field with unique values. It gets ignored (although it may be used for some derived variables).

These columns come from reference tables, so their values are repeated many times.

Figure 6.1 Typical data mining records.

(or record or case) that, by understanding patterns at the row level, provides useful insight. Since much data mining is focused on customers, each row often corresponds to a separate customer. Although this is often the case, for practical or legal reasons, this is not always true.

Privacy laws in some countries make it more practical to focus on households. Or, data is often available only in systems that do not talk to each other, making it more feasible for a row to be at the account level. Or, in the case of web applications, the unit might be based on a cookie stored on a computer. This roughly corresponds to a user, but several people may use a single computer and a single person may use several computers. In other applications, a row can refer to anything from a printing run to an inventory item.

Not all data is always available for all customers, so the data is often limited to a subset of customers with valid values in certain fields. For a direct mail campaign, rows should refer to customers with valid addresses. For a telemarketing campaign, rows should refer to customers with valid telephone numbers. For an e-mail campaign, rows should refer to customers with valid e-mail addresses. During the data mining process, this suggests limiting the data mining to those customers with valid mail addresses, telephone numbers, or e-mail addresses.

Use of a subset of the data occurs in other ways. Perhaps the initial campaign will be targeted to prospects in New Jersey—so it will focus only on data from New Jersey initially. Perhaps the initial campaign will be only for Elite Club members, so it will focus only on them for the data mining effort.

The rows are the level of granularity and the unit of action. Next we need to know what data the rows contain.

The Columns

The fields or columns represent the data in each record. Each column contains values. The *range* of the column refers to the allowable values for that column. Numbers typically would have a minimum and maximum value. Categorical fields would have a list of observed values for their range.

A histogram, such as those shown in Figure 6.2, shows how often each value or range of values occurs. So, the vertical axis is a count of records and the horizontal axis is the values in the column. This figure shows some common distributions, such as the normal distribution that looks like a bell-shaped curve (statisticians call this a Gaussian distribution) and the uniform distribution.

The distribution of the values provides some very important insights into the columns. Statistical methods are very concerned with distributions; fortunately, data mining algorithms are a bit less sensitive to them. Here, we will illustrate some special cases of distributions that are important for data mining purposes.

Columns with One Value

The most degenerate distribution is a column that has only one value. These unary-valued columns, as they are more formally known, do not contain any information that helps to distinguish between different rows. Because they lack any information content, they should be ignored for data mining purposes.

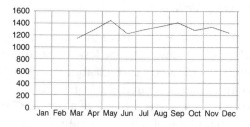

This histogram is for the month of claim for a set of insurance claims.

This is an example of a typically uniform distribution. That is, the number of claims is roughly the same for each month.

This histogram shows the number of telephone calls made for different durations.

This is an example of an exponentially decreasing distribution.

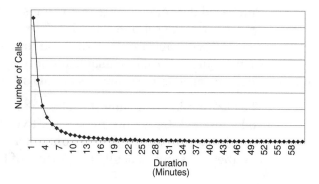

This histogram shows a normal distribution with a mean of 50 and a standard deviation of 10. Notice that high and low values are very rare.

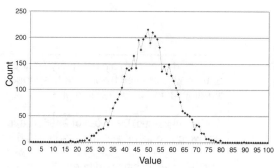

Figure 6.2   Common data distributions.

Having only one value is sometimes a property of the data. It is not uncommon, for instance, for a database to have fields defined in the database that are not yet populated. The fields are only placeholders for future values, so all the values are uniformly something such as "null" or "no" or "0."

Another cause of unary-valued columns is when the data mining effort is focused on a subset of customers. The fields that define this subset all may contain the same value. If we are building a model to predict the loss-ratio (an insurance profitability measure) for automobile customers in New Jersey, then the state field will always contain "NJ." This field has no information content on the subset of data that we will be using. We want to ignore it for modeling purposes.

Columns with Almost Only One Value

In "almost-unary" columns, almost all the records have the same value for that column. There may be a few outliers, but there are very few. For example, retail data may summarize all the purchases made by each customer in each department. Very few customers may make a purchase from the automotive department of a grocery store, or the tobacco department of a department store. So, almost all customers will have $0 for total purchases from these departments.

Purchased data often comes in an almost-unary format as well. Fields such as "people who collect porcelain dolls" or "amount spent on greens fees at golf courses" will have a null or $0 value for all but very few people. Some data, such as survey data, is available for only a very small subset of the customers. These are all extreme examples of data skew, shown in Figure 6.3.

The big question with almost-unary columns is: "When can they be ignored?" To be ignored, the values must have two characteristics. First, almost all the records have the same value. Second, there are so few having a different value that they constitute a negligible portion of the data.

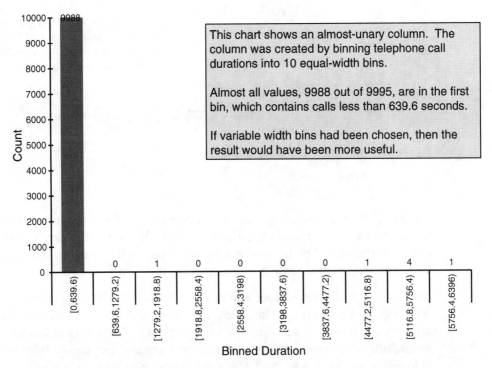

This chart shows an almost-unary column. The column was created by binning telephone call durations into 10 equal-width bins.

Almost all values, 9988 out of 9995, are in the first bin, which contains calls less than 639.6 seconds.

If variable width bins had been chosen, then the result would have been more useful.

Figure 6.3   Histogram for an almost-unary field that is probably useless for data mining purposes.

What is a negligible portion of the data? It is a group so small that even if the data mining algorithms identified it perfectly, the group is too small to be significant.

Before ignoring a column, though, it is important to understand why the values are so heavily skewed. What does this column tell us about the business? Perhaps few people ever buy tobacco because only a few of the stores in question even sell tobacco, and those that do offer only a very limited selection. Identifying customers as "tobacco-buyers" in this case may not be useful.

An event might be rare for other reasons. The number of people who cancel their telephone service on any given day is negligible, but over time the numbers accumulate. So the cancellations need to be accumulated over a longer time period, such as a month, quarter, or year. Or, the number of people who collect porcelain dolls, although very rare in itself, may suggest an important segment of collectors when combined with other fields.

The rule of thumb is that even if a column proves to be very informative, it is almost-unary when it is not useful. That is, fully understanding the rows with different values does not yield actionable results. As a general rule of thumb, if 95–99 percent of the values in the column are identical, the column—in isolation—is likely to be useless.

Columns with Unique Values

At the other extreme are columns that take on a different value for every single row—or nearly every row. These columns identify each row exactly. Examples of such columns are easy to come by:

- Customer names
- Addresses
- Telephone numbers
- Customer ids
- Vehicle identification numbers

These columns are also not very helpful. Why? They do not have predictive value because they uniquely identify each row. In doing so, they prevent data mining algorithms from finding patterns contained in multiple rows.

One caveat, which will be investigated later in this chapter is this: Sometimes these columns contain a wealth of information. Lurking inside telephone numbers and addresses is important geographical information. Vehicle identification numbers encode year, make, model, and country of origin. Customer numbers may be sequentially assigned, telling us which customers are more recent. And so on. These are cases where the important features (such as geography and customer recency) should be extracted from the fields as derived variables. However, once the useful information has been extracted, the original columns should be ignored.

Ignoring Columns Synonymous with the Target

When a column is too highly correlated with the target column, it can mean that the column is just a synonym. Here are two examples:

- "Account number is non-NULL" may be synonymous with response to a marketing campaign. Only responders who opened accounts are assigned account numbers.
- "Date of churn is not NULL" is synonymous with having churned.

Another danger is that the column reflects previous business practices. For instance, we may find that all customers with call forwarding also have call waiting. This is a result of product bundling; call forwarding is sold in a product bundle that always includes call waiting.

Or perhaps previous prospecting campaigns focused on a particular segment of customers, such as people with children and under 40. Well, all responders will have these characteristics, so the age and number of children may not be useful for data mining purposes. This, by the way, also illustrates why the data miner needs to know who was contacted, as well as who responded.

It is important to ignore columns that are synonymous with the target.

Roles of Columns in Data Mining

Different columns play different roles in data mining. Three fundamental roles are

Input columns. Used as input into the model.

Target column(s). Used only when building predictive models. These are what is interesting, such as propensity to buy a particular product, likelihood to respond to an offer, or probability of remaining a customer. When building descriptive models, there does not need to be a target.

Ignored columns. Columns that are not used.

Of course, different tools have different names for these roles. Figure 6.4 illustrates the "Type" node in SPSS Clementine. This is the node that sets the role for each column. In this case, there is a single TARGET (or OUT direction in their terminology), which is typical for most predictive data mining applications.

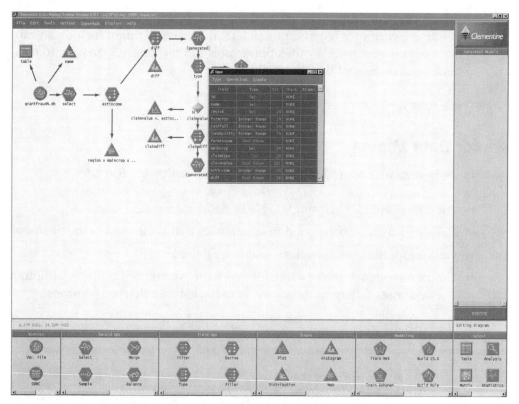

Figure 6.4 Column roles in SPSS Clementine.

TIP

Ignored columns play a very important role in clustering. Since ignored columns are not used to build the clusters, their distribution in the clusters can be very informative. By ignoring columns such as customer profitability or response, we can see how these "ignored" columns are distributed in the clusters. In doing so, we just might discover something very interesting about customer profit or responders.

In addition to the fundamental roles, there are a few more advanced roles as well. These roles are used under certain specific circumstances. Here are some examples from SAS Enterprise Miner:

Identification columns. Uniquely identify the data. In general, these columns are ignored for data mining purposes.

Weight column. Specifies a "weight" to be applied to this row. This is a way of creating a weighted sample by including the weight in the data. A record with a weight of three counts three times as much as a record with a weight of one.

Cost column. Specifies a cost associated with a row. For instance, if we are building a customer retention model, then the "cost" might include an estimate of each customer's value. Some tools can use this information to optimize the models that they are building.

These roles are illustrated in Figure 6.5.

Data for Data Mining

In short, data for data mining needs to be in the following format:

- All data should be in a single table or database view.
- Each row should correspond to an instance that is relevant to the business.
- Columns with a single value should be ignored.
- Columns with a different value for every row should be ignored—although the information they contain may be extracted into derived columns.

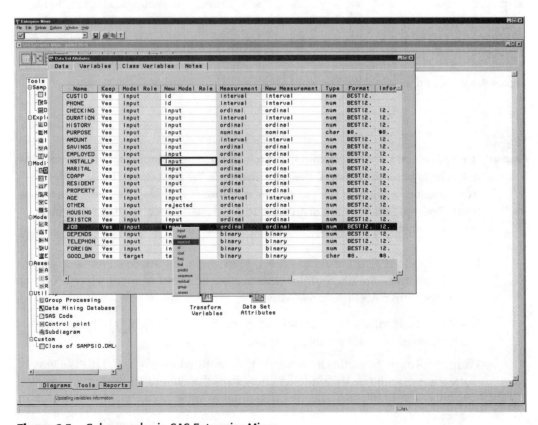

Figure 6.5 Column roles in SAS Enterprise Miner.

- For predictive modeling, the target column should be identified and all synonymous columns removed.

This is not, alas, the format that data typically comes in. Let's take a look at that now.

What Does Data Really Look Like?

In the real world, data is not, to say the least, data-mining-ready. The biggest challenge in data mining is transforming the data into the format needed by the data mining algorithms. Understanding this challenge begins by understanding data in the real world.

Where Data Comes From

Where does the data come from? Everywhere! Data is spread throughout an organization, on a myriad of different systems. Some of these systems are used to run the business (operational systems). Some of these systems are used for reporting purposes and business intelligence (data marts, data warehouses, and sometimes desktops). And sometimes the line is blurry, such as when the same system is used to run part of the business and to do reporting.

These systems come in many flavors. Often the data will be stored in a relational database, such as Oracle, Informix, Sybase, DB2, or SQL Server. Data can also be in flat files, log files, or other esoteric file structures. Fortunately, most operational systems have the ability to export data. Data mining typically takes place on a separate platform, requiring that the data be imported from other systems.

What Is a Relational Database?

Data sources are often relational databases. This brief section reviews relational databases (RDBMS). If you are already familiar with them, skip to the next section. The basis of relational databases goes to research by E. F. Codd in the early 1970s on the properties of a special type of sets composed of tuples—what we would call rows in tables. From this, he derived a set of operations that form a relational algebra (see Figure 6.6). These operations are in addition to set operations, such as union and intersection.

In nonscientific terminology, the relational operations are as follows:

- Filter a given set of rows based on the values in the rows.
- Select a given set of columns.

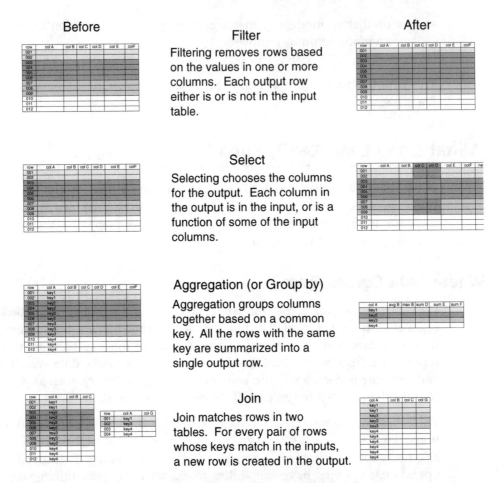

Figure 6.6 The four major querying operations of a relational database.

- Group rows together to aggregate the columns.
- Join two tables together based on the values in the columns.
- Sort the rows by the values in one or more columns for output purposes.

SQL, developed by IBM in the 1980s, has become the standard language for accessing relational databases.

A common way of representing the database structure is to use an entity-relationship (E-R) diagram. Figure 6.7 is a simple E-R diagram with five entities and four relationships among them. In this case, each entity corresponds to a separate table with columns corresponding to the attributes of the entity. In addition, keys in the table represent the relationships.

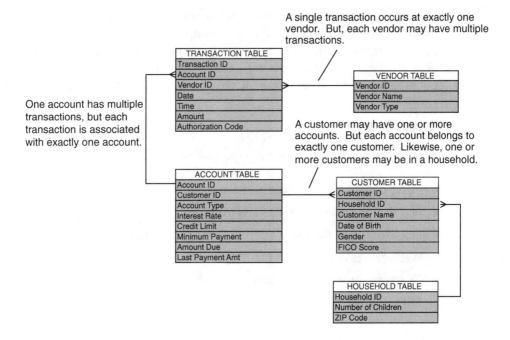

An E-R diagram can be used to show the tables and fields in a relational database. Each box shows a single table and its columns. The lines between them show relationships, such as 1-many, 1-1, and many-to-many. Because each table corresponds to an entity, this is called a *physical design*.

Sometimes, the physical design of a database is very complicated. For instance, the TRANSACTION TABLE might actually be split into a separate table for each month of transactions. In this case, the above E-R diagram is still useful; it represents the *logical* structure of the data, as business users would understand it.

Figure 6.7 An entity relationship diagram describes the data for a simple credit card database.

One nice feature of relational databases is the ability to design a database so that any given data item appears in exactly one place—with no duplication. Such a database is called a *normalized* database. Knowing exactly where each data item is located is highly efficient in theory, since updating any field requires modifying only one row in one table. When a normalized database is well designed, there is no redundant, out-of-date, or invalid data.

The key idea behind normalization is creating reference tables. Each reference table logically corresponds to an entity, and each has a key used for looking up information about the entity. In a relational database, the "join" operation is used to look up values in the reference table.

Relational databases are a powerful way of storing and accessing data. However, much of their design is focused on updating the data and handling large numbers of transactions. Data mining is interested in combining all the data together. Typically, data mining uses many queries, each of which requires several joins and several aggregations—a veritable army of killer queries.

Operational Systems

Operational systems are the systems that run the business, such as:

- Point-of-sale (POS) systems in retail
- Automatic Teller Machines (ATMs)
- DDA (demand deposit systems) in retail banking
- Web servers and e-commerce databases
- Telecommunications switches
- Billing systems

Operational systems offer a very rich source of data. This is the data collected directly at the point of customer contact and offers the most potential. If the operational system does not collect the data, though, it is not available (until the system is changed). Some real examples follow.

- Many telephone switches do not record when a customer turns off call waiting, even though turning off call waiting often indicates dual-use lines (voice and fax or voice and data). The data would be very informative, but is simply not available.

- A surprising number of web-based systems do not keep track of customers, using even imprecise technology such as cookies. Without the ability to track repeated but disparate visits to a site, an important source of information is lost.

- The mortgage, private banking, and demand deposit (checking and savings accounts) systems in a bank may not share a common customer ID. Without a common customer ID, it is not feasible to get a complete view of a customer.

These examples illustrate a basic truth: *Operational systems define the data potentially available for data mining.* When these systems do not collect useful data, then businesses have to resort to more expensive and incomplete sources, such as surveys, market profiles, and guesswork.

Operational systems also have some other constraints. These are the legacy systems where data is stored for operational efficiency instead of human understandability. Because they are business-critical systems, there may be established and arduous procedures for obtaining data from them. Other imperatives, such as getting monthly bills out, rightly take precedence over business intelligence activities. In short, the data is not readily accessible and is cumbersome to get at.

The data also tends to be rather dirty, a topic discussed later in this chapter. The lack of cleanliness comes from several factors. Data that is used will generally be clean. So, it is generally true that the "amount owed" line from a billing system is accurate (and often follows an audited trail to the general ledger system). However, the contact telephone number in the billing system may be rarely used—and unlikely to be accurate, even where the field is populated.

Also, the data in operational systems embeds business rules. Here is an example from the retail world. When a customer returns an item, in theory, the amount of the return is in the "amount returned" field. Except sometimes, when it stands out as a negative amount in the "amount of sale" column. What is the difference? When a customer returns one item *and* purchases other items, then the return is a negative amount. When a customer just returns an item, it is just a return. This is a business rule embedded in the data. And, because a return is represented in two very different ways, such rules make it difficult to interpret values in the data without understanding the business process.

Data Warehouses

Data warehouses are databases that, in theory, store all the data that a company or department collects or purchases from outside sources. All the data is in one nice, clean place. Data warehouses are quite popular with the result that the term encompasses many different beasts. Here, the term is used to mean "normalized" data stores that attempt to store large amounts of relatively raw data across an entire enterprise. By contrast, "dimensionalized" data stores, discussed in the next section, summarize the raw data along business dimensions.

Data warehouses are generally relational databases containing dozens or hundreds of tables described by hundreds or thousands of fields. Data is brought into the system, cleaned, and verified. Often, there is a corresponding metadata system, describing the tables, fields, references tables, and so on. As with any other large, enterprise-wide systems, data warehouses struggle to keep up with the business.

Not all data sources may be available. The data warehouse is often designed and then data is incrementally loaded. As businesses change, particularly by entering new markets and through mergers and acquisitions, data warehouses struggle to keep up with the new sources of data.

Only a subset of data is included. The data warehouse is loaded from the operational systems. Therefore, the warehouse contains only the subset that someone, perhaps several years ago, thought was important. Often there is a time lag before updates in the operational system filter into the warehouse.

Not all the data is used. A general principle of data mining is that only data being used has any hope of being clean. Data mining applications are often the first to bring together large amounts of data from disparate systems—and hence data mining often reveals unclean data even from a warehouse.

The most voluminous data may not be warehoused. Because disk, memory, and processors still do cost money, the most detailed records—at the transaction level—are often not stored in the warehouse. Their volumes are tremendous and the processing power needed to handle them is very large.

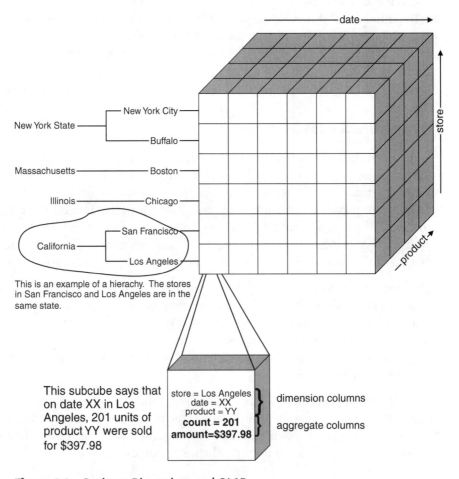

This is an example of a hierachy. The stores in San Francisco and Los Angeles are in the same state.

This subcube says that on date XX in Los Angeles, 201 units of product YY were sold for $397.98

store = Los Angeles
date = XX
product = YY
count = 201
amount=$397.98

} dimension columns

} aggregate columns

Figure 6.8 Business Dimensions and OLAP.

Data warehouses are very useful sources of data. In fact, a commonly asked question is "Can you do data mining without a data warehouse?" The answer is, of course, yes. And, although data warehouses are a good source of data, they are not perfect.

Data Marts and OLAP

Data marts and online analytic processing systems (OLAP) handle business intelligence for business users. These systems handle the reporting, slicing, and dicing needs of a department. These systems are specialized for the reporting and online analysis applications that use them. However, multiple OLAP systems can share business dimensions, in which case the set of OLAP systems behaves in much the same way as a normalized data warehouse.

OLAP, in particular, focuses on making data accessible along several predefined dimensions. Figure 6.8 is a simplified example for a retailing application. Here the dimensions are date, product, and store.

Numerical fields are calculated for each *date-product-store* triple, such the number of items of that product sold on that particular date at that particular store. More complicated information, such as the average dollar amount of the transactions containing those items, or the original cost of the items, could also be stored. The data is stored at the *date-product-store* granularity of information. The building blocks of OLAP are these units of information. And queries about dates, products, and stores are processed very quickly.

OLAP systems then build hierarchies on their dimensions. That is, they make it easy to form weeks, months, quarters, and years from dates. And to form counties, states, and regions from the location of stores; and also to group stores as "urban stores" and "suburban stores." These hierarchies make it possible to ask rather sophisticated questions about the data, and then to get answers quickly.

Multidimensional systems are immensely powerful for reporting and investigating data. Data mining, though, thrives on detail and OLAP presummarizes data along particular dimensions. There is a tension between customer relationship management and OLAP, because the customer dimension is usually too large to include in an OLAP cube.

Despite this tension, though, the two technologies coexist harmoniously. During the data exploration phase, OLAP systems can be invaluable for understanding the data and the business. For instance, knowing that younger wireless phone users are more likely to churn provides some insight that may help in building a churn model. However, when using the OLAP for data exploration, it is important to realize that the data going into the OLAP system may be different from the data used for data mining—it may represent a different subset of customers or products, or the data may come from different time frames. In general, it is a good idea to reverify any hunches on the data actually being used for data mining.

Also, data mining predictions can be applied to the dimensional data. For instance, in the standard OLAP cube, perhaps we want to add a new calculated value that is a prediction of how many products would be sold in each store on a given future day. This prediction would then be available in the system, and available for slicing and dicing and reporting. The cube could then also be used for measuring the effectiveness of data mining, by easily showing the accuracy of the predictions.

Survey and Product Registration Data

Surveys, polls, and product registrations are examples of self-reported data. That is, customers are being asked to tell you something about themselves. Surveys are near and dear to the hearts of marketers. One reason for this affinity is because they often provide the only data available about customers and their behavior that is combined with other attributes, such as demographics. Since many surveys are conducted on only a few hundred or few thousand people, the data fits inside a desktop spreadsheet. And perhaps the biggest advantage is that the surveys are conducted or outsourced directly from the marketing department. Often, the cumbersome process of working with IT can be circumvented.

A similar data source is product registrations. These are the postcards or online forms that ask users to check a box for estimated household income, number of pets, where they saw the product, and so on.

These types of self-reported data should always be treated cautiously:

- First, anytime people are asked questions, they have the opportunity to answer none of them. The people who respond are self-selected as a group of people more likely to respond to questions. This is an example of sample bias. The people in the survey do not necessarily represent the entire population, so you have to be careful about using the responses as representative of the whole population.

- People may not always give accurate responses or the responses may be keyed-in with errors. Even if only 10 percent of the responders are inaccurate, this can have a large effect on the analysis. There is no way to tell which 10 percent of the answers are inaccurate—and the inaccuracies may merely reflect errors that occur when typing responses into databases.

- Although self-reported data often gets saved for future use, past surveys may not be comparable to more recent surveys. Consider survey of Web users in 1996. The same survey may have quite different results from the one taken now. Back in 1996, Web users were much more likely to be white, male, American, earn high incomes, and work in the high-tech industry. As time goes by, Web users are becoming more and more like the general population. The differences in survey responses may be due only to shifting demographics.

- It can also be challenging to match survey data to the customer database. That is, often the only identifying information on the survey is the customer's name, and this must be matched to the customer database—if you want to tie survey responses to customer billing, promotion, and usage histories.

- And, perhaps the biggest problem from the data mining perspective is that survey data is quite incomplete. So, it is not possible to actually use responses from surveys as inputs into models. The simple reason is that the model could be run only on people who have responded to the survey.

Of course, having pointed out all these deficiencies, it is also important to point out that surveys can be quite useful. It is possible to adjust the results of a survey for sample bias, by taking into account the responses for different subgroups of the population. Polling agencies use these types of adjustments to determine public opinion, with a margin of error less than 3 percent. By assuming that people lie consistently, it is possible to reduce the impact of inaccurate data.

And, like data mining, surveys are often used to provide insight into customers. The results may point at a new way to market a product, or a new theme for an advertising campaign, or a new list to purchase. The survey data itself is often valuable as the primary source of data. It can also be valuable to try to predict survey responses using other data. For instance, perhaps we can predict who the "soccer moms" are by using internal data sources (that is, "soccer moms" may have particular and distinctive patterns in their data). The predictions may not be 100 percent accurate, but they would give us the ability to identify important demographic segments in the customer base.

External Data Sources

External providers are a very valuable source of data. Some of these suppliers augment existing data with additional fields. Here are some examples:

- Doing a credit check on a potential or current customer. In this case, additional credit history and credit worthiness data is provided by a credit bureau.

- Using an outside agency to add demographic, psychographic, or Webgraphic data. This data contain columns such as "number of children," "amount paid in greens fees," and "number of Web sites visited."

- Using an outside agency to do address correction, householding, and similar functions. In this case, the agency is using external data to provide cleaner and more complete columns of data.

- Using an outside agency to "score" records. The credit score developed by Fair, Isaac and Company, called FICO, is very commonly used by the credit card industry to estimate credit worthiness.

These are a few of common examples. Another interesting source of data in the United States is the Census Bureau, which provides detailed data about ZIP codes and census tracks.

WARNING

Data provided by outside bureaus can be an important source of data. However, there are some important caveats:

- Only a subset of your customers are likely to match their database.
- Even customers who match are likely to have missing data.
- The process of matching customers takes time, introducing additional time lags into the modeling process.

Even with these caveats, external data is useful for data mining, especially for acquisition modeling.

Other suppliers provide lists that meet certain criteria. Do you want to sell golf clubs? Well, buy a list of people who have subscribed to a golfing magazine or paid greens fees at a country club. There are an astonishing number of lists that are available.

Data mining can help determine the right list to purchase. However, whenever purchasing external lists for finding new customers (prospecting), there are two things to keep in mind. First, all your competitors might be using the same list. You have no control over it. Second, you want to be careful in thinking about the privacy of the people on the lists. We will be talking about privacy implications later in the book.

The Right Level of Granularity

Having established where data comes from, the next big question is what do the rows correspond to? This is really a question about the size of the unit of data mining—its granularity, so to speak. Consider the question of "what is a customer" to the credit card group of a retail bank. The example E-R diagram had several different ways to answer this question:

- A customer corresponds to an account.

- A customer corresponds to an individual who may have more than one credit card.
- A customer corresponds to a household, containing all credit cards held by all individuals in the household.

All of these are valid answers. The purpose here is not to choose among them, but to illustrate that there are different levels of granularity. An important point is that, regardless of which definition is chosen, different data is available at different levels of granularity.

Ignoring the vendor table in the E-R diagram, this simple example has data at four different levels:

1. Transaction data at the transaction level, with an account key
2. Account data, with a customer key
3. Customer data, with a household key
4. Household data

To get this all at the household level takes a bit of work. Well, the HOUSE-HOLD TABLE is fine—it provides a beginning. Let's add something from the CUSTOMER TABLE, such as the number of customers in a household or the average FICO score. This requires aggregating the customer table at the household level, and calculating the desired fields.

Next comes the ACCOUNT TABLE. This table can provide the number of accounts, the total amount due, the total last payment, and so on. But we need this information at the *household level*. First, look up the household ID in the CUSTOMER TABLE, using the customer ID; then aggregate the ACCOUNT TABLE by household; then join this into the result.

This is starting to get complicated. (Processing the TRANSACTION TABLE is left as an exercise.) Even in this simple example, combining these disparate sources of data into a single table (as needed for data mining purposes) is a challenge. Figure 6.9 illustrates the processing that needs to be done. First, data that is at a too-detailed level needs to be aggregated to the right level, which may involve looking up the key. For instance, to aggregate accounts at the household level may first require looking up the household key for the account number, and then doing the aggregation.

Aggregating more detailed records is a form of summarization. The big question is which summaries should be calculated. Some features are quite basic, such as the total number of transactions and the total amount of the transactions. However, other features might prove useful as well, such as the number of transactions that are greater than $100 or that take place more than 50 miles

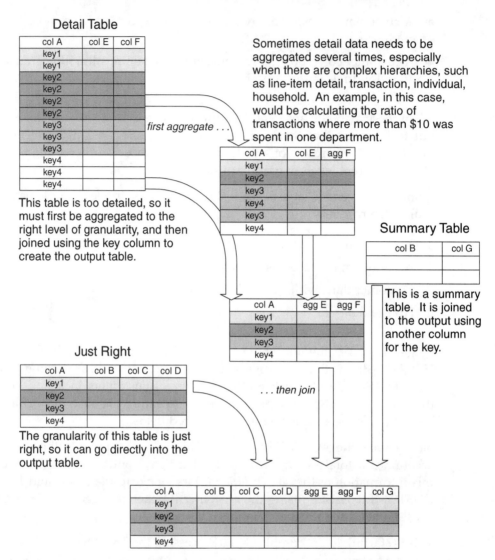

Detail Table

col A	col E	col F
key1		
key1		
key2		
key2		
key2		
key2		
key3		
key3		
key3		
key4		
key4		
key4		

first aggregate . . .

Sometimes detail data needs to be aggregated several times, especially when there are complex hierarchies, such as line-item detail, transaction, individual, household. An example, in this case, would be calculating the ratio of transactions where more than $10 was spent in one department.

This table is too detailed, so it must first be aggregated to the right level of granularity, and then joined using the key column to create the output table.

col A	col E	agg F
key1		
key2		
key3		
key4		
key3		
key4		

Summary Table

col B	col G

This is a summary table. It is joined to the output using another column for the key.

col A	agg E	agg F
key1		
key2		
key3		
key4		

Just Right

col A	col B	col C	col D
key1			
key2			
key3			
key4			

The granularity of this table is just right, so it can go directly into the output table.

. . . then join

col A	col B	col C	col D	agg E	agg F	col G
key1						
key2						
key3						
key4						

Figure 6.9 Combining data from multiple sources is a multistep process that involves aggregating tables and joining tables together.

from the customer's home address. Finding the right features is part of the art of data mining.

The second operation is matching records in different files based on a common key (also called joining). This is the process, for instance, for matching purchased information at the customer level with other information. This match may occur on arbitrary fields, such as ZIP code, area code, state, county, etc.

In practice, aggregating and joining files (or tables) are expensive operations, both computationally and in terms of disk storage. Bringing two large tables together on a single machine can saturate networks. Complex joins and aggregations in a relational database are killer queries. Storing data and intermediate results can use a lot of disk space. These are all issues that recur in practice.

A different problem occurs when the data has already been summarized along particular dimensions, such as for OLAP tools. The summarized data does not usually contain data about a single account or a single customer. The OLAP data can, however, be included in data mining by appending it to the records, using other fields as keys. For example, it would be possible to include response rates by ZIP code or churn rates by age and gender when these are available.

Different Ways to Measure Data Values

So far, the discussion has focused on the bigger picture of data and how to get it into the single data mining table. Now, the discussion turns to the values in the fields, and some important properties with respect to data mining. These properties constitute the *measure* of the columns.

Order is the most important measure property. Is it natural to say that one value is less than or greater than another? Two gallons is bigger than one gallon; 10:30 AM on 4 Feb 2001 is earlier than 2:14 PM on 4 Feb 2001; $100 is less than $120. These are examples of values with a natural order. However, New York and California do not have such an order. Is "New York" greater or less than "California"? It does not even make sense to ask the question. States, status codes, and colors have values that are typically unordered. Columns that have no natural order are called categorical (or, sometimes, nominal).

Ordered columns come in different flavors:

- *Ranks* have an order but do not permit arithmetic. So, "low" is less than "medium" and "medium" is less than "high." However, it makes no sense to perform arithmetic on these values.

- *Intervals* have an order and allow subtraction, but not necessarily summations. Dates, times, and temperatures are the most common examples. It makes sense to ask the number of days between two dates. However, it is not possible to double a date or add two temperatures.

- *True numerics* support arithmetic. It makes sense to add true numeric values and to perform other types of arithmetic.

Data for data mining usually comes in the form of strings and numbers. The form of the data does not necessarily tell you about the measure! Many code fields contain numbers, but the numbers are not ordered. Sometimes codes have an order even though they are stored as strings. Determining the right measure requires understanding what the data represents. Figure 6.10 provides an example of overriding a value in Enterprise Miner.

Categorical

Categorical columns have a well-defined set of values that they can take on. These values are usually category labels, without a natural order. This lack of order is an important feature. For instance, it does not make sense to say that "Alabama" is in some sense closer to "Alaska" than to "Georgia" because "Alabama" and "Alaska" are adjacent alphabetically. State codes are an example of categoricals.

Sometimes, categorical variables are represented as numbers. In fact, it is not uncommon to see databases where "Alabama" is represented as 1, "Alaska" as 2, and so on. The fact that the codes are represented as numbers does not mean that the values are ordered. Since some data mining tools treat all numbers as true numeric, it is important to override the default when the numbers represent categories.

Neural networks and k-means clustering are examples of algorithms that want all their inputs to be true numeric. This poses a problem for categorical data. The naïve approach is to assign a number to each value, but this introduces a spurious ordering not present in the original data. The solution is to introduce a flag variable for each value. Although this increases the number of input

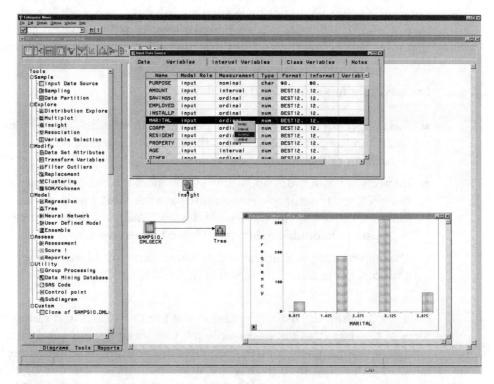

Figure 6.10 Informing Enterprise Miner that a code, stored as a number, is really categorical.

variables, it eliminates the problem of spurious ordering and improves results. Another approach, described by Dorian Pyle in his book *Data Preparation for Data Mining* (Morgan Kaufmann, 1999), is to look for a natural ordering of the categoricals. This allows the categoricals to be replaced by true numerics

Rank

Ranks are similar to categoricals, except they have a natural ordering. Hmm, doesn't this mean that we can do arithmetic on them? Not always. An example of a rank is income ranges. We may divide income into different ranges, say less than $10,000 per year, $10,000–$30,000, $30,000–$60,000, and over $60,000. These ranges have a natural ordering, but it makes no sense to take the average of the ranges. Of course, it would be possible to calculate the average if the distributions of the values within each range were known.

Often, ranks appear as a result of binning true numerics. Binning can balance an uneven distribution of values, as shown in Figure 6.11, and this is one way to manage outliers (rare data values that are excessively large or small). The most common approach to binning is to try to find bins that put the same number of values into each bin. The width of each bin will usually differ, but the height (or weight) of the values in the bins will be roughly equal. An alternative is equal width bins, where all the bins have the same difference between the maximum and minimum value (regardless of how many values fall into them). Equal width bins can make a skewed distribution even worse, and equal height bins eliminate outliers.

Sometimes, some columns in external data are only available as ranks. For instance, demographic information such as salary typically is reported as a range instead of a fixed value. This may also be true of information gathered through surveys and other means: "Check the box of your total household assets," which is then followed by several choices, each of which is a range.

Interval

The next type of data are those where intervals can be defined on them. The intervals are the difference between two values. Although we can take the difference of two values, other types of arithmetic do not always make sense on these values.

This may sound a bit strange, but it is actually very common. Consider dates and times. It makes sense to ask how many days are there from November 11, 1999 to February 2, 2000. However, it does not make sense to try to add November 11, 1999 to February 2, 2000. The interval between them is easily calculated, but other arithmetic does not work.

Equal-height bins balance the values that go into each bin. The width of the bins varies considerably but approximately the same number of rows fall into each one. Equal-height bins are not sensitive to outliers; only the width of the last bin needs to be adjusted.

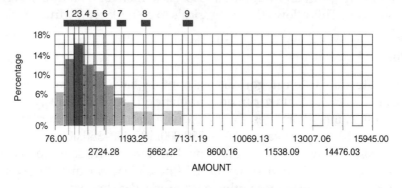

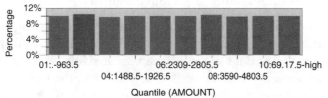

With equal-width bins, on the other hand, all bins have the same width. Equal-width bins make a skewed distribution worse and are very sensitive to outliers. Some bins may be empty.

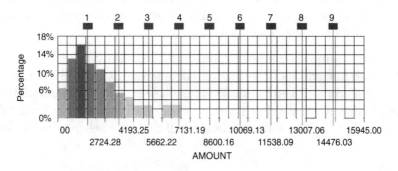

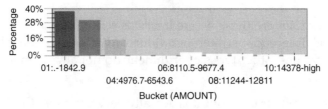

Figure 6.11   Binning true numerics creates ranks.

True Numerics

Columns that support a full range of numeric operations are called true numerics. These include total amount purchased, or a time series of stock prices, and so on. True measures are stored as numeric values, although not all numeric values are true measures.

This distinction can make a difference when working with neural networks, because all inputs into a neural network must be numeric—the neural network performs rather complex mathematical operations on them. Most neural network software includes tricks for converting other types of data into numbers. This is true of other statistical approaches as well. However, decision trees do not perform mathematical operations on values in columns, so they either bin numeric data or treat them as ranks.

Text, Pictures, and Audio

Not surprisingly, there are other types of data that do not fall into these nice categories. Text, audio, and images are becoming increasingly common. And data mining tools do not generally support them.

Because these types of data can contain a wealth of information, what can be done with them? The answer is to extract features into derived variables. For instance, an address may be stored as a text field. As such, it is not particularly useful, since every record (or almost every record) has a different address. The text, though, might contain an apartment number, which indicates whether someone lives in a single-family house or in a multi-unit building. Or, it might contain a rural route number or a PO box—any of which provide some information. Although the address field is not particularly useful, the flags "is-multi-unit," "is-po-box," and "is-rural-route" may prove very useful.

How Much Data Is Enough?

There are many ways of asking how much data is enough. How many rows? How many columns? How many bytes? How much history? As a general rule, more data is better, but there are some important considerations.

When building a prospect model, for instance, perhaps only a few dozen fields may be available, and these are purchased from an outside bureau. There are not many columns but there could be millions and millions of rows. On the other hand, building models on existing customers, or subsets of existing customers, may reduce the number of rows and greatly increase the number of columns. In some cases, the number of rows numbers in the millions, and the number of columns in the hundreds or thousands.

Answering the question of how much is enough starts by knowing how much data is available. Often, the amount of data available is much larger than the amount needed for the data mining tools, because it will be aggregated and summarized during data preparation. This is especially true of transaction data, such as point-of-sale data, call detail records, and web hits. On the one hand, such detailed data is being used for data mining, because the detail provides important features. On the other hand, the data mining algorithms are probably running on tens or hundreds of megabytes of data—instead of terabytes.

Another consideration is the size of the population. Are there 10,000 current customers? Are there 100,000,000 prospects? In general, it is a good idea to have tens of thousands or hundreds of thousands of rows available for data mining. And, when there are too many rows for practical consideration, the number can be reduced using sampling. For some tasks, such as data discovery and visualization, less data is often more practical.

Data mining tools can impose limits on the data size as well. Some tools keep data in memory for efficiency reasons, so available memory limits the size of data. And, even if the tools support larger data sizes by spilling over to disk, the performance degrades so much that you want to keep everything in memory anyway. Fortunately, memory is getting cheaper and more available. And a few hundred megabytes is sufficient for many data mining applications. On the other hand, regardless of the tool, neural networks have theoretical limits on minimum data size (see the sidebar).

The amount of data required for data mining varies with the application, as well as on how much data is available. Also, it is important to be sure that there are enough instances representing rare events of interest. Tools can have upper limits on the amount of data they support—or at least practical limits due to the hardware on which they are running. And some data mining algorithms, such as neural networks, require a minimum amount of data to avoid overfitting.

Derived Variables

The discussion so far has talked about variables in the original data sources. Derived variables are calculated columns not in the original data. One large class of derived variables consists of the aggregation values accumulated when summarizing data to the right level of granularity.

This section covers common reasons to create derived variables and some issues when working with them. There are, of course, a virtually infinite number of ways of combining columns, using mathematical and statistical functions. Derived variables work best when they represent underlying behaviors in the data.

Neural Networks and Data Size

Because they are so flexible, neural networks have theoretical minimums on the amount of data needed to train them effectively. Remember that a neural network really consists of a bunch of weights.

In a fully connected neural network with one hidden layer and one output, the number of weights is given by $h * (n + 2) + 1$, where h is the number of hidden units and n is the number of inputs. Each edge has a weight associated with it. In addition, each node in the hidden layer and each output node has an additional weight, called the *bias*. Other types of neural networks would have slightly different formulas for the number of weights.

If there are more weights than instances to train the network, then there is a very, very good chance that the network will simply memorize the training set (overfitting). As a general rule of thumb, there should be *at least* 10 training instances for every weight in the network, and this is very, very liberal. When building a network that predicts categorical values, it is a good idea to have this number of training instances for each category—and more instances per value is better.

Consider a network with 50 input variables and 10 hidden nodes. It has 511 weights. There should be at least 5,110 instances for training the network. In fact, this is too few. It is much better to have at least 10 instances for every category being predicted. So, if there is a binary output, there should be at least 10,220 instances.

TIP   The most effective derived variables are those that represent something in the real world, such as a description of some underlying customer behavior. Randomly combining columns with fancy functions is unlikely to produce useful results. That is why automated tools are unable to do a good job of creating derived variables.

Issues in Working with Derived Variables

Many data mining tools have the ability to create simple derived variables, by transforming values in other columns. These transformations are a valuable part of data mining. In fact, when deploying models, it is important to consider where the variables are being created to be sure that they are created for new data as well.

However, some derived variables are more naturally created during the data preparation steps. The aggregation process creates a form of derived variables.

During data preparation, it may also be practical to look up information in reference tables, create new "modified" distribution variables, and so on.

Often, several derived variables have very similar information content. For instance, when analyzing telephone data, the overall number of calls made during a given time frame is very similar, in terms of information, to the total length of time on the telephone during that time period. Consider the behavior of making no calls for one month. There are many ways that this behavior might be found in derived variables: the number of local calls and long distance calls are both zero, and the time spent on local calls is zero, and the time spent on long distance calls is zero. It is important to remember that several different derived variables may really be identifying the same behavior.

Traditional statistical techniques, such as regressions, can have problems when there are highly correlated input variables. However, data mining techniques can handle highly correlated inputs, so this is not a problem. The only issue is that the number of columns can affect the run-time performance of building models. And, in the case of neural networks, having too many inputs can prevent the network from converging on a good model during training.

Handling Outliers

It is not uncommon for some values in a column to be quite rare or far out-of-bounds from other values in the column. These values are referred to as outliers, because they lie outside the expected values of the data. Here are some examples.

In analyzing affinity card data from grocery stores, some affinity cards often have very, very large monthly totals. Most cards have monthly totals up to a few thousand dollars per month. Some, though, are in the tens and hundreds of thousands per month. These larger values are examples of outliers, and so suggest further questioning. What causes them? Sometimes frequent shoppers forget their card. To allow the shopper to take advantage of frequent shopper specials, the check-out person assigns some special card number.

Another example comes from looking at customers in the credit card group of a major regional bank. Most customers live in a few hundred ZIP codes in the bank's region. However, there is a much larger number of ZIP codes that have very few customers. This is an example where most ZIP codes are outliers because they contain just a handful of customers. On the other hand, almost all the customers are in the most common ZIP codes.

And, outliers can also indicate collection problems. Once, in analyzing transactions of files being sent between computers, it was surprising to find that a significant number had negative transmission times. This indicated problems with the time synchronization of the computers.

Here are five approaches to working with outliers.

Do nothing. Some algorithms are robust in the presence of outliers. For instance, decision trees are mainly concerned with the rank of numeric variables, so numeric outliers do not have a big effect on them. On the other hand, a few outliers can seriously disrupt a neural network.

Filter the rows containing them. This can be a bad idea, because it can introduce a sample bias into the data. However, in the case of the retail data, ignoring the cards with large purchases actually removes some "noncustomer" cards and might improve results.

Ignore the column. This is extreme, but not as far-fetched as it may sound. The column can be replaced with reference information about the column. For instance, instead of ZIP codes, we might include some information about the ZIP code—number of customers, number of residents, average income, and so on. Some of this data is available from sources such as the United States Census Bureau (www.census.gov).

Replace the outlying values. This is a very common approach. The replacement value might be "null" if your data mining tool handles null values effectively. It might be "0," or the average value, or a reasonable maximum/minimum value, or some other appropriate value. In some cases, it makes sense to predict a value, using the other input fields to infer a reasonable value that will not disturb the true distribution of the data.

Bin values into equal height ranges. An example would be low, medium, and high for salaries. Binning values places them into ranges, so outliers fall into their appropriate range. Many data mining tools support binning directly in the tool.

As just described, binning applies to true numerics. However, it can also be applied to categoricals, when there are large numbers of them. There are two approaches in this case. Consider the ZIP codes. What we really might want is to use all the ZIP codes where there are more than, say, 100 customers. And then combine the rest of the ZIP codes into a "too-small-to-care" ZIP code. That is, we are grouping together, into a single category, the rarest ZIP codes while keeping information about the larger ZIP codes.

The other approach occurs when the categories naturally fall into a hierarchy. For instance, ZIP codes in the United States fall into counties, which are parts of states, which are parts of regions. Instead of using the ZIP codes directly, we might group them into states. Or, the ZIP code itself represents its location, so we might use only the first three digits of the ZIP code. Hierarchies are particularly important for certain types of data, such as product codes and geography.

Combinations of Columns

An important class of derived variables are those that perform calculations on values from multiple columns. These take data that is already present in a row and calculate new values. This is area where creativity and experience are very helpful. Here are some examples of useful derived variables:

- height^2 / weight (obesity index)
- Debt/earnings
- Passengers * miles
- Credit limit – balance
- Population / area
- Minutes of use / number of telephone calls
- Number of calls longer than two minutes / number of calls
- Activation_date – application_date
- Proportion of sales of cereal to total sales
- Number of web pages visited / total amount purchased

Although creating derived variables is as much art as science, there are a few pointers to keep in mind. First, the purpose of the variables is to find useful information, so they are a good way to incorporate hunches into the data. "Hmm, the age of the insurance agent is not related to customer acquisition, but I think there is some relationship. Let's look at the difference in ages between the prospect and the agent." This suggests adding the difference in ages as a derived variable.

It is usually not necessary to derive large numbers of variables that convey similar information. Consider the two variables:

- Age_diff = agent_age – prospect_age
- Age_ratio = prospect_age / agent_age

These contain almost the same information. If the prospect is older, then age_diff is positive and age_ratio is greater than 1. When they are about the same age, the age_diff is about 0 and age_ratio is about 1. Although usually not harmful, it is not particularly useful to include a lot of strongly correlated variables. The data mining algorithms typically need only one variable to identify any given feature of the data. Choose one of the variables and move on to something else.

When taking ratios, another problem is handling divide by 0. What to do? Some tools offer a special function to handle this situation. SGI Mineset, for instance, has a convenient function to handle this situation.

```
divide(minutes_of_use, num_telephone_calls, 0)
```

The function divide takes a third argument that says what to do when divide-by-0 is a problem. Many tools (including Mineset) support conditionals:

```
if (num_telephone_calls == 0) then 0;
else minutes_of_use / num_telephone_calls;
```

When such a function is not available, a quick and dirty approach is to add 1 to the denominator:

```
minutes_of_use / (num_telephone_calls + 1)
```

Of course, this only works when the denominator is greater than 0.

Summarizations

Summarized derived variables are the result of looking up information along dimensions in a record. We have already seen summaries in the context of OLAP, and the idea here is almost the same. For instance, instead of including the ZIP code, we might include the average customer profitability for customers in that ZIP code. Conceptually, we summarize the data by ZIP code to determine the average customer profitability. Then, we add the information back in for every customer, using the ZIP code as the key.

Notice that multiple customers will have the same value, because they reside in the same ZIP code. This is often the case. Yet, these summarized derived variables are often the most useful because people in different ZIP codes with similar demographics will have similar values of the derived variable.

When possible, it is a good idea to calculate the summarizations on the same data being used for data mining, as opposed to using the results from the separate OLAP system. This is because other systems may be doing the calculation on slightly different sets of data.

Chapter 11 presents a case study about churn in the wireless telecommunications industry. It is a truism that the past is the best predictor of the future. So, in this case study, it is helpful to look at historical churn rates along different dimensions. One that is particularly useful is the churn rate by handset type.

Why is it more useful to include the churn rate by handset, rather than just the handset type itself? Every month, new handsets may appear on the market and older handsets become less common. The data mining models will not recognize new handsets, and fewer and fewer customers have the older handsets that the model does recognize. However, there is no problem in just including a historical churn rate of 0 for new handsets and applying the model.

Also, the number of customers with different types of handsets varies widely. As the algorithms try to find patterns among the handset types, they can become confused because most handsets have very few users. Imposing an ordering using the historical churn rate eliminates this problem.

Another useful variable was churn rate by demographics, in particular, by gender and age. This variable is useful because it combines two different variables (gender and age) in a way that the data mining algorithms might not easily detect.

One of the challenges is the performance of adding such summarization columns. Using SQL, the expression looks something like:

```
CREATE TABLE CHURNLOOKUP AS
   (SELECT C.HANDSET_TYPE,
                SUM(CASE (C.IS_CHURN) WHEN 'Y' THEN 1 ELSE 0) as
num_churn
                COUNT(*) as num_total
   FROM Cust_Info C
   GROUP BY C.HANDSET_TYPE) ;

CREATE TABLE CHURNTABLE AS
   (SELECT C.*, CL.num_churn / CL.num_total AS handset_churn_rate
    FROM Cust_Info C, CHURNLOOKUP CL
    WHERE C.HANDSET_TYPE = CL.HANDSET_TYPE
 ) ;
```

Without trying to understand this, it is obviously a complicated query. This can be a computationally intensive process, especially when adding multiple summarizations. Often special-purpose code is used for this purpose.

Extracting Features from Single Columns

Many of the columns available for data mining actually contain a wealth of information. However, this information is embedded in specific codes and in our own domain knowledge. This occurs when the values have other attributes attached to them.

As a simple example, the dates 4 July 2000 and 25 December 2000 both share a property—they are holidays (in the United States). Recognizing this simple fact requires incorporating domain knowledge, along with the value. In other words, knowing the data is not enough. It includes additional features that can be included as other variables, such as is_holiday.

This is true of a number of different types of data. Here are some common examples.

Features from Dates

Dates contain a wealth of information about behavior. Some of the more interesting features to extract from dates are:

- Day of the week
- Day of the month
- Month of the year
- Day of the year
- Quarter of the year
- A holiday or not
- Standard workday versus nonworkday

These features can be added as separate columns into the data. Some tools provide extensive date functions that can calculate most of these values. Other tools provide at least rudimentary capabilities, such as calculating the number of days between two dates. This is powerful enough to calculate the day of the week, for instance:

```
(days_between(date, "01/01/1999") + 4) % 7
```

produces a value of 0 for Monday, 1 for Tuesday, etc., up to 6 for Sunday. We usually have the week start on Monday and end with Saturday and Sunday together, so it is easier to notice weekend patterns.

When summarizing data it is often useful to look at behavior that happens on different days of the week, or on workdays versus nonworkdays. These fields might contain, for example, the total amount spent on the weekend and the total amount spent during weekdays. These variables need to be created when summarizing the detailed data.

Data may have multiple dates as well. In this case, it is often useful to calculate the number of days between important events. An example would be calculating the average number of days between purchases.

Features from Time

Specific times do not contain quite as much information at dates. However, they do indicate the hour of the day and morning, afternoon, evening, and late evening.

As with dates, it is often useful to look at other data by time, such as by hour of the day or by period of the day (morning, afternoon, evening).

There is a danger when using time stamps from computers. It is important to remember the time zone of the user, as opposed to the time zone of the computer. As more and more data comes from e-commerce systems, the users may be arbitrarily spread around the globe.

WARNING

When using the date and time fields from data collected over the Web, remember that you usually want the date and time where the inquiry originated. Because of time zone differences, this is unlikely to be the time on the computer processing the request.

Features from Other Types of Data

Other types of data contain interesting features:

- *Telephone numbers* contain country codes, area codes, and exchanges—all geographical information. The standard 10-digit number in North American starts with a 3-digit area code followed by a 3-digit exchange and a 4-digit line number. In most databases, the area code provides good geographic information. The exchange within the area code can also distinguish between landlines and wireless phones.

  Outside North America, the format of telephone numbers differs from place to place. In some cases, the area codes and telephone numbers are of variable length making it more difficult to extract geographic information.

- *Addresses* are stored as strings. They contain a few extractable features, such as whether it corresponds to a multi-unit dwelling (by having an apartment number), and whether it contains a post-office box.

- Probably the most interesting feature of the address, the *ZIP code*, fortunately is usually stored as a separate field. In the United States, the 5-digit ZIP codes have a hierarchical structure. The first digit is the region, so all ZIP codes starting with "0" are in Puerto Rico and New England. This continues up to the leading "9" in California ZIP codes. The first three digits correspond to a district. Often, it is valuable to truncate the ZIP code to three digits to get geographic information.

- The Web provides yet another form of addressing—*web addresses*. The only extractable feature from a web address is the domain name, and especially the suffix. The suffix sometimes can identify countries, educational establishments, nonprofits, and government. The domain name can identify users from the same company, governmental department, and so on.

- *Universal product codes* (Type A UPC) are the 12-digit codes that identify products passed in front of scanners in the United States and Canada. The first six digits are a code for the manufacturer. The next five encode the specific product, and are controlled by the manufacturer. For instance, one of them often contains the "amount" of the product. The final digit has no meaning. It is a check digit to verify the data. More information about them is available through the Uniform Code Council (www.uc-council.org). Scan codes outside North America have different formats. More information about them is available through the standard organization, EAN International (www.ean.be).

■ *Vehicle identification numbers* are the 17-character codes inscribed on automobiles that describe the make, model, and year of the vehicle. The first character describes the country of origin. The second, the manufacturer. The third is the vehicle type, with 4–8 being specific features of the vehicle. The tenth is the model year; the eleventh is the assembly plant. The remaining six are sequential production numbers.

These are examples of the types of codes and strings that appear in data. It is important to extract the component information from these codes for data mining purposes.

Time Series

Some data occurs repeatedly at specific time intervals. Probably the most common time series data are customer billing records, which provide monthly snapshots of customer behavior. Billing data has the additional advantage that it is usually quite clean—numbers on bills typically are audited for correctness since they feed into the company's balance sheet.

When using times series data, the series are usually normalized to the last date available for each record. Figure 6.12 shows this normalization. Several customers leave (or churn) at different points in time. To build a model to describe these customers, we want to reorient their data relative to the date they left. So, instead of a fixed month, the month is relative to each customer's final month.

This is the first step in working with time series. However, this approach does remove information about particular periods of time, such as seasonality. Adding derived variables back in can recover the lost seasonality information. Examples of such variables are

■ Proportion of a customer's yearly purchasing that occurs during the holiday season

■ Average length of telephone calls made during weekends and during the week

■ Total amount of interest paid in the first quarter of the year

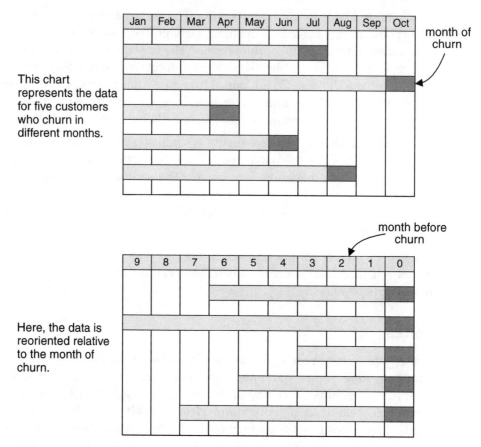

This chart represents the data for five customers who churn in different months.

Here, the data is reoriented relative to the month of churn.

Figure 6.12 Reorient time series relative to the event in question.

This information would otherwise be lost after reorienting the time-series data. Adding new derived fields makes it possible to find time-related patterns.

Regular time series, of course, have many features that are not related to seasonality. Within a single time series, the following may be of interest:

- Total (or average) values in the time series, such as total amount spent over the period

- Rate of growth of the times series, such as the ratio of the first and the last values or ratios between success values

- Number of values that exceed thresholds, such as the number of times that the customer used a credit card more than three times during the month

- Variance of the time series, which gives a measure of how wildly the values change

Usually, the data actually contains several variables with historical time series values. For wireless telephone billing records, for instance, there is the number of calls, amount billed, length of calls, number of local calls, number of long distance calls, and so on. Interactions between these series can be quite interesting, so these series generate other series: average length of calls per month, proportion of local calls to all calls, amount billed per call, and so on. In short, time series offer many opportunities to add derived variables.

When there are several time series, the number of derived variables can multiply very quickly. Although handling large numbers of variables is not a problem, it is not useful to have many variables that describe the same behavior. Earlier, we emphasized an important point about derived variables: those that represent customer behavior are generally the most useful.

For the wireless telecommunications data, we might categorize some types of behavior:

Steady customers. These are customers whose total wireless usage remains constant over the time period.

Growing customers. These are customers who are spending more and more time on the phone.

Receivers. These are customers who receive most of their calls.

Senders. These are customers who send most of their calls.

Next, we can assign scores to customers, based on their usage patterns, for each of these categories. So, there would be a score that measures how steady usage has been, and another score measuring the growth in telephone calls, and so on. These scores are derived variables and will often condense a myriad of potential variables into a manageable few.

In the next section, we will see a case study that uses some of these ideas to categorize customer behavior.

Case Study: Defining Customer Behavior

The credit card group of a major retail bank has identified three types of profitable customers:

- *Revolvers* are customers who maintain a large balance on their credit card. These are highly profitable customers because every month they pay interest on large balances.

- *Transactors* are customers who have high balances every month, but pay them off. These customers do not pay interest, but the processing fee charged on each transaction is an important source of revenue.

- Convenience users are customers who periodically charge large bills, such as for vacation or large purchases, and then pay them off over several months. Although not as profitable as revolvers, they are lower risk while still paying significant amounts of interest.

The marketing group believes that these three types of customers are motivated by different needs. So, understanding future customer behavior will allow future marketing campaigns to send the most appropriate message to each customer segment. They want to predict customer behavior six months in the future.

This case study investigates different methods of defining these behavior patterns. All of these methods derive segmentation attributes from customer data.

Data

The data available for this project consists of 18 months of billing data, including:

- The credit limit
- Interest rate
- New charges made during the month
- Minimum payment
- Amount paid
- The total balance in each month
- The amount paid in interest and related charges each month

The rules for the credit cards are typical. When a customer has paid off the balance, there is no interest on new charges (for one month). However, when there is an outstanding balance, then interest is charged on both the balance and on new charges. How can we use the data to segment customers?

Segmenting by Estimating Revenue

Estimated revenue is a good way of understanding the value of the customer. As we will see, though, the value does not give as much insight into customer behavior as we would like. And, estimating revenue assumes that the costs for all customers are the same. This is not true, but it is a useful approximation since a full profitability model is quite complicated, difficult to develop, and offers little additional value to the revenue estimate.

Table 6.1 illustrates one month of billing for six customers. The last column is the estimated revenue. This consists of two parts. The first part is the amount

Table 6.1   Six Credit Card Customers and One Month of Data

	CREDIT LIMIT	RATE	NEW CHARGES	BEGINNING BALANCE	MIN. PAYMENT
Customer 1	$500	14.9%	$50	$400	$15
Customer 2	$5,000	4.9%	$0	$4,500	$135
Customer 3	$6,000	11.9%	$100	$3,300	$99
Customer 4	$10,000	14.9%	$2,500	$0	$0
Customer 5	$8,000	12.9%	$6,500	$0	$0
Customer 6	$5,000	17.9%	$0	$4,500	$135

	AMOUNT PAID	INTEREST	TRANSACTION REVENUE	EST. REVENUE
Customer 1	$15	$4.97	$0.50	$5.47
Customer 2	$135	$18.38	$0.00	$18.38
Customer 3	$1,000	$32.73	$1.00	$33.73
Customer 4	$75	$0.00	$25.00	$25.00
Customer 5	$6,500	$0.00	$65.00	$65.00
Customer 6	$135	$67.13	$0.00	$67.13

of interest paid. The second is a percentage of new transactions, which is estimated to be 1 percent of the new transactions.

The estimated revenue is a good way to compare different customers with a single number. The table clearly shows that someone who rarely uses the credit card (Customer 1) has very little estimated revenue. On the other hand, those who make many charges or pay interest create a larger revenue stream.

However, estimated revenue does not differentiate between different types of customers. In fact, a transactor (Customer 5) has very high revenue. So does a revolver who has no new charges (Customer 6). In fact, revenue has little relationship to customer behavior. Frequent users of the credit card and infrequent users both generate a lot of revenue. And this is to be expected, since there are different types of profitable customers.

Estimating revenue has other difficulties. The real world is more complicated than this simplified example. Each customer has a risk of bankruptcy where the outstanding balance must be written off. Different types of cards have different rules. For instance, many cobranded cards have the transaction fee going to the cobranded institution. And, the cost of servicing different customers varies, depending on whether the customer uses customer service, dispute charges, and so on.

In short, estimating revenue is a good way of understanding which customers are valuable. But it does not give much information about customer behavior.

Segmentation by Potential

In addition to actual revenue, each customer has a potential revenue. This is the maximum amount of revenue that they could possibly bring in each month. The maximum revenue is easy to calculate. Simply assume that the entire credit line is either in new charges (hence transaction revenue) or in carry-overs (hence interest revenue). The greater of these is the potential revenue.

Table 6.2 compares the potential revenue with the actual revenue for the same six customers during one month. This table shows some interesting characteristics. Some not-so-profitable customers are already saturating their potential. Without increasing their credit limits or interest rate, it is not possible to increase their value.

Comparing actual revenue to potential has another nice feature. It normalizes the data so the wealthiest customers do not necessarily always show up as the most valuable. The customer with a $10,000 credit line is far from meeting his or her potential. In fact, Customer 1, with the smallest credit line, comes much closer to achieving potential value.

Customer Behavior by Comparison to Ideals

Since estimating revenue and potential does not differentiate among types of customer behavior, let's go back and look at the definitions in more detail.

Table 6.2 The Potential of Six Credit Card Customers

	CREDIT LIMIT	RATE	INTEREST	TRANSACTION	POTENTIAL REVENUE	ACTUAL	POTENTIAL
Customer 1	$500	14.9%	$6.21	$5.00	$6.21	$6.09	98%
Customer 2	$5,000	4.9%	$20.42	$50.00	$50.00	$18.38	37%
Customer 3	$6,000	11.9%	$59.50	$60.00	$60.00	$34.72	56%
Customer 4	$10,000	14.9%	$124.17	$100.00	$124.17	$25.00	20%
Customer 5	$8,000	12.9%	$86.00	$80.00	$86.00	$65.00	76%
Customer 6	$5,000	17.9%	$74.58	$50.00	$74.58	$67.13	90%

First, what inside the data tells us who is a revolver? Here are some definitions of a revolver:

- Someone who pays interest every month
- Someone who pays more than a certain amount of interest every month (say, more than $10)
- Someone who pays more than a certain amount of interest, almost every month (say, more than $10 in 80% of the months)

All these definitions might make sense to business users. However, to do analysis we have to choose one of them. This is an example of why communication between the data miners and the business users is very important.

All of these definitions have an ad hoc quality (and the marketing group had historically made up definitions similar to these on the fly). What about someone who pays very little interest, but does pay interest every month? Why $10? Why 80 percent of the months? These definitions are all arbitrary, often the result of one person's best guess at the definition. It is worth investigating further.

From the customer perspective, what is a revolver? It is someone who makes only the minimum payment every month. So far, so good. For comparing customers, this definition is a bit tricky because the minimum payment changes from month to month and from customer to customer.

Figure 6.13 shows the actual and minimum payment made by three customers, all of whom have a credit line of $2000. The revolver makes payments that are very close to the minimum payment each month. The transactor makes payments closer to the credit line, but these monthly charges vary more widely, depending on the amount charged during the month. The convenience user is somewhere in-between. Qualitatively, the shapes of the curves help us humans understand the behavior.

Manually looking at the shapes is an inefficient way to categorize the behavior of several million customers. Shape is a vague, qualitative notion. We want a score. One way to create a score is by looking at the area between the "minimum payment" curve and the "payment" curve. For our purposes, the area is the sum of the differences between the payment and the minimum. For the revolver, this sum is $112; for the convenience user, $559.10; and for the transactor, a whopping $13,178.90.

This score makes intuitive sense. The lower the score, the more the customer looks like a revolver. However, it does not work for two cardholders with different credit lines. Consider an extreme case. If a cardholder has a credit line of $100 and was a perfect transactor, then the score would be no more than $1200.

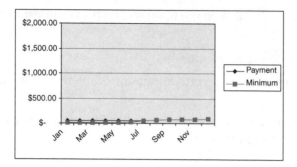

A typical revolver pays only on or near the minimum balance every month.

This revolver has maintained an average balance of $1070, with new charges of about $200 dollars.

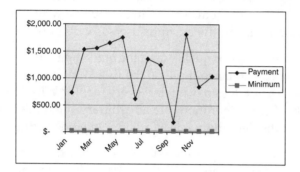

A typical transactor pays off the bill every month. The payment is typically much larger than the minimum payment, except in months with few charges.

This transactor has an average balance of $1196.

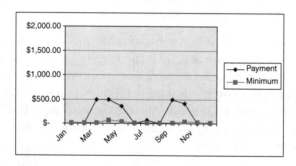

A typical convenience user uses the card when necessary and pays off the balance over several months.

This convenience user has an average balance of $524.

Figure 6.13 Actual and minimum payment for three credit card customers with a credit line of $2,000.

And yet an imperfect, but very good, revolver with a credit line of $2000 has a much larger score.

The solution is to normalize the value by dividing each month's difference by the total credit line. Now the three scores are 0.0047, 0.023, and 0.55 respectively. When the normalized score is close to 0, it means that the cardholder is close to being a perfect revolver. When it is close to 1, the cardholder is close to being a perfect transactor. Numbers in between represent convenience users. This provides a revolver-transactor score for each customer.

This score for customer behavior has some interesting properties. Cardholders who never use their cards would have a minimum payment of $0 and an actual payment of $0. These people look like revolvers. That might not be a good thing. One way to solve this would be to include the estimated revenue potential with the behavior score, in effect, describing the behavior using two numbers.

Another problem with this score is that as the credit line increases, a customer looks more and more like a revolver. To get around this, the ratios could use the monthly balance instead of the credit line. When nothing is owed and nothing paid, then everything has a value of 0.

Figure 6.14 shows a variation. This score uses the ratio of the amount paid to the minimum payment. It has some nice features. Perfect revolvers now have a score of 1, because their payment is equal to the minimum payment. Someone who does not use the card has a score of 0. However, transactors and convenience users both have scores higher than 1, but it is hard to differentiate between them.

This section has shown several different ways of measuring the behavior of a customer. All of these are based on the important variables relevant to the customer. Different measures are more valuable for finding different features of behavior.

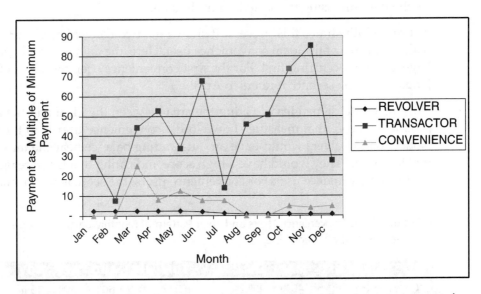

Figure 6.14 Comparing the amount paid as a multiple of the minimum payment shows distinct curves for transactors, revolvers, and convenience users.

The Ideal Convenience User

The measures in the previous section focused on the extremes of customer behavior, revolvers, and transactors. Convenience users were just assumed to be somewhere in the middle. Is there a way to develop a score that is maximized for the ideal convenience user?

The answer is "yes." First, we have to define the ideal convenience user. This is someone who, twice a year, charges up to his or her credit line and then pays off over four months. There are few, if any, additional charges during the other 10 months of the year. Table 6.3 illustrates the monthly balances for two convenience users as a ratio of their credit lines.

This table also shows a problem. The curves describing the behavior of convenience users have no relationship to each other in any given month. They are out of phase. In fact, there is a fundamental difference between convenience users on the one hand and transactors and revolvers on the other. Knowing that someone is a transactor exactly describes their credit card behavior in any given month—they will making many charges and pay off the balance. Knowing someone is a convenience user is much more ambiguous. In any given month, they may be paying nothing, everything, or making a partial payment.

Does this mean that it is not possible to develop a measure to identify convenience users? Not at all. The solution is to sort the 12 months of data and to create the measure using the sorted monthly data.

Figure 6.15 illustrates this process. It shows the two convenience users along with the profile of the ideal convenience user. Here, the data is sorted, with the largest values occurring first. For the first convenience user, month 1 refers to January. For the second, it refers to April.

Now, using the same idea of taking the area between the ideal and the actual produces a score that measures how close a convenience user is to the ideal. Notice that revolvers would have an outstanding balance near the maximum for all months. They would have a high score, indicating that they are far from the ideal convenience user. For convenience users, the score is much smaller.

Table 6.3 Two Convenience Users and Their Pattern of Monthly Balances, Expressed as a Percentage of Their Credit Line

	JAN	FEB	MAR	APR	MAY	JUN	JUL	AUG	SEP	NOV	DEC
Conv1	80%	60%	40%	20%	0%	0%	0%	60%	30%	15%	70%
Conv2	0%	0%	83%	50%	17%	0%	67%	50%	17%	0%	0%

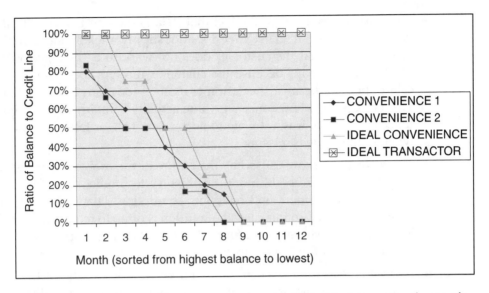

Figure 6.15 Comparison of two convenience users to the ideal, by sorting the months by the balance ratio.

This case study has shown several different ways of segmenting customers. All make use of derived variables to describe customer behavior. Often, it is possible to describe a particular behavior and then to create a score that measures how each customer's behavior compares to the ideal.

Dirty Data

Data is always dirty. Throughout the book, there will be many examples of dirty and missing data, along with explanations of how to work with it.

THE CURSE OF DATA MINING

Data mining likes to look at lots and lots of data—both while preparing the data and when building the models. Many fields in data are collected—and nobody ever looks at them. Data mining tries to use these fields, and discovers missing and dirty data . . . the curse of data mining.

Missing Data

Missing data is one kind of dirty data. These are fields whose values are not filled in, often represented by NULLs in relational databases. Although all missing values look the same, they occur for different reasons:

- *Empty values* occur when the fact that data is missing is relevant information. For instance, if a customer does not supply a telephone number, that could indicate that the customer does not want to be bothered with telephone calls, perhaps because the customer receives too many marketing calls or perhaps because the customer receives too many bill collection calls. This is a case where the missing value actually contains valuable information. In this case, it is valuable to add a new true-or-false field indicating whether the value is missing.

- *Nonexistent values* are caused by the nature of the problem. For instance, if a model wants to use 12 months of history to predict some future event, then recent customers will have lots of missing data, since they lack 12 months of history. In this case, the solution is often to reformulate the problem. Build a separate model for customers who have 12 months of history and another for those who do not.

- *Incomplete data* occurs when data sources cannot supply all the relevant data. This is a big issue with outside vendors who provide overlays for data. In this case, a noticeable number of customers will not match, and will have missing values. Or, when data is coming from multiple divisions, such as the demand deposit group, the credit card group, and the mortgage group of a bank, many customers do not have relationships with all the divisions. Sometimes it is helpful to build separate models. Sometimes it is helpful to replace the missing values with derived values, such as the total number of relationships with the bank, the total amount in deposit accounts, and so on.

- *Uncollected data* is missing because it is never collected. For instance, most telephone switches do not record when a customer turns off call waiting; and if they do record this as an event, they do not pass the data through to the billing system. The consequence is that there is no way to determine which customers turn off call waiting, without significant modifications to the operational system.

What can be done about missing data? Actually, the situation is quite similar to handling outliers:

Do nothing. Some algorithms (such as many decision tree implementations) are fairly robust when there are missing values. If there are few missing values, they may not materially affect the models.

Filter the rows containing them. This can be a bad idea, because it might introduce sample bias into the data. In other words, if there is a systematic problem in the systems that produce the data, the rows may not be representative of the overall population.

Ignore the column. Focus on the complete data by ignoring columns with missing values. If only a few columns have spotty columns, often it makes sense to ignore them, or to replace them with indicator flags that just say whether the data was present.

Predict new values. Using decision trees or neural networks, it is possible to use other columns to predict the missing column. A less refined approach is to insert the average value or most common value into the column.

Build separate models. Often, it is possible to eliminate much of the problem by segmenting the customers based on what data they have available. This approach is particularly useful for nonexistent missing values.

Modify the operational systems. And wait until the data is collected—admittedly not the most practical short-term solution.

There is no simple cure-all for missing data. The curse of data mining is that it looks at lots and lots of data—and finds problems.

Fuzzy Definitions

Another class of dirty data occurs when the data does not have clean, consistent definitions. Data mining algorithms assume that the values in fields mean the same thing from one row to the next. That is, when the same value appears in multiple rows it means the same thing each time.

Consider retail point-of-sale systems in North America that produce data with a column for the UPC. Another field is the "amount" of the transaction. Embedded in the UPC is a subfield that says what the amount means. A "1" in the amount field could mean 1 apple, or 1 box of cereal, 1 six-pack of beer, or 1 pound of meat. In other words, the field means different things in different records—a problem for data mining.

Mergers and acquisitions cause dirty data, too. Having to translate one set of codes to match another introduces the possibility of error. Sometimes, multiple codes appear in the data, so there may be several codes that mean the same thing, such as "account open." But each has a different nuance in its definition, so they are not exactly the same (if they were, it would be more likely that they would have been combined). In this situation, two records may have different codes, but they almost always mean the same thing.

Fuzzy definitions can also occur at the record level. The definition of the population may be fuzzy. What exactly is a current customer? What about customers who have been late paying their bills? Or, how are separate sites of the same business customer handled? Often, the answers to these and similar questions are answered on an ad-hoc basis. So, the available data may include "customers" that are not really customers.

Incorrect Values

Incorrect data are fields whose values do not correspond to valid values for the column, or are unreasonable in some other way. There are numerous causes of incorrect data.

Some data is input incorrectly. Sometimes, this is due to the nature of transcribing information, such as misspelling someone's name or address. Sometimes, the cause is less innocent. In one data set we once looked at, almost 5 percent of the individuals were born in 1911. And, more surprisingly, almost all were born on November 11th. An incredible coincidence? Probably not.

In this case, the customer service representatives were responsible for inputting the date of birth. And, since knowing the age was so important to the company, the designers of the system made date of birth a mandatory field. The representatives could not skip over it; they had to fill it in with something. They quickly learned that hitting the "1" key six times was the quickest way to fill in the field and move on. Voila! A significant portion of the database has a birthday of 11/11/1911.

Sometimes the problem is not people but other programs. Another database had hundreds of state codes. Or, rather, hundreds of two-character codes in the state field. Now, many databases share state code fields with more than fifty values. Databases readily admit Puerto Rico, Gaum, and the Virgin Islands as states. Even Canadian provinces are common in states fields. Two hundred values, though, is a bit excessive. This was due to a programmer error. The city field contained 15 characters, followed by 2 characters for the state field. When the city name exceeded 15 characters, it simply overwrote the state. Hence, "North Miami Beach" (with 17 characters) would find itself with a state code of CH instead of FL. Subsequent processing did not use the state code; it used the ZIP code, so the problem was never found.

Another problem is timing. Old codes are still being used in the database, although they should have been supplanted by newer codes. An extreme case of this occurred when analyzing grocery data—and later learning that there were two types of cash registers. The NCR and IBM point-of-sale systems each used separate but overlapping sets of department codes. Oops!

And sometimes, data is simply collected incorrectly. Dates and times are collected without time zone information, so they cannot be compared from geographically disperse areas. Clocks are not set correctly, so timestamps are invalid. Customer numbers are not available, so arbitrary customer numbers are put in. Data is miskeyed when it is entered into the computer. And so on.

Occasionally, the data is stored incorrectly. The same key field, say a customer number, is a string in one database and a number in another. A social security number contains hyphens in one database but no hyphens in another, so they cannot easily be joined. The data warehouse "guesses" at the best value for missing fields . . . and puts in an unusable value.

Incorrect data occurs in all systems. As we mentioned in Chapter 3, one of our favorite quotes came from an unnamed CIO who claimed that his data must be clean because "no humans ever touch it; it is collected automatically." And, in fact, almost half the time values were incorrect . . . because humans never touched the system clocks on the computers, either.

Lessons Learned

Data mining is fundamentally about data. And data preparation is a key part of data mining. This chapter covered many of the important topics about data, and these will be revisited in the case studies:

- Data mining algorithms want data in a tabular format. Rows are the unit of data mining (often at the customer level). Columns describe attributes of the rows.

- Data mining algorithms do not treat all columns the same. Most are inputs, one may be a target, and some may be ignored. Columns may be ignored for many reasons—three common reasons are unary-valued columns, identification columns, and columns redundant with the target.

- In the real world, data comes from data warehouses, operational systems, data marts, OLAP systems, and external sources. Important data may be on people's desktops. There is no such thing as a perfect data source.

- Data is not ready for data mining in the real world. Many separate transformations are needed to transform real data into a data mining format, especially aggregations and joins.

- To be useful for data mining, values in columns should be categories, ranks, intervals, or true numerics. More complicated data types, such as text, are generally not used, although features may be extracted from them.

- Much of the art of data mining is in creating derived variables. These express features about the data.

- Data is always dirty.

This chapter started with an allusion to a story about thirsty sailors surrounded by a salty sea, making an analogy to business people surrounded by data in need of information. Data mining holds the promise of quenching the thirst, but only after the data has been well prepared.

CHAPTER 7

Building Effective Predictive Models

The third pillar of data mining is building effective models. Predictive modeling, often the primary purpose of data mining, has historically been a specialized function within companies. Data mining, though, is supposed to make predictive modeling easy. Well, easy may be too strong a word, but at least it is no longer necessary to spend years taking actuarial exams or to have a doctorate in statistics to make predictions. That's the good news.

The bad news is that predictive modeling is still a tricky business, and we often see people making mistakes when building models. No predictive model is going to be correct 100 percent of the time—if it were, the model really would be too good to be true. The purpose of building models is to use the predictions to make better *informed* business decisions, such as who receives a telephone sales call or which banner ad to show on a web page. If the predictions are not good, then the so-called "informed" decisions will be worse than decisions made with no information at all! So, some care has to be taken when building predictive models. Otherwise, we might as well roll dice.

This chapter begins with a discussion of what a good model really is. We will see that the most common way of looking at model performance—the lift chart—can reveal quite a bit about what is going on.

The most important goal when building models is stability, which is just another way of saying that the model should make predictions that will hold true when applied to unseen data. This, in turn, requires understanding the data going into the model, the time frame, and a host of other factors that are covered in more detail throughout this chapter. And, the most important insight in this chapter is this: The best model is not the one with the highest lift when it is being built. It is the model that performs the best on unseen, future data. Although there is no 1-2-3 recipe for building perfect models, this chapter covers the fundamentals needed to build effective models, and we will see these lessons applied in the case studies in later chapters.

Building Good Predictive Models

Fortunately, the basic process for building predictive models is the same, regardless of the data mining technique being used. Success depends more on the process than on the technique. And this process depends critically on the data being used to generate the model. Garbage-in, garbage-out is an adage that applies especially well to predictive modeling.

Chapter 3 introduced the basic methodology for data mining, as well as lift charts to measure performance. This section will go more in depth into this area, illustrating some common problems that can be diagnosed by examining lift charts. It will also discuss why producing effective models is challenging, regardless of the techniques being used.

A Process for Building Predictive Models

The first challenge in building predictive models is gathering together enough preclassified data. Since the next chapter covers this area, we can skip the details here. In preclassified data, the outcomes are already known. And, because these known examples will be used to teach the model about the data, this set is called the *model set*.

Figure 7.1 shows the basic steps in building and applying a predictive model:

1. The model is trained using preclassified data in a subset of the model set called the *training set*. In this step, the data mining algorithms find patterns of predictive value.

2. The model is refined, using another subset called the *test set*. Why does the model need to be refined? In order to prevent the model from memorizing the training set, thereby ensuring that the model is more general and will work better on unseen data.

3. We can estimate the performance of the model, or compare the performance of several models, by using a third set, entirely distinct from the first two. This holdout set is called the *evaluation set*.

4. The model is applied to the *score set*. The score set is not preclassified and is not part of the model set. We do not know the outcomes for this data. Presumably, we will use the predictive scores to make more informed business decisions.

Of course, the details of these steps do depend on which data mining technique is being used and on which tool is being used, but the overall process remains the same.

Another way of looking at this is from the perspective of the patterns in the data. The model wants to learn all the patterns in the model set. Well, not quite all the patterns—just the patterns that are likely to be relevant for prediction. When the model trains on the training set, it learns to recognize the patterns in the training set. These patterns are a combination of the general patterns in the model set and of the specific patterns in the training set.

But the patterns specific to the training set are not useful. By using the test set to refine the model, the model can "unlearn" these extraneous patterns. The test set allows the model to generalize better. Finally, using the evaluation set, we can estimate the model's performance.

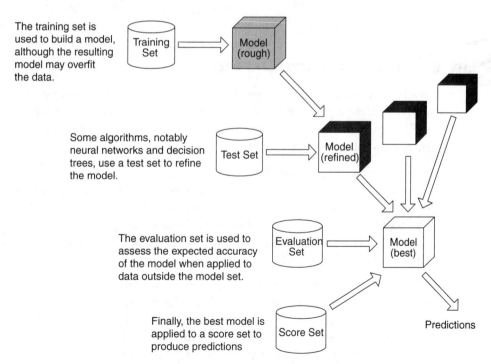

Figure 7.1 Building and applying a model is a multistep process.

The evaluation set is particularly important because most modeling efforts involve building several models. From these models, the one with the best performance will be chosen. Different tools have different levels of automation handling this aspect of model building. Almost all data mining tools have some mechanism for building a model and then scoring it (it would not be much of a tool if it did not do this). Some require the user to do all these steps manually, building one model at a time, estimating the performance on the evaluation set, and repeating for other models. At the other end of the spectrum are tools that fully automate the process, building and comparing dozens or hundreds of models and then choosing the best one.

Finally, the model has to be scored. This usually introduces time-dependency into the modeling process, because the score set is often more recent than the model set. In fact, the model may be used repeatedly over time. In such cases measuring the model's accuracy is important in order to know when the model has to be rebuilt.

You must also do something with the score. Typically, the score has a value or confidence, and when it exceeds some threshold, you take action. Setting this threshold is important. For instance, if you know that you will be contacting only 20,000 people per month in an outbound telemarketing center, then the modeling effort should be focused on getting the best 20,000—not on getting the best results overall.

Lift as a Measure of Performance

We have seen how lift is a good measure of model performance. In fact, lift and cumulative gains charts can provide important insights into the model, as well as measuring performance. In addition, they can compare model performance on different sets of data.

Figure 7.2 shows a cumulative gains chart comparing the results of a model on the test and evaluation sets of data. This is an example of a good model, not only because we see decent lift, but also because the results on the test and evaluation set are similar. As should be the case, the performance on the training set is better than the performance on the test set, which in turn is better than on the evaluation set.

The cumulative gains chart for decision trees actually consists of a collection of line segments (see Figure 7.3). Each of these segments corresponds to one of the leaf nodes in the decision tree. Each leaf node gets a different score, but the score is the same for all records that land there, so they are all grouped together. This grouping results in a slanted line on the cumulative gains chart. If we can actually see the slanted lines, then there are not very many leaves in the decision tree. Depending on the data, having few leaves may be a good thing or a bad thing.

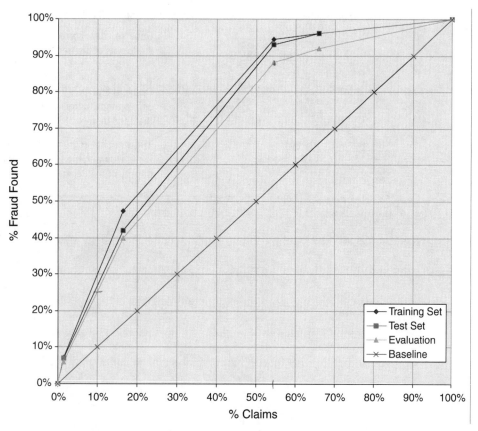

Figure 7.2 Example of a good lift chart where performance on the test and evaluation sets are similar.

Sometimes, the lift curves are close to the baseline, as in Figure 7.4. In this case, the model does not provide much lift. Normally, this would be an indication of a poor model. However, it is important to keep in mind what the theoretical maximum lift could be. This chart actually shows the results from modeling which customers are likely to want call waiting. The line in the middle shows lift curve for the model, but it doesn't seem so good. The top 10 percent of the customers account for only 16 percent of the customers with call waiting. What is happening?

In fact, 55 percent of the customers already had call waiting—quite a high number. So, even if all the top scoring customers had call waiting (the theoretically best model), then they would account for only 18 percent (10 out of 55 percent) of the customers with call waiting. Finding 16 percent is actually pretty good then. It is important to keep in mind the theoretical maximum as well as the baseline when interpreting these charts.

The cumulative gains chart for a decision tree consists of a series of flat line segments.

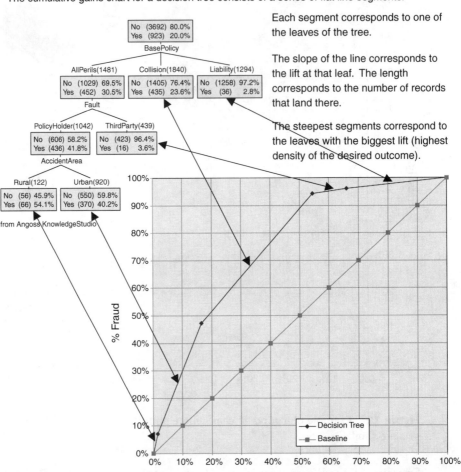

Each segment corresponds to one of the leaves of the tree.

The slope of the line corresponds to the lift at that leaf. The length corresponds to the number of records that land there.

The steepest segments correspond to the leaves with the biggest lift (highest density of the desired outcome).

Figure 7.3 The relationship between a cumulative gains chart and a decision tree.

Of course, when the lift curve is close to the baseline, it often means that the model is not very good. Perhaps adding derived variables, obtaining new data, or trying a different modeling technique will do a better job. Or the problem may be related to the technique. For instance, if a neural network has too many input nodes it can converge on a very suboptimal model—requiring the removal of variables to improve model performance.

Figure 7.5 shows one of the classic signs of overfitting. This is a curve for the evaluation set of a model, and it shows two things. First, the model does not perform very well—the lift curve is pretty close to the baseline. However, there is also an interesting feature in the curve; it has a dip in it around 20 percent. What is causing this? The answer, in short, is overfitting. The model has memorized the training and test sets and is not able to generalize very well. At

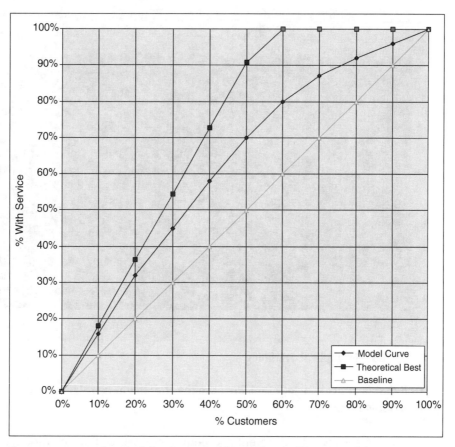

Figure 7.4 Keep in mind the theoretical best when judging a model.

about the twentieth percentile, in fact, what the model predicts is actually worse than a random guess. This is evident because the slope of the line at that point is almost horizontal (and not because the curves almost touch) meaning that there are very few "Y"s in this region.

Overfitting is the bane of modeling, and evidence readily shows up in the lift curves. A good lift curve starts almost vertical and gradually becomes horizontal. The "W" shape is one example of a curve characteristic of a poor model. Another common defect is jagged edges. When overfitting does occur, it is necessary to revisit the model. Try removing hidden nodes in a neural network or increasing the minimum leaf size in a decision tree.

TIP

The lift curves in cumulative gains charts can show evidence of overfitting. But what can you do about it? For neural networks, try modifying the network so it has fewer nodes in the hidden layer. For decision trees, try making the pruning criteria stricter.

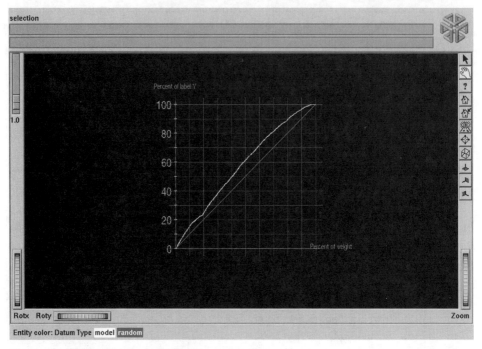

Figure 7.5 Example of overfitting.

Or if that is difficult in your tool, increase the "minimum leaf size"—a parameter that most tools support.

Figure 7.6 shows yet a different problem. Here we see that the model seems to do very well. In fact, it zooms up to the top long before exhausting the data. This means that the 60 percent of the records with the lowest score have exactly zero examples of the outcome. What we see is a correlation between the input and the output—a situation that can indicate bad inputs, or a lot of insight. There is still more work to do to understand what is going on, to figure out whether inputs are improperly correlated with the output. Even when there is no improper correlation, it is usually a good idea to build a new model on the portion of the population that does contain the outcome of interest.

We will see this chart again in Chapter 10 (the case study on best next offer models) and learn that, in fact, there is a strong correlation between some of the inputs and the output of the model. Without giving away the whole story, we can say that it is not hard to predict that most people do not have an unpopular product.

A normal model should do a bit better on the training set than on the test set, and a bit better on the test set than the evaluation set, although the performance on all these should be similar. The curves should start with a steep

This is a cumulative gains chart used in the cross selling case study. This portion of the cumulative-gains chart is suspicious because it is entirely flat.

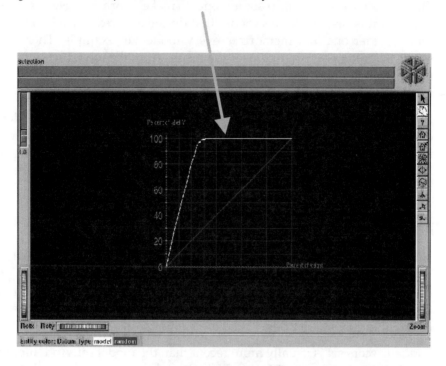

A flat line in a cumulative gains chart can indicate a strong correlation between the inputs into the model and the output being predicted.

Figure 7.6   When a cumulative gains chart looks too good to be true, it just might be.

slope and gradually become more horizontal. In a cumulative gains chart, the curve for the training set should be above the curve for the test set, and both should be above the evaluation set (although they should be close). If these curves are inverted, then it is worth investigating further. When the curves look very different from these rules, it is worth revisiting the model.

Model Stability

Building a model is like test-driving a car. The car should handle well not only on a sunny, clear day when it is brand-new and driven for the first time, but also in all kinds of weather and road conditions. We want the performance of the car to be stable over time and in different situations.

The same principle applies to predictive models. A *stable* model is one that behaves similarly when applied to different sets of data. Not only do we want a model that produces good results on the model set, but we also want to have confidence that the model will work well on other sets of data.

This confidence allows us to use a model to make informed business decisions. After all, it is easy to make a model that does really, really well on the model set. Consider one that memorizes every model set example. Then, when it scores an unknown record, it uses the results from the model set—if there is a match, and if not, it produces a random guess. Well, this model is entirely unstable. It will do no better than random for the score set.

Another aspect of model stability is that the performance of models degrades over time because the score set becomes more and more different from the model set. When a model is being deployed in an application, it is very important to measure the performance of the model and rebuild it when the performance becomes unacceptable.

The Challenge of Model Stability

Unfortunately, when we are building the model, the only data that we have to work with is the model set. So, one of the big challenges in data mining is producing models that will remain stable on different sets of data, and among these, especially the score set. The model set and the score set are likely to be different for several reasons.

First, the score set is usually more recent than the model set. And, more recent data is likely to be a bit different. There have been additional marketing campaigns, customer contacts, new products, changes in the marketplace, and macro-economic changes. It sounds daunting; later in this chapter we will discuss how to enable models to slide forward in time.

Other problems arise because the score set and the model set are samples from the general population. And the samples might be different. For instance, if we are trying to predict the propensity of customers to purchase a product, we will eliminate anyone who already has the product from the score set. This can introduce skew. Or, we might decide to score a subset of the customers for business reasons, such as those from California or those who have a second telephone line. Once again, the model set and the score set may be qualitatively different.

What does this mean? It means that it might be hard to make a stable model because the data we used to build the model is different from the data being scored. Statistics provides detailed explanations for understanding sampling and modeling. Without diving into the mathematics, we can say that data mining, fortunately, uses large amounts of data (tens or hundreds of thousands of rows, for instance). And having lots of data reduces the impact of these issues.

Remember, the evaluation set is part of the model set. It gives only a rough guide for the accuracy of the model on unseen data.

When a model does well on the model set but not on the score set, then it has overfit the model set. This type of overfitting can be a function of the model set. The data used to build the model is too different from the score set, so the patterns found in the model set do not apply. Although these situations are less likely to arise when using large quantities of data, it is always important to keep the challenge of model stability in mind.

Working with the Model Set

The model set is the preclassified data used to build a model. It is important to remember that a predictive model is only as good as the data used to create it. One way of thinking about predictive models, in fact, is as a summarization of the model set, a way of distilling the information in the model set so it can be applied to other data.

Since a larger model set has more information, we just want to collect as much data as possible. Well, this is not always true—sometimes more is better, sometimes not. Working with model sets can be a bit counterintuitive. Understanding how they influence models is critical to effective data mining.

This section will cover the important facets of the model set. We will see many of the ideas presented here repeated in the case studies.

Divide and Conquer: Training, Test, and Evaluation Sets

As discussed earlier, the model set needs to be split into three components, the training set, the test set, and the evaluation set. Each of these components should be totally separate. They should not have any records in common.

Most data mining tools provide at least some support for splitting the model set. In particular, the test set is important when using most flavors of decision trees and for neural networks. The test set is actually part of these techniques. It is used to make the model more general; that is, to prevent it from overfitting the training set. Since both the training set and the test set are used to create the model, they cannot be used to evaluate its performance.

Support for the evaluation set is not always available in tools. In this case, part of the model set needs to be manually separated from the rest and held back. Once the model has been trained, the evaluation set can be scored to get an idea of how the model performs on unseen data.

The evaluation set must be completely different from the training and test sets. Otherwise, the evaluation of the model's performance is cheating. The model should do well on the data it was trained on. In fact, one way to "cheat" when showing the results of models is to show the results on the test set instead of the evaluation set; this makes the results look better since the data mining techniques use the test set to optimize the model.

How should the model set be distributed among the training, test, and evaluation sets? This is a good question. If you really want to know the answer, try building models with different proportions. We have found that a split of 60-30-10 percent works well in practice (although at least one popular tool has a default split of 40-30-30 percent).

How the Size of the Model Set Affects Results

In general, bigger is better. Models trained on larger model sets tend to do a better job of prediction because the model set has more examples from which to learn. When working with model sets of different sizes, there are some things to keep in mind. In general, you want at least several thousand records in the model set—and model sets with hundreds of thousands of records are not uncommon.

Why Bigger Is Not Always Better

There are several reasons why a larger model set may not be the best choice. First, there is usually a fixed amount of time for doing the modeling. During this period of time, the model set has to be constructed, models built and tested, and then the results deployed. Building models on larger model sets takes more time. This time could sometimes be better spent investigating other parameters, obtaining different types of data, or creating new derived variables. Any of these could have a larger effect on the performance of the model than the number of records. So when there is a trade-off with time, sometimes it is better to work with a smaller model set, at least initially.

Similarly, the tool being used may limit the size of the model set. For performance reasons, some tools try to keep all the data in memory. Even if they do not, the extensive file processing required for really large model sets may make them unattractive for performance reasons. Sometimes, the right approach is to experiment with a sample of the data and then build the final model on a larger model set.

There are even some technical reasons why bigger model sets may not produce better results. Often, what we are trying to predict is a rare event, such as fraud or purchasing a brokerage account. Say the rare event occurs in 1 percent of the records in a data set that has a million rows. The model built with 50,000 rows and a density of 20 percent may produce better models than the one built with a million rows and a density of 1 percent—in fact, it almost surely will, since the second model will probably just predict a single outcome. We will address this topic later in this chapter when we discuss oversampling.

Adjusting Model Parameters

There is often a relationship between the parameters used to build a model and the size of the model set. The parameters are often represented as minimum sizes. For instance, when building decision trees, it is often valuable to have a minimum node size. A rule of thumb is to set this to around 50 or 100 to prevent overfitting the data (although improved pruning algorithms are making this less important). However, it really needs to take into account the size of the model set. A value of 100 is 10 percent of a model set that has 1000 rows; it is only 0.1 percent of a model set that has 100,000. This difference can result in drastically different models being produced.

The same situation arises with neural networks as well. With a larger model set, it may be possible to have a larger number of hidden nodes. If the number of hidden nodes is fixed, though, then models built with a smaller model set are more likely to overfit the data.

How the Density of the Model Set Affects Results

Let's say that we have built a model to categorize something, and we are looking at how well it performs. Of the records with the top score, half are predicted to be "dark" and half "light." How well is this model performing?

There is not enough information to answer the question. If 5 percent of the model set originally consisted of records marked "dark" (and the rest marked "light"), then the model is performing well. Without modeling, only 5 percent of those records would be "dark." Instead, the model is getting 50 percent—that is a lift of 10, a good result. However, if the density was 30 percent "dark," then the model is not doing as well. And, if the model set had a density of 50 percent, then the model is doing nothing at all! The top scoring records are equivalent to a random sample.

The density of the model set affects the interpretation of the results of the model. This is particularly important when comparing the performance of different models, or when combining multiple models together. The next section talks about how to control the density of the model set, using a method known as oversampling. The discussion on oversampling begins with sampling.

Sampling

Sampling is the process of creating a data set containing fewer records than were contained in the original data set. When building predictive models, the samples should be *representative*. That is, the sample should look as much like all the data as possible (statisticians have a name for all the data: the *population*). All values should be present in the sample and the distribution of values in the sample should be about the same as in the unsampled data. For instance, a representative sample of people from the United States would have more Californians than North Dakotans.

Statisticians have proven that the best way to obtain a representative sample is by taking random records. This may sound easy, but randomness is more common in our daily lives than it is on deterministic machines such as computers. Fortunately, there are pseudorandom number generators available in most programming languages, spreadsheets, and even in some databases and data mining tools. Pseudorandom numbers are, for our purposes, sufficiently random, and computers can calculate them easily.

When trying to create a sample, it is tempting to try to find an easy way to get it; for instance, by taking all records with fields in a particular range of values, or data from a limited geographic area range. This is a very, very bad idea for predictive modeling, because the resulting records are biased; they do not represent the whole population. For example, consider what might happen if we were to use a range of customer IDs to sample down a database of customers. Perhaps customer IDs might be assigned by geography, so the modeling results would apply only to certain areas. Or customer IDs might be assigned sequentially, so the range might apply to customers who joined at about the same time—another bias we would like to avoid.

TIP

Sometimes a random number generator may not be available or you might need more control over how the sample is generated (to repeat it in the future or on a different computing system, for example). It is possible to use a mathematical function on an numerical ID to kind-of, sort-of, mimic a random sample. An example is to multiply the ID by one prime number and then take the remainder of the result when divided by another prime number. For example, 101 is one prime number and 17 is another. So if you wanted about 10 percent of the original data, you might select the rows where `(rownum * 17) % 101 < 10`.

A good check of whether a sample is representative is to verify that the field values look about the same in the sample and in the original data (in statistics-speak, have about the same distribution). For categorical values, all the values should be represented in the sample; the most common values in the sample should be the most common values in the original data. For numerical values, the mean and standard deviation should be about the same. If the values in the sample are noticeably different from the values in the data as a whole, then generate another sample.

What Is Oversampling?

Oversampling is the process of creating a model set by taking more of the rare outcomes and fewer of the common outcomes, as shown in Figure 7.7, to adjust the ratio of outcomes in the model set. When there are only two outcomes, we typically want the rarer outcome to occur in about 10–40 percent of the model set—and ratios near 20–30 percent often produce good results.

The idea behind oversampling is quite simple. Consider the case when there are 1,000,000 records and 1 percent are "dark" and the rest "light." This means that there are 990,000 "light" examples and 10,000 "dark" examples. Almost any model built on this data set will say that a given record is "light"—and it will be right 99 percent of the time. But it is not a useful model since it does not distinguish between the two types of records.

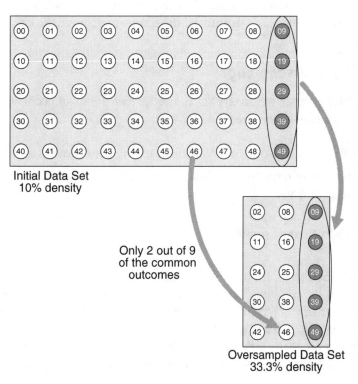

Initial Data Set
10% density

Only 2 out of 9
of the common
outcomes

Oversampled Data Set
33.3% density

Figure 7.7 Oversampling increases the frequencies of the less common outcomes. In this example, the density is increased from 10% to 33.3%—an oversampling ratio of 3.33.

Reducing the size of the model set to 100,000 records, where 90,000 are "light" and 10,000 are "dark," makes it more likely that data mining algorithms will produce a good model. Because the original data started out with only 10,000 "dark" examples, this oversampled data set will have all the "dark" ones and just a small fraction (90,000/990,000 or 9.09 percent) of the "light" ones.

Oversampling has its limits. Because there are only so many "dark" examples, it is not possible, for instance, to create a model set that has 500,000 examples of which 10 percent are "dark." To do this, there would have to be 50,000 "dark" records—but there are only 10,000 in the original data.

This is a typical occurrence. Oversampling increases the proportion of the less frequent outcome or outcomes. What we are really doing is taking all of the examples of the rarer outcome and a mix of just enough of the rest to get an appropriate density.

When there are more than two outcomes, oversampling works in the same way. All the records with a given outcome are called a *stratum* of the data. Oversampling works by taking different proportions from each stratum. For this reason, statisticians call oversampling *stratified random sampling*. This name is quite informative. It means that the sampling is done separately for each possible outcome—each stratum of the data—to achieve the right balance in the model set.

When to Use Oversampling

Often, the outcome that we are trying to model just does not occur very often in the data. There are several reasons for this:

- The outcome may be quite rare, such as tracking breakdowns in machinery
- The outcome may have to be validated before it can be used for modeling, such as cases of fraud
- The outcome may be for a short amount of time, such as customer churn or charge-offs in a single month

Regardless of the cause, though, modeling techniques do not do a good job when almost all the data has a single outcome. If 99 percent of the data is "no fraud" and 1 percent is "fraud," then it is very easy to devise a model that is accurate 99 percent of the time—just predict that everything is "no fraud." Although this is accurate, it is not valuable because we are really interested in the "fraud" cases—and the model predicts none of them. The solution is oversampling.

Oversampling Can Go Too Far

Instead of reducing the size of some of the strata, another approach to oversampling data is to use row weights greater than 1 to make the rarer examples more important or to actually make multiple copies of them. Sometimes when there are not enough samples, this approach can help. However, we do not recommend it.

In addition to the approach described above, some tools support weighted model building. In this case the weight of each "fraud" record would be 1, but each non-fraud would have a weight of 0.01 (we prefer to have the maximum weight be 1). However, weights can only be used when the tools support them.

The trick of using weights greater than 1 has a fatal flaw. It is very easy to generate models that overfit the data. Consider the extreme case where one record has a very high weight and is the only example of a desired outcome. There is no way to build a model, because even though the weights may balance, there are no patterns to find. When actually copying records into a new data set, there is an additional problem. The test and evaluation portions of the model set are likely to contain copies of the same records—unless you prepared them very carefully.

Using weights or copying does solve the problem of increasing the density of the model set without reducing its size. When using weights, it is a good idea for the maximum weight to be 1 and for all other weights to be less than 1. However, if there are very, very few samples of certain outcomes, then predictive modeling may not be the best approach. There are more sophisticated techniques being researched for working with such sparse data. One interesting idea is to replicate the rare outcomes. Instead of copying them entirely, though, tweak the values in all the other fields. The resulting model set is not a real set of data, but it is close. And it might prove useful for modeling.

Oversampling, Lift, and Scores

A predictive model produces a score, often expressed as a likelihood of some result. The scores produced on an oversampled model set are different from the scores on the original, not-oversampled data. Oversampling *changes the meaning of the scores.* Therefore, you must be careful when reporting lifts, and take into account the density of the model set.

Say the records with the best score have a lift of 2. Is this good or bad? Consider these three situations:

- The model set has a density of 1 percent. In this case, the lift of two corresponds to a density of 2 percent for the best records. This may be a disappointing result.

- The model set has a density of 45 percent. In this case, the corresponding density is 90 percent—a much better result.

- The model set has a density of 50 percent. Here, the corresponding density is 100 percent—an incredible result.

One property of the scores does not change. A higher score is better, regardless of oversampling. The numbers are not absolute. The sidebar explains how to convert a score generated by a model built on an oversampled model set into a likelihood on the original data.

A related issue arises when you want to choose a particular number of records, such as choosing the 10,000 customers with the highest scores for a marketing intervention. The best approach is to apply the model to the score set and to choose the top scoring records. Sometimes, this is not possible, and we really want a threshold value. It is possible to estimate for a particular score threshold, the number of records that will have that score or greater. Of course, the

Calculating Predicted Lift when Using Oversampling

Often, when we build predictive models, the purpose is to assign a score to new records and then to choose records whose score exceeds a certain threshold. Often we choose the threshold either to optimize a function (such as profit) or just to get a certain number of records.

It is tempting to believe the lift values and scores generated on the oversampled model set. However, these are only useful at that oversampling rate and not on the original data density. How do we convert lift values on the model set into lift values on the original data, removing the effect of oversampling?

The model assigns a score to every record. For this explanation, we assume that there are just two outcomes (such as fraud/not-fraud or churner/not-churner). The rarer outcome is the one that we want to predict. To determine the lift, we use the density of the outcomes after scoring; that is, a subset that is twice as dense as the model set has a lift of 2. The lift tells us how much better we are doing.

So, the density of a subset is the number of rare outcomes divided by the total number:

$$\text{DENSITY}_{\text{model set}} = (\text{\# of rares}) / (\text{\# of rares} + \text{\# of not-rares})$$

An oversampling rate of OSR simply says that every "common" outcome in the model set corresponds to OSR common outcomes in the original data. On the other hand, every rare one corresponds to exactly one rare one in the original data. Figure 7.8 illustrates what is happening.

threshold value is just like the scores on the records and has to be adjusted for the original density.

Oversampling affects the number of records as well. Estimating the number of records is a bit tricky. Just because a threshold value corresponds to 1 percent of the oversampled model set does not mean that the adjusted threshold will correspond to 1 percent of the original data. In fact, it won't. In one example, the score threshold for the top 1 percent, based of the oversampled model set, corresponded to just 0.07 percent of the score set. Even the threshold at 10 percent yeilded lass than 1 percent of the score set. The sidebar explains this as well.

Modeling Time-Dependent Data

Time frames play a critical role in building effective predictive models. The time frame for predictive modeling has three important components, as shown in Figure 7.9:

1. The **past** consists of what has already happened and data that has already

---

To calculate the predicted density, we simply multiply the number of "rare" instances by 1 and the number of non-rare instances by OSR.

$$DENSITY_{orig\ set} = (\text{\# of rares} * OSR) / (\text{\# of rares} * OSR + \text{\# of not-rares})$$

To estimate the corresponding lift on the original data set, the calculated density is divided by the density of the original set.

Consider a situation where the density for the top 1 percent of the scorers is 90 percent versus a 30 percent density in the model set. The lift (of this segment) on the model set is 3. Now consider that the original data really had a density of only 1 percent, so OSR is 30. The predicted density of this segment is then 90/(90 + 10 * 30) or 23.1 percent—it has gone down just a bit. However, the lift has jumped from 3 to over 23!

There is one caveat, though. Say the segment accounted for 1 percent of the data in the model set. The relative size of the segment changes, as well as its lift. This can have important implications when you are trying to predict how well the model will perform on the original data.

If the 90 percent response rate was occurring for the top 1 percent, then the size of this group decreases. In this case, 90 percent of the group are churners, so they stay the same size; the other 10 percent get multiplied by 30. The formula for the new size is:

```
New size = old size * (DENSITY + (1—DENSITY) * OSR) / OSR
```

So the lift of 23 occurs for the top 0.13 percent in this case, instead of the top 1 percent.

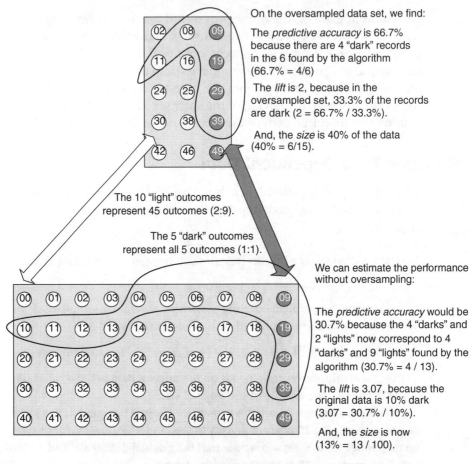

A data mining algorithm assigns its top score to 40% of the oversampled Model Set, giving a lift of 2.

On the oversampled data set, we find:

The *predictive accuracy* is 66.7% because there are 4 "dark" records in the 6 found by the algorithm (66.7% = 4/6)

The *lift* is 2, because in the oversampled set, 33.3% of the records are dark (2 = 66.7% / 33.3%).

And, the *size* is 40% of the data (40% = 6/15).

The 10 "light" outcomes represent 45 outcomes (2:9).

The 5 "dark" outcomes represent all 5 outcomes (1:1).

We can estimate the performance without oversampling:

The *predictive accuracy* would be 30.7% because the 4 "darks" and 2 "lights" now correspond to 4 "darks" and 9 "lights" found by the algorithm (30.7% = 4 / 13).

The *lift* is 3.07, because the original data is 10% dark (3.07 = 30.7% / 10%).

And, the *size* is now (13% = 13 / 100).

On the original data (without oversampling), the top scoring segment of this model corresponds to 13% of the data and a lift of 3.

Figure 7.8 In an oversampled data set, some of the records represent multiple other records.

been collected and processed. At all times, data about the past is available (assuming that it has not been deleted). The past actually mimics the overall structure of the data. The **distant past** is used on the input side of the data; the **recent past** determines the outputs; a period of **latency** represents the present.

2. The **present** is the time period when the model is being built. Data about the present is not available because it still is still being generated by operational systems.

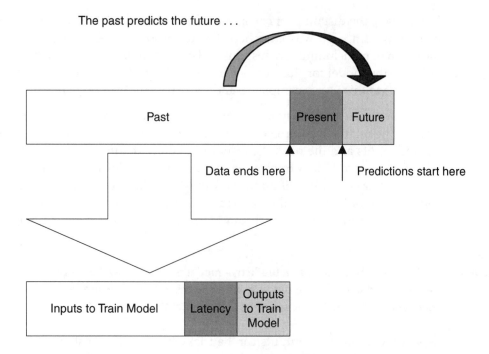

The past predicts the future . . .

Past | Present | Future

Data ends here | Predictions start here

Inputs to Train Model | Latency | Outputs to Train Model

To build an effective model, the data in the model set has to mimic the time frame when the model will be applied.

Figure 7.9 Models are built and applied in the present. When building a model, the past needs to "look" like the present.

3. The **future** is the time period for prediction. Typically, it combines the model built on data from the past applied to data from the past and present.

These three very different time frames are important in building effective predictive models.

Model Inputs and Model Outputs

Defining the output of the model is usually a bit tricky. Sometimes, we are lucky and the problem is very well defined. For instance, perhaps we are going to repeat a marketing campaign from last year. We have data about the customers from before the campaign, and we know exactly who responded to the campaign (since it is presumably finished after almost one year).

In this data, the distant past consists of all the data available before last year's marketing campaign was launched. The recent past consists of the data after the campaign, including any responses. The present is the period when we are building the model for this year's campaign. Finally, the future represents the responses to this year's campaign, and these have not yet occurred.

All the input data must be available prior to any of the data used to determine the outputs. In the relatively simple example just given, it is not difficult to separate out the inputs and the outputs. Data from before the initial campaign date is used for the input; data from after that date is used for the output. Also, the types of data are quite different, and they are likely to come from different sources. The only output data used is the response variable. Any other older data can be used as inputs (including responses to even earlier campaigns).

PREDICTIVE MODELING TIP
All data used as inputs into a predictive model must occur earlier in time than any of the data used to create the outputs. Violating this rule creates models that look very, very good on the model set and yet fail to predict the future well.

Separating inputs and outputs can be tricky in other circumstances, especially when the inputs and the outputs are coming from the same data source. As with other data mining efforts, predictive modeling usually requires adding in derived variables. These derived variables must follow the same law: Any variables used in the derivation must occur earlier in time than the output variables.

Figure 7.10 illustrates an oversight that once happened to one of the authors. In this case, we were working with the credit card group of a large regional bank to build a model to predict customer behavior. We had 18 months of data at hand and were interested in predicting customer behavior segments:

- Revolvers are cardholders who maintain large outstanding balances and pay lots of interest.
- Transactors are cardholders who pay off their bills every month, hence paying no interest.
- Convenience users are cardholders who charge a lot and then pay off the balance over several months.

We determined customer behavior by calculating the behavior on the last six months of the data. This left 12 months of data for the inputs into the model.

Alas, one derived variable was the total ratio of outstanding balances to the total credit line, for the most recent 12 months in the data. This variable violated the law that input come strictly before outputs. What effect did this derived variable have? With the variable in place, the model achieved an accu-

The intention was to have 12 months of history predict six months in the future.

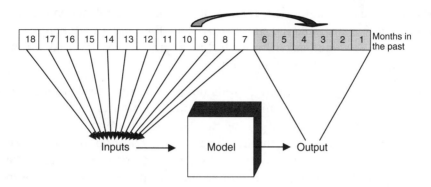

But one derived variable used data from the past twelve months, crept in, and skewed the results.

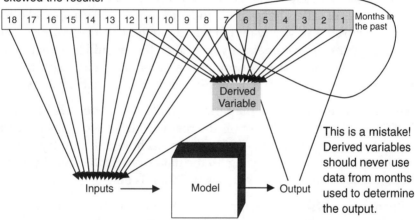

Figure 7.10 Never use the output months as input, so be careful of how derived variables are defined.

racy of over 90 percent—an exceptionally good result, considering that the model was predicting three outcomes (so the baseline accuracy would be about 33 percent). Without the variable, the model accuracy fell to under 70 percent. This result, while still good, illustrates the dramatic influence of this variable.

How did we find this problem? In this case, the model results looked suspiciously good, good enough to make us stare at all the input variables to verify their correctness. One way to prevent this from occurring is to keep track of the time frame used for every derived variable. Using a careful naming convention for the variables, where the time frame for the variables is included in the name, would have prevented this problem.

Latency: Taking Model Deployment into Account

It takes time to build models. It takes time to score models when they are being built. These statements are not just truisms; they must be taken into account when building models. In more technical jargon, we say that a model has latency, because it takes time to run.

Of course, what is important here is not just the time for running the model itself. This is usually insignificant on today's computers. Much more important is the time required for getting the data, transforming the data into inputs for the model, and deploying the output. In fact, although it may take only a fraction of a second to assign a model score to a given record, it can take weeks or longer to complete the entire operation, from collecting the data from the input systems to deploying the results.

An example will help to clarify why this is important. Let us say that we are in the business of selling something and we want to make a special offer for customers who are likely to want to make a purchase during August. Our goal, of course, is to make customers buy more than they would have without the offer, and we have a database that contains all customer purchases throughout the year, along with a bit of demographic and marketing data about each customer.

Now, it is June and we are preparing to build the model. We have the data for last September through May (in the real world, we would want data from at least one year ago as well). A typical approach would be to try to predict who made a purchase in May, using all the data from September through April, as in Figure 7.11. This sounds reasonable, but it is not.

Why not? Let us see what happens in July, when we want to create the mailing list. To predict who is going to make a purchase in August, we need the data from December through July—the inputs into the model that makes a prediction for August.

July data is not available now. It is still July, and all the data has not been collected yet. So, let's wait until the first of August. Is July data available yet? Not likely; at most companies, it might take one or two weeks to get such data through all the relevant systems. So, about in mid-August, we have the July data. Then it takes a day or two or three to process the data and apply the model. Finally, in the middle of the month, the mailing list is ready. And if we are lucky, it will get there before the end of the month. By then, we can hardly affect August sales. It is too late.

This is a bad thing. The problem goes all the way back to the beginning. When designing the model, we did not take latency into account. Instead of using September–April data to predict May, we should have used September–March

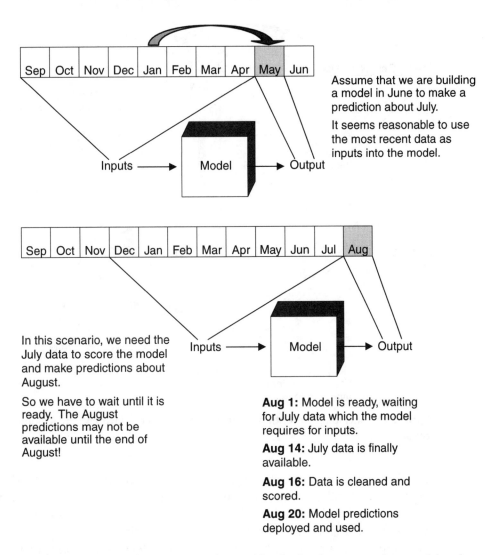

Assume that we are building a model in June to make a prediction about July.

It seems reasonable to use the most recent data as inputs into the model.

In this scenario, we need the July data to score the model and make predictions about August.

So we have to wait until it is ready. The August predictions may not be available until the end of August!

Aug 1: Model is ready, waiting for July data which the model requires for inputs.

Aug 14: July data is finally available.

Aug 16: Data is cleaned and scored.

Aug 20: Model predictions deployed and used.

Figure 7.11 Real world concerns, such as waiting for the data, can render a model useless.

data to predict May. April data is not used; it represents the latent or modeling month, used to score and deploy the results as shown Figure 7.12.

In this happier scenario, we have the results for the August mailing in mid-July instead of mid-August—and the mailing can go out on time. A much happier result.

Taking model latency into account has another nice benefit. Sometimes, what you are trying to predict is rather complex behavior. For instance, consider a wireless telephone customer who decides to switch carriers. There are several

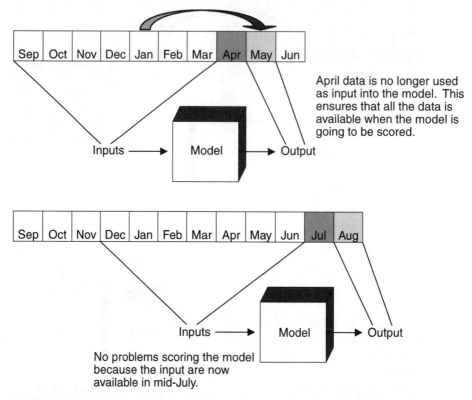

Figure 7.12 Including a month of latency takes model deployment and scoring into account.

steps in the process. First, she may decide that she's going to switch. Then she might research other offers, and, at some later point in time, she informs the company—most likely, not until after she has already signed up with a competitor. The company assigns a churn date sometime after that. Presumably, she stopped using her cell phone when she first decided to churn; that was the point in time when the decision was made. However, her actual churn date is later. Invariably, the last month of usage for churning customers shows a large rate of decline—however, it is not useful because the customers have already decided to leave.

To prevent churn, we want to reach them *before* they make the decision, not after. During the final month, churners will show a large decline in usage; this is the time period when they stopped using the phone but before the churn was formally recorded. If we look for customers with big usage declines during the previous month, then the churn prevention campaign may be wasted on customers who are already commmited to leaving. Including a month of latency helps avoid this problem.

Time and Missing Data

One of the most common problems when trying to build a predictive model is missing data. Although there are some sophisticated modeling techniques for handling data with missing values, the best solution is usually to modify the original systems to collect the data of interest. Alas, this is quite time consuming.

However, there is one class of missing data that can often be avoided entirely when building models— the problem of insufficient historical data for many of the inputs. It typically arises because the inputs to the models go back further in time for some records than for others. This is particularly true when the number of customers is growing rapidly, as in Figure 7.13. Because of rapid customer growth, many customers have little historical data.

For example, say we have 18 months of billing data for credit card customers and we want to build an attrition model. This credit card group has been growing rapidly, so half its current customers were not even around 18 months ago. In this situation, attempting to build the attrition model on the entire customer base means having to deal with lots and lots of missing data values in the billing history.

The approach to solving this problem is to redefine the problem. Instead of building an attrition model for all customers, build an attrition model for customers who have been around for at least 18 months. Voila! The missing data problem has disappeared.

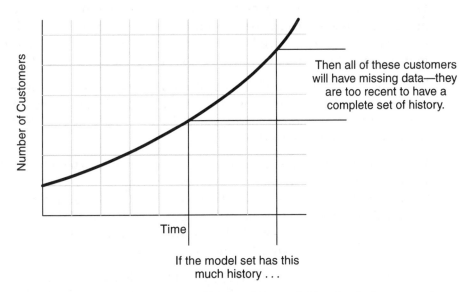

Figure 7.13 Rapid customer growth is usually a good thing, but it also means that many customers are lacking historical data.

What is the effect of limiting the model to customers who have been around for 18 months? Many of the effects are beneficial. In many industries, recent customers have very low attrition and churn rates—especially because introductory offers or contracts make it attractive to stay for some amount of time. Also, longer term customers often have higher estimated customer lifetime values—you have had more opportunity to cross-sell and up-sell them—so losing them may be disproportionately bad. The factors driving churn for newer customers are likely to be different from longer-term customers. Also, the model is working on a defined customer segment and there is no reason why another model can't be built on the more recent customers (just using less or no historical data).

The only downside is that the model set is now a bit smaller—perhaps even less than half the size. This is a reasonable compromise in most cases—eliminating many missing values just by solving a slightly different, but perhaps more relevant problem.

Building Models that Easily Shift in Time

One of the central issues in building models is ensuring that models built on historical data will still work to predict the future. The crux of the issue is that the models may overtrain on the past, having no predictive power for the future. Also, the performance of predictive models generally decreases over time, as the lag between the model set and the score set gets larger and larger.

When using a model on a regular basis, it is important to measure its performance over time to ensure that it retains predictive power. But, is there anything that we can do, when building the model, to help ensure that it shifts more easily in time, and that it will be useful to predict the future?

The answer is yes, there definitely is. Consider a problem where the available data consists of twelve months of historical data, for something like a customer attrition or customer charge-off model for a single month. What data do we incorporate into the model?

Figure 7.14 illustrates a first approach. This approach uses ten months of history to make a prediction one month in the future. One month of latency is taken into account, so only 11 months of the data are being used. However, this model is very likely to find patterns in older months that may no longer be valid when the model is deployed. In a sense, the model has overfit on history—and unfortunately, the history will be a bit different when the model is being deployed.

A better approach is to use less history for the model, but to have more months of data in the model set. Figure 7.15 illustrates this. Now the model is using only six months of history instead of 10; it is still predicting one month into the

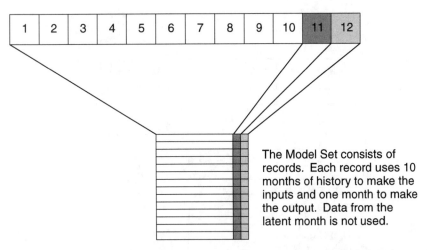

The Model Set consists of records. Each record uses 10 months of history to make the inputs and one month to make the output. Data from the latent month is not used.

Figure 7.14 Using all the history for each record has the drawback that the model may learn peculiarities from the past that do not apply to the future.

future. The model set actually has five different windows on the data. Some records are making predictions for month 8, others for months 9, 10, 11, and 12.

This has the effect that the model can more easily shift into the future, because it is not being tied to a particular time frame in the past. Overall, it should make the model more stable. It also has a secondary benefit: The number of records available for the model set has multiplied by 5, since there are five windows on the data. When there are relatively few records and a relatively large amount of history, using multiple windows can increase the size of the model set and improve the results of the data mining algorithms.

Of course, using less history can go to extremes as well. In general, more history is better. And for most applications, that means having something like 13 months of history, so the data contains behavior for an entire year. For this reason, it is nice to be able to work with 18 or 24 months of data, to allow multiple windows in the model set.

Notice that in this example the same month of data plays different roles in different records in the model set. This is okay. Some records are making predictions about month 8, so the data from month 8 is an output for these records. For the records making predictions about month 12, though, month 8 is on the input side. And for the records where output is for month 9, month 8 does not even appear—it is the latent month. There is no problem with having the same month of data play different roles in the model set.

PREDICTIVE MODELING TIP

To build more stable models that shift easily in time, use time windows in the model set. The model set will then contain rows from different time frames, and the resulting models should shift over time more easily.

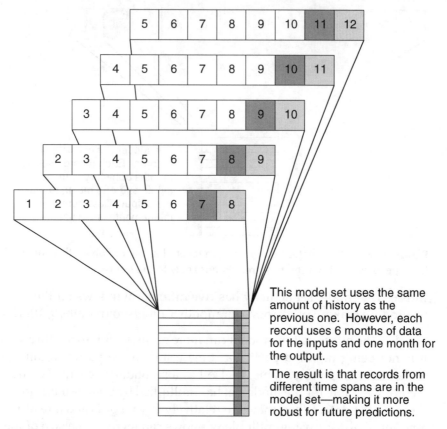

This model set uses the same amount of history as the previous one. However, each record uses 6 months of data for the inputs and one month for the output.

The result is that records from different time spans are in the model set—making it more robust for future predictions.

Figure 7.15 A better approach is to use the historical data to make a model set with overlapping time spans, allowing the data mining algorithms to learn about patterns that are not fixed at one point in time.

Naming Fields

The time element of data can be tricky to deal with. A simple mistake—including data that is too recent as input into the model—can have big consequences. And unfortunately, these consequences are usually not apparent until the model has been deployed.

One way to avoid these problems is by adopting a naming convention for variables. This convention helps ensure that inputs occur before outputs, that derived variables do not accidentally use the future, and that models shift more easily in time.

The convention is to append the time frame to each field that involves a time series. So instead of a field called "balance" or "amount_owed," the fields would look like "balance_01" or "amount_owed_11."

For example, assume that the units are in months, and the modeling month is given a value of 0. No variable should end in 0, since data from the modeling month is not valid input data. The data from the previous month would have 01 appended, from two months before, 02, and so on. Because we are counting backwards, it is much harder to inadvertently include future data.

For derived variables, it is necessary to include the earliest and latest time units in the name. So the names might be like "total_03_01" for the total balances for the three months just before modeling.

Notice another effect as well: the field names are not tied to a specific month, so it is more natural to include overlapping months of data in the model set. For instance, the model set might have three components of data:

```
Jan, Feb, Mar → May
Feb, Mar, Apr → Jun
Mar, Apr, May → Jul
```

The records for these three would all look the same. The field balance_01 would refer to March data in the first case, to April data in the second, and May data in the third.

Using Multiple Models

Predictive models are very useful. In fact, if one is useful, then perhaps several are even better. The more the merrier, right?

Well, as it turns out, this is often the case. There are many different ways to combine multiple models. The key is remembering the first picture in this chapter: predictive models take a set of inputs and produce one or more outputs. The output(s) can be fed into other models. The inputs can be a subset (or superset) of what is available.

In this section, we discuss some of the more common ways that models are combined. These techniques do not depend on the nature of the model—they work with neural networks, decision trees, and other types of regressions. Figure 7.16 illustrates methods discussed in this section.

Multiple Model Voting

Voting is one of the most common ways to combine multiple models. Each model makes its own prediction. All of these predictions are then compared. When all the models agree, the confidence is usually much higher. The resulting model, combining many smaller models, is sometimes called an *ensemble model*.

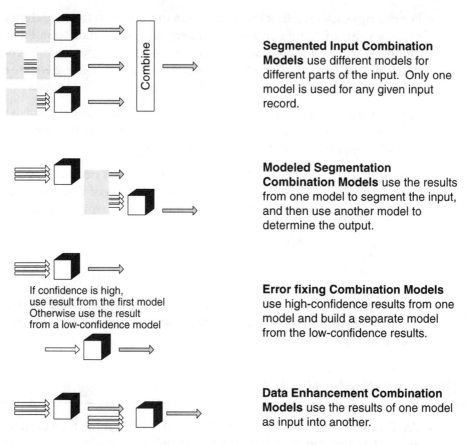

Segmented Input Combination Models use different models for different parts of the input. Only one model is used for any given input record.

Modeled Segmentation Combination Models use the results from one model to segment the input, and then use another model to determine the output.

If confidence is high, use result from the first model Otherwise use the result from a low-confidence model

Error fixing Combination Models use high-confidence results from one model and build a separate model from the low-confidence results.

Data Enhancement Combination Models use the results of one model as input into another.

Figure 7.16 Multiple models can be combined to produce more effective results.

Replacing an Existing Model: A Simple Matter of Voting

Often, the business comes to depend on certain models; in particular, models that are used over and over. These include using modeling for solving predicting information such as customers' propensities to churn, customers' propensities to not pay, and the best next offer to make to each individual customer. Models such as these are put into production and replacing them is a significant issue.

A good way to replace such models is using the champion challenger approach. The new model is considered a challenger to the existing model, the champion. Replacing the champion requires doing the following:

1. (alpha) Develop the new model and deploy it side-by-side with the old model. The results from the old model are used.

2. (beta) Start using the new model results, but keep the old ones around.

3. (release) Dispense with the old model, when you believe that the new one is performing better.

This is a good example of having two models vote. During the alpha stage, the two models vote, and when they disagree, the results from the old model are used. During the beta stage, the two models vote, and when they disagree, the results from the new model are used. Eventually, the newer model replaces the old model.

Of course, this is the simplest scenario. Perhaps there are several models contending to replace the new one. Then, during the alpha phase, all the models would vote, with the vote for the older model having a greater weight. This may weed out a few of the possible models. During the beta phase, these models would vote while still being able to compare them to newer models. Finally, the old model can be retired.

Often, replacing models does not need to be such a cumbersome process because the newer models are known to be better once they have been tested. This example, though, shows how multiple models vote and decide tie-breakers.

Multiple Outcomes—Best Next Offer Models

Multiple model voting is quite useful for determining the best offer to make to a customer. In Chapter 10, there is a case study about an online bank that wants to put up a banner ad offering one of a few dozen products—a mortgage, a certificate of deposit, a home equity line of credit, a brokerage account, and so on. Which banner should they put up for any given customer?

This is a good example of a problem where multiple model voting can provide the solution. What is a good approach for building a predictive model for this problem?

Well, one approach is to train a single model with multiple outputs. The single model would distinguish between all the different types of outputs in one swoop. This works okay when there are few choices—fewer than four, say. But it does not work well at all when there are dozens of possibilities.

Model voting provides a solution. The approach is to build a separate model indicating the propensity of a customer to purchase any given product. This requires building a separate model for each different product. All the product propensities are then voted on to choose the product for the best next offer. There are many ways to combine the results. The simplest is to choose the product with the highest propensity. It may also be desirable to include profitability information, business rules, and other information during voting. In fact, combining the propensities is sometimes called *conflict resolution*, highlighting the fact that different business units have different interests in the result.

This approach is likely to produce better results than a single model. Why? A separate model for each possible offer allows the model to specialize on that product. Another advantage is that it makes it easy to add new products or remove old ones. It is simply a matter of adding or removing one of the propensity models; the rest of the models and the voting algorithm do not have to change.

Trying Multiple Techniques

Multiple model voting can also be used to combine different types of models. This is one way to combine different techniques, such as combining decision trees and neural networks. It can also occur using just a single technique, but with different parameters. For instance, voting is how you can combine multiple neural networks having different topologies (different numbers of hidden nodes).

How do the models vote? The simplest way is to take a majority vote of the results of the model (for categorical predictions) or the average (for numeric predictions). The majority vote works well when there are an odd number of models (such as three) and two outcomes—which is happily a common situation. When there is an even number, some rule is needed to break ties.

A slightly more sophisticated way to combining the results from models is to consider the predictions as evidence with a confidence. Statistics gives us a way of combining the evidence, as shown in Figure 7.17, for three models with two outcomes.

When do you want to do this? Well, it works best when using a tool that supports different types of models. Even without support for voting inside a tool, it is not difficult to implement. Take the input and score it with each model—adding new fields for the "predicted value" and the "predicted confidence." This can be accomplished in most tools without too much difficulty. It is important to remember to exclude, as input, the predictions from earlier models. Then, the data set has all the predictions in different fields and a few mathematical formulas can turn them into a single value.

It just so happens that there is a flavor of decision tree that does all of this work for you. An *option tree* is just like a decision tree, except at the highest levels in the tree, it produces multiple trees that then vote on the outcome. Few products support option trees; one of the few is SGI MineSet.

One of the downsides to using model voting is that it takes longer to train and score the models. This is our experience with option trees. Although they almost always produce marginally better results (although this is not guaranteed), it takes longer to build them.

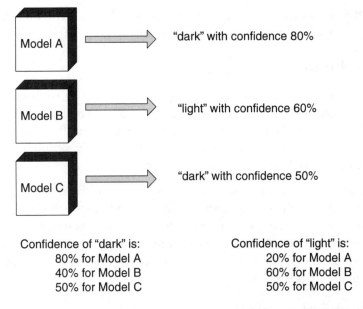

Confidence of "dark" is:
    80% for Model A
    40% for Model B
    50% for Model C

Confidence of "light" is:
    20% for Model A
    60% for Model B
    50% for Model C

To combine the confidence values, we look at them as evidence. That is, we combine the probabilities from the separate models, assuming that they are independent.
How much evidence do the models provide that the outcome is "dark"? How much evidence that the outcome is "light"?

The evidence for "dark" is 80% * 40% * 50% = 16%.
The evidence for "light" is 20% * 60% * 50% = 6%.

And the total amount of evidence is 16%+6% = 22%

The confidence of "dark" is the ratio of its evidence to all the evidence or 16%/22% = 72.7%. The corresponding confidence of "light" is 27.2%.

Figure 7.17 An example showing how to combine confidences from multiple models.

TIP

When different models are going to vote on a result, be sure that all the models were built with the same oversampling rate. If not, you will need to adjust the scores to get confidence levels that can be compared to each other.

One common mistake happens when the base models are created on model sets with different oversampling rates. As discussed in the section on oversampling, the scores generated by such models are not comparable. They need to be adjusted to remove the effect of oversampling. Notice that this is true even when the scores are converted into confidence levels. With an oversampling rate of 10, a score of 0.5 is really 0.091 on the original data.

Segmenting the Input

Another common way of combining models is to segment the inputs into the model. For any given class of input, exactly one model is being built, focused on that particular class. Notice that this is different from multiple model voting. In voting, all models are applied to all the inputs. In segmented input models, only one model is used for any given input.

One of the consequences of segmenting the input is that the resulting models are built on smaller model sets. Regardless of the modeling technique, smaller model sets increase the risk of overfitting the data—so it is worth rechecking all the parameters to verify that they make sense on smaller model sets. In particular, check the size of the hidden layer in a neural network and the minimum leaf size for a decision tree.

When Is Segmenting Useful?

There are two primary reasons for segmenting the input into models. The first is to handle missing data. Data may be available for some records but not for all of them:

- Outside data, such as demographics, is available only for the subset of the customer base that "matches"
- Historical data, such as billing information, is available only for customers who have been around for a sufficiently long time
- More detailed data, such as credit card or ATM transactions, are available only for customers who have those products
- Customers acquired through mergers and acquisitions may have different sets of data available
- And so on

Instead of working with the missing data in a single model, it is often more efficient and effective to build different models for different groups of customers.

The second reason is to incorporate business information into the modeling process. For instance, it may be known that platinum cardholders behave differently from gold cardholders. Instead of having a data mining technique figure this out, give it the hint by building separate models for platinum and gold cardholders.

Segmenting Using Clustering

One way to segment the data is by using an automatic clustering algorithm. The clustering algorithm is used to assign each record to a cluster, and then each cluster is treated as a different segment.

This can be effective when the data falls into different clusters that behave differently. In this case, a better model may be built for each cluster than for all the data—because training the model does not have to relearn the clustering.

This method, though, does not always produce better results, because the models are being built on smaller model sets. If such obvious clusters appear in the data, business users often know about them. In fact, information from business users often suggests more pertinent segmentation. Less obvious clusters may not have predictive power. When time is available, it is often worth experimenting with clustering to see if it produces superior results.

How to Do It

There are two ways to segment the input: either inside the tool or outside it. To a greater or lesser extent, all data mining tools support this functionality inside them. In some, such as SPSS Clementine, it is easy and a natural part of the user interface. It supports splitting the data and building different models on it. SAS Enterprise Miner supports the functionality, but it can take some work to find the "filter outliers" node and use it correctly. And then you have to use it multiple times to partition the data for each segment.

One of the advantages to using the tool to segment data comes when the model is being deployed. The more work done in the tool, the easier it is to use that tool's methods for deployment.

The alternative is to segment the data outside the tool by building separate input files for each segment. This may be desirable even when the tool supports segmentation, because it allows the model developer to experiment with each segment independently, or even for different people to build models for different segments at the same time. Remember, though, that if the models are going to be combined, then the scores must be adjusted to take oversampling into account.

Other Reasons to Combine Models

Multiple model voting and segmented input models are the most common reasons for combining models. However, there are other ways that are worth mentioning, because they may prove useful at some point.

Modeled Segmentation

Modeled segmentation is closely related to segmented input models. The big difference is that for segmented input models, the segmentation is known in advance. For modeled segmentation, another model determines the segmentation. Often, the purpose is to build results only for one of the segments.

Why is this useful? It turns out that some marketing problems fall directly into this method because the problem implicitly contains a segment. For instance, what if you are doing a mailing and you want to know how much each prospect will be worth. There are really two parts to the answer: who will respond (binary) and how much are they worth (continuous).

Another example was a marketing campaign for an automobile manufacturer. The goal of the campaign was get them in to test-drive a car. This really has two parts: who is going to respond and which car should they drive. Their solution used a neural network to determine who was likely to respond and then used a decision tree to figure out which car.

Fixing the Errors

This is really a variant on model voting, where multiple models are cascaded based on their confidence (technically, this method is known as "boosting"). A given model gives a prediction. If the model has a low level of confidence, then another model is used to determine the outcome. This can be repeated as many times as necessary.

The big difference from what we have seen so far is how the models are trained. In the previous examples, all the models have been built on either all the data or a specific segment of the data. This method of combining models is different.

The second model, the "error-fixing model," is trained using rejects from the first model, where the rejects are determined by low levels of confidence. That is, the model set for the first model is scored with confidence values. All the records with a confidence lower than some threshold are used to train the error-fixing model. The presumption is that a different modeling technique may be able to produce better results for this segment of the data.

This same idea may be used for screening purposes. Some predictions have a cost associated with them. For instance, the prediction of fraud on a particular credit card or a telephone card implies that the card will be rejected, so you want to be very sure about the prediction. An initial model may be used to find the most likely fraud cases, along with a large number of nonfraud cases. Then, a more detailed model run on the likely fraud cases may isolate the specific cases of fraud for further action. This is particularly useful when the first model runs in an operational environment, that screens out most cases of non-fraud.

The use of cascading models based on error results occurs in the nonautomated world as well. Medical exams are often structured this way. Less expensive, noninvasive tests are first run to find the likelihood of some disease, such as AIDS or cancer. If the test is positive, then more invasive and expensive tests follow—effectively and efficiently screening a large population for the disease at a lower cost.

Enhancing the Data

The last way of combining models that is discussed here is simply to use models to add new features to the input, sort of as an enhancement of derived variables. For instance, a cluster field can be added based on the results of clustering. This field does not have to be used for segmentation; it can be used at the whim of the modeling algorithm, if the algorithm finds it useful.

Actually, there are some common applications of using other models to enhance data. This is because outside service bureaus often add (at a price) propensity scores to the data. Probably the best known is the FICO score available for credit card processing. This score, or similar scores, sometimes find their way into in-house models that do a better job than the purchased scores.

Another case where enhancing the data can be useful is to replace missing values. In some cases, missing values can be predicted from the data that is available.

Experiment!

The good news is that there is no one right way to build a predictive model. The bad news is the same: there is no simple recipe for building the best model. So, the task of model building needs to be faced as a learning process. Even when building models for the nth time, there is still a lot to learn.

The best way to figure out what to do is to try out different things and see how they work on your data in your environment. Of course, this advice is not always practical because of the constraints facing any real-world problem. This section discusses some of the different things that you might want to test.

The Model Set

The model set is a good place to start. Once the data fields have been chosen, there are two interesting features of the model set: size and density (controlled by the oversampling rate). Generally, the more data you have the better, so you want to build models with tens or hundreds of thousands of records. At the same time, the ratio of the rarer outcome should comprise about 15–35 percent; otherwise, modeling techniques tend to overlook the outcome.

Table 7.1 shows an example of results for different model sets on different sizes and densities of data. It clearly shows the importance of density and model set size. The "Reported Lift" column is the lift reported by the model. The "Predicted Lift" adjusts the reported lift for oversampling. This is the lift predicted for the original data density, in this case 0.8 percent.

This adjustment is important; the best predicted lift has the lowest reported lift! And its lift, on a model set with 50k records and 30.5 percent density, has a lift over twice that of the worst performing model. This chart illustrates the fact that larger model sets are usually better. For a given density, say around 10 percent, the model built on 50k records is better than the one on 20k; and the one on 100k is better still. At the same time, density plays an important role, so the best model is actually the one with a density of 30 percent on 50k records. In this case, there were only about 15,000 records with the rarer category, so it was not possible to test a model set with a size of 100k and a density of 30 percent.

The model set is also split into three different sets for model building. Generally, using 60 percent for the training set, 30 percent for the test set, and 10 percent for the evaluation set works well, particularly when the model set is large. It is worth trying other values, although we tend to find that changing these ratios does not have much effect on the models being built (unless some of them become very small); it does seem best to have a training set larger than the other two, however.

Table 7.1 Model Set Size and Density Can Have a Big Impact on Reported Lift and on Predicted Lift

SIZE	DENSITY RATE	OVERSAMPLING LIFT	REPORTED LIFT	PREDICTED
20K	10.3%	12.9	3.60	5.47
20K	17.9%	22.4	3.26	7.38
50K	9.9%	12.4	3.71	5.61
50K	17.8%	22.3	3.08	6.45
50K	30.5%	38.1	2.61	11.68
100K	10.0%	12.5	4.52	7.75
100K	17.9%	22.4	3.60	9.34

Different Types of Models and Model Parameters

It is also valuable to try out different types of models and different model parameters. If available, see whether a neural network produces better or worse results than a decision tree. There is no right answer between the two.

Neural networks let you control the size of the hidden layer and some parameters related to the learning method, the momentum and learning rate. Some tools also let you control more arcane features, such as the type of activation function and the network topology. Although there are rules of thumb for setting these parameters, it is useful to see how different sets affect the results. It is particularly useful to try different sizes of the hidden layer.

Similarly, there are many choices within decision trees. Different tools give different types of control, of the splitting function, of the number of splits allowed at each node, option trees versus decision trees, the minimum leaf size, maximum depth, and so on.

Table 7.2 compares six different model types, all decision trees. All the decision trees use the same parameter settings except for two. The GINI models use the Gini function for measuring the diversity of splits (corresponding to the original CART algorithm); the ENT models use entropy (corresponding to C4.5). The other change was whether 2-, 3-, or 4-way splits were allowed in the tree. What is most interesting about this comparison is that there is no clear winner. Although these parameters definitely affect the results, no one of them uniformly produces the best results on all sets.

Time Frame

It is also worth investigating how the time frame affects the models. To make a model that shifts more easily through time, it is a good idea to have a model set that consists of multiple different periods of data. With respect to the time frame, though, there are still some options.

The first is the total amount of historical data to use. In general, this is a given part of the environment—so much data is available and you want to use all of it for modeling purposes. Sometimes, though, it might be better to take less history because too many records are lacking a complete history or because market conditions have changed dramatically over time. A shorter history also allows the model set to be more mixed in terms of time.

A second question is on the output side of the model. What is the time frame of the prediction? For specific intervention campaigns, the time frame might be one month or one quarter. However, it is worth considering how the data will be used. Does a flag that indicates propensity to churn indicate it for one

Table 7.2 Comparison of Predicted Lift for Six Different Types of Decision Tree Models

SIZE	DENSITY	OVERSAMPLING RATE	ENT2	ENT3	ENT4	GINI2	GINI3	GINI4
20K	10.3%	12.9	4.74	3.91	4.40	4.46	4.41	4.18
20K	17.9%	22.4	4.45	4.68	4.93	4.29	4.63	-
50K	9.9%	12.4	3.71	3.51	3.66	3.75	3.65	3.65
50K	17.8%	22.3	4.37	4.32	4.20	4.21	4.39	4.16
50K	30.5%	38.1	5.60	5.48	5.17	5.39	5.38	5.22
100K	10.0%	12.5	3.51	3.53	-	3.46	3.55	3.54
100K	17.9%	22.4	4.40	4.36	4.29	4.30	4.30	4.37

month? For three months? For the calendar year? Similarly, how long does a best next offer last? For a specific amount of time? Until the next purchase?

Models can sometimes be improved by increasing the time frame for the outcome. This is especially true for infrequent occurrences where there may only be relatively few records in a short time span. For instance, few customers charge off in any given month; but over the course of six months, there are several times as many—providing a richer model set.

Lessons Learned

The main theme of this chapter has been building stable models. Stability is important, because we want to have confidence that predictions made by the model will hold on unseen data. That is the point of making predictions, after all. Important points are the following:

■ The model set consists of three components, the training set, the test set, and the evaluation set. It is important to understand model performance on all these sets of data.

■ The density of the model set has a big influence on the model. Oversampling lets you control the density. At the same time, understanding the effect of oversampling on the results is important.

■ The model time chart allows us to see what time frames of data are used for inputs and for outputs. All inputs must occur before the outputs, and it is usually wise to leave a latent period as well.

■ Using multiple time windows in the model set helps ensure that models are more stable and can shift in time.

- Naming the fields by appending their time frame can help avoid time frame mistakes.

- Combining models is an important part of data mining and the basis for models such as cross-sell models. When combining models, it is important to understand the effects of oversampling.

Finally, there is no one solution that works for all problems. Experimenting with the model set, model parameters, and the time frame can lead to better and more stable models.

CHAPTER 8

Taking Control: Setting Up a Data Mining Environment

Like the paths to Buddhist enlightenment, there is no single path to introducing data mining into a company. In the end, we want to create an environment conducive to data mining, both technically and business-wise. Success is much less dependent on the choice of particular tools and algorithms than it is on creating the right environment.

Data mining is only as powerful as the organization that implements it, and every organization is different. This chapter tells four stories about four different data mining environments in four different companies. The first three focus on setting up a data mining environment for the first time. Although each company is new to data mining, each is starting from a different place. This is quite typical, since no two business environments are identical; they often differ in strategy, customer focus, data warehousing infrastructure, market positioning, analytic skills, and so on.

The last story goes into more depth and demonstrates how technology can catalyze data mining—when used well. This is the story of Eddie Bauer, Inc., a major multichannel retailer. Eddie Bauer is not new to data mining, especially on the catalog side of the business. With a keen understanding of how data mining fits into their business, they have built an environment, using Tessera's Rapid Modeling Environment, to facilitate data mining and to automate many of the supporting functions. (At the time of writing this chapter, Tessera has announced that iXL, a leader in internet services, has acquired them.)

Getting Started

Building a data mining environment can be a very subversive activity, the beginning of a quiet revolution that will shift corporate focus from products to customers, from guesswork and opinions to analysis and fact. It is important to realize that data mining—in the context of customer relationship management—is not business as usual, when implemented successfully.

This point was hammered in several years ago when one of the authors was advising a medium-sized regional bank on setting up their customer-centric data warehouse. Although regional, this bank was quite sophisticated: It was one of the first to offer online banking, for instance, and they owned their automatic teller machines—all the better to print targeted messages on the back of ATM receipts. Internally, the bank had already developed an extensive customer data model and was in the process of populating parts of it. The bank was looking at data mining and other applications for the data warehouse.

During the second week of the visit, the branches received a mandate from upper management. The mandate was to sell a few hundred million dollars more in certificates of deposit during the coming quarter. Excuse me? Where is the customer? Are they going to force-feed CDs on customers who don't really need or want them? Are they going to direct money from other long-term investment accounts to CDs? So long as the executives and board members are thinking in terms of products—and increasing CD sales is a classic example of product-based thinking—data mining and customer-focus is revolutionary. The boards of more customer-centric banks ask questions such as "what is the average number of products per customer?" and "what are the projected revenues by customer segment?"

As we show several examples of companies setting up data mining environments, it is worth keeping in mind that this is only the beginning of a much longer process. Some large, successful marketed-oriented companies have dozens or hundreds of people devoted to data mining and marketing analytics. They have set up business processes so their results are used throughout the business, from the scripts used on outbound telemarketing to developing new products; from forecasting where the business is going to driving customer relationship management. What may initially seem as merely a choice between data mining vendors may end up having radical implications.

What Is a Data Mining Environment?

The data mining environment is the part (or parts) of an organization whose core competency is data mining. It includes several pieces:

- A recognized group that develops data mining skills

- Communication pathways into one or more business units, so the work is focused on business needs

- A set of tools, hardware, and software, to effect data mining

- Access to data throughout the organization and the ability to publish results so they can be acted upon

The definition is intentionally very broad. It is meant to cover large groups, such as those that exist at American Express and Capital One, that are very integrated into the corporate strategy. It is also meant to cover much smaller groups in their formative stages.

Four Case Studies

This chapter has four case studies that illustrate different ways that companies can start to build a competency in data mining. Every organization is different:

- They have different business priorities.

- They have different sources of business intelligence data.

- They have different strategies and commitments to data mining.

- They have different skills, both managerial and technical.

In the first case study, we look at an insurance company that is trying to build an internal competency in data mining. The business of insurance companies is built on anlayzing risk using probability and statistics, but the analytic skills reside on the actuarial side as opposed to the marketing side of the organization. The second case study, also from the insurance industry, concerns a company that is building a new line of business on the Web. Prospecting for customers on the Web requires a heavy investment in customer relationship management technology. The third case study examines a bank that is building data mining skills as part of its data warehousing efforts. Together, these case studies are illustrative of the different ways that companies build core data mining skills. The fourth case study shows how a catalog company—that depends on data mining for its core business processes—addresses the technical requirements for a data mining environment.

What Makes a Data Mining Environment Successful?

Here are five factors that are common to the first three case studies.

1. *A single person leads the effort.* All the case studies have an individual who is responsible for data mining. This individual usually has a track record of suc-

cess within the organization (or in another similar organization), understands the possibilities of data mining, and works as an evangelist to build a team and secure executive interest.

2. *A multidisciplinary team runs the process.* The leader is working with a multi-disciplinary team, split between technical and business units. This team needs to cover the gamut, from business users to data owners, from statisticians to managers. Often it consists of 8–12 people.

3. *The business units are involved from the beginning.* The purpose of data mining is to deliver results to the business units. No one "goes away" and returns with results. Important business units are involved from the beginning and throughout the process. Often, the marketing organization owns the process. Even when the Information Technology (IT) department is building the data mining competency, though, one or more business units need to be involved to drive the effort from the business side.

4. *IT is involved from the beginning.* Data mining is a technology and it needs to coexist harmoniously with other technologies in the organization. This is especially true because the data to be mined may be coming from virtually any other system. You don't want to surprise IT, even when it might mean making compromises on the choice of platform and tools (but don't compromise too much, either).

5. *A pilot project demonstrates the power of data mining.* A pilot project is very important to success. This project needs to be selected by the team and is usually run in close cooperation with an outside vendor or consultant with more experience.

WARNING

Choosing a good pilot project is an important ingredient for building a successful data mining environment. However, the pilot must be chosen as part of an effort to build internal skills. Many pilots fail because there is not enough interaction with the business units. The pilot needs to be part of the bigger effort to build an internal competency in data mining.

Case 1: Building Up a Core Competency Internally

This case study looks at a property and casualty insurance company that is building up a data mining practice. In this case, we were working initially with the car insurance side of the business, although the data mining group is intended to support multiple lines. When we met them, they were in the process of selecting a vendor by comparing proposals from about twenty different vendors.

Data Mining in the Insurance Industry

The insurance industry is a natural for data mining. It is filled with lots of data and lots of statisticians and actuaries who already make sense of all the data to manage risk. In fact, more than any other industry, data analysis lies at the heart of insurance—how else do they measure risk and price products? For instance, they determine the rates for car insurance (where the government does not already do that for them), based on factors that have caused expensive accidents in the past. So, if younger, male drivers have higher insurance rates, it reflects the fact that the insurance company has had to pay more money in claims made by younger, male drivers.

Given this historical background, it is surprising that insurance is a rather late arrival to data mining. There are several good reasons for this. Insurance is traditionally sold through agents who maintain the customer relationships far from the actuaries. Another important reason is that insurance is a highly regulated industry. Often, the companies have very little leeway in setting rates and sometimes have to offer insurance to anyone who asks for it. This is particularly true in car insurance in the United States, which is often highly regulated.

The regulation takes place on the state level, so each state operates almost like a separate business. Legal restrictions—as part of regulation—can determine what data can, and cannot, be used for any purpose, including marketing.

However, many of these restrictions are becoming less and less important. There are efforts to harmonize insurance laws among different states (in the United States). And other efforts give insurance companies more flexibility in pricing their products. Also, though some products, such as car insurance, are very heavily regulated, others, such as renters insurance, are much less so. So, there is a broad scope for action in insurance. As new competitors appear (especially on the Web), the incumbents know they have to take action.

Getting Started

The insurance company we were working with recognized the need for data mining expertise. They followed a traditional process:

1. They identified a team that would be responsible for data mining.

2. The team sketched out the business needs that they expected to address. This included describing a pilot project to demonstrate the success of data mining.

3. They developed an RFI (Request for Information) and sent it to about two dozen vendors. These included both data mining tool vendors and insurance-industry vertical market application vendors.

4. They chose a vendor, based on written responses to the RFI and on meetings with four finalists.

5. They performed a pilot project with the vendor.

6. After the pilot, they will move on with installation, training, and other projects.

The following sections dive into this process in a bit more detail.

Choosing the Team

The first step was to identify the individuals in the organization responsible for data mining. Although only three people would initially be using the tool, the team responsible for getting data mining started was a bit larger. It included the managers of the users, the IT group responsible for providing the data and hardware, and several marketing professionals who provide the business expertise for initial projects.

This team was responsible for advocating data mining and customer relationship management throughout the company. The team's focus was on building a competency: identifying likely requirements for data mining, defining a pilot project, learning about the vendors, and choosing a vendor with a good fit. The group was also responsible for preparing a budget, assessing the impact of the pilot project, and selling data mining throughout the company.

The team recognized that there was no one in the organization who had the right background for leading the data mining effort. However, they were fortunate enough to have an individual with strong analytic and business skills who had been working as a consultant on special analysis projects. They hired this individual during this initial process.

Sketching the Business Needs

They recognized several areas where data mining could add value to the company, and determined that there was a need to develop a core competency by creating a data mining group to serve the needs of marketing. The group would be located with marketing groups in the company's headquarters, as opposed to residing with the technical people at a satellite location.

To further the process, they settled on an business problem that would become the data mining pilot project. This example was to analyze data for automobile insurance in one state (New Jersey) in order to build a predictive model to estimate loss ratios for policies. Loss ratio is the insurance industry term for the ratio of claims paid out to premiums collected. It is a key driver of profitability. In general, the ratio is about 70 percent; that is, 70 percent of revenue from premiums is paid out as claims (although the percentage can differ significantly from this).

One of the challenges faced when approaching the business problem is the level of action. What is the right unit for analysis?

- Driver?
- Car?
- Policy?
- Household?

This is challenging, because these change over time. For instance, cars and drivers are added onto policies fairly often. Households may have more than one insurance policy, covering separate cars driven by different individuals. The unit chosen, in this case, was policy, which implied rolling up information at the policy level—including the number of cars, the number of drivers, the frequency that cars are added and dropped from the policy, and so on.

New Jersey was chosen because it had been used for previous pilot projects, so data was known to be available. Although rates are set statewide, and all car insurance companies have to offer insurance to everyone, there are a few ways to leverage customer information. The company can target marketing efforts to particular customers who are profitable, or by avoiding particular groups of customers who are not profitable. Because rates are set statewide, profitability has little to do with risk. That is, the least risky individuals could be very profitable, if the statewide rate structure makes their rates a little on the high side; or they could be quite unprofitable, if the statewide rate structure makes their rates a little on the low side. In the parlance of the insurance industry, they are looking for areas where the statewide rate structure is inefficient, and they want to exploit the inefficiencies.

An example from another insurance company, Fireman's Insurance Group, illustrates how insurance companies can learn from their data. It is well known that men who own sports cars are generally a higher risk than other car owners, and they pay a premium on their insurance. However, it turns out that if an individual owns a sports car and has another car used for routine trips, then the sports car is no higher risk than any other car. By focusing on owners of multiple cars who happen to have a sports car, and offering them reduced rates (where allowed), the car insurance company can grow market share with a minimum of risk.

Developing an RFI (Request for Information)

With a sketch of the business needs, the next step is to identify and approach vendors with an RFI. An RFI is a document sent typically to tens of vendors that specifies what the company wants to do and then asks vendors how they would approach the problem. Their RFI asked for some specific details:

- What are the vendor's tools and capabilities?
- How does the vendor approach training?
- How does the vendor solve business problems?
- What is the 5-year cost-of-ownership?
- What is the financial viability of the vendor?
- Does the reader have good customer references, preferably in the insurance industry?
- Does the vendor support the particular hardware (in this case an Alpha processor running UNIX)?
- How would the vendor approach the pilot project and how much would it cost?

Finding the vendor with the lowest price is not the purpose of the RFI. In fact, the chosen vendor turned out to be the one with the highest five-year cost of ownership because they could demonstrate the most value across the spectrum. Many other issues, vaguely called "vendor fit," are more important than price. Also, the team knew that there were no standards yet on choosing data mining software within their company. The result from this effort would probably result in a company-wide commitment to the tool.

Choosing a Vendor

Choosing a vendor was a two-part process. The first part was narrowing down the list of vendors based on the written proposals. The list was narrowed to four: SAS Enterprise Miner, SPSS Clementine, Thinking Machines (now Oracle) Darwin, and Unica Model 1.

The second step was having vendors each give a two-hour presentation on their solution. The presentations started with a 45-minute vendor presentation, followed by a 30-minute demonstration of the tool. The remainder was devoted to discussing the vendor's approach to the pilot project. The nature of the pilot project had been worked out in more detail, and these details were provided to each vendor as a written document.

The vendor presentations were scheduled on two consecutive days, in the morning and afternoon. One week later, the team made its final decision by voting. Each member of the team ranked each vendor in several categories. The rankings were added up and the vendor with the highest average ranking won. The team chose SAS Enterprise Miner on the first round of voting. Had the vote been inconclusive, the team was ready to proceed with the pilot using more than one vendor.

Where They Are Now

At the time of writing this chapter, the company is working on the pilot project. As expected, there were delays due to obtaining the right data in the right format—a very typical problem at this stage in the effort. At the same time, several members of the team have attended SAS training, to learn more about data mining in general and Enterprise Miner in particular.

All indications are that the pilot project will be quite successful. When it is completed, the data mining group will formally open for business.

Case 2: Building a New Line of Business

This case study is about another insurance company, a life insurance company. The life insurance business is quite different from the property and casualty business because whole life insurance is really an investment, and term life insurance often complements investments. Life insurance companies expect their competition in the future to be other financial services companies, such as banks and mutual funds.

Going Online

This life insurance company recognized the need for a direct insurance business unit that would supplement the agent networks where most of their life insurance is sold. The personal relationships that agents build are a very powerful way of keeping customers—in some cases, the agents actually collect the insurance premiums by visiting their customers every month.

However, these personal relationships are expensive. Selling insurance over the telephone has also proven costly, because the sales agents must be licensed to insurance agents—making them considerably more expensive than most telemarketers. The Web, though, offers a new approach. People interested in insurance visit the Web. A licensed insurance agent only needs to become involved when the insurance is actually purchased. In fact, this company has an internal goal of selling 25 percent of its policies over the Web by the end of 2003. The Web, of course, is only one component of the direct insurance business unit. It also included outbound telemarketing, direct mail, and advertising.

The process of purchasing insurance requires more than a few Web clicks. Life insurance still requires investigations into the health of the covered person and into determining the factors that affect the premiums. So, click-click-click will get a potential customer an initial quote on the Web, but the insurance does not become active until the customer's health is verified and other paperwork gets filled out. The process of successfully making it out of underwriting and actually paying a premium is called conversion.

The Environment

This company set up a separate division to build the direct business. On the Web side, one of the primary sources of leads are Web sites that compare prices among different carriers for a given type of coverage (such as www.quick-quote.com and www.insweb.com). With a click, these sites bring the prospective consumer to the company's Web pages.

However, click-throughs are not the only source of leads. Traditional sources of leads, generated by advertising and direct mail, are also very important. One of the great ironies of these campaigns, though, is that the agents get first pick of people who really want insurance. This is necessary to keep the agents happy, since they are still responsible for the majority of the business.

The new direct-insurance division is primarily a marketing group. One of its functions is marketing analytics, and, within the group, they set up a marketing analytics group. After looking at several data mining tools, they settled on SGI Mineset as their tool of choice. One of the strengths of Mineset is its extensive visualization of data, in addition to advanced predictive algorithms. Working closely with marketing people makes visualization particularly important.

The Prospect Data Warehouse

The key to selling life insurance is determining which prospects are likely to purchase it. The purchase is a one-time event, but it often comes only after multiple contacts to the prospect.

As part of the investment for building the direct side of the business, the company was building a prospect data warehouse. This is more challenging than a customer data warehouse for two reasons. First, you don't actually know who is in it because they are not your customers. When new names appear, they must be matched to the prospects, identifying information such as addresses must be updated even though you are not sending them bills on a regular basis, and so on. Second, the sources of information are, almost by definition, outside the regular business processes. The primary data sources for prospect data warehouses are often outside vendors and data sources.

Although the prospect data warehouse was part of the IT group, there was a very warm relationship between the warehousing group and the marketing data mining group. The ability to work together is a key success factor.

The sidebar discusses a very important issue in creating the prospect warehouse, the choice of an outside vendor to augment the data with demographics.

The Next Step

At this point, the company is in the process of launching the new line of business. They have the organization in place to analyze data and act on the results. They have the data available through the prospect data warehouse, and good relationships with the warehousing group. They have a tool that they are comfortable using. They have set up a small data mining group in the marketing department to use the tool.

Choosing Demographic Data for Prospect Warehouse

Data about prospects is notoriously poor, because they are not yet customers. To make it more useful, the plan was to augment the data with additional demographic data, purchased from an outside vendor. The augmentation process requires:

1. Sending a list of prospects to the vendors (or, in some cases, purchasing a list that meets specified criteria from them).
2. Having the vendor augment the list with additional fields, generally several hundreds of them, and returning the list back to the company.
3. Transforming and loading the data into the prospect warehouse.

There are several data suppliers in this area. The company decided to test overlays from three of them: Acxiom, Experian (formerly Metromail), and First Data. Only one vendor is really necessary. How does the company choose which one?

The most important requirement is that the data be valid for data mining purposes. In fact, it is worth paying a premium for better data. The company wanted to test the data for data mining, in a way that would somehow measure the value of the data instead of the skill of the data miners.

A subset of prospects that had been targeted for a previous campaign was chosen for testing. All three vendors were asked to augment the data for these prospects. The idea behind the tests was to build "naïve" models on the augmented prospect data—during a period of time that lasted for three weeks.

The naïve modeling test that proved most useful was the evidence model in SGI Mineset. Figure 8.1 provides an example of the evidence model, showing the conversion rate for customers who apply for insurance. That is, of the people who apply, who makes it through underwriting, and who purchases a policy at the price set by underwriting?

The input variables are sorted on the left by their importance to the outcome. Then each value of the variable (or bin for real numbers) has a little two-part box that shows the ratio of converters in that bin. We see in this chart that the most important variable is ius_duration_day, the amount of time spent in underwriting. People who spend very little time in underwriting are those that are easily rejected.

Continues

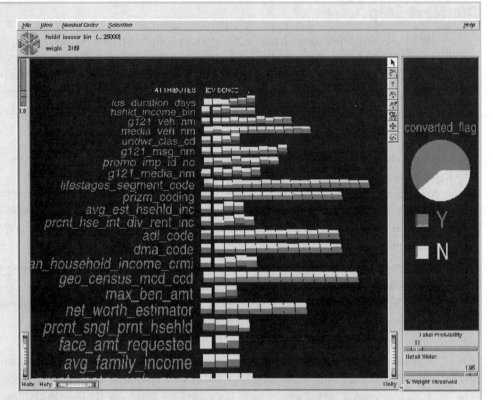

Figure 8.1 Evidence for conversion (making it through underwriting).

Choosing Demographic Data for Prospect Warehouse (*Continued*)

On the right, we see a pie chart that shows the ratio of converters. We can choose particular variables or values on the left side and interactively see the conversion ratio meeting the criteria.

The fourth data variable found by the evidence model is media_vehicle_nm. It turns out that the square at the very end corresponds to the Internet channel—and it has a very high conversion rate.

Evidence models handle sparse data very well, making it very appropriate for this test. And, the demographic data tends to be quite sparse, because, for instance, most households do not have any children in the 1–4 age bracket (and so on).

Figure 8.2 compares the evidence models for the three vendors. What is most striking is that all data performs about the same. This is all the more surprising since one of the vendors does offer a smattering of medical information, information that would likely affect life insurance. However, the health data is so sparsely populated that it does not affect the overall results.

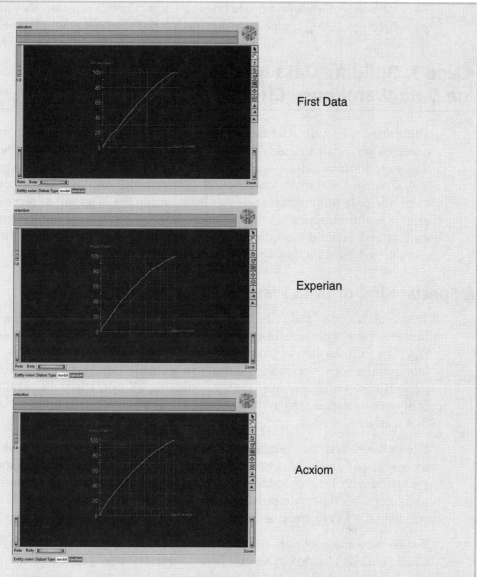

First Data

Experian

Acxiom

Figure 8.2   Comparison of lift of evidence models for three data vendors.

Part of this test also compared data from multiple vendors. The vendors were all able to augment about the same proportion of the data. And when fields could be compared, they almost always agreed. For instance, the estimated household income field did not vary significantly from one data vendor to another.

Having determined that the data all contained about the same information, the insurance company turned to other criteria for choosing the vendor. Because of previous experience and the ease of loading the data, they chose Acxiom.

The next step is to work on a marketing campaign. For this purpose, they are testing a direct marketing campaign, using models built by their new analysis group.

Case 3: Building Data Mining Skills on Data Warehouse Efforts

The third case study tells the story of a bank that is building data mining expertise on top of an ongoing data warehousing effort. In this case, the bank was very fortunate to be working with a vendor (then Tandem Computers, now Compaq) that really understands data mining. And, unlike the previous cases, the data mining expertise was built within the IT group to serve all the groups within the bank. However, once the bank built the computing in data mining and verified the quality of the data in the data warehouse, the bank reorganized the data mining efforts into different business units.

A Special Kind of Data Warehouse

This bank had decided to build their customer-centric data warehouse using hardware and software from Tandem Computers. The database, Nonstop-SQL, is a fully functional parallel relational database. At the same time, it also incorporates some very useful features for data mining. These features include performance enhancements, such as enabling all operations in parallel and compressing data stored in the database to reduce disk access times for queries that read a lot of data.

The database also has extensions that help some data mining operations run more efficiently. Several vendors, including SAS, Angoss, and SPSS Clementine, partnered with Tandem to take advantage of this functionality. By moving some of the complex data manipulations into the database, the tools can leverage the parallel server performance. In short, Nonstop-SQL is data–mining-ready.

To take advantage of data mining, Tandem set up the Advanced Data Mining Center (ADMC) located in Austin, Texas to work on pilot projects (www.tandem .com/prod_des/advdmcbr/advdmcbr.htm). (The ADMC is now part of Compaq's Database Engineering Center.) The ADMC is a good group to work with; because of their database backgrounds, they are intimately familiar with data.

The Plan for Data Mining

The bank identified a key resource in the IT group to head data mining efforts. This individual had a background in databases and was learning about statistics and data mining when he started the effort. His background in databases was very important, because access to the data is a key success factor for data mining, especially when the functionality is being built on top of a data warehouse.

As data was loaded into the data warehouse, more and more became available for data-mining purposes. The bank embarked on a data-mining pilot project:

1. *Identify business objectives.* They worked with the managers in the credit card group to identify business needs that could be addressed with data mining. The business was concerned with the behavior of customers over time; in particular, whether they would be transactors (who pay off their balances every month), revolvers (who pay the minimum balance and lots of interest), or convenience users (who pay off the balance over several months).

2. *Evaluate the Data.* The next step was evaluating the data for the project. In particular, to understand customer behavior in the manner described, they needed to have multiple months of billing data, with outstanding balances and amount paid just to define the behavior. Plus, there were other fields from the customer information file and historical billing records that could be used to predict future behavior.

3. *Prepare and transform the data.* The data in the data warehouse was in a very normalized format and it needed to be flattened for data mining purposes. This required appending the billing data to each customer record and adding derived fields.

4. *Explore and interpret the data.* Using two tools, Angoss KnowledgeStudio and Clementine (now owned by SPSS, Inc.), they analyzed the data to predict future customer behavior.

5. *Deliver results.* The final step was delivering the results back to the business to illustrate how data mining can be used for predicting behavior, and for other business problems as well.

Much of this work took place off-site at the ADMC, especially steps 2, 3, and 4. However, identifying the business problem required working with the credit card group inside the bank, since this group was chosen for the pilot. The work at the ADMC included demonstrations of SPSS Clementine and Angoss KnowledgeStudio running on the bank's data.

Data Mining in IT

The group responsible for the data mining pilot project was an ad hoc group. However, one individual had been identified as a key leader for data mining. He had both a background in databases and was familiar with analytics—a good combination for leading a new data mining group.

This group is responsible for building a core competency in data mining to take advantage of data in their data warehouse as well as other data sources. The group has taken a multiple tool approach, so they have since acquired SAS Enterprise Miner as well as other tools.

As they move forward, the data mining group is going to other groups in the bank offering data mining services. By centralizing the effort, they are learning about the available data and rapidly improving their modeling skills.

Case 4: Data Mining Using Tessera RME

With the advent of e-commerce and affinity card programs, retailers are starting to understand who their customers are and what they are purchasing. These changes are revolutionizing the industry, shifting the power from the manufacturers and distributors to the marketers. However, one corner of the industry has always been focused on customers—the catalogs. Chapter 9 describes a case study with a catalog vendor, which describes the business background, history, and data mining efforts in more detail. Here we are focusing on how to build an effective environment.

Eddie Bauer, Inc. is a major multichannel retailer. As a cataloger, they send out more than one hundred million catalogs each year. As a retailer, they have more than 500 stores. And their Web presence is an increasingly important part of the business. Eddie Bauer has also been a leader in integrating the different channels of their business. Instead of building artificial walls between the different divisions, they have concentrated on a single brand image delivered across multiple channels. In the area of database marketing, the catalog side has taken the lead. However, they have been very careful to recognize that good customers sometimes purchase from the catalog, sometimes purchase from stores, and increasingly purchase over the Web, even though different channels offer different products.

They have been a leader in managing data and in using it to run the business. Here, in this case study, we are going to take a look at their approach for building a data mining environment, using the Rapid Modeling Environment (RME) from Tessera Enterprise Systems (www.tesent.com). This case study is going to focus on the capabilities of the RME and how it enables effective data mining. (Although Eddie Bauer is happy to be mentioned as a user of RME, they are hesitant to disclose details about the business operations.) RME provides one example, and a good example, of a data mining environment. The experience at Eddie Bauer shows some technical functionality that is useful, regardless of the tools being used.

Requirements for an Advanced Data Mining Environment

As the data mining group matures, it needs to become a part of the overall business processes. This usually requires a higher level of support, from a technical perspective, than originally needed.

What type of support is needed?

- The ability to access data from many sources and bring it together as a single data mining table
- The ability to score already created models, on demand
- The ability to manage scores of hundreds of models developed over time
- The ability to manage dozens or hundreds of models developed over time
- The ability to publish the results of data mining (typically scores) back into the data warehouse and into other applications that need them

At the same time, the environment wants to enforce best practices for predictive modeling. For instance, where possible, it should verify that inputs are occurring before prediction variables. It should allow models to slide easily into new time frames, and it should integrate well with popular data mining tools.

An advanced data mining environment needs to tie data mining back into business processes. The bleeding edge companies developed technology in-house to manage models, deliver scores, flatten data, and so on. Now, there are an increasing number of vendors who are building solutions in this area.

Other vendors are working on similarly powerful systems. Ab Initio, which we will revisit in Chapter 12 (www.abinitio.com), has been working with AT&T on a powerful data mining environment that can take advantage of the volumes of data generated by one of the world's largest telephone companies. This environment features the ability to run SAS code in parallel, as well as other performance enhancements and aids to modeling. Torrent Systems (www.torrent.com) also has experience in this area, particularly with Knowledge Discovery One (www.kd1.com), a customer relationship management software and services company that has built their product line using Torrent's Orchestrate.

What Is RME?

RME focuses on the pre- and post-modeling activities that enable data miners to effectively deliver data mining results. The purpose of RME is to allow them to develop data mining applications quickly to business users. Along the way, RME provides a platform for solving technical issues that commonly occur when integrating data mining into business processes:

- Complex extraction of data from the customer warehouse
- Creation of samples from extracted data sets
- Registration of scoring code

- Scheduled application of the production models to the appropriate customer base

- Integration of scores back into the warehouse

With such technology in place, a company such as Eddie Bauer can improve its overall analytic capabilities by automating and facilitating many of the more cumbersome aspects of model development. RME is a good example of a data mining environment.

How RME Works

The RME System Architecture is built around SAS. Eddie Bauer has its data mining environment around their customer data warehouse, with the following subject areas (see Figure 8.3):

Household. Data about every household that has received a catalog or made a purchase.

Promotional History. Data about which households have received which catalogs or promotions. This also includes data about households who have requested catalogs.

Transaction. Detailed records of every purchase and return. This includes catalog sales, store sales, and web sales.

Product. Data about every product, including product hierarchies.

Store/Catalog. Data about every store and catalog, including size and so on.

In addition, RME maintains information about models and about household scores for the models. This is maintained in another subject area:

Model. Metadata information about models and the score tables corresponding to the models.

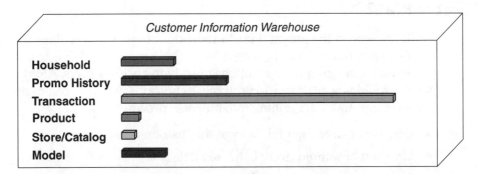

Figure 8.3 Subject areas for a typical customer data warehouse used by RME.

RME is a three-tiered distributed application, as shown in Figure 8.4. A three-tiered architecture provides flexibility for enhancing performance. The back end is the data warehouse, augmented as necessary to support the modeling metadata required by RME. The middle tier is the RME Server that executes processing functions and accesses the data warehouse. The front end is a graphical user interface running on users' desktops. The networks connecting these machines should be fast, because of the large volumes of data moving back and forth. For instance, database extracts are used for modeling, and scores must be loaded back into the warehouse.

The implementation at Eddie Bauer is particularly powerful. It allows users to be close to their data, while still being over one thousand miles away—the wonder of modern networks. The underlying hardware is a top-of-the-line (at the time of this writing) Sun Starfire System, running IBM's DB2 Universal Database. Although users are in Redmond, Washington, the machine is located in Illinois, where Eddie Bauer's parent company, Spiegel, has a major data processing facility. There are really three applications running on the machine: one for the data warehouse, which stores more than 600 Gbytes of data; another for the RME Server; and the third for an OLAP system using Sagent's decision support technology. That is, the RME Server and data warehouse are running on separate parts of the same physical parallel computer.

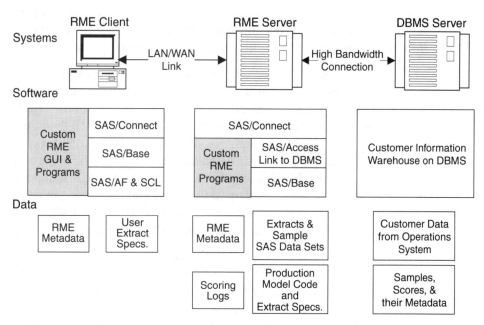

Figure 8.4 Systems architecture of RME.

The RME pays special attentions to metadata (information about data) to control GUI presentation, SQL and SAS code generation, and production scoring. This metadata is based on the physical schema of the data warehouse and on the business significance of the data. Populating this metadata is a principal activity in integrating the RME for an organization.

How RME Helps Prepare Data

The modeling process requires access to many different data sources. As explained in Chapter 6, customer-centric data warehouses store the *raw* data needed for data mining; this data is in many narrow and normalized tables. However for analysis, data miners need a composite customer profile, which is a wide, denormalized able. The creation of the customer profile involves retrieving and aggregating data from many different tables.

Extracting data from data warehouses requires several types of operations. *Aggregations* combine multiple records of data for a single household into individual fields. For instance, taking the sum of purchases over the past year is an example of aggregation. *Flattening* takes multiple records of data and appends them to a single household record. An example of flattening is taking the total purchases in each month during the past year, producing twelve columns. *Filtering* restricts the processing to including only the appropriate data for other transformations. Filtering works with aggregation and flattening, so it is possible to count the number of purchases that were in excess of $50 over the past year, or to count the number of shirts purchased during each of the past 12 months. RME handles the complex SQL querying and SAS code required to bring together data from multiple tables into a single, wide table.

The interface to RME Extraction is friendly. Users describe what the resulting data should look like using a graphical user interface. This is much, much friendlier than trying to express the complex data transformations as SQL code, and does not require expertise in a particular language. RME then translates the complex operations into a sequence of SQL queries and SAS procedures in order to produce the data in the desired format. Figure 8.5 shows an overview of this process. Selection, aggregation, and filtering, to the extent possible, take place in the data warehouse, where the relational database can exploit parallelism and other performance optimizations to extract the data in a customer-centric view. SAS code is then used to merge the different extracts together.

One of the powerful features of RME Extraction is the ability not only to do data extracts, but also the ability to store what is happening in an extract specification file. This file is part of RME's metadata environment. The same extraction process can then be used for scoring the model, eliminating the need for manual coding or for manually trying to repeat the extract. Also, the description can be used as the starting point for further modeling efforts. The speed of specification and

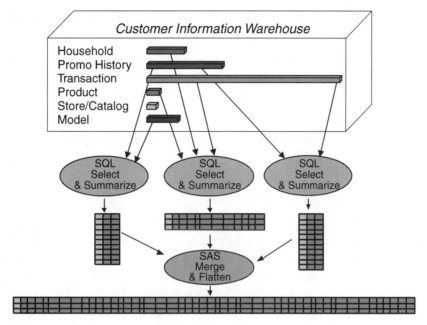

Figure 8.5 RME uses SQL and SAS to produce extracts.

generation encourages an iterative approach to data acquisition to ensure that the right data from the information warehouse goes into the modeling analysis.

How RME Supports Sampling

Sampling is an important part of data mining. Model development often takes place on a sample of the entire population. The smaller model set is useful, not necessarily because of limitations in tools, but because faster model building allows a greater amount of iterative experimentation. RME provides a rich support for sampling to support data mining efforts.

The two major forms of sampling are:

1. Random sampling, where households are taken from the general population to produce a representative, but smaller, model set.

2. Stratified sampling, where households are taken from the general population, and the resulting model set is defined to have a particular distribution for one of the variables. Stratified sampling is a more general form of oversampling.

Although the model is built on a sample of the population, it is able to score the entire population.

The RME Sampling Model facilitates sampling and works with RME Extraction. Sampling is a three-part process, as shown in Figure 8.6:

1. The user specifies how to create the sample using the graphical user interface. The customer ids and fields needed for the sample are included in the extract.

2. The sample is created from the extract, as a list of households that belong to the sample.

3. This list lives in the data warehouse, so the same sample can be used later.

4. RME Extract uses this list to generate the appropriate data for an extraction. This process automatically takes into account the nature of the sample and the specific needs of the extraction.

There are several advantages to this multipart sampling approach. First, the sample can be used for multiple extracts with a minimum of effort. The sample itself is a list of households, which is small, and it can be reused. Second, the extraction process knows about the sample so it can optimize its performance by working only on the appropriate data elements. Third, it is logically very easy to replace the sample by a new one.

How RME Helps in Model Development

At this point, RME has done the first half of its work. It has prepared the model set, which can then be used by SAS or imported into another tool. During the course of developing models, users will generally modify the data: They add new derived variables, remove unneeded fields, bin numeric values, or make other data transformations. Eventually, the data miner has produced a final

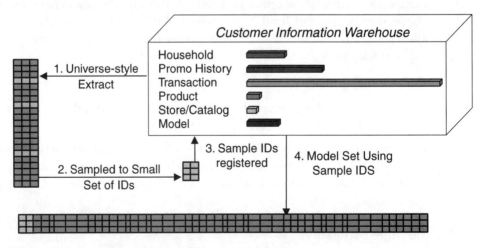

Figure 8.6 Sampling using a multistep approach.

model, which can also be described using SAS code. This is true even when the user is using SAS Enterprise Miner, SAS's graphical data mining tool.

RME basically stays out of the model development process itself, letting data mining tools focus on this area. Of course, during the course of creating a model, users may decide that they need more data or a different model set. In these circumstances, it is a simple matter to return to RME to iterate through the model development process.

The final step is bringing together the data transformations and model scoring code. Together, these represent the model, which can then be registered back into RME.

How RME Helps in Scoring and Managing Models

Once a model has been developed, RME kicks in again. Now, it must address the needs of registering models, scoring data sets, scheduling scoring operations, and so on.

Model Registration

RME registers models after they have been created. The model registration is smart:

- It understands the extract associated with the model, so it can ensure that exactly the right data is generated for scoring it.
- It recognizes when certain fields in the data are not used, and uses this information to optimize the extract.
- It allows the model to have date indicators instead of absolute dates, helping data miners work with time-dependent data.

This information is stored in the data warehouse as modeling metadata (along with other information such as who created the model, comments about it, and so on).

Customer Scoring

The scoring process then combines all of the steps that have been described so far. The process of scoring is depicted in Figure 8.7.

1. RME creates the appropriate extract for the model. Notice that the production extract does not have sampling, has been optimized to contain only the fields needed by the model, and date indicators are converted to actual date ranges.

2. The registered version of the scoring code is used to add scores to each household, in essence adding one or more new fields onto each household record.

3. The user can specify how to work with the scores. Often, the raw score is not as interesting as knowing into which decile the score falls, or which model produced the highest score.

4. The scores are loaded back into the data warehouse, where they can be used by other applications and fed to downstream marketing efforts.

The scoring process is fully automated. In production, it runs on the RME Server and data warehouse. RME can schedule production scoring to run at any time, to meet production schedules. For instance, if a catalog has a deadline where it needs the list of customers on Tuesday morning at 10:00 A.M. to meet printing deadlines, then production scoring is run on Monday at midnight (in case there is a problem, there is still time to run production scoring again). The production scoring process uses the latest version of the model registered for that mailing. Analysts can register new and improved versions of the model through Monday evening.

Over time, Eddie Bauer's database accumulates many scores for each household. After all, they mail out dozens of catalogs every year to their household base, and every household gets a score for each marketing effort—even if they were not chosen. This introduces yet another management issue. Over time Eddie Bauer archives old scores, keeping only a handful active in the ware-

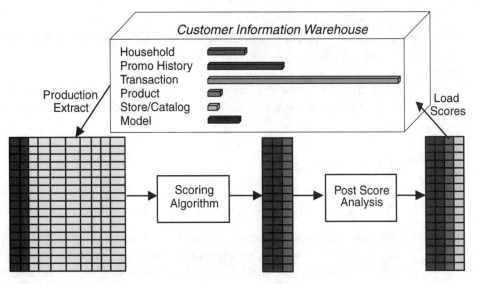

Figure 8.7 The scoring process.

house. For instance, Eddie Bauer calculates an estimate of "lifetime customer value" every month. Although the score exists for many months, only the most recent is available in the warehouse.

Lessons Learned

This chapter has used case studies to describe the data mining environments of four different organizations. When building a data mining environment, there are five critical factors for success:

1. Choose an effective leader who can work as an evangelist for data mining and secure high-level interest.

2. Build a multidisciplinary team that will work together, making joint decisions everyone can abide by.

3. Include business units from the beginning, since they are the ones that will ultimately determine the success of the data mining effort.

4. Include IT from the beginning, since they generally have access to most of the data and can procure hardware, networks, and software.

5. Demonstrate the power of data mining using a pilot project—a pilot project that is part of the effort to develop a competency in data mining.

As the data mining group grows, it will want to automate its processes. In particular, the preprocessing steps require loading data from many disparate sources, and identifying key features at the customer level. The post-processing steps require managing models, scores, and publishing results back into the data warehouse. A data mining environment can be the start of an internal revolution that shifts the company focus from products to customers. Building an effective environment is an important part of this shift.

Case Studies

The first two parts of this book are really preparation for the case studies. Part One explains the business imperative for data mining. Part Two focuses on the technical aspects of data mining. Here in Part Three, we see examples of real opportunities addressed by real companies. In the case studies, we see data mining applied to real world problems. Mastering data mining is best accomplished by learning from real world experiences.

Up to this point, we have many examples to illustrate the business and technical sides of data mining. How are the case studies different from these vignettes? The examples shown so far are intended to illustrate a single point: how to identify the business problem, or what decision trees are, or what is an example of data transformation? We hope that these vignettes have helped to convey important facets of data mining. However, they remain just that: pieces of the story.

The case studies take a more comprehensive approach. They start with background about the business and industry, and then move to the particular business problem. They explain what data is available, and what data is not available, and then show the data mining process. Where possible, the case studies give actual results. Each case study tries to show an entire cycle through the virtuous cycle of data mining.

The case studies have both positive and negative lessons. That is, we do not pretend that everything goes right in the course of doing data mining. Such an attitude would be disingenuous. Even worse, it might discourage others who are in the throes of data mining challenges. Imprecise business problems, lack of data, dirty and inaccessible data, bugs in data mining software—these are not unexpected events. As with any process, we learn from both successes and mistakes.

That said, the case studies clearly demonstrate the value of data mining. In every case, data mining is providing business value, and the speed-bumps on the road are merely inconveniences. The most important success factor is to let what's important in the business drive the data analysis—be open-minded and listen to the data.

Following the Customer Lifecycle

The most important application for data mining is customer relationship management. The first three case studies follow the customer lifecycle. They start, naturally, with the acquisition of new customers, then move to the building of cross-sell models for existing customers. The third is about customer retention. Although the case studies all illustrate the application of data mining to managing some specific point in the customer lifecycle, they differ in most other respects. They come from different industries, use different tools, show different approaches, and offer different lessons to be learned.

The acquisition case study is the story of Vermont Country Stores, a medium-sized catalog that sells practical but hard-to-find items that evoke a simpler era. VCS has been kind enough to let us show a snapshot of their customer acquisition process, which is fairly typical for the retail catalog industry. As the chapter points out, the catalog industry has some significant differences from other industries. In particular, the thousand or so largest catalogs in North America actually pool their data so they know about what customers are purchasing (although the data does not say from where, for instance, hiking gear was purchased). This allows catalogs to prospect using industry-wide information—something of a rarity.

Why would readers not involved with catalog retailing be interested in such a case study? There are several reasons. Some readers may just be curious why their mailboxes fill with catalogs. From a more business-perspective, customer acquisition is a very important process in many industries. Understanding how other industries approach it is a valuable exercise.

Perhaps the most important reason, though, is that the catalog industry is not like the rest of the brick-and-mortar retail world. Where most retailers work with anonymous transactions, catalogers know who their customers are—and their purchasing patterns over time. In this respect, the catalogers are more similar to e-commerce than to their geographic brethren. Their strengths in predicting who will buy what, when, and how often, are exactly the strengths that are emerging as critical on the Web. Catalogers have been among the first to exploit the Web, and to learn how to create a unified customer view, integrating the web-channel with their traditional catalogs and brick-and-mortar retail.

The second case study continues with the theme of e-commerce, now in the guise of Web banking. This chapter shows how to create additional value from existing customers, by cross-selling. Web banks offer dozens of products, and their goal is to figure out the best next-offer to make to each customer. One of the tenets of customer relationship management is that offering customers what they are looking for benefits both the customer and the company.

This case study demonstrates good experimental methodology in banking. The bank did a very good job determining what they wanted to measure and how they would do it. The results show the effectiveness of different models, as well as of their marketing message. They proved the value of both data mining and their approach.

There are several different approaches to building cross-sell models, and the one presented here builds the cross-sell model from individual propensity models for each product. Another approach, less favored by us, is to look at historical patterns of which products sold together, and then look for customers with some but not all of these products. This second, more market-basket approach, has a tendency to reinforce historical marketing efforts. It tends to build a box rather than enable thinking outside the box.

The third case study addresses one of the final steps in the customer lifecycle—customer retention. The market for mobile telecommunications is rapidly maturing in many markets. The maturation is actually happening more quickly outside North America than within. This case study looks at the leading cellular provider in a country where half the population already has mobile phones. At this point, retaining customers becomes as important to the bottom line as acquiring new ones. This shift from growth and customer acquisition to customer relationship management is a big change in the wireless industry.

This case study illustrates the importance of effective model building skills. Because the ultimate goal of the project was to build a churn management system, the client wanted to understand the model-building process as well as build an effective churn model. This provided the leeway to experiment with different types of models and model sets.

Together, these three case studies span three industries that have proven leadership in data mining: catalog retailing, banking, and telecommunications. They also span three important parts of the customer lifecycle. Together, they bring the lessons of Chapter 4 into the real world.

Gaining Insight into Business Practices

The customer lifecycle does not drive everything that is data mining. And there is more to data mining than building predictive models for customer-related events. Data mining is often about understanding the business and gaining actionable insights. The next three case studies focus on this aspect of data mining.

Before describing them, it is important to emphasize that predictive modeling and gaining insights are not mutually exclusive. There were some very interesting insights gained during the process of building predictive models in the first three case studies. As an example, the work described in Chapter 11 revealed an important segment of customers who "abused" the marketing rules to get discounts on new cellular handsets.

The first case study in this group takes on a big challenge. The challenge is big because the data is big. Telephone companies make records of every telephone call being made. These are called call detail records. There are literally billions of telephone calls made every day throughout the world, resulting in more than a terabyte (trillion bytes) of call detail records *every day*. All the large telephone companies are dealing with tens or hundreds of gigabytes per day. Their challenge is to figure out what to do with them—and whether it is worth the effort.

This case study is a voyage of discovery through call detail records—or actually several voyages from different companies, all of which wanted to remain anonymous. The voyage takes us away from the focus on predictive models, focusing instead on intelligent querying and visualization. It takes us from looking at anomalies in the data, to individual consumers, to business consumers.

The analysis of such large amounts of data is made possible only with the advent of parallel computing environments. Part of the case study describes a technology called dataflows that have proven to be very valuable for these types of projects. A word of advice to nontechnical readers: don't be put off by the description of dataflows. We have included them in the chapter because they are fairly easy to explain, they are a useful way to look at complicated data transformations, and most technical readers are probably not familiar with them. However, understanding dataflows is not critical for understanding the value of exploring detailed data that describes customer behavior.

The next case study also looks at an industry that collects a tremendous volume of data, the supermarket industry. However, in this case, they immediately summarize the data and throw away the individual transactions. Only then do they start to ask the hard questions.

The particular question being asked in this case was what differences are there in the purchasing patterns of Hispanic consumers versus non-Hispanics in Texas? This is the type of business problem that can result in big changes. The results can be used in many ways:

- Which products are distributed to predominantly Hispanic stores
- Which products are promoted, and where, and when
- The layout of stores and the placement of products on shelves
- Advertising in Spanish-language media

This case study looks at finding this information through very informed visualizations on presummarized data. The chapter also includes a smaller case study on using market basket analysis to discover interesting patterns in grocery data; in this case, for perishables.

The last of the case studies is the most surprising. It moves outside the realm of marketing entirely and shifts to the operational side of the business. Today, manufacturers are often massive generators of data. Many manufacturing processes have been automated, and those that have not are often still subject to central control. As a result, there are constantly many measurements being taken, whether the product is a computer chip, a roll of aluminum, or, in this case, a magazine.

Time, Inc. is a major publisher of magazines, spends hundreds of millions of dollars each year on paper alone. During the process of making the magazines, about 10–15 percent of the paper is wasted. Do the math. Millions and millions of dollars of paper are wasted. Since data is collected all through the printing process, it should be possible to identify the causes of waste.

And, indeed, it is possible. This chapter once again shows the power of flexible data analysis for tackling a complicated problem. Even though this problem has nothing to do with marketing, the result is still worth millions of dollars to Time, Inc. in lost savings.

Structure of the Case Studies

Each case study chapter is independent from the others. Although you can pick and choose among them, we do encourage you to read all of them and to learn from the combined experience. Even seemingly unrelated case studies can help improve your data mining efforts.

Even though the chapters are independent, we have tried to follow a common organization to help you follow them more easily. All start with an introduction that explains the case study and why it should be interesting.

Following the introduction is usually a section called "Business Problem." This explains the business problem that the case study is addressing. In some cases, the business problem is quite simple. In others, it is much more nebulous. Where useful, we have explained the process of arriving at the right problem, showing some of the pitfalls that arise when trying to do data analysis.

The next common section is about data. Data, more than anything else, determines the success or failure of a data mining effort. This section talks about the sources of data, important data transformations, and derived variables. The bulk of most of the chapters is then devoted to explaining the modeling and data mining process. Where possible, we have illustrated the chapters with actual results. Even where the results needed to be tweaked to protect the identity of the companies, they still are representative of the actual results.

All the chapters end with a section entitled "Lessons Learned." This section provides a bulleted point-by-point summary of the important ideas presented in the chapter. Earnest readers may be tempted to cheat by reading just the lessons. However, the stories, as told, are a much richer explanation of the data mining process.

Data Mining and Society

The first case study (about customer acquisition in the catalog industry) and the last case study (about saving paper in printing plants) have something very interesting in common: the companies have agreed to be identified. The reluctance of most companies to be identified is an interesting feature of data mining. This reluctance is often for competitive or regulatory reasons. However, much of it is based on the perceived role of data mining in society, and, especially, the privacy implications.

The final chapter in the book turns to the topic of data mining in the larger context. Throughout the book, we have highlighted the power of data mining and its applications. Data mining offers the promise of making economic transactions much more efficient, by reducing the cost of marketing and selling products and services. This benefits both the consumers (through lower prices, better service, and more relevant offers) and sellers (through higher margins and more customers).

As with many technologies, though, data mining must be used with care. Whenever we look at historical data, there is the danger of repeating mistakes from the past, instead of learning from them. This is true of illegal, discriminatory practices as well as of poor business decisions. In practice, incorporating a business focus into data mining mitigates this risk.

Another big issue is privacy. This is especially true as the Web grows in popularity and makes data readily available. It may be surprising to many people, but (in the United States at least) it has always been possible to find lists of who got married, how people died, who owns a particular license tag on a car, and so on. Possible, yes. Feasible, no. Looking up one item of information might require one or two trips to government offices. As such data becomes available on the Web, though, it is just a few clicks away. The easy accessibility of personal data used by the government highlights privacy issues.

The same is true of data collected through all the electronic interactions we have nowadays—from purchasing food in a supermarket, to making a hotel reservation, to enrolling our kids in school. Taken as a whole, there exists data—somewhere—about a surprising range of details about people's personal lives.

These privacy issues are mostly about the collection, storage, and matching of data. Data mining does exacerbate them, by offering powerful analysis techniques aligned to business needs. Chapter 15 has some examples of data analysis resulting in broken marriages and incorrect medical diagnoses. Interesting, though, is that such results are bad for the companies involved. What is the result? Often, better privacy policies and less data sharing among companies.

As you go through the next six case studies, keep in mind that data mining is a powerful technology. It affects not only our work lives, but it also affects us individually as members of society. The case studies provide good examples of using data mining in a responsible way, in a way that ultimately benefits everyone in the free market.

CHAPTER 9

Who Needs Bag Balm and Pants Stretchers?

Acquisition or response models are undoubtedly the most common application of data mining. For any business, no matter how large, the world population contains many more noncustomers than customers. It is the job of the marketing department to craft a message that will convince some of those noncustomers to become customers. What should that message be? That depends on whom you want to attract. Who do you want to attract? That depends on who is likely to be a happy, loyal, and profitable customer. Data mining, in combination with traditional market research, can shed light on both what the message should be and to whom it should be addressed.

Every industry faces this challenge in one way or another, but the nature of the customer interaction and the characteristics of the sales channels determine quantity and quality of the data available for mining and the types of communication that are practical. As an example, compare and contrast the banking and fast food industries. In banking, every transaction is linked to a particular customer about whom much is already known. Bank statements, ATM screens, and home banking Web sites all have the potential to be used for personalized messages chosen on the basis of information gathered throughout the history of the relationship. In fast food industries, on the other hand, most transactions are done anonymously with cash. There is no way to tell if a particular milkshake and large fries went to a regular customer or to a first-time visitor. Any communication is per force aimed at an entire market segment rather than an individual. The catalog industry, where this chapter's case study takes place, is somewhere between these extremes, but closer to banking than to fast food. No transaction is anonymous because the items ordered (and the catalogs themselves) must be sent to individual customers with known addresses. As in banking, customers can be tracked over time although the continuity is less assured. People are more likely to order from a catalog sent to a friend or a previous resident at their address than they are to use someone else's ATM card!

In this case study, we look at a company that has no doubt about its marketing message, but could use help finding the people most receptive to it. We start with the story of how Vermont Country Store (VCS) grew from a historic recreation and roadside tourist attraction in Vermont into the thriving catalog business it is today. We then introduce the business problem that is being addressed by data mining and describe the data that is typically available in this industry. The bulk of the case study describes how VCS applies predictive modeling to its business and how they were able to measure the return on their investment in data mining for response modeling in particular. After a look at future plans, the chapter ends, as usual, with a summary of lessons learned.

The Vermont Country Store

Many of the companies we write about in this book insisted on anonymity. The subject of this chapter was not among them, and no wonder! Any reasonably accurate description of this idiosyncratic, family-owned company with its quirky black and white catalog full of sturdy, useful items—jetsam left in the wake of the world's rush to electronic everything—would render it instantly recognizable, no matter what pseudonym was used. In any case, the Vermont Country Store was founded by a journalist and first rose to prominence through an article in the Saturday Evening Post in 1952; they have never been shy of publicity.

The company describes its mission as selling "merchandise that doesn't come back—to people who do." The merchandise itself is mostly composed of items that were once common but have slipped into disuse and become hard to find. As an example, the VCS catalog is Olivetti's largest remaining distributor of manual typewriters. The typewriters share the black-and-white newsprint pages with all manner of Americana from push mowers and hand-cranked ice-cream freezers to sensible shoes and cotton gingham by the yard. Not to mention a drugstore full of old-fashioned remedies and a pantry full of nearly-forgotten grocery products like Ovaltine and Postum. Clearly, what the Vermont Country Store is really selling is the image of a lifestyle. Not a flashy, modern lifestyle with its attendant headaches and stress, but a mythical, simpler life led by sensible, no-nonsense New Englanders in the hill towns of Vermont. Even the company Web site (http://vermontcountrystore.com—that's right, no www) invites us to click through to "an era when there was more time to savor the small pleasures of life." Of course, this particular vision does not resonate with everyone. The purpose of response modeling is to select a catalog mailing list that will include a high percentage of people for whom it does.

As with any catalog company, VCS wants to send theirs to people who appreciate and want to purchase the merchandise they have to offer. And, although their business is built on selling relics from the past, their approach is state-of-the-art.

How Vermont Country Store Got Where It Is Today

When Vrest Orton founded the Vermont Country Store in 1945, it was a return to his roots. In his 1983 book, *The Story of the Vermont Country Store*, he recounts how he spent his early childhood helping out in the country store run by his father and grandfather in the northern Vermont town of Calais. Vrest Orton became a journalist in the 1920s, writing for publications like the *Readers Digest* and *Saturday Evening Post*. In the 1930s, he and his wife lived in Weston, Vermont, where they became active in a variety of historical restoration projects. After spending the Second World War at the Pentagon, they returned to Weston with the idea of building a historical recreation of the country store his family had once owned. This was the project that became the Vermont Country Store. As he tells the story, he originally envisioned it as a side-line to his main career as a journalist, but it quickly became his principal business.

The store included a mail-order operation from the very beginning. In fact, the first 12-page catalog featuring 36 items went out to about 1,000 friends and acquaintances in 1945—ahead of the opening of the retail store in 1946. The retail store soon became a major local tourist attraction and a very successful business. In the 1970s, Vrest Orton's son, Lyman Orton became president of the company. As of this writing, Lyman Orton is still the sole owner of VCS and the chairman of its board of directors but the company is run by a President and CEO brought in from outside the family. Under Lyman, the catalog business really took off and by the 1980s, the catalog accounted for more than 80 percent of company revenues. The company has certainly not lost sight of Yankee thrift; the main catalog, the *Voice of the Mountains* (see Figure 9.1) costs under 40 cents per piece to produce and mail—a fraction of the industry average.

The 1980s were a boom time for the mail order industry as a whole and VCS in particular. Some years, the company's revenue increased by 50 percent. Without any modeling or, indeed, much targeting of any kind, response rates to catalog mailings were high by today's standards. By the 1990s, higher paper costs, higher printing costs, and a glut of new catalogs killed the boom. VCS continued to do well, but they did become aware of the need to target customers more effectively. In 1995, the company did an analysis of its strengths, weaknesses, opportunities, and threats and came up with a strategic plan. Central to this plan was a data warehouse that would store transaction detail

The Vermont Country Store
The Orton Family Business Since 1946
WESTON, VERMONT

Figure 9.1 The *Voice of the Mountains*, the main VCS catalog.

data by household from 1989 (the earliest year for which tapes were available). The primary impetus for the data warehouse was the inability to use historical data to answer marketing questions related to past activity. A secondary goal was support for analytic modeling.

Order processing is handled on an HP 3000 computer, which has 200 order takers entering transactions. These transactions accumulate on the operational system until the marketing department requests an update for the data warehouse. This tends to happen every six to eight weeks in preparation for a mailing. The data warehouse is implemented in Oracle on a UNIX system from Sun Microsystems. The end users are all in the marketing department. Marketing analysts use Cognos Impromptu or native SQL queries for decision support.

At this writing, in 1999, the mail-order catalog accounts for most of the $60 million in sales volume for the Vermont Country Store. Most of the company's 350 employees are employed in the mail-order business taking orders or working in the distribution center. Others work in the company bakery making the old-fashioned crackers sold in the food section of the catalog. And of course, there would be no case study without those all-important folks in the information technology and marketing departments at the corporate headquarters in Manchester Center, Vermont.

TIP

Don't assume that just because your company is not measured in billions of dollars and tens of millions of customers, it is too small to take advantage of data mining. A smaller company may be able to get by setting up a data mining environment on an existing computer alongside other applications. If there are only one or two analysts, they can share a software license and the investment in training will not be large. The potential savings or extra profit available through data mining will be smaller at a small company, but so will the expenses.

One thing that makes this case stand out from others in this book is the size of the company. Although $60 million is certainly nothing to sneeze at in a family-owned business, it is tiny in comparison with the large banks, insurance companies, and telephone companies that we are used to working with. The company maintains a culture that makes it feel even smaller than it is—there is, for example, the never-yet-broken promise of no layoffs, and the fact that the company has never felt the need for an 800 number for taking catalog orders (here VCS may be helped by the fact that Vermont's area code, 802, apparently looks like a free call to many customers from out-of-state). Even the vendor who sold VCS its data mining software was unsure whether it would be possible for such a relatively small company to justify the expense of the software licenses and training. They were amazed when VCS reported a return of over 1,000 percent on their investment in data mining!

Predictive Modeling at Vermont Country Store

Predictive modeling of the kind we discuss in this book has only recently been introduced at VCS. In this section we focus on how the company convinced itself that mastering data mining was worth the time, effort, and money expended. VCS went about this in a very methodical way, by applying data mining to a well-defined business problem with measurable results.

The Business Problem

Catalogs are never (well, rarely) simply mailed out at random. They are always mailed to a list and the list is always chosen in some deliberate way to achieve some particular goal, such as maximizing the number of orders or the number of items per order or the total revenue due to the mailing. Whatever method used to select the mailing list is a model in the broadest definition. The most frequently used model in this industry, and the one against which all others were compared at Vermont Country Store, is called RFM, which stands for Recency, Frequency, Monetary segmentation. RFM analysis is explained in the section "The Technical Approach," later in this chapter.

A model must have a target. In the catalog world, there are several possible goals including increased response rate, increased overall revenue, decreased mailing costs, increased overall profit, increased reactivation of dormant customers, higher order values, and lower returns. For this study, the goal was increased

Data Mining at Larger Catalogers

At the other end of the spectrum from Vermont Country Store is Fingerhut, a wholly owned subsidiary of Federated Department stores, that has long been acknowledged as a leader in database marketing and the application of data mining to the catalog business. In addition to its flagship Fingerhut catalog, Fingerhut owns Figi's, a specialty food and gift catalog company, and several other women's apparel and general merchandise catalogers. Recently, Fingerhut has leaped wholeheartedly into e-commerce with equity positions in a variety of online retailers such as PC Flowers and Gifts and Hand.com in addition to its own online business.

VCS is a relatively small company with revenues of $60 million from selling practical, if eccentric, merchandise to a fairly well-heeled customer base. Fingerhut, with 40 times as many employees, takes in approximately 33 times the revenue (around $2 billion a year) selling equally eccentric, but decidedly more down-market merchandise to consumers, many of whom may be more concerned with the size of the "four easy payments" than the actual price of the item purchased.

VCS has a list of around a million and a half people who get its regular catalog, whereas Fingerhut mails out 400 million catalogs yearly—more than a million a day. It is at companies like Fingerhut, where the sheer scale of the operation means that a tiny reduction in cost per mailing or a tiny increase in response translates into millions of dollars, that data mining collects its best publicity.

As a dedicated database marketing firm, Fingerhut maintains multiple terabytes of transaction history and a customer file with 1,400 (mostly null) entries for each of 30 million households. This customer database has been mined in many interesting ways.

One application is customer segmentation based on a combination of the customer file, the order histories, and demographic data. For example, Fingerhut discovered that its customers triple their purchasing in the 12 weeks after a change of address. This lead to the creation of a special movers' catalog featur-

revenue per catalog mailed. This is a function of both response rate and order size and so would be a good candidate for a multimodel approach that combines a response model with a revenue model in order to come up with an expected value for the catalog mailed. The approach at VCS, however was to go after high spending responders directly with a single model.

The Data

One of our first introductions to data mining (although it wasn't called that yet) was in the airline industry, back in the days when airlines were a heavily

---

ing home furnishings, kitchen appliances, telephones, and the like, but without jewelry or cosmetics.

Another application is "mailstream optimization," which means figuring out who should receive which catalogs and when, or, more importantly from the point of view of cost savings, which catalogs *not* to send to which customers. In initial tests, mailing expenses dropped 8 percent while revenue declined by only 1.5 percent. Fingerhut reports that it now saves $3 million a year by not mailing catalogs it otherwise would have.

A third example is the use of a neural network model to predict staffing needs in the call center based on catalog mailing schedules and historical response.

In addition to supporting its own catalog business, Fingerhut's Business Systems division provides direct marketing and information management services to other companies in the industry.

The focus on database marketing has been there since the beginning. Manny Fingerhut, who started the company that bears his name in 1948 and retired from it 30 years later when it was a quarter-billion dollar company, was a pioneer of modern direct marketing. The company started out selling plastic car-seat covers by mail. They gave buyers 30 days to pay while somehow convincing suppliers to wait 60 days for their money.

In a very early example of database marketing, the seat covers were marketed directly to a list of people registering new cars in the state of Minnesota, where Fingerhut is based. The product was even offered on an installment plan without any credit checks. The company figured that any buyer who could afford a new car was good for the price of seat covers as well—a rudimentary form of predictive modeling. We got this account from one of Manny's acquaintances from the good old days, so we aren't sure that it is entirely accurate, but we hope so because it makes a great story!

Today, about 70 percent of Fingerhut's sales come from the catalog, and the other 30 percent come from direct mail, outbound calls, and the Internet.

regulated industry in the United States. At that time, airlines filed detailed information on all their flights with the Civil Aeronautics Board. Information collected included the number of revenue passenger miles (RPM) and load factors for each flight. The government also recorded the full itinerary for every ticket coupon ending in 0 (a tenth of the trips taken). These databases were made available to the public through computer time sharing services. As long as the industry remained a placid, noncompetitive world where routes and fares could be changed only with government approval, these databases had limited appeal. But when competition dawned, the airline industry had something that most industries lack—full and trustworthy information on the performance of the industry as a whole. This could be used, for instance, to identify city pairs with many two- and three-coupon trips (trips requiring two changes of plane), but no nonstop service. The pooled data from all airlines allows any one airline to measure its performance against the industry and to spot opportunities in markets it is not serving.

Since leaving the airline industry, we have generally not had the luxury of being able to use data supplied by competitors. Your wireless phone company knows all about your cellular calling habits, but nothing about your land-line communications. In the case of the airlines, this pooling of data came about through government regulation, but ended up being very good for competition. In the catalog world, there is a similar source of pooled data, but it has nothing to do with government. An industry co-op called Abacus (now part of DoubleClick—see sidebar) collects detailed data from its 1100 member companies who comprise most of the mail-order businesses in the United States. The member companies submit data about their own customers and what they are ordering. Abacus combines the information submitted by the member companies in order to create an industry-wide view of the purchasing habits of anyone who orders things from catalogs.

Abacus does not reveal which customers are shopping from which catalogs. (There is a thriving market in that information in the form of mailing list rentals, but that is another story.) They do reveal how frequently customers place orders for how much money in what categories. So, a seller of camping equipment could submit a prospect list to Abacus and for each name matched find out how often that person has ordered in this category recently, but not whether the order was placed with Eastern Mountain Sports or L.L. Bean.

In addition to this external data, every cataloger has a "house file" containing information on its customers, both active and lapsed. The contents of the house file will vary from company to company, but at the very least it will contain mailing addresses along with a summary of each customer's activity at the level required for RFM analysis. It may include much more. The database used for modeling at Vermont Country Store includes

Abacus-Direct, DoubleClick, and the Convergence of Two Industries

As this chapter was being written, the merger of Abacus-Direct and DoubleClick was announced. This is yet another indicator of how fast the worlds of catalog marketing and e-commerce are converging. Before the merger, Abacus-Direct Corporation was the most important source of information on catalog shoppers in the United States. Abacus is a membership organization whose 1100 members are catalogers that account for nearly all the catalog shopping done in the U.S. These companies pool their data at Abacus in a database of over 2 billion transactions. This allows Abacus to build predictive models based on shoppers' behavior across the industry, not just with a single company. The results of these models are made available to the members in the form of scores without revealing competitive details about what individual consumers are buying from whom.

DoubleClick, meanwhile, is a Web advertising firm that offers a number of services to advertisers that would be impossible in "old media." For instance, for around $5000 a month Data Miners could ensure that any search on the Alta Vista search engine that used the phrase "data mining" would cause a banner ad for our company to appear along with the search results. The ad would be "clickable" so that people interested in data mining could be brought right to http://www.data-miners.com. Every time someone clicked, the event would be recorded in a database at DoubleClick where we, the advertiser, could watch the click-through count rise in real time. More importantly, we could vary the creative content of the ad and watch what happens to response, or we could put out multiple versions of the banner and watch to see which gets the most click-throughs.

DoubleClick can also customize an ad based on the geographic location of the person arriving at the page (well, more accurately, the geographic location of the ISP of the person arriving at the page). For example, the Alta Vista search engine's main site is hosted in the United States, but for a recent three-month period, anyone visiting that site from Israel saw a banner ad in Hebrew advertising the Golden Pages, an Israeli telephone directory. Of 40,000 Israelis who saw the banner, an impressive 22 percent clicked through. This high response rate was undoubtedly due to the novelty for Israelis of being addressed in their own language on the Web. SK Telecom, a Korean wireless telephone company, did the same thing with ads in Korean and also saw very high click-through rates.

- Household ID
- Number of quarters with at least one order placed
- Flags indicating payment by personal check, credit card, or both
- Number of catalogs purchased from

- Number of days since last order
- Number of purchases from the various different catalog types (*Apothecary, Green Mountain Mercantile, Goods and Wares, Home, Voice of the Mountains*)
- Dollars spent per quarter going back several years

Internal data of this kind is augmented with outside information about a household's industry-wide purchasing by product category and by demographic data.

The Technical Approach

Vermont Country Store wanted a controlled, scientific comparison of advanced data mining techniques such as neural networks and decision trees, which would require an investment in new software and training, with the current practice of using RFM models and various kinds of demographic segmentation.

VCS decided to test the new methods by applying data from past mailings and calculating how well they would have done had they used a mailing list produced by the new models instead of the one they did, in fact, use. This approach is attractive because it makes use of historical data that is readily available in the house file and does not require any actual test mailings. The difficulty is that the new models will suggest sending catalogs to people who did not actually get them and not sending catalogs to people who did. The latter case is easily handled—any expenses incurred by sending catalogs to people who would not have gotten them if the new model had been used can be subtracted from the total expense of the mailing, and any revenues due to those customers can be subtracted from total revenues. But what about the people that the new model would have added to the mailing list? For these people, we need to be able to estimate the probability that they would have responded and the revenues that would have resulted. This is a data mining problem in itself.

Choice of Software Package

VCS was new to data mining and so made a survey of software packages that might help them incorporate this new technology into their marketing process. After looking into several software packages, VCS settled on Enterprise Miner from SAS Institute. Although they found some other packages easier to use, such as Unica's Model 1, they liked the greater degree of control they felt was afforded by Enterprise Miner. The fact that user-written SAS code could be called from Enterprise Miner also appealed to the analysts at VCS. In short, it felt like a package that could not be outgrown.

The Baseline—RFM and Segmentation

Recency, frequency, and monetary analysis, or RFM, is a term used to describe a family of models where the input variables are constrained to three old favorites:

- How long has it been since the customer's most recent purchase?

- How often has the customer made a purchase in some predefined length of time?

- How much money has the customer spent over the measured time period?

The direct marketing industry knows from long experience that each of these variables is a powerful response predictor in its own right. A mailing list sorted by recency will have much greater response in the top decile than in the bottom decile. The same goes for lists sorted by frequency or amount spent. The idea of RFM analysis is to get all three variables working together.

Creating RFM Cells

To create an RFM score, the mailing list is sorted three times—once by each of the three input variables: recency, frequency, and monetary value. Each time the list is sorted, it is divided into equal slices. In Figure 9.2, the list has been divided into quintiles—a common choice. The people in the top quintile are given a 5, the people in the next lower quintile a 4, and so on. In this manner, each customer is given three scores, ranging from 1 to 5. Taken together, these scores are the coordinates of a particular cell in an RFM cube. Customers who fall into the same cell of the RFM cube are said to be in the same "bucket" and will receive the same treatment. Customers who have very recently made a purchase, buy frequently, and spend lots of money are in RFM bucket 555. A customer who has made a recent purchase, buys frequently, but doesn't spend much money might be in bucket 542.

Note that although the RFM codes look like numbers and have some degree of ordering in that we can say that a customer in bucket 555 is "better" than one in bucket 111, these codes are not *scores* in the sense that we use the word in this book. We cannot use the RFM codes to sort a mailing list because that would give too much weight to the R column and not enough to the M. There is no reason to expect that customers in bucket 511 are better than customers in bucket 115. (Quite the opposite, in fact—a customer who has spent a lot of money but not recently and not often may be just the one to target.) RFM codes should be treated as categorical, much like ZIP codes or telephone area codes.

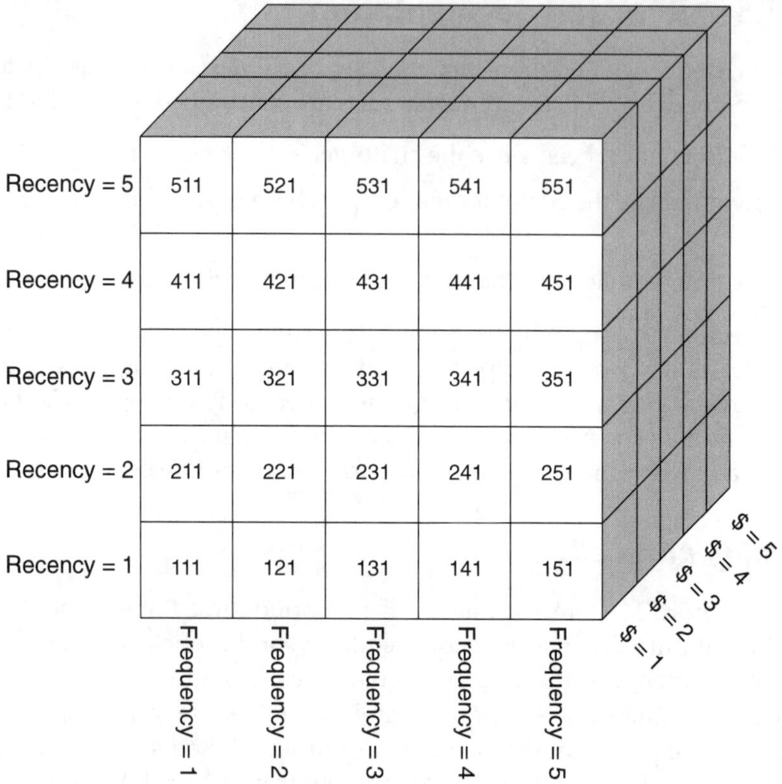

	Frequency = 1	Frequency = 2	Frequency = 3	Frequency = 4	Frequency = 5
Recency = 5	511	521	531	541	551
Recency = 4	411	421	431	441	451
Recency = 3	311	321	331	341	351
Recency = 2	211	221	231	241	251
Recency = 1	111	121	131	141	151

Figure 9.2   RFM cells.

Using RFM Cells

Once every customer has been assigned to an RFM bucket, these buckets can be used to predict response to a mailing. The procedure is to do a test mailing to a random sample of the database in which all the RFM buckets are equally represented. Some cells will respond better than others. The RFM buckets can now be sorted by their response rate to the test mailing. For a mailing list with 1 million names, there will be an average of 8000 people in each of the 125 (5 cubed) buckets. If a mailing of 100,000 pieces is planned, we would mail to the top 12 buckets and fill out the remaining 4000 with half of the 13th.

Alternatively, the response rates from the test mailing can be used to calculate the profitability of mailing to each bucket. The break-even response rate is the cost per piece divided by the net profit from each sale. So, if it costs a $1.00 to contact a customer and the average profit per order is $40, this ratio is 0.025, suggesting that it will be profitable to mail to any RFM bucket that achieved a response rate of greater than 2.5 percent in the test mailing.

Of course, response rate is not the only thing that varies by RFM cell, so all kinds of analysis can be done, for example, by using recency, frequency, and monetary as dimensions of an OLAP cube.

Segmentation

Segmentation simply means making different offers to different market segments—groups of people defined by some combination of demographic variables such as age, gender, and income, or by certain lifestyle indicators. VCS has done fairly well with segmentation. For example, they recently created a catalog aimed specifically at people aged 53 to 71. They designed a catalog that, in a departure for VCS, included color pictures of the actual merchandise. Interspersed with the color images were black and white images from the 1950s and 1960s, when members of the target audience were in their teens or young adulthood. The catalog was tested by mailing it to members of the target audience and to a control group of people from the same RFM buckets but outside the targeted age group. There was a substantially higher response from the target segment—one which would not have been predicted by RFM analysis.

Segmentation of this kind generally relies on common sense, but it too can be improved through data mining. The various branches of a decision tree represent naturally occurring segments. So do the clusters found with automatic cluster detection algorithms. Sometimes these techniques reveal market segments that no one has thought of before.

The Challengers—Neural Networks, Decision Trees, and Regression

The track record of RFM models at Vermont Country Store was mixed. Although they have had some success with them in the past, the marketing department felt that they were now less effective than they had been. They also felt that as the owners of a customer database capable of providing much more information, it was silly to base their models on only three variables. They also felt that the hundreds of buckets produced by RFM analysis were a bit unwieldy and wanted to investigate data mining techniques that produce a single numeric score.

SAS Enterprise Miner provides three modeling techniques that fit the bill: neural networks, decision trees, and ordinary regression. Models were built using all three techniques and compared to the results of several earlier mailings made of the basis of RFM. The models were applied to several historical mailings. One interesting wrinkle is that there are actually two versions of some of the catalogs—a 96-page book and a 120-page book. Many of the models built lists that would have increased the profitability of the 120-page book at the expense of the 96-page book by moving valuable customers from one to the other.

The Neural Net Model

The neural network was applied to two different mailings of the general merchandise catalog. Key input variables were recency, first quarter orders, beauty, and number of *Voice of the Mountains* catalogs received. This model achieved a predicted increase in sales of 2.86 percent over the baseline.

In this case, the neural network model did not do as well as the other two. Since this technique was new to VCS, this may reflect the fact that neural network models are less tolerant of naive users than decision tree models and can benefit from more extensive data preparation as well as a greater degree of experimentation with model parameters.

The Regression Model

We have not discussed regression much in this book, because it is generally considered to be "statistics" rather than "data mining." This distinction is a bit arbitrary since data mining is first and foremost about creating predictive models and that is exactly what regression is for. Presumably, the reason that many data mining tools do not include a regression module is that it is hard to market regression as a leading edge technology. For the same reason, we have not given much attention to regression in this book, but if you are interested, the sidebar contains an introduction to the concept.

The regression model built for this study was applied to a catalog that VCS calls the "Holiday Catalog" that comes out in October, and to the Christmas catalog that comes out shortly thereafter. Inputs to the regression model were RFM code, number of categories purchased, average items per order, fourth quarter purchases, and food purchases. Using this model achieved a predicted increase in sales of 3.89 percent over the baseline for the Holiday mailing and 4.99 percent for the Christmas mailing.

The Decision Tree Model

The decision tree model did the best of all, apparently because it was able to make good use of a wider range of variables to find many small pockets of profitable customers. Variables that proved useful included beauty, number of categories, months since last order, food, bath, women's footwear, hosiery, and outdoor. This model achieved a predicted increase in sales of a spectacular 12.83 percent.

Regression

Regression, in one form or another, is the most common form of predictive modeling. The most common form of regression is linear regression. A regression equation combines all of the input variables (called *independent variables* in statistics) in a formula to predict the target variable (called the *dependent variable* in statistics). A linear regression is one where the equation takes the form of a straight line through a space of as many dimensions as there are variables.

In a regression model, as in several other techniques we have discussed, the training data is viewed geometrically. The value of each field of the training record (including the target field) is used to define the position of a point in space. The regression equation describes the "line of best fit" through these points; that is to say, the line that minimizes the average distance of the points from the line. This line turns into a predictive model when the value of the dependent variable is unknown. Its value is predicted by the point on the line corresponding to the values of the independent variables for that record.

In Figure 9.3, the line $z = 3x - 17$ is the best fit through the cloud of dots that surrounds it. We can use the formula to predict a value for an unknown z given a known value of x.

Regression is a standard workhorse of predictive modeling, but it is not without problems. It works only with numeric data and can be very sensitive to the data distribution.

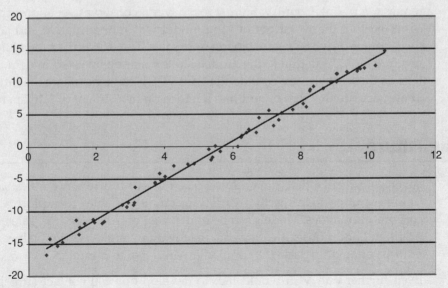

Figure 9.3 A linear regression.

The decision tree model got the best results, but it was not without problems. Chief among them was the fact that many records ended up in the same leaf node and therefore received identical scores. This is not desirable, because the whole point of having scores is to be able to sort a list. If many records have the same score, there is no meaningful way to sort them. One way of addressing this problem would be to build a separate model just on the records that arrived at the oversized node.

Determining What Would Have Happened

The previous section reported "predicted increases in sales" ranging from 2.86 percent for the neural network model to 12.83 percent for the decision tree model. How were these calculated? What happens when the new model would send a catalog to someone who was not picked by the RFM model? The answer is simple. The comparisons among models are based on equal circulation. The actual historical mailing went to 1.4 million people drawn from the house file. Each of the challenger models is used to score the house file and the top 1.4 million people are selected. Wherever the new model picks a customer who was also picked by the RFM model, his or her actual spending is recorded. When the model picks a customer who was not picked by the RFM model, we assume that he or she would have spent the average amount spent by customers with the same score who *were* picked by the RFM model.

Calculating the Return on Investment

To calculate the return on investment from using the new data mining techniques, Vermont Country Store took a very conservative approach. They assumed that the worst-performing model was representative and so based their figures on a 2.86 percent increase in sales. The ROI is the ratio of the extra revenue brought in due to the models, to the money invested in data mining. Both of those figures are confidential, but VCS is happy to share the ratio itself: They calculate that this project had a return on investment of 1,182 percent.

The Future

Given returns like that, data mining has a bright future at VCS. Plans for the future include models with a variety of target variables to explore alternate corporate strategies. Models can be built based on response rate, sales dollars, profit dollars, house file growth, reactivation, higher order values, lower returns, or anything else the company would like to improve.

Even further out, VCS would like to develop optimal contact strategies for each customer, offering each one only those catalogs to which they are likely to respond at a profitable level.

Expected Benefits

Vermont Country Store expects to see benefits from the new approach that go beyond better response rates, including:

Fewer keys to keep track of. The data mining techniques yield a single score no matter how many variables go into the model. That frees VCS to use input variables that were previously left out in order to prevent an explosion of customer "buckets."

Fresh Segmentation. The same people tend to end up in the best RFM buckets time after time, and there is a danger of "exhausting" these people by targeting them too often.

Reactivation. The new models are already finding large numbers of responders among segments overlooked by the RFM models. The recency and frequency components may be to blame. Consider the case of seasonal buyers who buy only at Christmas, or only when it is time to open up the summer place at the lake. They buy infrequently and so at any given time their most recent purchase may not be very recent, and yet, if reached at the right time, they may respond very profitably.

Lessons Learned

The most important lesson of this chapter is that it is not only huge, multinational corporations that benefit from data mining. Vermont Country Store is a medium-sized, family-owned company with a talented, but small marketing team. Despite their size, they are a showcase of best practices in database marketing and are successfully applying advanced data mining techniques while some much larger companies dither on the sidelines.

CHAPTER 10

Who Gets What? Building a Best Next Offer Model for an Online Bank

This chapter describes the way the online division of a major bank used data mining to improve its ability to perform cross-selling. Although this particular engagement took place in a bank, cross-selling is an important application of data mining for any company that offers its customers a wide range of products or services. Cross-selling is a way to make existing customers more valuable—something that is bound to be of interest in any industry.

Things move fast in Web World! During the six months from the start of the engagement described in this case study to the time we could measure results in the field—one trip around the virtuous cycle of data mining—the number of customers using the online banking service rose from 200,000 to 1.5 million. This chapter starts with some background on the banking industry to set the stage for the introduction of the business problem. Next there is a discussion of the importance of cross-selling to increased customer profitability and loyalty. There are several approaches to building cross-sell models, so before getting into the technical details of the model-building effort, we introduce our preferred approach. The chapter ends with some observations about how the job might have been done even better were it not for limitations of the data and the constraint to work at Internet speed.

Gaining Wallet-Share

The banking industry in the United States is going through many changes. After the Great Depression of the 1930s when many banks failed throughout the world, the United States reacted differently from most countries. Whereas Canada, for instance, nurtured a few large national banks that would be too strong to fail, the U.S. worked to limit the potential damage from any one bank's demise. For decades, federal regulations kept banking separate from other financial services such as insurance and brokerage. These regulations prevented banks based in one state from offering their services in another. In recent years, these restrictions have been relaxed, leading to a wave of consolidations as the U.S. market for financial services comes to resemble those of other rich countries.

When financial institutions merge, one of the justifications usually given is the opportunity to cross-sell products and services—when a customer comes in for a new car loan, what could be more natural than to offer him or her car insurance at the same time? But not all cross-sell opportunities are so obvious or so easy to capture. If the bank that issued your credit card is acquired by another bank that offers mortgages, you may not even realize that the credit card issuer has other services. In fact, you may have no idea what bank even owns your credit card—after a few mergers, it gets rather confusing. In any case, when you buy a new house, it is no easier to call the credit card issuer to inquire about a home loan than to call any other bank or mortgage broker. So, if they are going to deliver on the promises they have made to shareholders in order to sell their merger plans, the banks will have to do more than simply offer a broad array of services; they will have to get their customers to sign up for them. This requires determining precisely which products should be offered to which customers and figuring out how best to reach them with the message. In a word, cross-selling.

The challenge for today's large banks is to shift their focus from market share, which they have already purchased, to wallet-share, which is a bit more elusive. Instead of merely increasing the number of customers, banks need to increase the profitability of the ones they already have. Today, a typical retail bank actually loses money on a majority of its customers! Institutions that succeed in increasing the number of accounts per customer tend to grow both profits and customer loyalty. If you have a checking account at one bank, a home improvement loan from another, and a car loan from yet another, none of them is guaranteed to be your first choice when you go shopping for a mortgage or an IRA (individual retirement account). By contrast, if your checking account, home improvement loan, and car loan are all at the same institution, you are likely to call that institution "my bank" and it will be the first place you turn to when you are in need of additional financial services.

Selling additional services to the customers you already have is referred to as *cross-selling*. The closely related case of getting existing customers to trade up to more profitable products is called *up-selling*. Cross-selling and up-selling are natural applications for data mining because in general, you know much more about current customers than you could possibly find out about external prospects. Furthermore, the information gathered on customers in the course of normal business operations (balances, preferred language at ATMs, average number of credits and debits per month, payment history, home address, and the like) is much more reliable than the data purchased on external prospects. This case study shows how one bank built on data drawn from its customer information file to improve its ability to cross-sell new products to existing online banking customers by determining each existing customer's *best next offer*—the offer that is most likely to elicit a positive response from that customer.

The Business Problem

Our client was one of the largest banks in the United States with assets on the order of $100 billion and millions of customers. The online banking division is a small part of that, with fewer than half a million customers at the time of this project, but its aggressive plans call for double-digit yearly growth rates.

The project had immediate, short-term, and long-term goals. The *long-term* goal was to increase the bank's share of each customer's financial business by cross-selling appropriate products. Armed with a best next offer model, the bank would be able to greet each customer with a clickable banner ad for the next product he or she is most likely to want. The same model could, of course, guide other channels such as e-mail, traditional direct mail, and outbound telemarketing as well.

The *short-term* goal was to support a direct e-mail campaign for four selected products (brokerage accounts, money market accounts, home equity loans, and a particular type of savings account). E-mail is a very cheap channel for contacting customers. There is almost no monetary cost for sending an e-mail—that is, sending one e-mail costs about the same as sending one million. If the channel is so cheap, why do we care about accurately targeting e-mail? After all, the bank could just send messages to all online customers. It is still important to target e-mail effectively because customers, who might read one targeted e-mail message, are less likely to read 30 random messages. And, perhaps more importantly, customers who have given their permission to be contacted by e-mail will change their minds and withdraw their permission to be contacted if they begin receiving too many off-target messages.

The *immediate* goal was to take advantage of a data mining platform on loan from SGI to demonstrate the usefulness of data mining to the marketing of online banking services. This demonstration would justify the purchase of data mining software and the hardware on which to run it. The initial modeling work was

WARNING

Unsolicited e-mail falls somewhere between old fashioned junk mail and the dreaded dinner-time phone call in terms of its ability to annoy and alienate a customer. To avoid having your e-mail messages regarded as "spam," be careful to use them sparingly and only to convey information that is likely to be of interest to the customer. By signing up for online banking, customers have implicitly expressed a willingness to transact business on the net, but you should be careful to get their explicit permission to be contacted electronically with important information about their accounts. That way, your marketing messages will not be truly unsolicited and may even be welcomed as useful information.

done on-site. The four models used for the initial e-mail campaign were developed during this first phase using the MineSet data mining package running on a two-processor SGI Origin 200 server and a SGI O2 client workstation. Later stages of the project were performed at the DSS Lab (www.dsslab.com) in Cambridge, Massachusetts using a nearly identical software and hardware configuration.

The Data

The initial data comprised 1,122,692 account records extracted from the Customer Information System (CIS). The represents a snapshot of all online accounts as of February 1998. The 143 variables extracted for each account included internally generated data, such as account opening date and account balances, along with personal data provided by the customers themselves, such as names and addresses. The CIS also contained a small amount of externally purchased demographic data.

The customer data was available only as snapshots in time of account-level data. The particular snapshot used for modeling was June, 1998. Although the snapshot contained some historical data such as balances for the last several cycles, the fact that our view of the customers was essentially frozen did hamper our ability to apply some of the best practices for building cross-sell models described later in this chapter. In particular, it was not possible to model current holders of accounts of a particular type at the moment just prior to their having obtained that particular account. Instead, we had to work with the current account holders as they appeared in the snapshot month.

In preparation for the data mining engagement, analysts at the bank created a SAS data set containing an enriched version of the extracted data. The SAS data set included derived variables that the bank had found to be useful in the past such as the lag between the date a person first becomes a bank customer and the date they first sign up for online services. As usual, many more derived variables were added during the course of data mining and some of the existing variables had to be transformed in order to accommodate limitations of the data mining algorithms. Table 10.1 shows the variables extracted from the customer information system.

Table 10.1   Variables Extracted from the Customer Information System Focus on Single Accounts

TYPE	DESCRIPTION
Char	Account Number
Char	Statement County
Char	Employee Account Flag
Num	AOL User Flag
Num	Open Date
Char	Prime Household Phone Number
Char	Acquired From
Num	Account Status
Char	Area of Dominant Influence (ADI)
Char	Acxiom Prime Household Demographic Information
Char	Household Estimated Minimum Annual Income
Char	Estimated Household Net Worth
Char	Statement ZIP
Num	Balance #1: CURRENT CYCLE
Num	Balance #1: CYCLE-1
Num	Balance #1: CYCLE-2
Num	Balance #1: CYCLE-3
Num	Balance #1: CYCLE-4
Num	Best Balance: CURRENT CYCLE
Num	Best Balance: CYCLE-1
Num	Best Balance: CYCLE-2
Num	Best Balance: CYCLE-3
Num	Best Balance: CYCLE-4
Char	Credit Card Decline
Char	Debit Card #1 Checkcard Flag
Char	Debit Card #2 Checkcard Flag

Continues

Table 10.1 Variables Extracted from the Customer Information System Focus on Single Accounts *(Continued)*

TYPE	DESCRIPTION
Num	Members in Household
Char	Microvision Household Description
Char	Household Metro
Num	Household Number
Char	Premier Banking Household
Char	Solicit (Y/other=N)
Num	Internet User
Num	MS Money User
Num	Credits Count
Num	Debits Count
Char	Product Code
Char	Private Banking Household
Char	Product
Num	Quicken User
Char	Subproduct
Char	Customer ID
Num	Debit Card use 60-day, Card 1
Num	Balance Inquiries 60-day, Card 1
Num	ATM Payments Encl, Card1
Num	POS
Num	Network ATM use 60-day, Card 1
Num	Bank ATM use 60-day, Card 1

From Accounts to Customers

The data extracted from the customer information system had one row per account. This reflects the usual *product-centric* organization of a bank where managers are responsible for the profitability of particular products rather than the profitability of customers or households. The best next offer project required pivoting the data to build *customer-centric* models.

To be useful for cross-selling, the 1.2 million account-level records extracted from the customer information system had to be transformed into around a quarter million household-level records. This was accomplished using SAS to group all the accounts for a given tax identification number and then transpose them into a single customer record with a set of columns for each account type. In cases where the bank was aware that multiple members of a household had accounts, one of them was chosen as the primary ID for the household and used to identify all household members. This allowed each newly created customer record to represent all accounts belonging to an entire household. The new customer record contains a count for each product indicating how many accounts of that type the household has (0 in most cases) along with the associated balances. The resulting table had many more fields than the original extract of account data. The abbreviated Table 10.2 gives a feel for the kinds of variables that were available as inputs to the model.

Table 10.2 Illustrative Sample of Variables Used as Input to Models

HOUSEHOLD-LEVEL FIELD DESCRIPTIONS
Account county
Address state
Age of latest asset management product
Age of latest business brokerage product
Age of latest business credit card
Age of latest business time deposit
Age of latest business interest checking
Age of latest business installment direct loan
Age of latest business loan
Age of latest business credit line
The variables whose names start with age say how many months the customer has had an account of this type. This information is derived from the account open date.
America Online user flag
Acquired from
Time with bank
Credit card declined flag
Express check card #1 flag
Express check card #2 flag
Bank territory
Bank county
Months since express check card was used
Bank employee household

Continues

Table 10.2 Illustrative Sample of Variables Used as Input to Models *(Continued)*

HOUSEHOLD-LEVEL FIELD DESCRIPTIONS
Number of people in household
Microvision household description code
Premier (high value) household
Time between becoming bank customer and going online (months)
True if delay greater than 30 days
Number of credits
Number of debits
Months on line
Number of products held
Pseudo tax id (real tax IDs not used to protect customer privacy)
Count of asset management products
Count of business brokerage products
Count of business credit cards
Count of business time deposit accounts
Count of business interest checking accounts
Banking products fall into families such as "credit cards" or "demand deposit accounts." The variables starting with the word "count" are derived variables that say how many the customer has in each account family.
Uses Quicken
Number of balance inquiries last 60 days—card one
Number of ATM payments last 60 days—card one
Number of POS uses last 60 days—card one
Network ATM use last 60 days—card one
Bank ATM use last 60 days—card one
True if customer has any business product
True if customer uses Quicken bill paying feature
True if customer uses MS Money
True if customer uses Quicken
Many of the fields are flags that are true if the customer uses a particular service or has exhibited a certain behavior.
True if customer has at least one student loan
True if customer has at least one time deposit
True if customer has at least one unsecured line of credit

Table 10.2 *(Continued)*

HOUSEHOLD-LEVEL FIELD DESCRIPTIONS
True if customer has at least one wholesale DDA product
True if customer has private banking services
Balance for asset management products
Balance for business brokerage products
Balance for business credit cards
Balance for business time deposit accounts
Balance for business interest checking
Clearly, account balances can be very predictive.
Total balance over all customer's accounts
True if customer has total balance over $50,000
County of residence or "other"
Customer tenure bin
Telephone area code or "other"
Household standard metropolitan statistical area or "other"
First 3 digits of postal zip code or "other"

Note that many of the variables used as inputs to the model-building process are derived variables that were not part of the original extract. Some values, such as length of tenure, have been binned into ranges. Others, such as total balance, are values calculated from the original fields. A few are flags added to reflect groups of people that the bank considered interesting, such as people who tried online banking within 30 days of becoming a bank customer and people whose total deposits with the bank were over $50,000.

Defining the Products to Be Offered

The customer information system recognized several hundred different products, many of which are simply small variations on a theme. This level of product differentiation is too detailed for the kind of marketing campaign we were supporting. For example, the bank might make someone an offer of a savings account without trying to determine which of several variants would be most likely to appeal. These variants offer different interest rates based on total balances at the bank, other types of accounts, and so on. In fact, there are business rules for determining which savings account is most appropriate for a given customer—data mining can figure out that a savings account is appropriate and then business rules take over to determine which one in particular.

TIP

Often the number of product codes is often dauntingly large. And, when there are too many codes (more than a few dozen) it is difficult to develop good cross-sell models—there are simply too few instances for each one. Often, many of the codes refer to the same type of thing, such as a checking account or a home mortgage, with just minor (from the point of view of marketing) differences between them. Look for a hierarchy that describes the products at the right level.

There is a budgeting application that rolls up account types into a hierarchy of product category, account type, and subtype. The four major categories are deposit account, loan, service, and investment. The marketing people decided that, with a few modifications, the account-type level of this preexisting hierarchy would serve well. From a marketing perspective, some of the account types are essentially the same, such as certificates of deposit (CDs) and time deposits (TDs). These account types were combined into a single category.

The product categories were used as the target variables for modeling. That is, a model predicted who would have CD/TD, or home mortgages, or whatever. The individual product types were retained as input variables. Table 10.3 shows the 45 product types used for the best next offer model. Of these 25 products are ones that may be offered to a customer as part of this campaign. Information on the remaining (business-oriented) account types are used only as input variables when building the models.

Table 10.3 Product Types Used in the Best Next Offer Model

PRODUCT CODE	PRODUCT DESCRIPTION	TO BE MODELED	ACCOUNT HOLDERS	COMBINE WITH
ASM	Asset Management	No		
BBK	Business Brokerage	No		
BCC	Business Credit Card	No		
BCD	Business Certificate of Deposit	No		
BIC	Business Interest Bearing Checking			
BIL	Bill Pay	Yes	106,949	
BLD	Business Loan Division	No		
BLN	Business Line of Credit	No		
BMM	Business Money Market	No		
BMR	Business Market Rate	No		
BMS	Business Money Market Savings	No		

Table 10.3   *(Continued)*

PRODUCT CODE	PRODUCT DESCRIPTION	TO BE MODELED	ACCOUNT HOLDERS	COMBINE WITH
BNC	Business Non Interest Checking	No		
BSV	Business Savings	No		
CC	Credit Card	Yes	154,738	
CD	Certificate of Deposit	Yes	10,646	TD
CUS	Custody	No		
DLR	Installment Dealer Loans	Yes	2,693	
ELC	Equity Line of Credit	Yes	10,952	
EXL	Express Lease	Yes	2,792	
GRP	Group Retirement Programs	No		
GUR	Wholesale Loan Guarantors	No		
IBC	Interest Bearing Checking	Yes	40,233	NIC
IL	Installment Direct Loans	Yes	12,545	
IRA	Individual Retirement Account	Yes	13,074	
IRB	Individual Retirement Account Brokerage	Yes	2,045	
IRF	Individual Retirement Account Mutual Funds	Yes	5,339	
LOC	Line of Credit	Yes	53	ULC
ML2	Second Mortgage	Yes	519	
MMA	Money Market Access	Yes	1,823	
MMS	Money Market Savings	Yes	35,841	
MRA	Market Rate Account	Yes	19,467	
MTG	Mortgage	Yes	2,444	
NIC	Non-Interest Bearing Checking	Yes	370,420	IBC
PAN	Platform Annuities	No		
PMR	Premier	No		
RBR	Retail Brokerage	Yes	5,297	
RP	Retirement Programs	No		
RPS	Retirement Programs Securities	No		

Continues

Table 10.3 Product Types Used in the Best Next Offer Model *(Continued)*

PRODUCT CODE	PRODUCT DESCRIPTION	TO BE MODELED	ACCOUNT HOLDERS	COMBINE WITH
SAV	Saving	Yes	52,314	XTR
STG	Mutual Funds	Yes	3,880	
STU	Student Loans	Yes	7,430	
TD	Time Deposit	Yes	3	CD
ULC	Unsecured Line of Credit	Yes	33,165	LOC
WDA	Wholesale DDA	No		
XTR	Linked Savings	Yes	219,695	SAV

The marketing campaign supported by the best next offer model was aimed at individual consumers, not businesses, so none of the business account types were used as target variables in the cross-sell models. Information on business accounts was retained as input to the models. It seems quite likely, in fact, that someone who has both business and personal accounts may behave differently than someone who has only personal accounts. With that in mind, one of the derived variables we added was a flag indicating whether a person has any accounts classified as business rather than personal. If people who own their own businesses really do exhibit different behaviors with respect to their personal accounts as well, a business products flag will allow that pattern to be found.

Approach to the Problem

To accommodate both the short- and long-term goals of the project, we wanted the best next offer model to be built up from component models for the individual products. Our approach was to build a propensity-to-buy model for each product individually. The individual propensity models can be used to sort a list of prospects for each product so that those most likely to respond to a product offer are at the top of the list. Then, once each customer has been given a score for every product, the scores can be combined to yield the best next offer model: Customers are all offered the product for which they have the highest score. Of course, we had to take special care that the scores developed by each individual propensity-to-buy model were *comparable* to the scores developed by other models. This approach meant that we could start with the four models needed to support the near-term e-mail campaigns for brokerage, savings, home equity, and money market accounts, and scale up to the larger campaigns in later stages.

Comparable Scores

To be useful for the best next offer model, the scores from the various product propensity models must be comparable. But what does it mean to be comparable? We came up with the following list of requirements:

1. All scores must fall into the same range: zero to one.

2. Anyone who already has a product should score zero for it.

3. The relative popularity of products should be reflected in the scores. That is, the average score for popular products should be larger than the average score for less popular products.

The first requirement is really only that all scores should fall within the same range. The range zero to one is nice because it is the way probabilities are normally expressed and these scores may be thought of as the probability that a customer in a given leaf will want the product being modeled. The second requirement reflects the bank's wish to avoid trying to sell people accounts that they already have. Even for products where it might make sense for the customer to have more than one (such as one credit card for reimbursable expenses and another for purely personal expenses), it is likely that the bank would want to send a different message to promote the second instance of the product. The point, after all, is to make the bank appear to understand its customers needs. That means avoiding communications that might make the bank just look plain dumb!

It is the third requirement that poses the biggest problem. Many algorithms designed to accommodate requirement one would grant the people most likely to want a given product a score of one and the people least likely to want it a score of zero regardless of the number of people who might possibly want the product. To see the problem with that, imagine two products, one that could be used by anyone, and one that can be used only by left-handed people. The vast majority of people are right-handed and so have no interest in the left-handed product. Any system that gives right-handed people a higher score for the left-handed product than for the ambidextrous product is misleading. It is fine for the occasional left-handed person to score very high for the left-handed product, but the *average* score for that product will necessarily be much lower than the score for the ambidextrous product, reflecting the fact that most customers are not interested in it at all. At the bank, many more online customers are interested in the bill paying service than in student loans. This almost certainly reflects the true nature of the customer population, so given a set of customers who have neither, we should expect more of them to be offered bill paying than to be offered student loans.

If It Walks Like a Duck, …

Our approach to cross-selling starts by building models that characterize the current customers for each product. Prospects (any customers who do not already have the product) are then given a score based on the extent to which they *look like* the existing account holders for that product. The precise definition of what it means to "look like" an existing customer depends on the data mining technique employed. A clustering-based approach would assign the prospect to a preexisting cluster and use the relative popularity of the various products within that cluster to assign scores. A memory-based reasoning approach would be similar except that instead of using preexisting clusters, all the customers within a certain distance of the record to be scored would be surveyed and their "votes" translated into scores. In this instance, we used a decision tree–based approach, which assigns the prospect to a leaf node of a decision tree built for the product in question and uses the percentage of existing customers at that leaf to assign a score for the product; this score is the product-propensity score for that product.

The data mining algorithms for clustering and decision trees were introduced in Chapter 5 of this book, and described in detail in our earlier book, *Data Mining Techniques for Marketing, Sales, and Customer Support* (1997, John Wiley & Sons). For now, the approach can be summed up by the oft-paraphrased words of Richard C. Cushing: "When I see a bird that walks like a duck and swims like a duck and quacks like a duck, I call that bird a duck."

WARNING

A model developed for cross-selling *within* a given customer population is not likely to translate well to another population or to work well on prospects from the population at large. A model developed for existing customers is likely to make use of variables that are not available for the general population of noncustomers. Even where the same variables are available, the new population may be very different from the population used to develop the model. A cross-sell model should not be used to screen outside prospects. There is an amusing (and no doubt apocryphal) story that illustrates the point. According to this story, an English village petitioned British Rail to have the London-bound train that passed through town each morning stop to pick up passengers. The railroad did some research and determined that no one in that village was ever waiting for the train. The request was turned down.

Pitfalls of This Approach

There are a couple of pitfalls inherent in this approach to building cross-sell models. You need to be aware of them to avoid falling in.

Becoming a Customer Changes the Way You Behave

The first problem is that the propensity models score prospects based on their similarity to current customers, but current customers may look different than they did at the time that they signed up for the product. Certificates of Deposit (CDs) provide a good example. CDs are essentially interest-bearing savings accounts where the customer promises to leave a certain sum on deposit for a predetermined period. In return for giving up immediate access to the money, the customer earns a higher interest rate. It is a safe guess that people who own CDs probably do not have large balances lying around in their ordinary savings accounts, because they would move this money into CDs. Does that mean that we should look for CD prospects among the customers with low savings balances? Surely not! Prior to purchasing a certificate of deposit, the CD customer must have had the purchase price available somewhere. Of course, there is no guarantee that the somewhere else was another account at the same bank, but in many cases it probably was.

The best approach is to build models based on the way current customers looked just before they became customers. Unfortunately, this approach requires a fairly sophisticated data warehouse (and a fairly complex query) to get the requisite data. For each current holder of a particular account, this requires going back in time months or years to get a snapshot of his or her other accounts in the month prior to opening the particular account. For each product, there could be a different base month for each customer. Furthermore, each product would be modeled on a completely different data set because each product has a different population of customers with different account opening dates. As is often the case in the real world, it wasn't possible to obtain data in just the right form so we had to make do with a current snapshot instead.

To reduce the impact of the problem, we were careful not to use variables that seemed particularly likely to be misleading for a given product. A derived variable, total balance, dampened the effects of transfers between different accounts owned by the same customer. Fortunately, decision-tree models make it easy to spot which variables are being used to make a classification. If a model is relying on a variable that is likely to be influenced by the very thing that the model is trying to predict, it should be removed from the input list.

Current Customers Reflect Past Policy

Looking at the bank's data, it is clear that some products are much more popular than others. To some extent, this reflects naturally occurring patterns: More people have use for checking accounts than for home equity lines because more people pay bills than own homes. In other cases, a current policy

WARNING

A model that does a very good job of finding people who have a particular product may be useless for identifying prospects for that product if it has simply learned to recognize some behavior that only people with the product exhibit. We have seen many examples of this problem, including one amusing case of a model that was very successful at classifying people with voice mail—the model determined that people who tend to make a lot of short duration phone calls to the voice mail retrieval number are very likely to have voice mail. True, but not terribly useful for identifying prospects!

of the bank is reflected in the data: You don't get to be a private banking client unless you are very wealthy. Data mining will find both of these patterns—more people will be offered checking accounts than home equity lines and only the very wealthy will be offered private banking. But what if the current makeup of the population reflects some policy that is no longer in force? For example, the low number of mortgages reflects the fact that this bank historically has steered clear of the home mortgage market. If that policy should change, many people who might in fact be interested in a mortgage will not be identified simply because people like them where never offered mortgages in the past.

Although nothing of the kind was suggested in the current case, a particularly pernicious form of this problem involves past discrimination, or "red lining." If a bank had a past policy of not granting mortgages in certain ZIP codes, that would show up in the model as low propensity for mortgages in those ZIP codes which, if not caught, could lead to a perpetuation of the discriminatory practice. Similarly, if a certain product traditionally has been offered only to suburban men, this sort of best next offer model will continue to pick them as the most likely prospects, ignoring urban women.

Building the Models

At the bank's suggestion, the first model was built for brokerage accounts. These are of particular interest because they are highly profitable and relatively underutilized. (Of 462,799 online customers in June of 1998, only 4,685 had brokerage accounts.)

Finding Important Variables

Before actually trying to build models, we needed to become more familiar with the data. The first step was to use MineSet's statistics visualizer to look at the distributions of all the input variables. This initial data profiling revealed a few possible anomalies such as a few accounts that were over 100 years old. According to the bank, which was founded in the nineteenth century, there really could be accounts that old because some kinds of account get passed down through generations. Even so, we decided that these outliers were unlikely to aid the modeling process. In general, though, the data appeared clean and consistent.

Using the Column Importance Tool

The first data mining algorithm applied was MineSet's column importance tool. The column importance tool finds a set of variables which, taken together, do a good job of differentiating two or more classes (in this case, people with brokerage accounts and people without brokerage accounts). The top three variables found by column importance are not the three with the greatest individual discriminatory power (for that, MineSet provides an evidence visualizer). Rather, it finds a *combination* of variables that work together to increase the purity of the classification. The column importance tool is often used to select the best variables to map to the axes of a scatter plot for data visualization.

The column importance tool discovered that the most significant factors for determining whether someone has a brokerage account are:

- Whether they are a private banking customer
- The length of time they have been with the bank
- The value of certain lifestyle codes assigned to them by Microvision (a marketing statistics company)

Of course, sometimes a variable is very predictive only because of past marketing patterns. We were worried that this might be the case for the link between private banking and brokerage. Suppose that all private banking customers are automatically given brokerage accounts. Or suppose that brokerage accounts have never been marketed to ordinary customers. As a precaution, we decided to rerun the column importance algorithm with the private banking variable removed. As it turned out, MineSet was able to achieve the same level of accuracy without making use of the private banking flag. The new top predictors were:

- Whether the customer has been labeled as a member of a "premier household"
- The length of time they have been with the bank
- The existence of and balance in a money market account
- The Microvision code

Saying that someone is from a "premier" household is just another way of saying that they have a lot of money in the bank, and it is hardly surprising that rich people are more likely than others to have brokerage accounts. However, the third variable is an interesting one. At first glance, it might seem that money market accounts are just another way of saying that a customer has a lot of money. The column importance tool does not say whether the correlation between the variables it picks and the target outcome is positive or negative. Further investigation showed that people with money market accounts are far *less* likely than other wealthy customers to have brokerage accounts. Apparently, tastes differ even among the rich—some like stocks and so open a brokerage account, others prefer bonds and open a money market account.

Using the Evidence Classifier

The next tool we tried was the evidence classifier and its interactive visualizer. The evidence classifier uses a data mining algorithm called "naïve Bayes" to build a predictive model. Naïve Bayes models treat each variable independently and measure the effect that different values of the variables have on the outcome. These independent contributions are then combined to make a classification. The evidence visualizer in MineSet sorts variables in order of their contribution to a prediction and shows the probability of a particular outcome for each value the variables take on. See Figure 10.1.

For this particular problem, it is hard for any classifier to do a better job of classification than the very simple rule, "No one has a brokerage account." A model that takes in whatever evidence is thrown at it and comes out with the prediction that the customer will not have a brokerage account will have an error rate of less than 2 percent. What is really interesting is not the prediction, but the *strength* of the prediction. The evidence visualizer allows you to explore interactively the way that the probability of having a brokerage account changes as you select various possible combinations of inputs. For example, clicking on the attribute for private banking causes the piece of pie representing brokerage customers to grow from a tiny sliver of 1.1 percent in Figure 10.2 to a respectable slice of 11.7 percent in Figure 10.3 This is a lift of over 10 using a single variable.

Building a Decision Tree Model for Brokerage

The actual brokerage model was built using MineSet's decision tree tool. The decision tree algorithm builds a classifier by finding a series of splits that breaks the data into smaller and smaller groups that are purer and purer in the attribute under study. A decision tree for the brokerage variable will have many branches

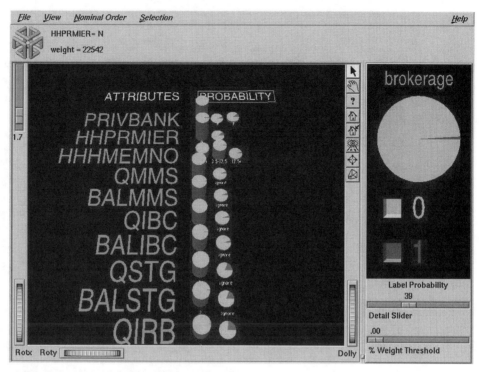

Figure 10.1   The MineSet evidence visualizer.

and levels, but at the leaves there will be groups that are either mostly nonbrokerage (the majority of leaves) or mostly brokerage. Each path through the tree to a leaf containing mostly brokerage customers can be thought of as a "rule" for predicting that an unclassified customer who meets the conditions of the rule is likely to have *or be interested in* a brokerage account.

Building a good decision tree for brokerage accounts took some time and some careful experimentation with parameters. The initial tree, obtained by accepting all the default parameters and just pressing the button, had exactly one node labeled "nonbrokerage." When the density of the target variable is so low (only 1.2 percent of the customers had brokerage accounts), it can be hard to beat such a simple model. One approach is to create a cost matrix that punishes the model for misclassifying a brokerage customer as a nonbrokerage customer much more severely than for misclassifying a nonbrokerage customer as a brokerage customer. Another approach is to use oversampling to increase the percentage of brokerage customers in the model set to give the model a better shot at learning how to recognize a brokerage customer when it sees one. The latter approach proved most effective. The final tree was built on a model set containing about one quarter brokerage accounts.

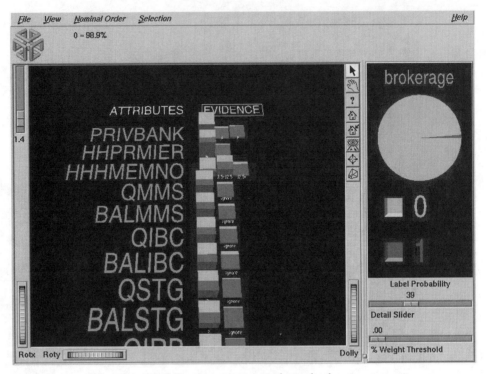

Figure 10.2 The prior probability that a customer has a brokerage account.

Record Weights in Place of Oversampling

MineSet has a number of features and default settings that betray its origins as a university research project prior to its adoption by SGI. The default settings for parameters, such as the minimum number of records that must be present in a decision tree node in order for it to be considered a candidate for further splitting, seem to have been chosen with the tiny data set of iris flower measurements that is commonly used for testing data mining tools. In a small data set environment, record weighting is used to achieve the effect of oversampling the records having some particular feature of interest without having to throw away any of the rest of the records in the training set.

MineSet does not provide any direct facility for oversampling; instead, it provides record weighting. Weighting causes some records to be treated as more important than others. When weighting is used, MineSet bases all of its splitting decisions on the total *weight* of records in each class rather than the *number* of records. Weighting can be used to achieve the same effect as oversampling by increasing the relative importance of the rare records. The proper approach is to lower the weight of records in the common class rather

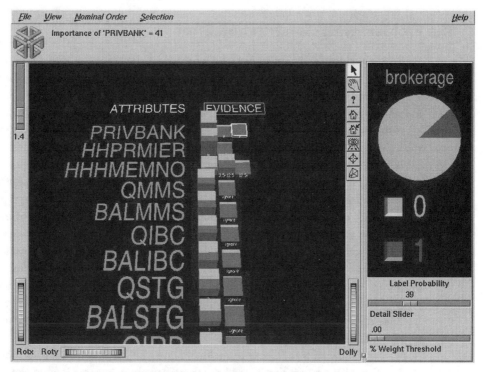

Figure 10.3 The probability that a private banking customer has a brokerage account.

than increasing the weight of records in the rare class. By experimentation we found that adjusting weights to bring the weight of rare records (brokerage accounts, in this case) up to 20 or 25 percent of the total worked quite well.

WARNING

When using weights to increase the relative importance of a rare class such as responders to a direct mail campaign, a natural tendency is to give responders a weight of 10 while giving nonresponders a weight of 1. This is wrong! This will cause each responder to be seen 10 times meaning that peculiar features of single records will come to seem like regular patterns thus exacerbating the problem of over-fitting. The proper approach is to leave each responder with a weight of 1 while decreasing the weight of each nonresponder to 0.1.

Allowing One-Off Splits

One of the parameters that the user can control in MineSet's decision-tree tool is whether the algorithm should consider one-off splits on categorical variables that take on many values. Normally, the tree building algorithm used by

The Problem with Classification Error

MineSet considers decision trees to be primarily a classification tool. When constructing a decision tree, it tries to find the tree that will be the best classifier. The expected use of a classifier model is to assign records to one of a small number of categories such as good/bad or responder/nonresponder. Unsurprisingly, classifiers are measured on their ability to make correct classifications. MineSet uses the classification error rate as a measure of how good a model it has built. Since we are using the decision tree for a different purpose, the classification error rate is a meaningless measure for our purposes. Since only 1.2 percent of the population has brokerage accounts, a model that ignores its inputs and predicts that no one has a brokerage account has a classification error rate of only 1.2 percent, which sounds very good. This is, in fact, the classifier that MineSet first built (see Figure 10.4). The one-node decision tree is a very good classifier, but it is of no help deciding to whom we should send e-mail recommending a brokerage account. The decision tree we ended up using does an excellent job of scoring as measured by lift, but has a classification error rate of around 8 percent because it optimistically classifies many people as brokerage customers who do not, in fact, have brokerage accounts.

The best decision tree for our purposes is one that has many different leaves, each with a different proportion of brokerage accounts. In most leaves, the proportion will be close to zero, but in some it will be quite high. Even among the majority of leaves where the proportion of brokerage accounts is quite low, it will be higher in some than others and we will use that information to order a list of prospects. When a decision tree is used as a propensity model rather than as a classifier, it should be measured on the lift produced by using it to score a list of prospects, not by its classification error rate.

MineSet will either split a categorical variable on every single value (so that a split on State, for instance, might produce 50 child nodes), or not split on that variable at all since some of the child nodes will get too few records. Allowing one-off splits causes MineSet to consider splits based on a single value of a categorical variable.

Several of the bank's decision trees included a one-off split on the state variable with its home state forming one branch and all other states forming the other. In Figure 10.5, the initial split is on the variable PRIVBANK which takes on three values, N, P, and H. The split puts the value N (for no private banking) on one branch and labels the other branch "other," lumping together the two flavors of private banking. We have found that this kind of split is often useful and worth the extra time it takes to calculate. Descending the left branch of the tree—the one that corresponds to the one-off split—we see in Figure 10.6

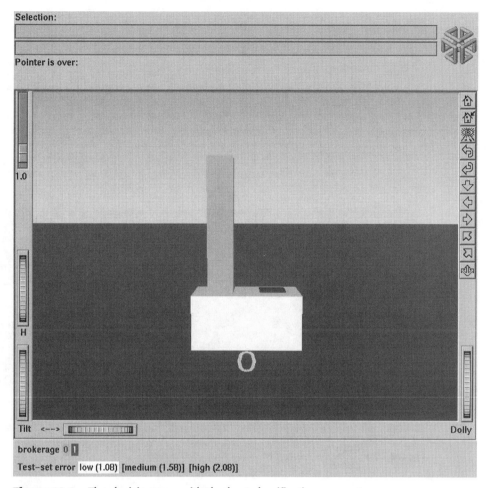

Selection:

Pointer is over:

1.0

H

Tilt <--->

Dolly

brokerage 0

Test-set error low (1.08) [medium (1.58)] [high (2.08)]

Figure 10.4   The decision tree with the best classification error rate.

that for people who are not private banking clients, the balance in a business checking account is the most important discriminator between brokerage customer and nonbrokerage customers.

Grouping Categories

Even with one-off splits enabled, MineSet refuses to consider categorical variables that take on more than some set number of values. Although this limit is user-settable through a variable in an options file, increasing the limit is not really the answer because MineSet's designers have a point: The algorithm is not likely to make good splits on a categorical variable that takes on hundreds of values. Unfortunately, some of the variables that MineSet rejected seemed likely to be very predictive for certain cases. Some of these discarded variables

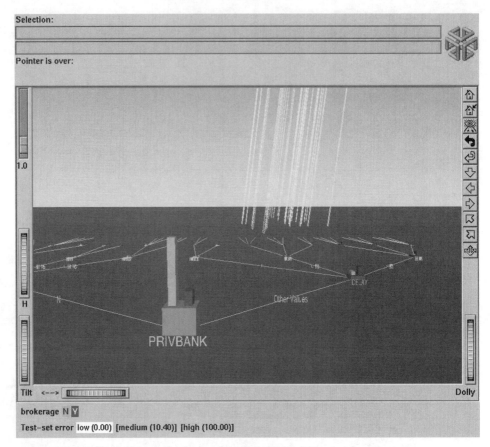

Selection:

Pointer is over:

1.0

H

N

PRIVBANK

Other Values

DE AY

Tilt <--> Dolly

brokerage N Y

Test–set error low (0.00) [medium (10.40)] [high (100.00)]

Figure 10.5 The decision tree that provides the best scores.

required a bit of work to save. Examples include `zip3` (the first three digits of the zip code, used as a geographic marker), `account county`, `area code`, and `metropolitan statistical area`. All of these variables had the characteristic that although there were hundreds of values in the data, most accounts had one of the top 20 or 30 values. It seemed a great pity to have to throw away data for counties where thousands of the bank's customers reside just because hundreds of far-flung counties in other states had a handful of customers each.

Our approach was to lump all values below a certain threshold into a catch-all "other" category, allowing splits to be made on the more populous ones. That way, if there is something special about residents of a certain wealthy and populous suburban county, the model can make use of that information even though no similar information is available for other counties that are less well-represented in the customer population.

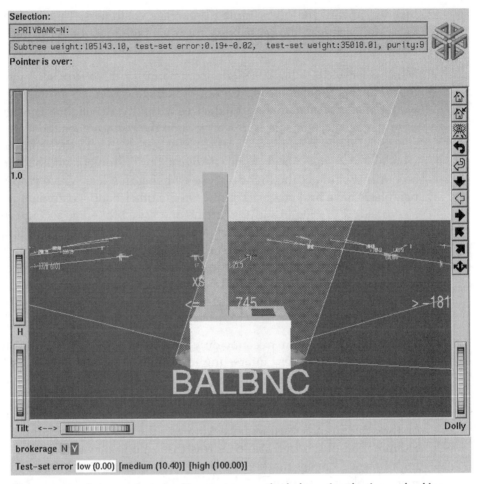

Selection:
:PRIVBANK=N:
Subtree weight:105143.10, test-set error:0.19+-0.02, test-set weight:35018.01, purity:9
Pointer is over:

1.0

H

Tilt <-->   Dolly

brokerage N

Test-set error low (0.00) [medium (10.40)] [high (100.00)]

Figure 10.6 For nonprivate banking customers, the balance in a business checking account is the next most important variable.

Influencing the Pruning Decisions

MineSet provides various parameters for controlling the size, depth, and bushiness of the decision trees it builds. Some of the defaults, such as the minimum number of records that are allowed in a node seem ill-chosen. Through experimentation we arrived at settings of 0.1 for the pruning factor, 50 records for the minimum allowed in a node, and no explicit limit on the tree's depth.

Backfitting the Model for Comparable Scores

The tree was originally built using records' weights to increase the importance of brokerage customers. However, the scores in this tree were unnaturally inclined toward the oversampled brokerage customers. To get proper score values at each leaf, the probability for brokerage must be recalculated using *unweighted* data.

MineSet provides a backfit model command for this purpose. To get scores that reflected the true proportion of brokerage customers in the population, we ran the original data through the tree without any weights. The percentage of brokerage accounts at each leaf became the *raw score* for the leaf. We then converted the raw score to a *mail score* by setting to zero the score of anyone who already was a brokerage customer. So, customers without brokerage accounts would get the highest score by being in a leaf where many of their neighbors have brokerage accounts. On the other hand, customers would get a zero score by being in a leaf where no one has a brokerage account (there are quite a few leaves like that) or by already having a brokerage account. Customers with brokerage accounts won't get the solicitation, but will increase the score of other records at their nodes. Note that it is impossible for a customer to get a score of 1 for any product because that would mean that all customers in his or her leaf already have the product, in which case they will all get a score of zero.

The resulting decision tree not only does a fine job of scoring brokerage prospects, it is also very interesting to visualize. Private banking is the split variable at the root node, confirming what we learned from the column importance tool and the evidence visualizer. For those on the private banking branch of the tree, length of tenure was the next most important variable, but for those on the other branch, business checking was the next most important variable. Examination of the tree also confirms that among private banking clients, a high-balance money market account is a strong predictor that you will *not* have a brokerage account.

A Worrisome Lift Curve

Like most data mining tools, MineSet includes the ability to generate cumulative response graphs to show the *lift* due to a model. The lift curve for the brokerage model in Figure 10.7 shows that if all prospects are sorted according to "propensity for brokerage accounts" score as given by this model, then all responders will be found in the top 25 percent of the list.

Normally, a response curve this good is a warning that something is amiss. Most often, a curve that flattens out at the top, meaning that all of the target population has been found in a relatively small part of the general population, means that the input variables are somehow providing the definition of the target variable. In this case, however, it simply reflects the fact that brokerage accounts are rare and that it is easy to identify large groups of customers who

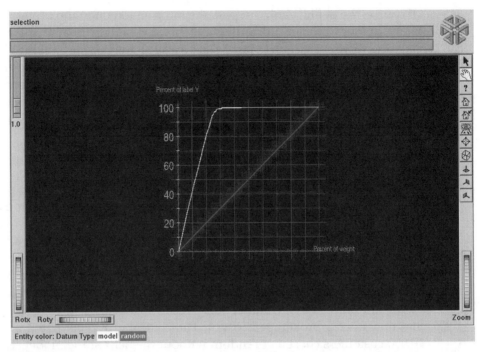

Figure 10.7   The model finds 100 percent of the brokerage accounts in the top 30 percent of the test set.

are not interested in them. Most people get a score of zero or very close to zero for brokerage account, and the actual brokerage customers are found among the few who have higher scores. We can expect similar lift curves whenever we are searching for something that can easily be ruled out for most of the population: Inuit speakers in France; Macintosh users at a bank; curling fans anywhere but Scotland. In any of these cases, the algorithm does not have to work very hard to find the bottom 98 percent of the population. In cases like these, it makes sense to filter out the boring 98 percent of the population in advance. Had we restricted ourselves to only customers with at least $50,000 in the bank, the lift curve for the brokerage model would have had a more usual shape and told us more.

The Problem with Private Banking Clients

So now we know that private banking clients who don't have money market accounts are the best prospects for brokerage accounts. Unfortunately, we are not allowed to contact them. All communications with the private banking clients go through their private banker—that is what it means to be a private banking client. Such customers are too valuable to be bothered by mere marketing campaigns.

Of course, the online bank can pass the information on to the private banking group, but they probably already know this anyway. Fortunately, all is not lost. Since the very first split in the tree takes away all the private banking clients on the right-hand side, the left-hand split remains as a perfectly good model of who, among the rest of the population, is a good brokerage prospect. The lift curve of this model is not as good as for the complete model, but it is much more useful because it identifies prospects that the bank is allowed to contact.

Brokerage Model Performance in a Controlled Test

When the brokerage model, without the private banking clients, was put to the test, it did a respectable job of finding brokerage candidates given the general unpopularity of that product. To perform the test, the bank created three groups of 10,000 people each: a model group, a control group, and a hold-out group. The model group consisted of 10,000 people who got relatively high scores from the brokerage model. (Recall that a high score is any score higher than the density of brokerage account holders in the population, not a large number.) Everyone in the model group received an e-mail message suggesting that they open a brokerage account. The control group consisted of another 10,000 customers chosen at random without the help of the model. They, too, got the e-mail solicitation. The hold-out group had the same characteristics as the control group, but its members did not receive the brokerage solicitation. The results were as follows:

- The response rate of the model group was 0.7 percent
- The response rate of the control group was 0.3 percent
- The response rate of the hold-out group was 0.05 percent

The improvement in response rate from the control group to the model group means that the model generated a lift of 2.3, albeit from a low base. The extremely low incidence of members of the hold-out group simply wandering in and asking for a brokerage account shows that the e-mail solicitation was effective. The improvement in response rate from no solicitation to untargeted solicitation was much greater than the improvement from untargeted solicitation to targeted solicitation.

Building the Rest of the Models

The models for the rest of the product groups were built following essentially the same procedure as for the brokerage model. For any product that was used by 25 to 75 percent of the total population, we did no weighting and no backfitting, but built the models directly from the June data. For checking accounts (interest-bearing and noninterest-bearing combined), we used weights so that records of people *without* checking accounted for 25 percent of the population. For most other products, we used weights to bring the density of account holders up to that level. The model parameters that worked well for brokerage also worked well for savings, money market, and home equity accounts, so we applied them to all the other models as well.

Getting to a Cross-Sell Model

Once all the individual propensity models had been built, the next step was to combine them all into a cross-sell model as shown in Figure 10.8. Conceptually, this is very simple: every customer is given a score for each product. The scores can be thought of as vote counts for the products. A customer's best next offer is the product for which he or she has the most votes. In fact, this query is difficult, if not impossible, to express in SQL since for each customer we want to return not the highest score, but the product corresponding to the highest score. In this case, the client implemented this part of the model in SAS code. Of course, there is no reason that we have to pick only one best next offer. Each customer now has an individual ranking of all products. We may want to offer the top three or the top five instead of the single highest scoring product.

A Market Basket Approach to Cross-Selling

The approach to building cross-sell models that we advocate here—building individual propensity models and letting them vote—is not the only possible approach. Another technique is based on affinity grouping or market basket analysis. The cross-sell module of Unica's Model One package appears to use this approach.

The affinity grouping approach to cross-selling starts by noticing what clusters or constellations of products are already owned by current customers. Customers who have some, but not all of a common constellation are assumed to be good prospects for the missing pieces. For example, if someone buys graham crackers and marshmallows, but not chocolate bars, we can assume that they have simply forgotten how to make s'mores and remind them with a coupon from Hershey or Nestlé.

A problem with this approach is that in an environment such as the bank in the case study, customers are likely to start out with just a single product (a checking account or savings account) that ends up being part of every bundle. Only after the customer already has several products can we start to recognize the distinct pattern into which he or she is falling. Where there are strong affinity groups, our approach will pick up on them. If current buyers of marshmallows tend to have chocolate bars and graham crackers, then any shopper with graham crackers and chocolate bars will get a very high score for marshmallows and we will pick them as the best next

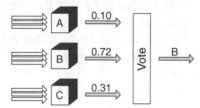

Figure 10.8 Combining multiple models to find the best next offer.

In a More Perfect World

Now that we have seen an actual case study involving the construction of a cross-sell model, it is time to step back and outline the steps we would follow to build one under ideal conditions.

1. Determine whether cross-selling makes sense for this company. For cross-selling to make sense there should be a variety of products (at least five) that might reasonably appeal to a large number of customers. The products should be complementary, or at least not mutually exclusive. People are unlikely to want a gas stove *and* an electric stove.

2. Determine whether sufficient data exists to build a good cross-sell model. It should be possible to recapture the state of a current customer at any point in his or her tenure to whatever resolution historical data is kept.

3. Build propensity models for each product individually, making sure that the models produce comparable scores. The target variables for each model should reflect the way customers who now have the product looked at the time period immediately before they made the purchase. Our preferred approach is to assign each prospect to a leaf node of a decision tree built for the product and to use the percentage of existing customers at that leaf to assign a score for the product.

4. Except in the case where a customer gets a zero score for all products, each customer will have some product or products for which they have a higher score than the rest. That product is the best next offer.

Lessons Learned

This case study illustrates many important things about cross-sell models.

- A cross-sell model may be constructed by combining several independent models each of which predicts the propensity of a customer to buy a particular product. Combining models in this way requires building models whose scores are comparable.

- Before building customer-centric models, it is often necessary to transpose product-centric data to create a model set with one row per customer and columns for each of the products.

- The product definitions found in operational data may not match the product definitions most useful for model building. Often, similar products such as checking accounts with different minimum balance requirements can be lumped together into a single product. In other cases, it may be useful to split a single product category, such as credit cards, into two or more products such as high-limit credit cards and low-limit credit cards.

- Having a particular product is likely to change a customer's behavior. Therefore, it is important to avoid mistaking patterns that stem from product ownership for patterns that indicate a propensity to own the product. The best way to deal with this problem is to build models based on the behavior exhibited by current product owners before they acquired the product.

- The current composition of the customer population is largely a reflection of past marketing policy. This is one of the many factors that necessitates intimate business knowledge for successful data mining. Without access to this kind of historical information, data miners will "discover" the target markets of the past rather than the desirable prospects of today.

- An error-prone model that produces scores that allow records to be sorted is much more useful than an accurate model that yields the same prediction for all records. A model that predicts that no one will respond to an offer is likely to be right more often than a model that goes out on a limb and predicts that some people will respond positively, but the latter model can be used to select targets for a mailing while the first one has no practical use.

- Oversampling and record weighting are good ways to trick data mining algorithms into producing models that will recognize rare events.

- A very high cumulative response curve with a steep slope at the start and a shallow slope at the end is indicative of too easy a task. Models that only predict what everyone already knows are reassuring as evidence that the algorithms work, but have little value beyond that.

CHAPTER 11

Please Don't Go!
Churn Modeling
in Wireless Communications

In this chapter, we learn about building a churn model for a mobile telephone company. *Churn* is the word used in the telecommunications industry to refer to customers, so a *churn model* predicts which customers are likely to leave in the near future. Building churn models is a common application of data mining, across many different industries. And, more specifically, almost every mobile telephone company in the world (in competitive markets) is doing, or is on the verge of doing, churn modeling. Those that aren't, aren't competitive. In addition, churn scores can be used for various purposes, beyond just developing marketing campaigns to retain customers.

The model building in this case study was actually the first step in building a churn management application. Such an application is an excellent example of incorporating data mining into business processes. And, data mining was leading the effort at the outset instead of being retrofitted at the end. Building an application changes the nature of the data mining effort (see Figure 11.1). Instead of trying to find the single model with the best lift, the project needed to find the best way to build churn models in general. After all, we want the application to be as automated as possible with intelligent defaults along the way.

This case study also provides examples of good modeling practices, which we have been discussing throughout the book. Data is key; there are some interesting ways of transforming data into what is best for churn modeling. The final result of this effort was a model that combined four different decision tree models. It is also an example of SAS Enterprise Miner in action.

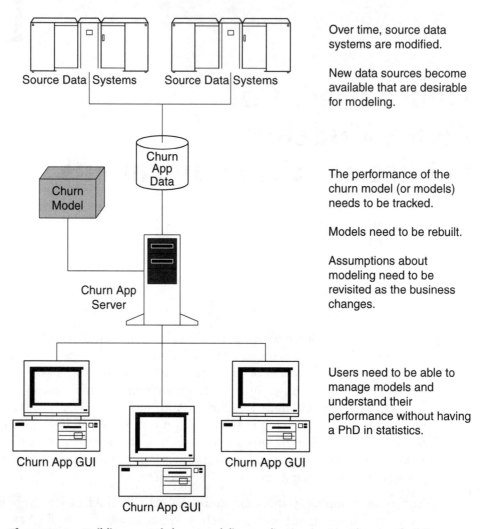

Figure 11.1 Building a good churn modeling application is more than just building a good model.

As with all the case studies, we start with some background on the industry.

The Wireless Telephone Industry

Every reader of this book is the customer of at least one telecommunications company—and probably several. Some of us may have different carriers for local telephone calls and long distance; some may use a dial-around service for international calls. Some may also carry a pager served by one company and a mobile telephone served by another.

Our own experience as customers often provides valuable insight when doing data mining. Why would we or our friends or colleagues change service providers? Service plans may no longer be competitive, or our handset may be too old. Changes in job responsibilities may change priorities, such as increasing or decreasing the need for international calling. It is interesting to consider how available data may reflect these different situations.

Our experience provides insight at the micro level, but these answers are not the whole story. This industry differs from other retailing and service industries. Even though no two companies are exactly alike, mobile telephone companies are more similar than different, offering similar services to similar markets using similar technology.

A Rapidly Maturing Industry

Once upon a time, wireless telephones were so popular that the leading service providers did not have to worry about customer churn. Many, many more customers would join than would leave in any given year. Such a period of exponential growth cannot last forever, since eventually everyone will have a mobile phone, saturating the market. Figure 11.2 illustrates the growth in the number of customers in a typical market, such as cellular. As we see, the number of churners and the effect of churn on the customer base grows significantly over time.

Figure 11.3 more clearly shows the increasing effect of churn. Initially, for every customer who churns, there are several new customers who sign up for the service. The focus during this stage is rightly on getting more and more new customers. Even eliminating churn entirely during this stage of rapid growth has little effect on the number of customers. As the market matures, the churn rate rises until each new customer merely replaces one who is leaving.

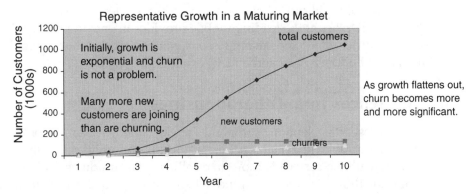

Figure 11.2 As exponential growth levels off, churn becomes a bigger and bigger problem.

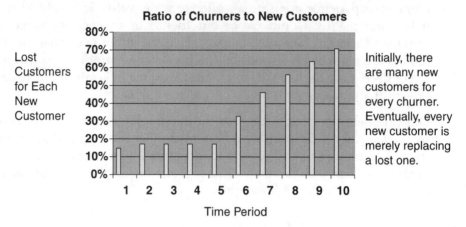

Figure 11.3 The number of churners gets larger and larger, choking off growth.

There is some limit on the total number of customers (such as the size of the population), so growth must stabilize at some point.

That is, as more and more people use cellular phones, the business shifts away from signing on nonusers in the general population. In a mature market, growth comes from three areas:

- Cross-selling and up-selling: maximizing the profit of existing customers
- Retention and up-selling: keeping profitable customers and getting rid of (or upgrading) unprofitable ones
- Poaching: stealing new customers from competitors

The cellular telephone market is in the process of maturing. Many parts of the world already have a more saturated market than the United States. This includes many developing countries, where a shortage of landline telephones has led to the rapid diffusion of wireless technologies. The case study in this chapter took place at the leading mobile provider in one of these newly developed countries. It contains many lessons, not only about churn modeling, but also about building good and effective models in general.

Some Differences from Other Industries

In many respects, telephone companies are just another example of the service industry, similar to financial services, insurance, and utilities. In other respects, selling telephone service is more like selling retail products. There are some important things to keep in mind when working in the mobile telephone industry:

Sole service provider ("customer monopoly"). Telecommunications companies tend to be "customer monopolies"; that is, any given customer tends to use only one provider for a particular service (although they may have a choice of many providers). This differs from other industries where customers have a choice with every purchase and customers' wallets are often split among two or more competitors. Being a "customer monopoly" implies that telecommunications companies have much more complete knowledge about their customers' behaviors relative to their products than do other industries.

Relatively high cost of acquisition. Subsidies for handsets and the need for credit checks raise the cost of acquiring customers beyond the usual marketing costs. The stream of revenue generated by each customer over time determines his or her value to the company. This implies that retaining an existing customer is much more valuable than attracting a new one, since retention efforts avoid up-front acquisition costs.

No direct customer contact. Customers almost never have face-to-face contact with their telephone providers. In fact, the only telephone contact is often only for customer service—and then usually only when there is a problem to report. This implies that telecommunications companies generate their image through brand management and direct marketing.

Little customer mindshare. Users of mobile telephones may not associate the service with their cellular carrier, except when service problems arise. After all, the telephone itself often carries the name of the handset manufacturer—Ericsson, Motorola, Nokia, Samsung, and so on—so unlike the credit card industry, say, there is little mindshare for the service provider. At the same time, handset manufacturers are also competing for brand awareness.

The handset. As with many other retail products, the wireless industry has vanity appeal—in the form of handsets. Newer telephones weigh less, offer more features, and are generally more appealing to the customer base. Handsets turn out to play a very important role in churn modeling.

There is also a tremendous amount of data potentially available. Telephone companies use switches to route calls. These switches are actually among the most powerful computers around, and they record every single call and attempted call made over the network. Nowadays, cellular companies can also use their network of receivers to determine the precise location of a customer using a phone. This is a wealth of information for marketing purposes. This wealth, though, poses problems in data management, because the data volumes are so large and the data so dirty. In addition, using very personal information raises some ethical questions about privacy, which we will not delve into in detail. However, it is worth realizing just how invasive call detail information can be; marketing campaigns can backfire if they exhibit too much knowledge about customers.

The Business Problem

The largest mobile telephone company in a newly developed country had been investing in decision support technology for several years. The mobile telephone market in their country had recently been deregulated and several recent entrants were growing rapidly. At the same time, the market was maturing and they recognized the need to move from reactive marketing to proactive customer management. They and their handful of competitors already supplied mobile services to over one-third of the country's population, with each of the other competitors having about half the number of subscribers of this company.

The maturing of the market and the increasing competition was now leading the company to focus on existing customers, how to keep them, and how to make them more profitable.

Project Background

Churn modeling was just one of the responsibilities of their newly formed database marketing team. Another relevant project was an ongoing data warehousing effort, whose prototype was the primary data source for this churn modeling effort. During the course of this effort, the data warehouse was in the process of being migrated to a larger platform with more functionality, more data, and more history. The first release was scheduled for delivery several months after the completion of this project.

Another relevant project was a decision support application based on relational OLAP (Microstrategy's DSS Agent) in its beta testing phase. This system allowed business users to slice and dice marketing and sales data along a number of dimensions, such as handset type, region, and time of day. The OLAP system proved very useful for the churn modeling effort by allowing quick answers to queries such as "What is the churn rate in April and May for Club members versus non-Club members?"

Throughout the churn modeling project, the client was also interested in learning how modeling efforts in the future would interact with other systems. What other requirements does churn modeling impose on the data warehouse and on the data marts?

Specifics about This Market

The wireless market is quite developed in the market the company serves. The company has over five million customers, with a very significant portion concentrated in major cities. Every month, about 1 percent of the customer base churns. Table 11.1 is indicative of the customer base.

High value customers belong to the "Club," which is analogous to frequent flyer programs at airlines. Customers qualify by generating enough revenue on their telephone. Membership entitles people to special discounts, promotions, and coupons.

People in this country depend heavily on their cellular phones. The typical customer makes about a dozen calls per day, not counting in-coming calls. The call volume at 10 P.M. is almost as high as it is throughout the day. This is in sharp contrast to the United States where call volumes decrease much more noticeably during off-peak and nonbusiness hours.

One of the reasons for the widespread use of mobile telephones in this and other developing markets is that mobile phone customers do not pay for incoming telephone calls—the person placing the call pays for it. This has allowed many people in developing countries to obtain wireless phones when they do not have access to landlines. Although this pricing scheme has been a considerable boost to the industry, it also means that the business rarely collects incoming call data. Switches record both incoming and outgoing calls, but only outgoing call data is passed into the billing system since the incoming calls are not charged. This is an unfortunate lack of data, because incoming calls contain important indicators of customer behavior. For instance, changing service providers usually entails changing telephone numbers. Someone who receives incoming calls from many other people is less likely to churn because of the hassle of giving a new telephone number to dozens of other people.

Table 11.1   A Comparison of Club versus Nonclub Customers

SEGMENT	# CUSTOMERS	% OF CUSTOMERS	CHURN RATE
Club	1,500,000	30%	1.3%
Nonclub	3,500,000	70%	0.9%
TOTAL	5,000,000	100%	1.1%

Note that the numbers in this and subsequent tables are representative of the actual numbers, but have been modified to avoid revealing the client's identity.

Another feature of this market is that about two-thirds of the customers have automatic payment. This means that their cellular bill is deducted monthly from a checking account or occasionally from a credit card. Although house-holding information was not available for consumers, sometimes multiple bills were assigned to one account—such as for all telephones in a household—providing a rudimentary form of householding for a subset of the customer base.

What Is Churn?

It is easy to talk about churn and the business value of developing predictive models for it. In fact, it is even easy to determine who has churned inside the data, because every billing telephone number has a field for the deactivation date. So what's the problem in defining churn?

There are several different types of churn. This database marketing group had already divided churn into voluntary and involuntary, which is a useful distinction. *Involuntary churn* occurs when a customer has not been paying the bill for several months. Predicting involuntary churn is very valuable, since the information can be used to reduce losses.

Voluntary churn is everything that is not involuntary churn. Unfortunately, the drivers for voluntary churn and involuntary churn can be similar in some cases. *It is very important that the model for voluntary churn not predict involuntary churn accidentally as well.* If it does, marketing will waste resources on campaigns to customers who are not going to pay their bills!

The problem with the definition of voluntary churn is that it encompasses many different situations:

- Customers who move out of the service area
- Customers who pass away
- Customers who can no longer afford a phone
- Customers who are lured to other service providers
- Customers who want to purchase a newer handset

This final category, called handset migration, merits further explanation. This company offers larger handset subsidies for new customers than they do for existing customers. People are smart, so this policy sometimes encourages existing customers to churn and rejoin in order to obtain the larger subsidies.

Sometimes, customers downgrade their service without churning. An example would be a customer that switched to a plan where his or her handset accepted incoming calls but did not allow outgoing calls. Service downgrades are not normally considered churn, although they can have a large impact on the value of these customers.

The final question about churn is "when." We know that every customer who joins is eventually going to disconnect for some reason, so a churn model predicting who will churn in the next hundred years is easy to produce—everyone is going to churn. The question of "when" is directly related to how the information will be used.

All of these possibilities suggest that a more refined definition of churn may be useful to the business. This project did not try to differentiate between different types of voluntary churn. The best approach for differentiating is often to build a model of who is going to churn first and then to figure out why (using another model).

Another approach to working with churn is to build models that predict each customer's tenure—how long each will remain a customer. Such models require a sufficient amount of historical data, which was not available. In addition, the purpose of the effort described here was to produce a list for interventions during an upcoming month. As a result, a churn model was most appropriate.

Why Is Churn Modeling Useful?

With a definition of churn, lots of data, and a powerful data mining tool we can develop models to predict the likelihood to churn. The key to successful data mining is to incorporate the models into the business.

Because this was a real project, we can admit one of the primary business drivers was an executive who insisted on having a churn model by the end of the year. His reasoning was simply that churn is becoming a bigger and bigger problem and well-run cellular companies have churn models. He wanted his company to be the best.

Fortunately, there are many good reasons for churn models besides satisfying the whims of executive management (even when they are right). The most obvious is to provide the lists to the marketing department for churn prevention programs. Such programs usually consist of giving customers discounts on air time, free incoming minutes, or other promotions to encourage the customers to stay with the company. For the case study, the cellular company belonged to a conglomerate, and their promotions offered products from sister companies that were not at all related to telephone usage.

Other applications of churn scores are perhaps less obvious. Churn is related to the length of time that customers are estimated to remain; that is, the customer lifetime. The idea is simple: If a group of customers have a 20 percent chance of churning this month, then we would expect them to remain customers for five months (one month divided by 20 percent). If the churn score suggested a churn rate of only 1 percent, then we would expect the customers to remain for one hundred months. The length of the customer lifetime can then be fed into models that calculate customer's lifetime revenue or profitability (also called lifetime customer value).

Churn models have an ironic relationship to customer lifetimes. If the churn model were perfect, then the scores would either be a 100 percent chance of churning in the next month, or a 0 percent chance. The customer lifetimes would then be either one month or forever. However, because the churn model is not perfect, it can provide insight into the length of customers' lifetimes as well.

Quite a different application is for prioritizing customer segments. If a segment is more likely to churn, perhaps they should not get the fabulous new offer for a discount on a handset—that will only start making money after the tenth month. Of course, giving them the discount might also encourage them to stay. The issue is not clear-cut, but having a churn score helps the business make more informed decisions.

Three Goals

The churn modeling effort had several goals. There was a near-term goal of returning value by building a list of probable churners for a marketing intervention. The approach taken to build this list could then be automated into a churn management application. And this churn management application would, in turn, be part of a larger customer relationship management system. Working with three such diverse goals is a challenge in any project.

Near-Term Goal: Identify a List of Probable Churners

One of the first tasks in the project was to talk to representatives from the marketing department and to understand *how* they would use a churn score. There had been attempts to build churn models in the past.

In the initial discussion with marketing, they pointed out a disappointing experience: a previous list of 10,000 likely churners had fewer than 3000 Club members. For churn interventions, the highest value customers interested them the most.

The type of intervention that they had in mind was to offer incentives to a list of about 10,000 customers using their outbound telemarketing center. These incentives were not related to telecommunications; they were discounts on products from other companies in the conglomerate that owned this company.

The discussions with the marketing group narrowed the initial focus considerably. Instead of assigning a churn score to all the customers, the marketing department only needed the top 10,000 for a marketing campaign. Instead of looking at all customers, only Club members were of interest. Instead of a nebulous deadline, the marketing department could act on the list if they received it by the 24th of the month.

The new near-term goal for the first half of the project became the following: By the 24th of the month, provide the marketing department with a list of 10,000 Club members most likely to churn. The value of involving business users cannot be overstated. This process illustrates the need to involve the business users to define the problem.

Trying to second-guess business users is bad practice. Data mining benefits from their insights and any successful effort will include their input.

The first phase of this case study provides an excellent example. Before this case study, efforts to build a churn model disappointed the business users. Why? The business users wanted to focus on Club Members for their churn prevention campaigns, and the lists provided to them did not contain enough members. Discussions with the marketing department turned a fuzzy goal—building a churn model—into a concrete goal—providing a list of 10,000 Club members who are most likely to churn by September 24th.

If you are involved with a data mining effort, you should ensure that communication channels to the business users are open.

Medium-Term Goal: Build a Churn Management Application

The medium-term goal was to build effective churn models to support a churn management application (we'll call it CMA). CMA was to be a refinement of the models built during the first few weeks of the project. It includes the models "under the hood." The modelers were not responsible for building the interface, just specifying what and how the models would work in the application.

This part of the project required educating the client about important issues for building a modeling application. After all, data mining tools provide the algorithmic guts to such an application. Besides running churn models, CMA also needed to

- Manage models
- Provide an environment for data analysis before and after modeling
- Import data and transform it into the input for churn models
- Export the churn scores developed by the models

These associated activities shift the focus from merely building a data mining model to automating model building as much as possible. Users of CMA would not need a Ph.D. in statistics to use it. In fact, a prototype of CMA that focused much too much on the statistics of modeling provided too little help in maintaining, testing, and updating models. Of course, the database marketing team never used this prototype, since it did not meet their needs.

The need to automate the model imposed several new requirements on the data mining model building:

- Automated model building is incompatible with changing the modeling technique every month, since end users are unlikely to be able to make educated decisions about logistic regression versus decision trees versus neural networks, and so on.

- Automated model building is incompatible with manually pruning decision trees, since users are unlikely to understand the details of manual pruning.

- Automated model building is incompatible with clustering, since it is important to understand clusters from both a business and a technical perspective.

- Automated model building needs to have very reasonable defaults set for modeling parameters; that is, the application should be the repository for the best practices in building models.

The need for automation also precluded some hybrid techniques, such as building a decision tree, taking a bunch of the most significant variables, and feeding them to a neural network (or, to a logistic regression routine). Such techniques are risky without being overseen by knowledgeable people.

Of course, CMA *could* implement interfaces so more advanced users would have access to more enhanced functionality. The issue here is defining a basic user interface so users do not have to understand all the details of modeling.

Long-Term Goal: Complete Customer Relationship Management

The long-term goal of the database marketing group was to include churn management as just another facet of a complete customer relationship management system. This initial project provided a good backdrop for discussing the Virtuous Cycle of Data Mining and customer lifecycle modeling. This project focused on building a model; the business still needs to deploy the model and to measure its effectiveness over time.

Approach to Building the Churn Model

Building a churn model is a good example of the Virtuous Data Mining Cycle in action. In any business, there is always a first time for data mining efforts focusing on churn or customer retention. As a market matures, understanding churn and customer attrition become critical parts of managing the business.

Define Churn

There are many different reasons why customers cease being customers. The most obvious distinction is between involuntary churn, referring to the cancellation of a customer's service due to nonpayment, and voluntary churn. Voluntary churn still encompasses many different reasons, from customers who move out of the service area, to customers who pass away, to customers who are lured away by competitors. Both voluntary and involuntary churn are worth predicting.

When defining churn, it is very important that the available data support the definition. We cannot ask data mining to predict the reasons for churn if we do not know them ourselves (although undirected data mining, through clusters, rules, and visualization, can suggest possible reasons). Involuntary churn is very well understood, since it requires cutting off someone's service. So defining voluntary churn as anything that is not involuntary is quite reasonable, and we should just be aware of the different factors responsible for churn.

Inventory Available Data

Churn modeling depends critically on the data that is available. In the wireless industry, the handset is often the most important factor relating to churn, as the case study illustrates. A basic set of data would be

- Data from the customer information file, such as age, gender, ZIP code, etc.
- Data from the service account file, such as number of handsets, pricing plan, activation date, etc.
- Data from the billing system, such as number of calls, total amount spent, roaming (where appropriate), etc.

If possible, it is also desirable to include call detail information. However, it needs to be reduced to some important behavior measures, such as sphere of influence (the count of distinct numbers called), number of incoming calls, and similarity of behavior to prototypical users (how much this customer is like an all-business customer, or a stay-at-home parent, or a college student).

Although the hourly call summaries did not prove particularly useful for this case study, we have found on other projects that call-related information can be a big driver of churn. On another project, we discovered a cluster of churners who had stopped roaming in the third month of service. This cluster, it turned out, was highly price sensitive and therefore highly susceptible to churn. They would roam in the first month, get the bill in the second month, and, finding it too expensive, they would stop roaming.

Another valuable source of information is customer service data. This sometimes has a paradoxical relationship to churn: We have seen companies where customers who bother to call customer service are less likely to churn than those who don't, perhaps because customer service is actually able to solve their problems.

Build Models

Since churn is an ongoing business problem, building the models is not a one-time event, such as building a response model for a single marketing campaign. For churn modeling, it is a good idea to experiment to determine which model provides a good fit to the data and to the business needs.

Decision trees are a good choice for modeling, since they provide rules that business users can understand. Other techniques, such as neural networks or boosting, reduces the understandability of the model as the price of a bit of incremental lift.

An important part of building the models is determining the right set of derived variables to include with the model. We recommend including variables that explain phenomena in the real world as opposed to including mere mathematical transformations. For decision trees, many mathematical transformations are of little use, since the decision tree algorithms, unlike neural networks or regression, only use the relative ordering of values and not their magnitudes.

Important derived variables (apart from churn rates) include: growth rates of numbers of calls over time; proportion of calls of different types; changes in the proportions; and calls to customer service. When detailed call data is available, there is a much richer ability to include customer behavior.

Deploy Scores

There are several ways to deploy churn scores within an organization:

1. The most static way is to make them available in a data warehouse or data mart environment. This is quite useful for business people, but it is important that they understand what the scores mean and the limitations on churn models.

2. Churn scores can also be used for marketing intervention campaigns. In this case, the scores may be generated for only a subset of the customers (such as the highest value customers or segments targeted by a competitor).

3. The business side may also use the churn scores for ongoing prioritization of customers for many different campaigns. They may want to focus some

campaigns on customers who are not likely to churn, to increase the value of the responses.

4. Finally, churn scores can be used to estimate customer longevity as a factor in computing estimated lifetime customer value. This starts to enter a gray area, since the estimate of the churn probability is only loosely related to customer longevity and directly predicting longevity is a better solution in the long-term.

Measure the Scores Against What Really Happens

Whenever approaching a data mining or modeling effort, measuring the results is a very important part of the process. In the case of churn modeling, it is important to measure two things:

1. How close are the estimated churn probabilities to the actual churn probabilities for each group? Answering this question requires measuring the actual churn rates for different groups and comparing the probabilities.

2. Are the churn scores "relatively" true? That is, does a higher churn score imply a higher probability of churn, even if the predicted probability is off?

The relative values of churn scores are often more important than the absolute values, so the second measurement is more important than the first. In some cases, such as using the churn probability in a customer lifetime value calculation, the accuracy of the probability is very important.

As with many such projects, measuring the results takes place over a longer time span and was not available for the case study. However, a key success factor was approaching the modeling with an open mind—and this revealed an interesting segment of customers, described later in the chapter.

The Project Itself

The project itself took place over a two-month period, with a senior data miner present for three weeks during each month. In addition, two experienced SAS programmers were involved with the project on a part-time basis to build data sets and to score the final model. An additional resource was available part-time to work as a liaison to the rest of the company and to learn about modeling. This does not count the occasional involvement of the marketing department and specific IT resources for obtaining data.

During the first month, the modeling effort focused on the refined business problem of returning a list of 10,000 Club members likely to churn. The second month of the project focused on finding effective models that could be incorporated into CMA.

Building a Churn Model: A Real-Life Application

This section starts diving into some technical detail of the churn modeling effort. The next section covers the data used in the project. In combination, these sections contain useful guidelines for churn modeling, and are condensed into a more usable format at the end of the chapter.

Data is data, but there are many different ways to approach modeling. To find the best model, this project tested various hypotheses. In general, a churn modeling effort needs to make a number of decisions:

- The choice of tool
- The type of model to build and which parameters to set
- Algorithm-specific choices, in this case pruning decision trees
- How to segment the data for modeling
- The size and density of the model set
- How to handle the time element
- Which data to include in the model and how to calculate derived variables

Using the case study as a guide, the next few sections will touch on each of these issues. Of course, these issues are not specific to churn modeling and the lessons apply to many different modeling exercises.

The Choice of Tool

Often, the first decision made when starting a modeling effort is the choice of data mining tool. In this case, SAS Enterprise Miner Version 2 was already installed inside the company and several consultants had been using SAS extensively (although no employees actually had hands-on experience with SAS EM). The choice of tool, therefore, was decided before the modeling effort even began.

Segmenting the Model Set

Early in the project, the marketing department had specified an interest in two different segments of customers: customers who were Club members and those who were not. Club members account for about one third of the total customer base and are automatically chosen by being high-value customers in the past.

At this point, there was a choice. Is the right solution to build one model and include Club membership as a flag? Or is it better to build two different models, one for the Club members and one for the rest? And how can we make this decision?

First, we discussed the issue with the business customers. Are the drivers for churn likely to be the same for the two groups of customers? Because of the different incentives, longevity, and usage, it seemed likely that the drivers for churn would be different. The churn rates for the two groups were quite similar, so we decided to build different models for each group: Club membership would be unlikely to appear as significant (since the churn rates were similar), although the business felt it important.

A third segment eventually provided the most insight of all. This segment consisted of recent customers who had joined in the previous eight or nine months. They were included as a separate segment because they had insuffi cient billing history. In such cases, it is often simpler to build a separate model for them than to try to deal with missing data. Of course, this is possible only if enough people churn, and the client was "lucky" in this respect. The three segments could be characterized roughly as shown in Table 11.2.

Even though the most recent customers had a very low churn rate, there were enough of them to account for about 8 percent of the churners. Models on different segments had different performance characteristics. We will talk about the implications of this in the next section.

The Final Four (Models)

The three models contained a big surprise: The model for recent customers performed very, very well. In fact, as Figure 11.6 shows, different types of models were able to characterize very well those customers who had joined in the previous nine months and then churned.

This led to some further investigation. Perhaps customers who join at about the same time have similar reasons for churn, and this insight can be applied to the other customer segments. Well, not quite. It turns out that most customers who have been around for more than a year are already Club members.

Table 11.2   Churn Rates by Customer Segment

	# CUSTOMERS	% OF CUSTOMERS	CHURN RATE	% OF ALL CHURN
Club	1,500,000	30%	1.3%	37%
Nonclub	1,750,000	35%	1.5%	55%
Recent	1,750,000	35%	0.2%	8%
TOTAL	3,250,000	100%	1.1%	100%

SAS Enterprise Miner

SAS EM offers a graphical user interface that provides access to key data mining functionality, including various flavors of decision trees, neural networks, regression, and clusters. EM is a full functionality tool, including the capabilities for connecting to databases (using ODBC) and SAS data sets; sampling; adding derived variables; splitting the model set into training, validation, and test sets; comparing the results from different models; and deploying models as SAS code.

Figure 11.4 shows a common EM screen. The screen has two windows. On the left are available node types, on the right is a diagram used to generate four models.

The line of nodes at the bottom of the diagram is a good example of building a simple model. The first node (called "Recent Source") reads the data, in this case from a SAS data set. The "Data Partition" splits it into a training, validation, and test set (the SAS terminology for what we call the training, test, and validation sets). "Recent Tree" is the decision tree model built for this data. The "Assessment" node compares the results from this and other models. What happens in the "SAS Code" node is explained later in this chapter and was necessary for pruning the decision tree.

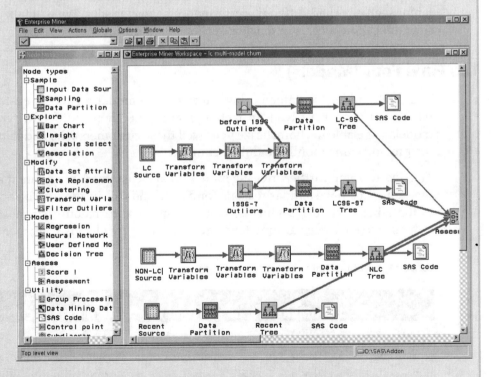

Figure 11.4 The SAS Enterprise Miner graphical user interface.

Figure 11.5 illustrates an EM session in action. This screen shot contains several different windows. On the upper left hand side are the available projects, each of which can contain multiple EM diagrams. The current diagram is in the background.

The Input Data Source window provides a view on the data being imported into the diagram. In this case, there are dozens of fields and one is highlighted: SET_YEAR. The histogram at the bottom of the screen shows the values for this variable.

The true power of EM is that it is built on top of SAS, which is a full-fledged programming and analysis environment for statisticians. This is a big advantage where SAS is already being used, although the reliance on base SAS steepens the learning curve for non-SAS users.

SAS Enterprise Miner (EM) is sold by SAS Institute (www.sas.com), whose statistical package is the most popular and widely used statistics software product.

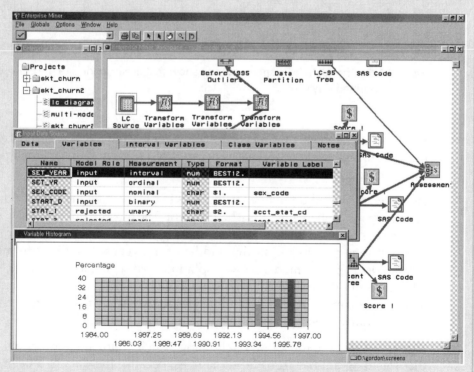

Figure 11.5   An EM session in action.

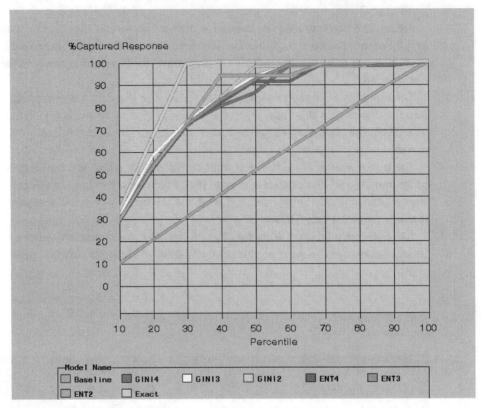

Figure 11.6 The captured response curves show that all six models for recent customers performed very well.

As Figure 11.7 shows, over 80 percent of the non-Club members were from the most recent complete year. That is because recent customers are ineligible for Club membership.

However, the idea did provide the impetus to test it out on the Club model. This histogram for Club members is a bit different. The most recent year has very few members, since membership is based on usage and billing for an entire calendar year. Customers who join in the middle of the year are unlikely to meet the thresholds. The Club model set was split into two segments, one for customers who joined in the previous two years (about 45 percent) and one for the rest (about 55 percent). The models built on these two segments provided an incremental improvement over using a single model for all the Club members.

Figure 11.4 showed the four models being built in a single EM diagram. Notice that this diagram has three input sources, because the data had been physically partitioned during the data transformation step (this was an arbitrary choice since EM could have filtered the data as well). The Club members seg-

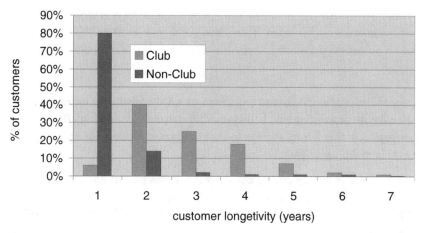

Figure 11.7 The proportion of customers in the two major segments by the year they joined (1 is the previous year, 2 the year before that, etc.).

ment is then split again in the diagram, for recent customers and older customers. Having all four models on the same diagram not only shows all the processing in a single view, it also makes it possible to score records and compare results easily.

Combining the four models into a single one requires two steps. First, the score set must be split into three parts, one each for Club members, non-Club members, and recent customers. EM takes care of splitting the Club members. Second, EM must convert the scores into a predicted rate of churn, taking the oversampling rate into account. The churn rate for each of the four segments of customers varies somewhat from each other, so the oversampling rate is different for the four. The predicted churn rate is then used for all customers, regardless of which model originally scored them.

For this work, SAS code was used to score the models instead of EM. EM easily converts models to SAS code by using the not-so-aptly-named "Score Model" node. SAS procedures were then used to calculate the predicted churn rate. The ability to export SAS code is quite useful in environments that already use SAS as a data transformation tool.

Choice of Modeling Algorithm

Decision Tree models have several advantages for churn modeling. During the exploratory phase of model development, their ability to handle hundreds of fields in the data helps to sift through the many basic and derived variables. This can be invaluable as an aid when brainstorming to figure out new fields to include in the model. Of course, decision trees also readily show which fields are highly significant for predicting the target variable. As we learned several times during this modeling effort, several variables were indeed too useful for predicting churn. These are variables such as the termination reason and termination date, which should not have been included as inputs at all.

Business users often have a strong sense of what constitutes important customer segments. Incorporating this knowledge can improve modeling efforts, and one way to incorporate this information is to build different models for each segment. When does this make sense?

- **When there is a clear and relatively stable definition of each of the customer segments, and the segments are nonoverlapping.**
- **When there are enough records to build effective models for all the different segments.**
- **When you are prepared to take a multimodel approach and combine the results from the models.**

Another advantage of segmenting the data is that it is often more feasible to partition the data and build several smaller models than to use all the data and build one big model. Each of the models can be tweaked for data in that segment, so the Club membership segment, for example, could contain length of time as a Club member and any special offers used by the member. Of course, building separate models for different segments is only advantageous when you believe that you can segment the customers better than the automatic data mining algorithms.

The explanatory power of decision trees is another advantage. Business users understand rules and understand the idea that certain variables are more important than others. These make decision trees a natural choice for applications involving not-so-technical end users.

Finally, it is pretty easy to automate decision trees. Although pruning decision trees is always a challenge (in a later section, we will discuss alternatives to the pruning that we used), the basic decision tree modeling process is quite simple: Assign a bunch of parameters to reasonable defaults, create the model set, throw the model set at the model, and just wait for the decision tree to come back. There is no need to choose the most important variables, or to figure out how to bin continuous values, or how to encode categorical variables, and so on. The algorithm is a natural for an automatic system such as CMA.

Different Types of Decision Trees

EM supports three different types of splitting function for generating decision trees: CHAID, Entropy, and Gini. The textbook definition of CHAID generally does not perform as well as the other two, so it was not considered for modeling.

One of the drawbacks to CHAID is that it can only handle categorical variables, so continuous values have to be binned somehow. EM has an implementation of CHAID that automatically bins continuous values. And, in fact, during the course of testing different models, it proved that EM's implementation of CHAID performs about as well as the other algorithms, even providing intelligent splits on continuous values.

EM offers the option of using multiway splits. Multiway splits are appealing, because they make it easier to isolate extreme values. Figure 11.8 illustrates what a typical EM diagram looked like during the exploratory portion of this project where different decision trees were tested (using Gini and entropy as splitting functions, and allowing 2-, 3-, and 4-way splits). Typically, six models were built on any particular model set or in testing any particular combination of parameters.

One purpose of building six models at the same time was to see which performed the best and to get familiar with the performance of the models on the data. Figure 11.9 shows a lift graph for several different models at the same time. The performance of the different types of models is generally pretty

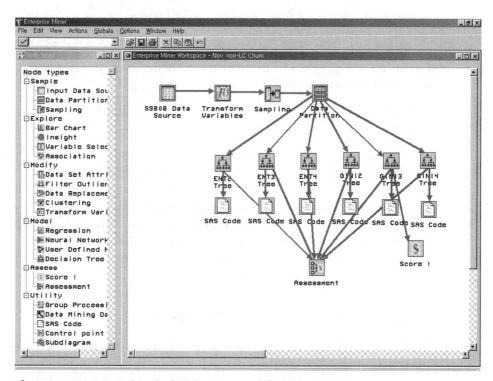

Figure 11.8   Comparing six decision tree models using SAS EM.

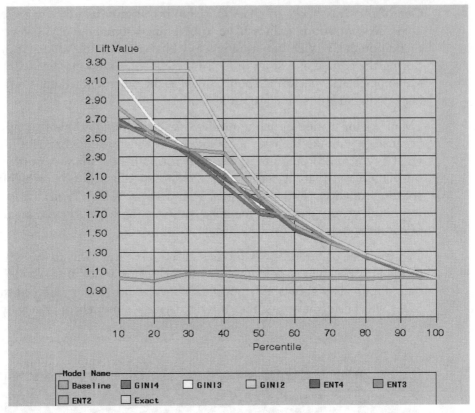

Figure 11.9 This lift chart for six different models; the line at the top represents the theoretical best the models can do.

similar, although it is not uncommon for one or two to be noticeably better than the rest.

Another important reason for building all these models was for the models to verify each other. Think of each model as giving a different view on the data, and their commonality provides insight. Which variables do the models consistently use? Which are different? Are the points where splits are made for continuous variables consistent? When one model is radically different from the others, the information from other models built at the same time helps us to determine if the model really is better (has it uncovered something in the data) or if the results are just a fluke.

Important EM Decision Tree Parameters

In addition to the splitting function and number of children, EM offers several other parameters for creating decision trees. We recommend that you think about the values for these parameters, because adjusting them can have a significant effect on the results. All of these parameters are accessed in EM by opening the decision tree node.

The *minimum size of a leaf node* determines the minimum number of rows from the training set that must land in a particular leaf node. EM refuses to consider any splits that do not meet this criterion. The smaller the value, the more likely the tree will overfit the training set. The larger the value, the more likely that the tree will miss important and relevant patterns. We found that on model sets with 50,000 records, a value of 50 was too small, and overfitting visibly affected the results. Raising the value to 250 for training sets with 100,000 and 150,000 rows improved the trees. Our recommendation is a value of between about 0.25 and 1 percent of the size of the model set.

When considering whether to split a node, EM has another parameter: It only considers splitting nodes larger than the *minimum size of a node to split*. The larger the value, more shallow the tree. The smaller the value, the deeper the tree. In general, we set this to twice the value of the minimum leaf size, typically using a value of 500.

These two values together determine how many records fall at each leaf. The more records there are at each leaf, the more likely that the results on the training set will hold for other sets of data. This is the law of large numbers.

EM also lets the user control the *maximum depth of the tree*. The default value of 6 is insufficient; for this effort, 10 was used. Because of difficulties visualizing trees online, the trees were often printed out. Deeper trees require much larger amounts of paper.

Pruning Decision Trees

The first decision trees built for the churn modeling project were too bushy; that is, they had too many leaves and were clearly overfitting the training set. The basic decision tree algorithm works by creating very large and very bushy trees. Lurking inside this large tree is a smaller tree that does a much better job of prediction (see Figure 11.10). To find the smaller tree, the decision tree algorithms measure the performance of the every node on the test set, eliminating leaves and nodes that do not improve predictability. This part of the algorithm is known as *pruning* the decision tree.

The details of EM's pruning algorithm are not appropriate for this chapter. However, it was obvious that the algorithm failed on these trees because they consistently produced the largest trees or trees with only one node. Arbitrarily setting the size of the tree to a lower level always yielded better results on the test (we usually use the term "test" set for what EM calls the "validation set;" and what EM calls the "test" set we call the "evaluation" set). This prob-

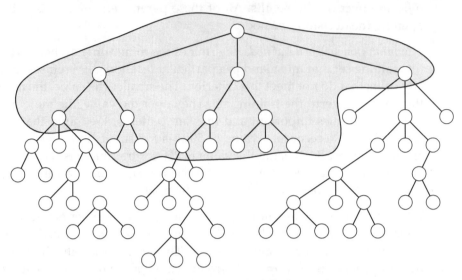

Figure 11.10   The challenge of pruning is to find the best subtree.

lem was particularly evident when using very sparse model sets, with less than 10 percent density of churners.

To fix this problem, the team developed SAS code to prune the trees for lift at a given percentile. That is, the code would find the subtree that produced the best lift on the top 1 percent of the data, or the top 10 percent of the data.

Increasing the density of churners in the model set to 30 percent greatly improved the performance of EM's built-in pruning algorithm. Even so, there were still some issues regarding churn. Looking at individual trees, it was possible to find highly suspect nodes that logically should have been pruned back. Fortunately, though, these nodes were in the minority and did not have a big effect on tree performance.

How Do You Know That Pruning Is Not Working?

Pruning is an issue whenever we use decision tree algorithms. Since pruning algorithms are buried deep inside the algorithmic code, it might seem difficult for mere humans to understand if pruning is working well. This is not the case—it is actually quite easy. Pruning is good when a tree is consistent—more specifically, when the results on the test set are similar to the results on the training set.

Figure 11.11 is a snapshot of part of a decision tree that has an example of bad pruning. This tree has three levels: At the top is the split for AGE > 35.5, followed by splits on `ZIP_RT`, and `TOT_CL` (EM happens to give the formula instead of the variable name). Each node has two columns of numbers. The first is for the training set and the second for the test set. The top two rows are the percentages of churners ("1") and nonchurners ("0"), followed by absolute counts, and then the totals.

Let's look at the `TOT_CL` level (where the arrow is pointing). There are three splits, resulting in the following ratios of churners for the training set: 48.9% churners, 41.8% churners, and 53.2% churners. There is some difference between 41.8% and 53.2%, so a split here does make sense.

Now look at what happens on the validation set. The results are 47.8%, 47.3%, and 47.3%—virtually identical and indistinguishable from the ratio on the parent node (47.5%). This is bad pruning. The data has overfit the training set and these leaves should have been pruned back.

In the actual case, this was a tree than ran on the non-Club members with additional fields for calls by day and calls by hour. Sometimes additional variables do not help. Since these were actually hurting the performance of the tree, the variables were removed from the model set.

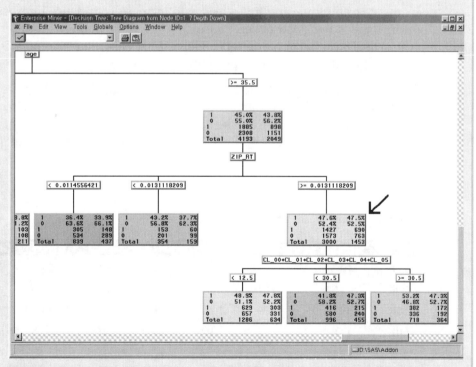

Figure 11.11   Below this node, the performance on the test set (second column) is quite different from the performance on the training set (first column), indicating a problem with pruning.

The Size and Density of the Model Set

The size and churner density in the model set definitely have an effect on performance. The previous section explained that low densities produced very poorly pruned decision trees. This section covers the efforts to find the optimal size and density for building models.

It is almost always true that using a larger model set will produce better models. However, the larger the model set, the longer it takes to build any given model. And longer build times mean that there is less time for experimentation and learning about the data. So small model sets can be useful.

Table 11.3 shows the predicted churn rates for different models built on different model sets. When measuring the effect of model set density, it is important to convert the model scores into predicted churn rates by taking into account the oversampling rate (explained in Chapter 7). The predicted churn rate for the top 1 percent of the validation set (the highlighted box is the maximum value in each row) is shown in Table 11.3.

The table clearly shows that the model set with 30 percent churners and 50k records uniformly produces a better lift for all six types of decision trees. One advantage of building multiple trees is to increase confidence in exactly this sort of knowledge. Also notice that increasing the density of churners for a given size always produces better model results. We did not extend this investigation beyond a density of 30 percent.

The table also shows that there is no single best model. Both Entropy and Gini sometimes give the best results; 2-way, 3-way, and 4-way splits are also spread among the best models. To choose one model over the others was hard, but necessary. The GINI-3 tree and ENT-2 tree gave almost identical results on the

Table 11.3 One Percent Lift for Different Models

SIZE	DENSITY	ENT2	ENT3	ENT4	GINI2	GINI3	GINI4
20K	10.3%	4.94	7.37	6.59	4.97	5.47	6.59
20K	17.9%	6.66	7.05	7.06	6.66	7.38	-
50K	9.9%	5.89	5.55	5.83	5.39	5.61	5.61
50K	17.8%	8.20	6.94	7.22	7.04	6.45	6.85
50K	30.5%	11.70	11.53	11.59	9.85	11.68	11.59
100K	10.0%	7.20	8.16	-	7.90	7.75	8.20
100K	17.9%	9.22	10.12	10.14	9.23	9.34	10.18

30 percent density model set. ENT-2, in general, either performed very well or very poorly among the six models; GINI-3 seems to have more consistent performance. For that reason, the final four models used GINI-3.

The Effect of Latency (or Taking Deployment into Account)

As we discussed in Chapter 7, the time element is critical to successful model building. It is critical to separate time into the past, the present, and the future. The past is data that is available when the model is ready to be deployed. The future is what we are trying to predict. The present is the time that it takes to gather the data, build the model, and deploy the results. Only data from the past can be used as inputs into the model. Data from the present and future is simply not available when it is needed. Keeping these time periods in mind is critical for building effective models.

Previous models built at this company exhibited the classic mistake of modeling the present instead of the future. The top part of Figure 11.12 shows this mistake. Several months of past data were used to predict the next month. For instance, February through May data was used to predict outcomes in June. Sounds correct, but not in the real world.

Now we want to apply the model to predict outcomes in July, and it is the end of June. When is the data for June available? Not for a while! In this company, the data is available by about the end of the second week of the month. So the model that predicts churn in July does not even have its data until the middle of the month. And then, how long does it take to transform the data, score the model,

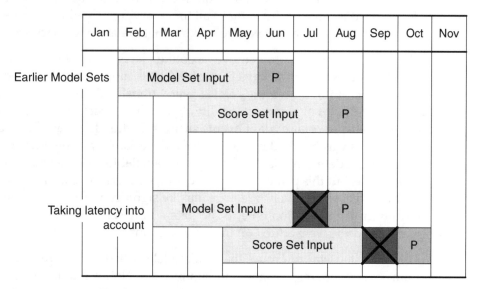

Figure 11.12   Taking latency into account means skipping a month.

deliver the scored list, and decide upon some action? At least another week. It is the end of the July before we can apply the model to predict July churn. Churners identified by the model have already left if the model is any good.

For this effort, we needed to leave a month of lag time to allow for scoring the model in the real world, as shown in the bottom part of Figure 11.12. The latency had another beneficial effect. In the models with no latency, one of the most significant factors of churn was when call volume dropped to zero in the most recent month. Well, in fact, this represented customers who had already turned off their handsets but had not yet formalized the process or there was a few-days delay in setting the deactivation date. In practice, these customers are not good candidates for churn prevention.

Translating Models in Time

The churn model uses data from the past to predict the future. This implies that the model must slide forward in time. Certain steps help to ensure that models can move forward in time.

The first step was to make all data relative to the "present." The present is the first day of the month of latency (which corresponds to the first day of the month when scoring will take place for the scoring data set). For the time series data, this implies making fields relative to the churn date rather than absolute time. Use names like CALL_1 and CALL_2 instead of CALL_JUN and CALL_MAY. Notice what happens with absolute names. A name like CALL_JUN may be four months before the churn date in the model set. However, it will then be six months before the churn date when the model is first deployed. It is more useful to make all time-varying behaviors relative to scoring month (which is equivalent to making them relative to the churn date).

The second step was to remove absolute dates wherever they occurred. Absolute dates almost always cause trouble as models are deployed further and further into the future. Dates were translated into days before the "present." But what about seasonality? Some things occur because of the time of year, because of important events such as the holiday season and back-to-school. This was handled by adding back in variables for the year and month of important dates. In this data set, the only available date was the service activation date, but this principal applies to other dates as well. When other dates are available, some other difference may be significant, such as the number of days from the activation date to the date a new service was added or additional handsets were added on the same account.

The third step was to ensure that the model set had a mixture of churn data from several months, as shown in Figure 11.13. Notice that in this chart, June

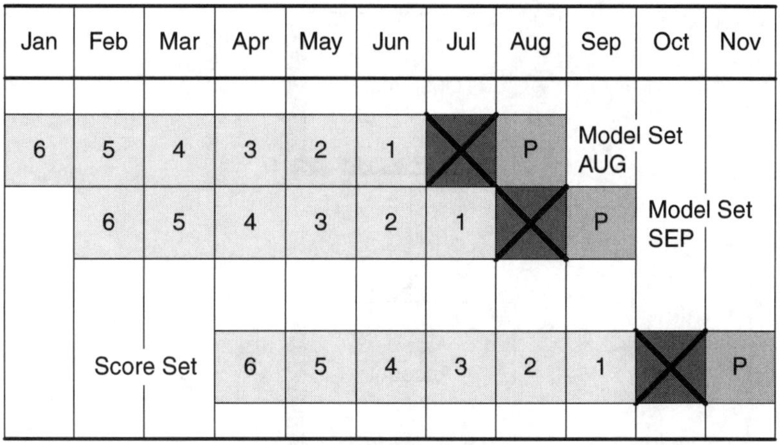

Jan	Feb	Mar	Apr	May	Jun	Jul	Aug	Sep	Oct	Nov
6	5	4	3	2	1	✕	P	Model Set AUG		
	6	5	4	3	2	1	✕	P	Model Set SEP	
	Score Set		6	5	4	3	2	1	✕	P

Figure 11.13   To avoid problems with time, a good model set (1) includes data from several months; (2) includes a month of latency; and (3) counts the months back from the month of latency.

data for a customer in Model Set Aug corresponds to month 1. The same data would correspond to month 2 for Model Set Sep.

This model time chart is typical. The modeling effort took place during the month of October, when data for Model Set Aug and Model Set Sep was available. By the end of the month, predictions for November could be made.

The Data

The primary source of data for this project was a prototype data warehousing system, using Informix on a multiprocessor Sun system. This system had a minimum amount of data modeling associated with it. Basically files from operational systems were downloaded into relational tables. Because much of the data came from the billing system, it was reasonably accurate and complete.

There were certain reference tables that were not available directly in the Informix system and needed to be added from other systems. However, no external data was incorporated into the model. At the time the modeling was taking place, approximately nine months of data was available for the project.

The Basic Customer Model

Figure 11.14 is a high-level entity-relationship diagram that describes the data in this project. The definition of customer is rarely obvious in most business environments, and the same is true here.

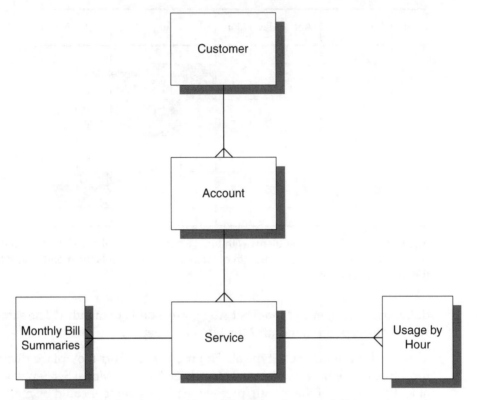

Figure 11.14 The important entities available for churn modeling.

The most important level is the service level. A *service* is the access to the telephone network provided to a single telephone number, usually associated with a single telephone handset. Churn at the service level was of primary interest, since one of the most important measures of the business is the number of active telephone numbers.

As mentioned earlier, most customers automatically pay their telephone bills through automatic payment on a banking or credit account. The *account* level refers to this actual account. Multiple services can share an account, for instance, when there are several telephones in a household. In fact, one of the billing plans, the family plan, provides discounts for multiple services that all pay from the same account.

The *customer* level is the least defined of all. It is used only when a customer signs up for a new service, and is not particularly useful for churn modeling. It is included here only to note that what is called a customer may not be the right level for modeling.

WARNING

■■■■ Much effort has gone into creating databases and creating names for important entities. When doing modeling for customer relationship management, it would seem natural to use the data at the customer level. However, this may not be appropriate. And, in some cases, the model of the customer does not even include an entity called "customer." Understand the data; don't just use the names.

From Telephone Calls to Data

Figure 11.15 provides a high-level view of how data about a call moves through various data systems. A receiver receives a signal from a handset and maintains contact with the handset. It, in turn, passes the call over to a telephone switch that records every call passing over the switch. This record is called a *call detail record* and it tells who is making the call, the number called, the duration, time of day, and so on. The switches also record dropped calls,

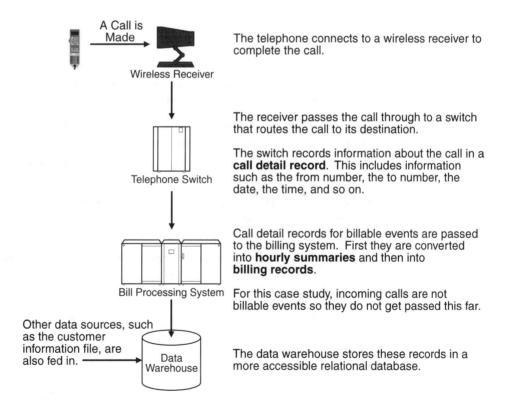

Figure 11.15 This is a high-level view of how data about a telephone call flows from the telephone into the data warehouse.

incomplete call attempts, and incoming calls, although these are not often used by the business. It is also possible to use data from the receivers to identify the exact location of the call. However, positional data (beyond the region covered by the tower) is not yet available for large-scale data mining efforts.

Call detail records for billable events are passed into the billing system, which categorizes and summarizes and slices and dices them to produce bills sent to customers. The billing system classifies calls into different categories, such as mobile-to-mobile calls, overseas calls, calls to value-added services (similar to 900 number in the U.S.), calls to directory assistance, and so on. The data in the billing systems provides a rough summary snapshot of customer behavior every month, and it is generally the only customer usage that is available for modeling. In addition, this project had access to some hourly summaries of data that provided some value for the segments containing Club members.

The billing systems, the call detail records, and other data sources are then fed into the decision support systems, such as the data warehouse that contains a history of data from the customer perspective. The first prototype of the data warehouse provided the bulk of the data used for this project.

Historical Churn Rates

One of the best predictors of churn in the near future is the recent history of churn, along different dimensions in the data. For this model, the historical churn rate was calculated along several different dimensions:

Handset churn rate. The churn rate for the handset was measured and then included in the data. The churn rates varied from 0.03 percent for the most popular and recent handsets to over 10 percent for older handsets with few users.

Demographic churn rate. The churn rate was measured for a combination of demographics including gender, age group, and geographic area, for a total of several hundred different combinations.

Dealer churn rate. The churn rate for each dealer where the customer bought his or her handset was included in the data.

ZIP code churn rate. The churn rate for the ZIP code of the customer's billing address (actually based on the first four digits of the ZIP code).

These churn rates turned out to be very significant in the churn models.

One of the best indicators of future behavior is past behavior. To predict churn, we want to include historical churn rates in the data. In fact, the business is quite aware that handsets are a major driver of churn—and the handset churn rate almost always turned out to be the most significant variable in the predictive models.

Data at the Customer and Account Level

The customer and account level contain basic descriptive information, including

- Social security number.

- ZIP code of residence. Summary demographic information for the ZIP code was not available for this project.

- Market id. The company split their service area into different marketing regions.

- Age and Gender. These fields would not normally be considered to be accurate. However, the social security number in the country where this study took place encodes the date of birth and the gender, and a valid social security number was required when signing up for service.

- Pager Indicator Flag. The company also offers paging services.

Typically, the information available at the customer level is rather sparse and often inaccurate because this data is usually self-reported at the time of purchase. And a network of geographically dispersed dealers usually collects this data. Front-line sales people who have little incentive to collect clean data rarely do. For this reason, we did not use other data, such as reported income, reported occupation, and so on.

Data at the Service Level

The data provides information at the service level that gives insight into the nature of the specific service:

- The activation date and reason for activation (and deactivation date for churned customers)

- The features ordered by the customer

- The billing plan

- Handset type, manufacturer, weight, analog versus digital, and so on

- Dealer where the service was activated

This data was judged to be quite accurate. Unfortunately, the network of dealers included both internal dealers and independent dealers, so consistent information about them was not possible to obtain. In particular, we would have liked to include information such as the size of the dealer and the actual price paid for the handset.

Data Billing History

The billing history contained monthly summaries for nine months. The billing history contained only a few different line items, such as:

- Total amount billed, late charges, and amount overdue
- All calls (number of calls and amount billed)
- Overseas calls (number of calls and amount billed)
- Fee-paid services, such as 900 numbers in the United States (number of calls and amount billed)
- Directory assistance charges

This data provided several time series for this modeling effort.

Rejecting Some Variables

During the course of modeling, it became obvious that certain fields were doing more harm than good, usually because the models were overfitting the training data. This case study employed several strategies for identifying and working with fields that hurt.

Variables that cheat. First, it is critical to eliminate future variables that are redundant with the target. In this data, termination reason and deactivation date were always very good predictors of deactivation! Fortunately, the decision tree made this obvious, so they could easily be removed when they were accidentally left in.

Identifiers. The second category consists of identifiers, such as customer ID, telephone number, and social security number, which are useless as inputs into models. They uniquely (or almost uniquely) identify every single row, giving the algorithm no new information about each row. Fortunately, EM does a good job of identifying these variables and eliminating them from the models.

Very high skew. At the other extreme are variables that are so highly skewed that all or almost all the values are identical. One of the parameters of the decision tree algorithm is the *minimum leaf size*. If all values for a variable are the same except for at most about *minimum leaf size*, then that variable can be safely ignored: the decision tree algorithm will never use it to split a node (including such variables merely increases the time it takes to build models).

Categoricals with too many values. The next set of rejected variables consisted of categorical variables with hundreds of values. The total number of churners in one month is only about 50,000. So, for categoricals with many values, there are at most a couple of hundred churners in any given category—and the values tend to be quite skewed. Clearly such categorical variables have some meaning, so it is not wise to eliminate them entirely. Here are some ways that this project worked with them:

- Values were grouped into larger units, such as dealer locations that were grouped into market areas.

- Additional lookup information was included for handset model, such as the manufacturer and the weight.

- Historical churn rate for value was included for variables such as dealer number and handset model.

Another approach not used in this project is simply to gather all the less frequently occurring values together into a single categorical.

Absolute dates. Absolute dates represent fixed points in time that make it unlikely that the model can be applied well in the future. As discussed earlier in this chapter, there are two sets of variables used to replace absolute dates. The first is the relative information for which this project used number of days before the present. It is sometimes useful to take the relative offset from other dates. The second is seasonality information that is included by storing the year and month, and sometimes the day of the month and the day of the week as separate variables.

Untrustworthy values. Some of the variables simply do not contain trustworthy data. This was particularly true of marketing data collected when new customers sign up for service. The sales force has little or no incentive to collect good data, so information about occupation, salary, and so on could not be relied upon. Other data, such as the weight in grams of handsets, was similarly known to be unreliable.

Derived Variables

There are two approaches to adding derived variables. One is to add only variables that make sense; that is, including variables which, if significant, can be explained to business users who are barely numerate (it is good to plan for the worst case). The second approach is to add combinations of variables that seem important, even if they do not make apparent sense. This project took more of the second approach.

The billing system provided several sets of time series data for each customer. These series contained six months of data for things like the number of calls per month and the amount overdue each month. For all of the time series data, additional variables were added:

- The summation of values over all months and their variance
- The ratio of each month's value to the total
- The ratio between successive months and between the first and last months
- Ratios within a month, such as the ratio of domestic and overseas usage to the total number of calls made in the month

In other words, the project took a very liberal approach to adding derived variables. In fact, many variables were redundant and would characterize a single situation. Take, for instance, a customer who stops calling during one month. Not only is the number of calls for that month 0, but so are the ratio of different types of calls within the month, the ratio of calls to the total, and the ratio of calls between months, and so on for units and usage. Although this situation is fairly obvious, others are subtler. The project was not long enough to take a more intelligent approach to the derived variables that would start to eliminate the redundancy. In fact, finding a small set of effective derived variables is a long-term learning task for the data mining group.

Besides, decision trees do a good job of sorting through hundreds of variables so people do not have to. There is a caveat, though. Two decision trees may not look alike in the variables that they choose, but they may be fundamentally similar. Each node divides the population into about the same sets for its children. The rules look different because different variables had close to the same effect.

Some additional derived variables proved useful as well. The age of the customer and the length of service both suggested interesting variables. For instance, what portion of a customer's life has he or she been a customer? This is the length of service divided by the customer's age. What is a rough estimate of the customer's worth so far? A rough estimate is the length of service in months times the average amount billed in a month.

A minor point about implementing the derived variables: Almost all the derived variables were added using SAS code instead of using the transform variables node in EM. One reason was the availability of seasoned SAS programmers. More important, though, the SAS code could easily be applied to data sets for the four segments without much trouble. Also, since SAS code is strictly text, it is easier to input when defining lots of variables. EM requires using both the mouse and the keyboard for creating new derived variables, which can be a cumbersome task for more than a handful. The transform variables node was used for a few on-the-fly derivations.

Lessons about Building Churn Models

One of the ideas we have stressed throughout the book is the need to be open-minded when approaching any data mining effort. This case study provides some lessons in building churn models. Some of these lessons are about the particulars of churn models. Others are more general.

It is important to listen to the data and to let it be the guide. At the same time, technical and business hurdles must also be overcome. Data mining requires being flexible and listening. This churn modeling effort reinforced these data mining lessons.

Finding the Most Significant Variables

History is the best predictor of the future, and churn is no exception. Topping the list of significant variables is the handset churn rate. It appeared at the top node in almost every tree built during the course of the project. Other historical churn rates, such as churn by demographics and ZIP code, were typically present in the trees as well.

Another very important variable was the number of different telephones in use by a customer. This variable was added rather late in the modeling process. It turns out that customers with multiple telephones are much, much less likely to churn than their counterparts with one telephone. Other important variables included the number of changes of features over time, age, and the market serving the customer.

In terms of usage, the most important billing variable seemed to be a decline to 0 usage in the most recent month. This was often expressed in different ways, such as very low values for ratios that included usage for the month. Surprisingly, billing data rarely appeared near the top of trees, although it was an important discriminator further down.

Listening to the Business Users

Before the project began, the primary goal was to create a model that could assign a churn score to all customers. During the first week of the project, the marketing group explained exactly what they needed in order to act on a model: a list of 10,000 names of Club members. The focus changed to meet the needs of the marketing group.

The next goal was to assign a churn score to all customers, presumably by building a single model. From discussions with the business users, though, it was evident that Club members and non-Club members were very different segments. This led to the decision to build two different models, and then combine them.

Listening to the Data

Data miners have two ears, one for listening to the business users and the other for listening to data. The two models suggested by the business users quickly became three out of the realization that not all customers would have six months of billing history. Recent customers became the target of the third model.

And then a very strange thing occurred. The model for churn for recent customers far and away outperformed the other models, as shown in the lift diagram in Figure 11.16. The churn model for recent customers provided lift, at the high end, of over 50, when oversampling is taken into account. This is a rare event in data mining, and we wish we could promise it on all engagements. It led to further investigation.

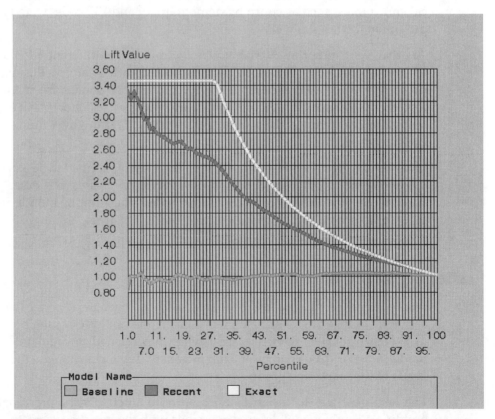

Figure 11.16 The lift curve for the segment of recent customers is close to the theoretical best possible.

Of course, one possible explanation might have been that the billing data was interfering with a good model. Could adding the billing data hurt model performance? This is not as far-fetched as it sounds; some variables, such as the ZIP code and dealer number, were known to hurt performance because the model used them to overfit the training set. This is a simple enough hypothesis to test. Happily, removing the billing data for the other segments produced worse models. Hooray for more data!

In fact, the actual explanation is quite interesting. Part of the decision tree for recent customers showed the following rules:

■ Number of handsets on the account is 1

■ Billing plan is family basic

■ Handset has a somewhat higher churn rate

This is a curious phenomenon. There should be multiple handsets on an account with the family plan. What is happening is that we are finding smart customers. Existing customers do not get any discounts on new handsets. Well, if they join the family plan, and add a new handset, and then cancel their old one—they can still get a discount. Being able to see the rule (using decision trees) has revealed an important and interesting customer segment.

Including Historical Churn Rates

This case study does illustrate one of the most important lessons in data mining: the past is often the best predictor of the future. For churn, the past is often in the form of churn rates. For each series of data, the churn rates should be calculated for the most recent month that data is available (see Figure 11.17), even though the month is different for different parts of the model set and score set. This helps ensure that the model can slide through time better.

There are a number of different churn rates that might prove useful:

■ Churn rate by handset model type

■ Churn rate by demographics (age, gender, etc.)

■ Churn rate by area (based on ZIP code or market ID)

■ Churn rate by usage patterns

This last one implies breaking down usage into a few dimensions, such as quintiles for total billing, total number of calls, and average duration of calls, and determining the churn rate for each cell.

In all these cases, the number of different cells should be between about 50 and 500. Although it would seem desirable to combine them (such as churn rate by

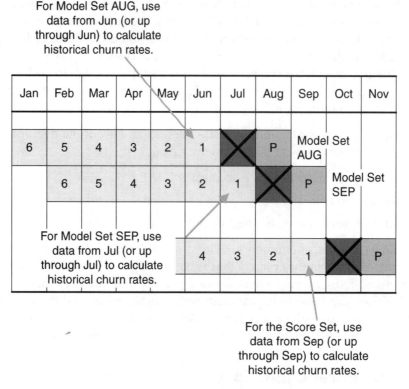

For Model Set AUG, use data from Jun (or up through Jun) to calculate historical churn rates.

For Model Set SEP, use data from Jul (or up through Jul) to calculate historical churn rates.

For the Score Set, use data from Sep (or up through Sep) to calculate historical churn rates.

Figure 11.17 When calculating historical churn rates, use the most recent month for each series of data.

handset model, age and gender, and area and usage patterns), the number of cells would exceed the number of churners.

Composing the Model Set

Figure 11.18 illustrates three possibilities for composing a model set.

The top is an extreme case using only one month of history. This model set contains churners for March through September. One advantage here is that the number of churners is about seven times larger than the number in one month. This can allow the model set to be larger and have a higher density. The middle is another extreme, using seven months of history with churners from only one month. This is rich in history, but does not have any "slide"—the resultant models may overfit September data and not be as useful for November.

At the bottom is a third possibility—predicting churn for multiple months in the future. In this case, four months of history is used to predict three months in the future.

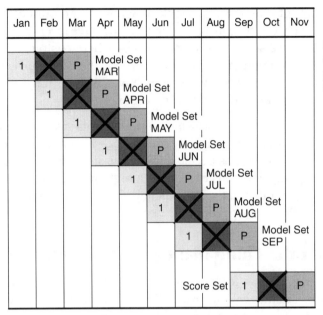

Jan	Feb	Mar	Apr	May	Jun	Jul	Aug	Sep	Oct	Nov
1	✕	P	Model Set MAR							
	1	✕	P	Model Set APR						
		1	✕	P	Model Set MAY					
			1	✕	P	Model Set JUN				
				1	✕	P	Model Set JUL			
					1	✕	P	Model Set AUG		
						1	✕	P	Model Set SEP	
						Score Set	1	✕	P	

Use seven windows, each with one month of history to predict one month into the future.

Jan	Feb	Mar	Apr	May	Jun	Jul	Aug	Sep	Oct	Nov
7	6	5	4	3	2	1	✕	P	Model Set SEP	
Score Set	7	6	5	4	3	2	1	✕	P	

Use one window with seven months of history to predict one month into the future.

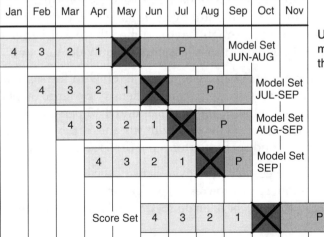

Jan	Feb	Mar	Apr	May	Jun	Jul	Aug	Sep	Oct	Nov
4	3	2	1	✕		P		Model Set JUN-AUG		
	4	3	2	1	✕		P	Model Set JUL-SEP		
		4	3	2	1	✕		P	Model Set AUG-SEP	
			4	3	2	1	✕	P	Model Set SEP	
				Score Set	4	3	2	1	✕	P

Use four windows, with four months of history to predict three months into the future.

Figure 11.18 Three very different ways of composing a model set from the same data.

Composing a model set is an issue particularly when the amount of historical data is limited. This may be the case for companies who have recently built a data warehouse (as in the case study), or for companies where customer growth is so rapid, that most customers have little history. For the case study, we used two months of churn. In general, we would have liked to have at least 13 months of billing data available for derived variables.

Another important factor in composing the model set is its size and density. We prefer to use model sets that have a density of about 20–40 percent churners, and for the model set to be as large as possible (depending on the total number of churners). Obtaining this high density requires a high oversampling rate, when predicting churn one month at a time. Predicting churn for three or six months in the future reduces the oversampling rate needed to get 30 percent density.

Building a Model for the Churn Management Application

Another important goal was to make a model that could automatically be rebuilt inside a churn management system. This imposed requirements on the modeling, such as avoiding manual pruning and other manual processes that would be part of a one-off modeling effort.

Much of the modeling effort was devoted to finding appropriate defaults for building trees. It was more important to be able to consistently build a good model than to build an excellent model only once.

Listening to the Data to Determine Model Parameters

During the course of building the churn model, many models were built whose purpose was only to test assumptions about modeling. One of the surprising results was the high density needed to get good results. With a 1 percent churn rate in any given month, oversampling was obviously necessary. However, without testing, we might have assumed that a 5 or 15 percent churn density would build good or, at least, essentially equivalent models.

And that would have been a bad assumption. Even with the same number of churners in two model sets, the one with the density closer to 30 percent performed better. A model set with 100k records and a 15 percent churn rate has the same number of churners as another with 50k and 30 percent churners. The models built on the second set outperform the first, for every type of model.

In fact, the studies showed that for a given density, the larger the model set, the better the results. In some cases, the results peak after the model set reaches a certain size. In this case, though, the team decided to build the models using a model set containing all the churners.

This also indicates one of the values of building multiple models with different parameters. If only one model was giving that result, then we might think it was a fluke. However, when six models yield the same conclusion, we can make an assumption about the model set.

Using a high oversampling rate has another advantage: all of the churners could be used for the model set. And, indeed, it was decided to build the final model sets using all the churners from two months and then mixing them with about twice as many nonchurners.

Understanding the Algorithm and the Tool

During the second week of the project, results were not looking as good as they should have. Particularly frustrating was the fact that the billing variables were not improving the model—at all. Why could this be? Such variables almost always provide some lift.

It took some investigation with EM to understand that the default algorithm for pruning decision trees almost always returned either the entire tree or the tree with a single node. In fact, manually setting the number of leafs on the tree almost always gave a better tree.

Fortunately, EM offers the ability to drop into the powerful statistical language of SAS. With this knowledge, we were able to write SAS code that does a good job of pruning the trees.

Lessons Learned

This chapter has described how to build a churn model, for a churn management application, using SAS Enterprise Miner. Four critical success factors for building a churn model are

- Defining churn, especially differentiating between interesting churn (such as customers who leave for a competitor) and uninteresting churn (customers whose service has been cut off due to nonpayment).

- Understanding how the churn results will be used. A churn model being used to estimate customer lifetime values is different from one that simply returns a list of high-valued customers for a campaign.

- Identifying data requirements for the churn model, being sure to include historical predictors of churn, such as churn by handset and churn by demographics.

- Designing the model set so the resultant models can slide through different time windows and are not obsolete as soon as they are built.

One of the challenges with churn modeling is that it is never a one-time event. Churn models play an increasingly important role in the mobile telephone industry and are examples of models that need to be incorporated into the business process.

CHAPTER 12

Converging on the Customer: Understanding Customer Behavior in the Telecommunications Industry

Throughout the world, companies that provide communications services are rapidly converging. They want to meet all of the communications needs of their customers:

- Local, long distance, and international voice telephone services
- Wireless voice communications
- Data communications
- Gateways to the Internet
- Data networks between corporations
- Entertainment services, such as cable and satellite television

The hurdles to convergence are as large as the opportunities. Each of these businesses has incumbents fighting hard to keep their customers—and looking for new services to offer them. Regulatory hurdles still prevent companies from offering all these services at the same time. However, the trend is apparent. Once, the value of a telephone company was measured in miles of cable and numbers of switches; increasingly, customers are becoming their biggest assets.

This trend places increasing reliance on understanding customers. The good news is that customer behavior is in the data, in the patterns of calls, data packets, and programming that they make and receive, as well as the more customary billing patterns, product mixes, and demographics. The bad news is that this is an incredibly voluminous amount of data. Each day, there are well over a billion telephone calls completed in the United States. Just describing all these telephone calls at the most basic level (who called whom and when) would require hundreds of gigabytes of storage every day. Technology is making storage and processing power cheaper. Even so, the volumes are daunting.

Data exploration plays a critical role in data mining, and, in many cases, spreadsheets, relational databases, and OLAP systems can yield significant insights into customers and the business. In other cases, visualization tools and geographic mapping tools are good choices. All these tools can work well, but what happens when the volume of data is large, very large?

This chapter demonstrates the insights gained from several data exploration projects. One of them involved approximately 20 gigabytes of data; another used a smaller amount of data for business-to-business data analysis; and another, over 125 gigabytes of data. The latter case was particularly interesting, because the technical work was completed in less than two weeks, using powerful hardware, and software that could readily take advantage of it.

The companies sponsoring these projects have declined to be identified for this chapter. They consider their data a key competitive advantage and are wary of highlighting the fact that they are involved in such work. This chapter combines experiences from several projects, mixing and altering them so that no company is recognizable while retaining the key characteristics of any project involving large volumes of transaction-level data.

This chapter highlights the power of parallel processing when it is successfully applied to problems with large amounts of data. Visualization is still one of the big challenges in data exploration. In other chapters, we demonstrate how packages, such as SGI MineSet, do a good job giving visual insight into data. In this case study, the visualizations are generally simple and almost all are done with the capabilities of desktop spreadsheets. The results presented here are all based on presentations given to business users.

This chapter introduces a powerful technology for working with large amounts of data. This technology is based on the idea of dataflows, and in particular on dataflows in a parallel computing environment. After introducing dataflows, the chapter introduces the business problem and then continues with a voyage of discovery with particular examples of finding and extracting patterns from call detail data. Business readers will be more interested in the results; technical readers will likely be interested in both the results and how they have been obtained.

Dataflows

A *dataflow* is a way of visually representing transformations on data. It is not necessary to understand them to follow the results presented in this chapter. Readers not interested in the technical detail can skip to the next section.

What distinguishes dataflows from other methods, such as flowcharts or algorithmic descriptions, is the focus on data and on how the data is transformed. Also, because dataflows focus on the transformations and not on the algorithms, dataflow compilers can implement the transformations in a parallel environment, significantly improving performance. The intention of this section is to give an introduction to dataflows that is sufficient to understand the results presented later in the chapter; it is not intended to be a tutorial or reference.

What Is a Dataflow?

A dataflow is a graphical representation of processing. That is, there are nodes in the graph (called *components*) that process data. These components are connected by edges. We can think of "data" flowing along the edges, with the nodes transforming the data throughout the dataflow graph. It turns out that dataflows are simple and very natural for expressing the types of data manipulations common in data mining. In addition, it is quite easy to run a dataflow on a parallel machine, taking advantage of multiple processors and disks.

Figure 12.1 shows a simple dataflow that reads a compressed text file, uncompresses it, and writes it back out. The compressed file is stored in a file called in.Z. The uncompressed version is in a text file, out.txt.

Each edge in the dataflow graph has an associated data type, described by the record format on each edge. The data in in.Z is a raw data stream; that is, a stream of bytes represented by the record description on the edge that has a single field, one_byte. Notice, though, that any number of records can flow over this edge, depending on the size of in.Z. The edge after the uncompress node has a record structure for a text file. This record contains a single field, one_line; that is, it is a string terminated by a newline character.

Dataflows can be considerably more complicated, as we will see throughout this chapter. However, the concepts remain the same. Edges carry data and associated information such as the types. Components transform the data. Next, we will discuss some fundamental operations of dataflows that we will find useful later this chapter. This is a whirlwind introduction intended to give only a taste of how dataflows work.

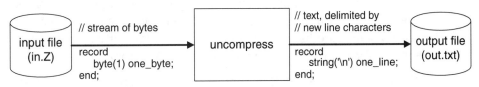

Figure 12.1 A basic dataflow to read a file, uncompress it, and write it out again.

Basic Operations

There are some basic building blocks that make dataflows useful for data analysis. To describe them, we will be using the terminology of Ab Initio (www.abinitio.com), the leader in graphical dataflow programming tools and the tool used for several of the projects incorporated in this chapter.

`Compress` and `Uncompress` make it easy to read and write compressed data files. Compression is a way of storing file data in less space, and these operations handle the processing needed to work with compressed files. (The Windows utility WinZip is a familiar example of a program to compress and uncompress files.) Interestingly, storing data as compressed files and doing the processing to uncompress them is often more efficient than storing the uncompressed data. Computer processors are many times faster than disks so it can take less time to read the smaller compressed file and uncompress it than to read the larger uncompressed file.

`Reformat` is a component that processes each input record individually to produce an output record. This is useful for dropping unneeded fields, adding derived variables, parsing dates, extracting parts of strings, and so on. `Reformat` can also convert text data (such as comma-delimited fields familiar to users of Microsoft Excel) into an internal format. The internal format increases processing speed, so it is quite common to have a `reformat` just after reading a text file.

The `reformat` component reads the description of the transformation from the aptly named transformation file. This file has a powerful language for expressing the many types of transformations that prove useful, including arithmetic operations, string operations, date functions, and more. One useful operation looks up a value in a table—we will be seeing several examples of this. The details of the transformation language, though, are beyond the scope of this chapter.

`Select` chooses certain records, based on selection criteria. This is the "if" statement and "where" clause of dataflow graphs. `Select` has an optional output for those that do not meet the selection criteria—the equivalent of an "else". The selection criteria can be arbitrarily complicated.

`Sort` orders all the records in a dataflow according to some key. The operations we have seen so far can just read one or a small number of records and generate an output record. `Sort` is different, because it must read all its input records before producing any output. In Ab Initio software, the `sort` operator is most efficient when all the records fit into memory.

`Aggregate` takes a dataflow that has already been sorted and produces summaries for all values of a key. This is basically the same operation as the

"Group By" in SQL, although `aggregate` is more powerful. The related operator, `HashAggregate`, does the same thing but does not require that the data
be sorted.

`Mergejoin` takes two dataflows that are sorted on the same key and matches
them. This is similar to a "join" in a relational database. It allows a dataflow
graph to match two files. We will see many examples of matching customer
information to the telephone numbers in call detail records. The aggregation and
merge components require transformation functions, similar to the `reformat`;
and, similarly, the syntax of this language is beyond the scope of this chapter.

These operations are quite powerful. They are sufficient for making dataflows
as powerful as relational databases on complex types of queries (the types that
we use in data mining). And, in fact, there are things that dataflows do
that cannot be expressed in SQL. On the other hand, dataflows are not a
replacement for relational databases. You would not want to use dataflows for
updating a single record in a large table. They are useful when you need to
read and transform lots and lots of data to get an answer.

Dataflows in a Parallel Environment

As mentioned earlier, one of the nice features of dataflows is that they can take
advantage of multiple processors and disks, when they are available in the environment. This scalability allows them to run on single machines, on networks of
PCs, on clusters of workstations, or on even more powerful machines.

Parallel programming in general is quite complicated. However, dataflows
prove remarkably expressive and powerful for data transformation operations.
The same dataflow graph can represent processing on a local workstation, or
on the most powerful parallel computer available. There are two enhancements
to dataflows that make this possible.

Parallel Operations

When there are multiple processors, most of the dataflow operations run independently on each processor. That is, a `reformat` operation runs on every
processor and reformats every record it encounters. Each component just
chugs along, oblivious to the fact that other processors are doing the same
thing. The `select`, `sort`, `aggregate`, and `mergejoin` all behave in the
same way, processing the data available on each processor.

There are some exceptions to this rule. These are operations that specifically work
on multiple processors at the same time (they are *synchronous* in the language of

parallel programming because the operations are synchronized on all processors). The three most important synchronous operations are described next.

Hash_partition takes each record in a dataflow and sends it to another processor based on values in the record. In other words, the hash_partition operation guarantees that all records with the same key value will land at the same processor. This makes it possible to bring together all the records with the same key value for some subsequent operation, such as a mergejoin or aggregate.

Gather takes all the records on all the processors and brings them together on a single processor. This is useful for creating a single output file.

Broadcast does the opposite of gather. It takes records from a single processor and sends them to all the others. This is one way of spreading data across all the processors.

In a system that is not parallel—that is, there is only one processor and one disk—these operations still work correctly by merely copying the data back to the same processor.

Parallel File Systems

The second enhancement involves storing data in such a way that each processor owns a part of the data. In Ab Initio, these files are called *multifiles* and they are really a parallel file system, as shown in Figure 12.2. We assume that each processor has one or more disks (actually file systems) that are locally accessible. The parallel file system stores a single parallel file as a collection of component files; each component file is assigned to one of the available processors. Voila! Each processor has data to work with. This structure has several advantages.

First, the size of a parallel file is larger than any individual file. This can be quite important when there are limits on the sizes of files. For instance, some file systems still have a limit of 2 Gbytes on the size of an individual file. Using parallel files makes it possible to store much more data in a single *multifile*.

Second, each record is located in one of the component files, so it is associated with a particular processor. This makes the parallel processing implicit.

Let's go back to Figure 12.1, which showed a simple dataflow graph that uncompressed a file. If the file in.Z is really a multifile, then the dataflow graph still works. As a parallel dataflow, this graph would automatically run on multiple processors. What happens?

The input multifile, in.Z, consists of a collection of input files, each local to one processor. Each processor runs the uncompress component on its com-

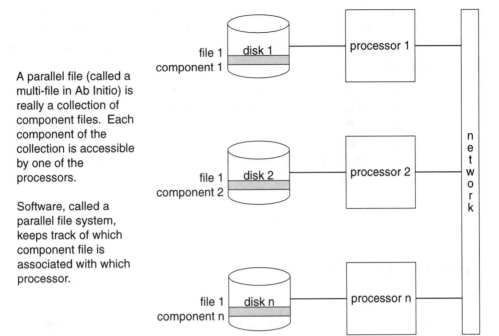

A parallel file (called a multi-file in Ab Initio) is really a collection of component files. Each component of the collection is accessible by one of the processors.

Software, called a parallel file system, keeps track of which component file is associated with which processor.

Figure 12.2   A parallel file system allows files to span multiple disks on different processors.

ponent file and then stores the result in another component file, for the output multifile out.txt. All we need to do to make this work is to tell the diagram that in.Z and out.txt are multifiles instead of files.

What is amazing here is that a simple dataflow graph can make dozens of processors and hundreds of disks work—with the same "programming" effort as doing the work on a single system.

Why Are Dataflows Efficient?

Dataflow graphs are important because they are powerful and efficient. The challenging task of analyzing over 100 GB of data in a week requires the most efficient tools possible. Using a relational database, it is quite possible that the data would not have been loaded with the indexes built in one week.

Why are the dataflow graphs efficient? Basically, they dispense with most of the overhead that traditional databases have. The basic processing is "read from file, perform operations in memory, write out file." The amount of disk I/O is minimized to just what is necessary. Data is only moved between processors when necessary. Processing takes place in memory, with no page faults, logging, unnecessary intermediate files, index updates, or wasted I/O.

A relational database, on the other hand, has a lot of infrastructure built in for functionality not needed for the types of data transformations that we need for data mining and exploration. This includes logging transactions, indexes, pages, and so on.

Another big advantage of the dataflow graphs is the ease of running them in parallel. Compared to most data transformation tools (such as programming languages), taking advantage of multiple processors and disks is easy. This immediately gives orders of magnitudes of speed-up when parallel hardware is available. Also, dataflows provide a much richer set of transformations than traditional SQL.

The end result is that using dataflow graphs and Ab Initio software makes it possible to do powerful, ad hoc analysis on very large amounts of data.

The Business Problem

This case study is a composite of multiple projects. What all these projects share is an understanding that the telecommunications business has shifted from an infrastructure business to a customer business. Whoever sells the most profitable services to the largest number of customers wins.

Understanding customer behavior is a critical part of this business strategy. And, the detailed transaction data contains a wealth of information, generally unexploited by these companies. Is mining this large amount of data worth the investment?

The sheer volume of call detail records has, historically, precluded their use for understanding customer behavior. This situation often leads to a pilot project to demonstrate the value of mining call detail records. The deliverable is a presentation to business users, rather than any immediate action. However, exciting results do lead to further work and to understanding customers better. In short, the business problem is to demonstrate the value of exploiting the great volume of call detail records.

Project Background

A typical project develops either to demonstrate the value of data in a data warehouse or to encourage a company to invest in a call detail data warehouse. The data project itself consists of several activities. Before the data mining work starts, the hardware and software systems that will handle the data need to be set up. The data has to be brought together.

The data mining work itself consists of three parts. The first part is investigatory work, determining what information is interesting. Talking to business people is the only way to accomplish this goal. The result is a list of interesting questions.

The data exploration is the next part. This can vary from one to several weeks, depending on a number of different factors, such as the amount of data, the specific problems being addressed, the quality of the data, and the power of the hardware and software. When everything works well, even hundreds of gigabytes of data can be analyzed in a matter of weeks.

The final part is bringing the results together into a coherent presentation—and getting the right people in the room to listen to it. Since these are demonstration projects, the presentation is the deliverable.

As mentioned earlier, this case study is a combination of several projects. One of the projects involved analyzing over 100 Gbytes of data on a massively parallel computer; another analyzed over 20 Gbytes; and a third, just a few Gbytes. For the purposes of describing the data, we will be referring often to the "big data" project because it best represents the challenges of working with large amounts of data.

Important Marketing Questions

Discussions with the business users highlighted several critical areas for analysis. These areas served as guidelines.

One area of interest was understanding the behavior of individual consumers. When do they use the telecommunication services? Who is likely to be working from home? What telephone numbers are forwarded to mobile phones? Who is using ISDN to connect to a computer network?

Another area was regional differences in calling patterns. This is important for demonstrating to regulators and pricing groups why different areas should be treated differently, from a regulatory or pricing perspective. The business side did not know exactly what patterns might illustrate such differences; that was left to the analysis team.

High-margin services provide another area of large interest. International calls account for a small fraction of all calls and a disproportionate share of profit. What could the data tell us about international calling patterns? With the Internet being an area with rapid growth, which customers use the Internet?

Of course, one of the prime motivations for the work was to support marketing and new sales initiatives. What marketing opportunities lie in the data, such as which customers need a specific product?

These are typical of the types of questions that call detail records can help answer.

The Data

The most voluminous of the data sources used for these types of projects are call detail records. At the same time, the structure of these records is usually fairly simple. For Ab Initio, they can be stored in comma-delimited text files, much like the files used to import data into spreadsheets, but much larger. Typically, the call detail comes from one of three sources:

Direct switch recordings. These are the records that are generated by the switch. Generally, these are the least clean, but the most informative.

Inputs into the billing system. Switch records eventually get transformed into billing records. These are cleaner, but not as complete. Some records, such as toll-free calls, may never make it into the billing system.

Data warehouse feeds. This is yet another source. The data will be rather clean, but will be limited by the needs of the data warehouse.

Of course, other sources of data are needed as well. Tables describing customers and other reference files are needed. We will talk about some of the more common ones. Interestingly, some of the most important information sometimes exists in spreadsheets on peoples' desktops. This is especially true of reference data, such as lists of access numbers for Internet Service Providers, international country codes, and the like.

Technically, the most interesting of these projects analyzed over one billion records on a massively parallel computer. We will be using ideas from this particular project as a guide, when talking about the data.

Call Detail Data

A call detail record is a single record for every call made over the telephone network. Because so many telephone calls are made, call detail records are a very, very, large data source. For instance, there are typically over one billion completed telephone calls every day in the United States. If about one hundred characters of information are kept about every call (a typical amount), then a single day's worth of data amounts to about 100 Gbytes of data. If this were stored on floppy disks, the stack would be about 781 feet high—two days' worth would be higher than the Empire State Building.

Often, call detail records are used by the billing systems to generate bills for customers. It follows that, as a data source, they include only those calls that are billable to the caller, so they do not include incoming calls (since the called person typically does not pay for these), toll-free calls, or calls on certain corporate networks. Also, call detail records can contain potentially billable events, such as turning on call forwarding or negotiating ISDN data transfers. Event records typically account for a small percentage of all the records.

Record Format

This describes the typical call detail record format. The important fields are described here.

from_number is a string representation of the telephone number originating the call. In North America, this is a 10-digit number (3-digit area code plus 7-digit telephone number). Telephone numbers have different formats in other parts of the world. In some countries, the length of telephone numbers can vary even within the country.

to_number is a string representation of the telephone number called.

duration_of_call represents the length of the telephone call (often measured in seconds). Records for billing events have durations of 0.

start_time is the time that the telephone call started.

band is a number that represents how the call should be charged. Examples are charge bands representing local calls, international calls, and so on.

service_field distinguishes between different types of billable event records, such as use of call forwarding.

Notice that there are really several different types of records bundled into this format. Local telephone calls would have a fixed maximum length for to_number that is the same as for from_number. For international calls, to_number could vary much more in length. And, billable events are represented by particular values in the service field.

Restructuring the Data for Exploration

Using Ab Initio dataflows has several advantages. In the "big data" project, the total amount of data exceeded 120 Gbytes of disk space as raw data, for about 1.6 billion call detail records. In a relational database system, these records would have occupied several times this amount of space. Because Ab Initio can read compressed files, though, the total space needed for the compressed files was less than 30 Gbytes—considerable savings in both disk space and in the time needed to read the files.

The data exploration was also focused on several key areas, so it made sense to structure the data to make the exploration more efficient. This was accomplished by using Ab Initio to read the original files and to produce new data files so that:

- Call detail records for telephone calls were placed into three categories: local and long-distance calls, international calls, and billing events.

- Data originating from one particular region was split into separate files for each week, based on start_time.

- The format of the files was changed from variable length text records to fixed length binary records to make processing more efficient. The format was slightly modified for each of the files. For instance, the billing events did not need duration_of_call, since the duration for all billing events is 0.

- The data was partitioned over the processors by from_number, so all the calls originating from the same telephone number were located on the same processor.

Customer Data

In addition to the call detail records, the project needed some basic customer information. Fortunately, telecommunications companies have made significant investments in building and populating data models for their customers. These data models generally describe residential and business customers using dozens of tables. Customer data is needed to match telephone numbers to information about customers, since customers can have multiple telephone lines.

The Customer Model

For the purposes of this project, there were only a few basic items of information required from the customer model. For instance, it was important to be able to identify all the calls from a single customer, even though that customer might have more than one telephone line.

Figure 12.3 shows a basic customer model with several important entities. The *telephone number* itself refers to a particular line with a particular telephone number and to the services available on that line. The *installation record* contains information about all the telephones installed at the same time. These are then rolled up into a *billing account*, which for a business may include dozens or hundreds of telephone numbers. Finally, the *entity* represents a given business customer. Large corporations, for instance, may have multiple billing accounts, spread throughout the world. For residential customers, there is no entity.

An additional entity in the customer model, *sales account*, represents information about the sales and marketing aspects of customers. For instance, it contains the market segment of the customer, the size of the customer (in employees or dollars), a code for the sales representative, and the line of business. Although sales account is not fully populated and the data is not as clean

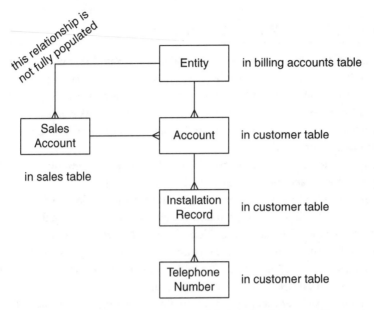

Figure 12.3 The basic customer model showing how to go from telephone number to customer information.

as we might wish, it is important because the ultimate audience for data mining projects is sales and marketing. The relationships on the billing side are more accurate, but less useful to the marketing side of the business.

 TIP The purpose of data mining is to return results back to the business. It is important to use data that business users understand and find valuable. The billing information may be more accurate than the sales account information. However, because sales account maps back to the structure of the sales and marketing organization, it is important to use it. Otherwise, the results are just more technical gibberish.

Original Data

In the big data project, the customer information used by the project was spread over three tables (out of dozens containing customer information). The customer table contained information on tens of millions of customers and billing accounts—and every row of data was needed. Once again, we were able to use dataflows to combine the data from the three tables into the format needed.

From these tables, the "big data" project used only a handful of fields. These include the telephone_number (used to match against from_number and to_number), the billing account, the line of business, and the sales account number.

Working with Data in a Parallel Environment

A parallel computing environment is a big advantage when doing data exploration, since the ability to use multiple processors can really speed up processing. For instance, running on 10 processors can make some processing 10 times as fast (so what takes one hour on a single processor might take only six minutes on a 10-processor system). However, a parallel environment also poses several challenges when laying out data.

On the system used for this project, all the processors had their own local disk, so managing where each record goes is part of the challenge.

As discussed earlier, Ab Initio stores large amounts of data in *multifiles*. A multifile is simply a collection of component files, where each one is local to a processor. We say that the data is *partitioned across the processors*. Sometimes, local files are limited in size (to 2 GB), so partitioning the data is even more important in these cases. Fortunately, Ab Initio hides much of the work required to keep track of the different disks, processors, and files.

There are many different ways to partition data. In general, it is most useful to partition the data by an important key, such as the telephone number. What this means is that all of the records corresponding to a given telephone number are available on the same processor.

The process of moving all the records to the right processor is called partitioning the data, as shown in Figure 12.4. When partitioning data, a function is applied to each key value to determine the right processor; this is often a hash function. Partitioning the data is usually an expensive operation because the sys-

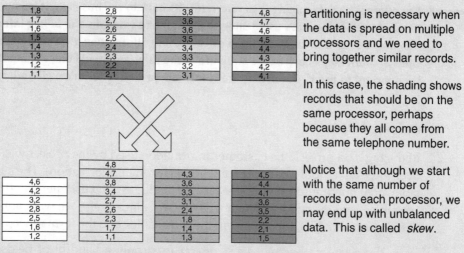

Partitioning is necessary when the data is spread on multiple processors and we need to bring together similar records.

In this case, the shading shows records that should be on the same processor, perhaps because they all come from the same telephone number.

Notice that although we start with the same number of records on each processor, we may end up with unbalanced data. This is called *skew*.

Figure 12.4 Partitioning data sends all the records with the same key value to the same processor.

tem has to send almost every record from the processor where it lives to another—a vast amount of data movement. So we want to minimize the amount of partitioning to make the dataflow graphs run faster.

One of the big challenges in data mining is combining data from multiple files. In the terminology of relational databases, this is called a *join*. For instance, each call detail record contains a from_number. The customer data for that telephone number is in a different table. For much of the analysis, we need to join the two files on a key; in this case, the telephone number.

Figure 12.5 illustrates the process for two large tables. First the records in both files are partitioned using the key. This means that all records with the same key are accessible on the same processor. Then, the records in each file are sorted on the processor. Now, it is a simple matter of matching up two sorted lists.

When one of the files is small, it is often more efficient to copy the entire file to all the processors. Ab Initio supports this method of doing joins using the lookup tables. Lookup tables are also used by reformat operations.

Laying out the data in a parallel environment can have a very significant effect on the performance of the data analysis. Partitioning the data correctly can greatly speed up the processing time.

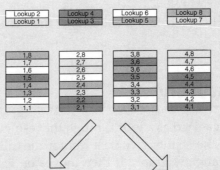

Figure 12.5 Joining files requires partitioning at least one of them.

One of the complications that arises when trying to match telephone numbers to customers is that the same telephone number can be assigned to different customers at different times. So, the TELEPHONE_NUMBER table actually has an effective date as a field. In the interest of speed, the project did not use the effective date field, running the risk of some inaccuracies. However, ownership of telephone numbers typically changes rather slowly over time and, in this case, we verified that fewer than 0.1 percent of the telephone numbers in the table were duplicates with different effective dates. Ignoring the effective date did not materially affect the analysis.

Auxiliary Files

Call detail analysis typically requires additional reference tables. These generally consist of anywhere from a few dozen to a few thousand rows, with data such as:

ISP access numbers, a list of access numbers of Internet service providers

Fax numbers, a list of known fax machines

Wireless exchanges, a list of exchanges (the first three digits of the telephone number) that correspond to mobile carriers

Exchange geography, a list of the geographic areas represented by the telephone number exchange

International, a list of country codes and the names of the corresponding countries.

A Voyage of Discovery

This section is organized as a tour through the results based on call detail. The first few parts of the results give us a feel for the call detail data and for analyzing it using dataflow graph. It then moves on to more complex dataflow graphs needed to understand customer behavior.

What Is in a Call Duration?

How long the calls last is a basic facet of customer behavior. More importantly, though, it can tell us a lot of information about data quality and give an indication if the data sources are producing reasonable values.

Once upon a time, telephone switches recorded a telephone call only when the call ended. This implied that calls that never completed never generated records—and hence were never billed. To get around this problem, very long telephone calls are broken down into chunks. Some switches break the calls into 8-hours chunks; others break them into 24-hour chunks. What do the call durations look like?

Solution Approach

The solution approach was to build a dataflow graph to generate the histogram of call durations, stored to the nearest second. This is sufficient—and, in fact, overkill. In eight hours, there are 28,800 seconds, far too much data to see on one histogram. The results were manipulated using a spreadsheet to get histograms by second, by minute, and by hour.

The dataflow graph needed to solve this is quite straightforward, as shown in Figure 12.6. The graph reads the compressed file and extracts the duration. Then, each processor creates a histogram of the durations (this is the first hash aggregate component), which the second hash aggregate then combines into a single histogram on a single processor. Finally, it is sorted before being output into a file.

Results

The results for seconds is pretty much what we expect, as shown in Figure 12.7. The first point, for 0 duration, has been eliminated since it is several times larger than any other point on the graph.

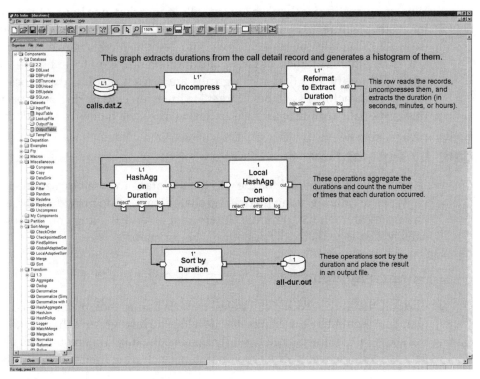

Figure 12.6 Dataflow graph to find durations.

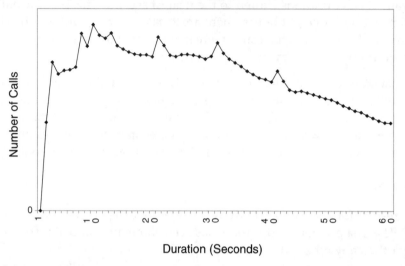

Call Duration Histogram by Second
for calls longer than one second
and shorter than one minute

Figure 12.7 Call duration histogram by second for calls longer than one second and shorter than one minute.

What is interesting is when we look at calls longer than one hour—there is a very interesting feature (in Figure 12.8): a peak at 24 hours. This is the peak we would expect if calls really are broken down into 24-hour pieces. However, some calls last longer than 24 hours. In fact, call durations range up to 46 hours—directly contradicting the fact that all long calls are broken up. The data does not lie. However, sometimes switches "forget" to break up calls during peak periods or, under special circumstances such as testing, the switch does not break them up.

Calls by Time of Day

A good way to get a feel for the call detail data is to break down when different types of calls are being made. The charge-band code provides a breakdown among local, regional, national, international, and fixed-to-mobile telephone calls. When are different types of calls being made?

Solution Approach

The solution is to read the call detail records and to look up the user-specified class represented by the charge-band field. The histogram is then produced for the six values of the charge band by hour of the day. This result was based on calls for a single week of the regional data (including international calls).

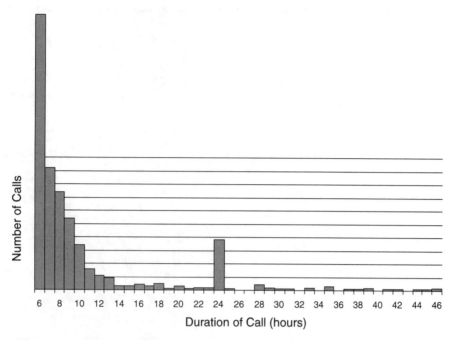

Figure 12.8 Call duration histogram by hour for calls longer than five hours.

The dataflow graph in Figure 12.9 illustrates the process. The data is read from the call detail file and uncompressed and turned into the internal record format. Then, another reformat component calculates the day of the week and the hour of the day for each call. The two hash aggregate components count the number of calls made during each hour of the week. The first hash aggregate creates the table on each processor for each partition of the data. The second combines these partial results into a single result, sorts, and saves the file. This graph illustrates how to do a group-by aggregation on a very large file, while doing some complicated calculations as well.

Results

The results are in Figure 12.10. This shows the pattern of calls made throughout the day. Seeing the calls by day-of-the-week and hour-of-the-day illustrates some interesting patterns. Generally, calls are very low in the early morning and increase noticeably during the day. These are only residential calls, and they show an interesting peak in the evening at about 8:00 P.M. or 9:00 P.M.—people making telephone calls after dinner. However, this peak does not exist on Fridays.

The results in Figure 12.11 are based on a similar dataflow that shows when, throughout a day, different calls are being made. There are peaks through the

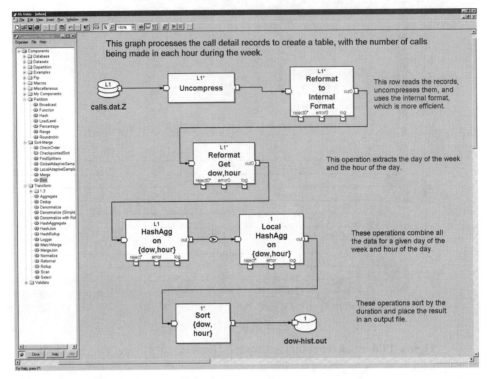

Figure 12.9 When calls are being made.

middle of the day and very little usage in the early hours of the morning. Throughout the day, local calls tend to dominate. However, looking at the proportion of calls throughout the day, we see that local calls are least likely in

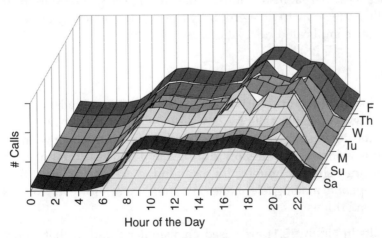

Figure 12.10 Number of calls by day of the week and hour of the day.

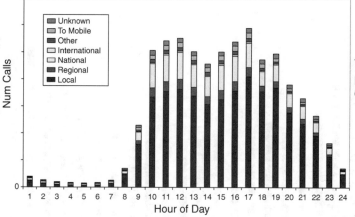

This is a typical pattern for telephone calls during the day.

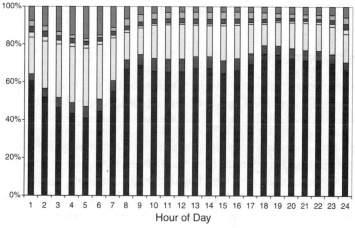

Using percentages, we see that long distance calls are much more likely during the early morning.

Figure 12.11   Looking at the proportions is also very informative.

the early hours of the morning and that international calls are a bit more likely during the night and early morning.

Because international calls are so important, this leads to further questions, such as the average duration of international calls and where the calls are going to. Figure 12.12 shows how the average duration of international calls varies significantly throughout the day. The shortest calls are during the day and the longest are during the night. Further investigation can determine which customers are price sensitive—that is, which customers call when the rates go down, differences between business and consumer usage, and so on.

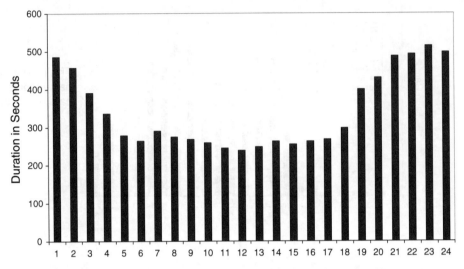

Figure 12.12 Average duration of international calls throughout the day.

Calls by Market Segment

The market segment is a broad categorization of customers. These categories include residential customers, government accounts, and different gradations of business (small, medium, large, and named accounts).

Market segments are units of action as well as customer segmentation since the sales organization is organized by market segment. For instance, there are separate divisions focusing on residential, small business, government, and large business accounts. This brings up some interesting questions about market segments. Are customers within market segments really similar to each other? What are the calling patterns between market segments, for instance?

Solution Approach

This is the first of the "hard" questions being asked about the call detail records, because this question requires looking up customer information about each telephone call. The solution is a table giving the number of calls made from each sales channel to each other sales channel. Transforming the call detail data into such a matrix requires a lot of processing power, because there are a lot of customers, and many, many more call detail records.

The market channel is available at the customer level, not in the call detail. Remember, the call detail only contains telephone numbers. For each record, from_number needs to be replaced by its market segment and the to_number needs to be replaced by its market segment. This requires "joining" the call detail data with the customer data—two times, once for each of the telephone numbers. This is the type of complex query often referred to as a "killer query" in relational database systems.

Once the call detail records have been transformed into (<from market segment>, <to market segment>, <other information>), then getting the information about calls between market segments is a simple matter of aggregating all the data by market segment.

The dataflow graph in Figure 12.13 illustrates the process of generating the table describing calls between market segments. The customer data is already partitioned and sorted by the telephone number. The call detail is similarly partitioned and sorted by the originating telephone number. The merge between these files requires no additional preprocessing.

However, for the merge between the terminating number and incoming number, the regional call data needs to be repartitioned and resorted by the terminating number. The bottom half of the graph partitions the files so they can be joined.

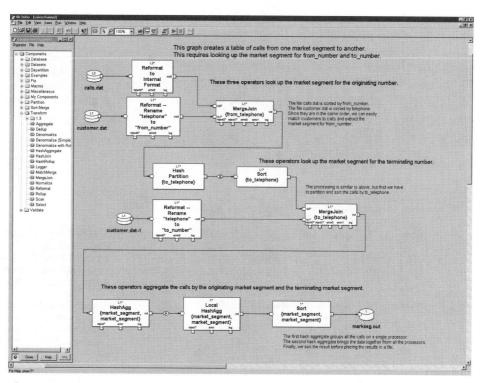

Figure 12.13 This dataflow graph looks up the sales channel for both the from_number and to_number fields and then aggregates by sales channel.

Results

The data in tabular format (see Table 12.1) gives some indication of the relative call volumes (all volumes are in thousands of calls).

Figure 12.14 gives a graphical view of the data. The top half shows that residential telephone calls predominate in the data, and in fact, calls from residence to residence are the largest proportion of calls. A major reason for this is that business calls are split among several different segments. The picture does not show rare market segments. There is always unclean data, and this is no exception. The marketing department did not recognize several market segments, alas. Fortunately, the mystery segments accounted for very few calls.

The bottom half shows the same graph with proportions instead of absolute numbers. Here we see that there is indeed a preference for calls within market segments. Each stripe represents the proportion of calls made from one market segment to another. What the graph shows is interesting. The "market segment" that makes the largest number of calls to residences is . . . other residences.

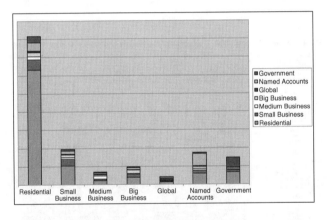

The raw number of calls between different market segments is interesting.

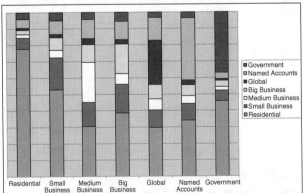

The real insight comes from looking at percentages. Calls are quite likely to remain within a market segment.

That is, government customers tend to call government customers, residential to residential, and so on.

Figure 12.14   Two views of calls between market segments.

Table 12.1   Representative Call Volumes (in 1000s) between Market Segments for one Week of Data

FROM SALES CHANNEL	TO SALES CHANNEL							
	RESIDENTIAL	SMALL BUSINESS	MEDIUM BUSINESS	BIG BUSINESS	GLOBAL	NAMED ACCOUNTS	GOVERNMENT	GRAND TOTAL
Residential	35,426	5,790	1,165	2,128	694	3,338	3,774	54,914
Small Business	3,136	2,139	560	963	246	1,008	549	9,554
Medium Business	907	482	941	358	157	448	168	3,898
Big Business	1,266	851	414	986	213	672	314	5,309
Global	504	202	134	157	627	280	78	2,150
Named Accounts	2,542	918	448	616	325	3,730	325	9,576
Government	1,870	549	168	302	78	347	3,046	6,630
Grand Total	47,555	11,883	4,301	6,194	2,554	10,528	8,568	8,325

The "market segment" that makes the largest number of calls to the government market segment is . . . government. And so on. This is a striking result that confirms the validity of the market segmentation.

International Calling Patterns

International direct dial (IDD) calls are a highly profitable, but highly competitive part of the telephone business. This data exploration explores only a few facets of international calling patterns, including the length of international calls throughout the day and the destinations of the calls.

There are many possibilities open for further analysis. What are the differences in patterns for residential versus business customers? Which customers primarily call one country (or even just one number in them) versus customers that call a wider variety of international numbers? How do customer's international calling patterns change over time? How do calling patterns change during the day? And so on.

Solution Approach

The solution approach is quite simple. First, we can identify international calls because they start with an international access prefix or (in North America) because they use certain area codes.

Second, we can extract the country code in to_number and look each up in an international country code table. The results can then be displayed in tabular format or as a map.

The dataflow graph for summarizing the data by country is quite simple (see Figure 12.15). The graph reads the international call data, looks up the country code (in the Reformat), and then aggregates the calls by country.

The complicated part of this graph is not apparent in the dataflow. Because the country code has a variable length up to six digits, extracting it from to_number takes a bit of work. The solution is to look up the first digit in the table of international country codes. If no match is found, then look up the first two digits, and so on until a match is found.

It is worth noting that this type of expression produces a very complicated join expression in a relational database, because it is basically what is called a "non-equijoin." Normally, when joining two tables, you are looking for exact matches between the two tables—such as using the entire telephone number to look up customer information. In a non-equijoin, the matches are not exact. Looking up countries requires matching just the first few characters of the called telephone number field. This type of processing is very expensive in a relational database.

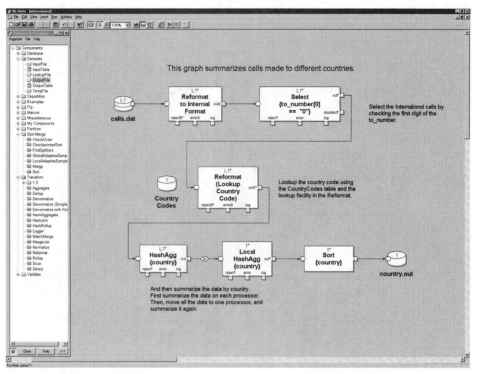

Figure 12.15   Ab Initio graph for extracting information by country.

Results

Figure 12.16 shows the average length of telephone calls for countries in Europe. It is interesting that calls to Eastern Europe are, on average, shorter than calls to Western Europe. However, calls to similar countries, such as Scandinavia or to the British Isles, are of similar length.

For instance, Tuvalu, a small country in the South Pacific, had what seemed like a disproportionately high call volume—even a few more than far more populous countries, such as Mexico. This is worth further investigation. It may suggest a spate of South Pacific holiday travelers. It might also be indicative of a call-back service or some other type of unusual telephone service.

An interesting use of the call detail data is for providing information to regulators, since they often prefer uniform rules for the entire country, state, or region. Often, regional differences can be quite striking. In one case, the average length of an international call was almost one minute longer in one region than in the country as a whole. This is regulatory ammunition for differential pricing schemes in different areas.

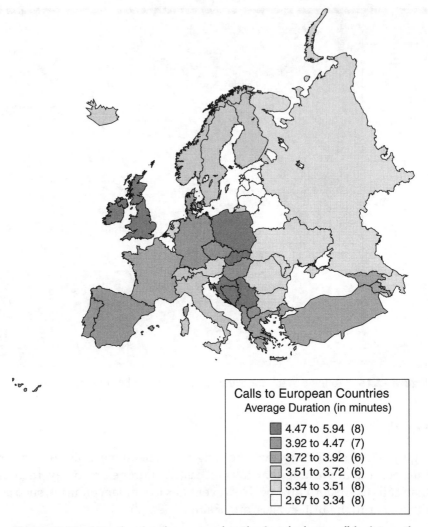

Figure 12.16 Map showing the average length of a telephone call for international calls to countries in Europe.

When Are Customers at Home?

Knowing when customers are at home has many potential uses. For customer service, it can provide times for maintenance and service repair. For marketing, it can provide times for reaching the customer by telephone. Of course, a company would want to be very careful before giving this information to any outside company.

The call detail records do not strictly say when someone is at home—we only know when someone is home and making a telephone call. However, by looking at this data over time, we can get an indication of customers' schedules.

Another possibility is using this information for customer segmentation. However people use their telephones throughout the week is likely to provide a rich source of information for identifying key segments of customers.

Solution Approach

The solution is to use the call detail records as indications of when a person is likely to be home. We assume that the behavior is a weekly behavior, so we want to look at the day of the week and hour of the day.

The dataflow graph in Figure 12.17 shows the steps in this process. First, the graph must identify residential customers. One minor complication here is that a single residence may have multiple telephone lines. For these usage profiles, it is useful to consider all telephones at the same time.

Next, the graph partitions the data by customer, and then brings together all the data about a single customer. The aggregate operator counts the number of telephone calls made in each hour period. The data is then brought together into a single file.

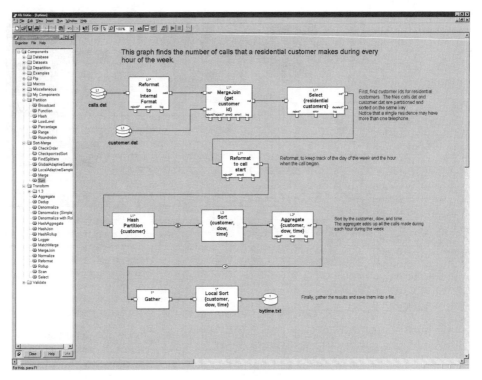

Figure 12.17   Ab Initio graph for extracting information by country.

Of course, this data includes only outgoing, billed telephone calls. It does not include toll-free numbers or incoming calls. We could modify the graph to look for incoming calls, but that does not provide a wealth of information—since we do not know if anyone was present to answer the call. Of course, we might also get confused by "automatic" out-going calls, such as those that might be made by a computer modem or a home security system, although these are relatively rare.

Results

Figure 12.18 shows when a particular customer is making telephone calls from home. The darker shading shows when more calls are being made. This graph shows several things:

- This customer is rarely home during the day.
- This customer is home making telephone calls on Saturday and Sunday, especially on Sunday.

	Monday	Tuesday	Wednesday	Thursday	Friday	Saturday	Sunday
11:00 pm							
10:00 pm							
9:00 pm							
8:00 pm							
7:00 pm							
6:00 pm							
5:00 pm							
4:00 pm							
3:00 pm							
2:00 pm							
1:00 pm							
12:00 pm							
11:00 am							
10:00 am							
9:00 am							
8:00 am							
7:00 am							
6:00 am							
5:00 am							
4:00 am							
3:00 am							
2:00 am							
1:00 am							
12:00 am							

The dark shading shows when calls are being made from a particular customer's home telephones. Notice the low volume of calls during the day on weekdays and the higher volumes on Saturday and Sunday.

Figure 12.18 When a particular customer is at home.

- This customer is home making telephone calls on weekday evenings, especially on Tuesdays and Thursdays.

Monday also has a light shading. This is probably because there was a Monday holiday during the time period we were looking at.

This illustration provides a profile of someone who probably works during the day and spends a fair amount of time at home in the evenings and on weekends. Other profiles would show people who work at home, who are retired, who own second homes, and so on. These types of patterns can be valuable for segmenting customers.

Internet Service Providers

The Internet represents a very important area for telecommunications companies. Many customers already connect to the Internet using modems—and these telephone calls are recorded in the call detail. There are many opportunities for using this information:

- Which Internet service providers (ISPs) are customers using?
- Do different segments of customers use different ISPs?
- Which customers own modems?

The answers to these questions are in the data.

Solution Approach

The first step is to identify calls to ISPs—accomplished by looking up the telephone numbers in a table of known ISP numbers. To find the market share for each ISP, the calls needed to be aggregated by ISP provider. This requires looking up the called telephone number in a list of known ISP telephone access numbers.

It was also interesting to compare the market share for different segments of customers, in particular for the small business customers versus residential customers. To accomplish this, we need to look up market segment information in the customer file.

Now that the ISPs have been identified, the calls can be aggregated by ISP and market segment. This shows market share by market segment. Another possibility is to aggregate the calls by entity. This tells us which customers are contacting ISPs, presumably by modem.

The dataflow graph, as shown in Figure 12.19, looks up both the ISP name and the market segment.

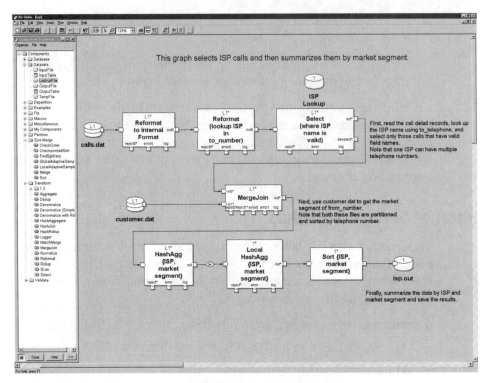

Figure 12.19 This dataflow graph finds information about ISPs.

Results

Figure 12.20 shows the market share for several ISP companies, based on the number of telephone calls being made to those companies. The pie chart on the inside shows the breakdown for small business customers. It is quite interesting that the market share for small businesses is quite different from the market share overall among the customer base.

In addition, we can identify thousands of businesses that placed at least one call to an ISP. This indicates that these businesses have modems and have at least a few people who access the Internet. The average call to an ISP turned out to be about nine minutes. However, some calls were significantly longer, with several coompanies having an average call in excess of three hours or more. This suggests, perhaps, companies that are using their ISP for large data transfers.

Private Networks

Many businesses operate from multiple sites and make large volumes of telephone calls and data transfers between the sites. Examples of such businesses

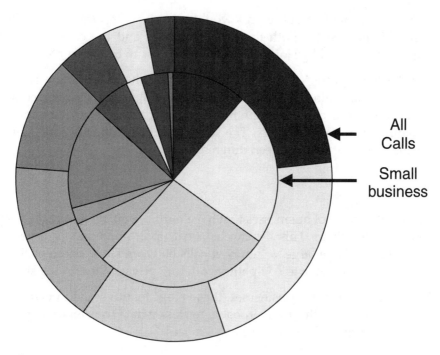

All
Calls

Small
business

Figure 12.20 The share of the small business ISP market differs noticeably from the overall market share.

are hospitals that have satellite clinics, retailers with multiple locations, and government offices. A property of these businesses is that they are likely to be making large volumes of calls between their different sites.

Another category of businesses are those that must exchange large amounts of data with other businesses, such as clinics and hospitals that send medical records between different sites or printers who receive images as data.

There is a telephone product designed just for this situation. *Virtual private networks* (VPN) are like dedicated circuits connecting the different sites, for data, voice, or both. And, for large volumes of telephone calls, they provide less expensive service than pay-by-call service. VPNs are a way of proactively responding to customer needs.

Which customers are good candidates for VPN?

Solution Approach

The solution is in the data. The customer table contains a list of companies and their different sites. What needs to be done is to determine the call volumes between the different sites using the call detail data.

Using a relational database, this would be quite complicated. The site information is needed for both the calling number and the called number, and requires two very large joins. Then the result has to be aggregated by site.

The Ab Initio graph (Figure 12.21) for finding this information is similar to graphs we have already seen. The business and site information comes from the customer file, and the graph has to find it for both the originating and terminating telephone numbers. The selection criteria finds all calls within one business entity going between different sites.

Results

The result is a list of businesses that have multiple offices and make telephone calls between them. This list can be acted upon immediately, especially for business that have large volumes of calls between sites. These business customers are vulnerable to competitors offering private networking services.

Interestingly, for some businesses, the average length of calls between sites is over an hour. Calls this long probably represent data transfers, suggesting further opportunities for offering them services.

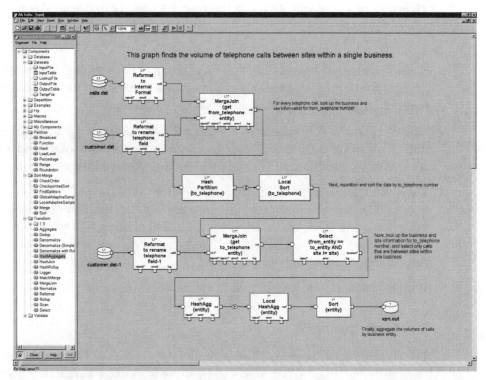

Figure 12.21 This dataflow graph finds businesses that make a lot of telephone calls between sites.

Concurrent Calls

There is a continuous business opportunity in providing more telephone lines to businesses that are saturating their current lines. Many customers, for instance, are small businesses that have a limited number of outbound lines connected to a larger number of extensions on employees' desktops. When do these customers need additional outside lines? When is the right time to offer upgrades to their telephone systems?

One measure of a customer's need for new lines is the maximum number of lines that are used concurrently. This information can also give other insight into customer behavior—such as when telephone usage peaks.

Solution Approach

Solving this problem requires counting up the number of telephone calls being made at any given time by a given customer. There is no simple function that looks over a bunch of telephone call data and gives the answer.

The solution is to break up each telephone call into two pieces, a record that indicates that a call is being started and another indicating that the call has finished. For instance, the three calls in Table 12.2 get converted into the six records in Table 12.3.

The next step is to sort all of these records by time and to perform one trick. The trick is to add a new "count" field to the data that is incremented by 1 for every start and decremented by 1 for every end (see Table 12.4).

Table 12.2 How Many of These Calls Are at the Same Time?

FROM_NUMBER	TO_NUMBER	DATE	TIME	DURATION (SECS)
Xxxxxxxxxx	Yyyyyyyyyy	980501	110322	742
Xxxxxxxxxx	Zzzzzzzzzzz	980501	110501	616
Xxxxxxxxxx	Aaaaaaaaaaa	980501	110842	52

Table 12.3 Breaking the Three Calls Are Equivalent to These Six Call Start-or-End Events

FROM_NUMBER	DATE	TIME	TYPE
Xxxxxxxxxx	980501	110322	start
Xxxxxxxxxx	980501	111544	end
Xxxxxxxxxx	980501	110501	start
Xxxxxxxxxx	980501	111517	end
Xxxxxxxxxx	980501	110842	start
Xxxxxxxxxx	980501	110934	end

Table 12.4 Sorting These Events and Keeping a Count Gives the Answer

FROM_NUMBER	DATE	TIME	TYPE	COUNT
Xxxxxxxxx	980501	110322	start	1
Xxxxxxxxx	980501	110501	start	2
Xxxxxxxxx	980501	111517	end	1
Xxxxxxxxx	980501	111544	end	0
Xxxxxxxxx	980501	110842	start	1
Xxxxxxxxx	980501	110934	end	0

What this says is that between the times of 11:03:22 and 11:05:01, there was one call in progress. From 11:05:01 to 11:15:17, there were two calls, and so on. This operation of adding the count is called a scan. It is not possible to do this inside a relational database using standard SQL.

What is interesting here is not the from_number but the office from which the call originated. So before doing the scan, all the numbers from a single company have to be brought together.

Note that this solution only takes into account the call detail records that the phone company passes on to the billing system. In particular, it does not include toll-free numbers or incoming calls. These were not available in the call detail data, because they are not billed to the calling number (which is what the billing system cares about). Assuming that these calls are recorded somewhere, the analysis can be extended for all types of calls.

The dataflow graph (in Figure 12.22) that implements this is the most complicated one in this chapter. The graph reads each call record and looks up the business entity for the from_number. The top two lines of components create, respectively, a call-start record and a call-end record. These are the two events that describe a telephone call.

All of the call event records for a single business entity are brought together by the partition component. Now comes the tricky part. These are sorted by business entity and time. Now we have an ordered list of all call events for each business. The scan calculates the number of concurrent calls (by adding 1 for a call-start and subtracting 1 for a call-end). Finally, the aggregation components find the maximum value of the count. And, the result is saved.

There is no way to represent this query using standard SQL. A stored procedure would be necessary to get the functionality of the "scan" operator.

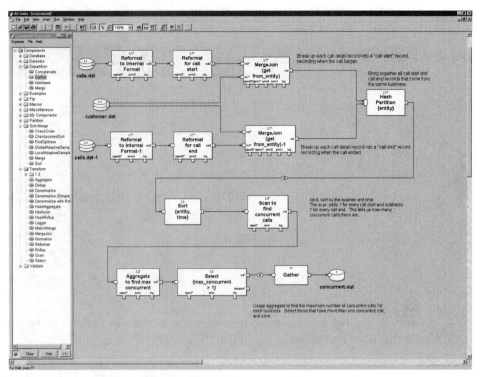

Figure 12.22   This dataflow graph finds concurrent calls at a business.

Results

A total of 21 sites had more than 30 concurrent outbound telephone calls. The highest number was an outbound call center. It is easy to look at the results in different ways. For instance, the top 10 corporate customers were almost all from the same line of business (see Table 12.5).

We would expect that the peak call volumes would occur during the day or evening hours. It is interesting that some sites had their peak number of concurrent calls between 10 P.M. and 7 A.M. In fact, a number of sites had five or more concurrent calls during this period, including one with a peak of 45 calls at 3:09 A.M.

Lessons Learned

Call detail records contain a wealth of information about residential and business customers (similarly, detailed transaction records in other industries

Table 12.5 Interesting—Nine of the Ten Corporate Accounts with the Largest Number of Concurrent Calls Are from the Same Industry

REGION	LINE OF BUSINESS	DATE OF MAXIMUM	TIME OF MAXIMUM	MAXIMUM
SW	IND12	10/31	15:56	27
SW	IND12	10/27	11:27	23
SW	IND12	10/28	18:30	18
SW	IND12	10/29	11:05	17
SW	IND48	10/29	11:10	16
NE	IND12	10/29	8:59	16
SE	IND12	10/27	9:48	15
SE	IND12	10/30	15:58	14
NE	IND12	10/31	15:42	14
SW	IND12	10/30	16:37	14

provide key information about customers in those industries). The purpose of this chapter is to show some of the compelling results:

- Customer behavior varies from one region of a country to another.
- Thousands of companies place calls to ISPs. These companies own modems and have the ability to respond to Web-based marketing.
- Residential customers indicate when they are at home by using the telephone. These patterns can be important, both for customer contact and for customer segmentation.
- The market share of ISPs differs by market segment.
- International calls show regional variations. In addition, the length of the calls varies considerably depending on the destination.
- International calls made during the evening and early morning are up to twice as long as international calls made during the day.
- Companies that make calls between their own sites are candidates for private networking (virtual or otherwise).

These results are combined from several data mining projects. Handling these large volumes of data is possible by taking advantage of parallelism, and thinking of the data processing as dataflows.

CHAPTER 13

Who Is Buying What? Getting to Know Supermarket Shoppers

The checkout scanners that so impressed former President George Bush, on what was apparently the only trip he made to a supermarket during his presidency, were originally installed for purely operational reasons. In the early days of the technology, supermarket managers were most attracted by the ability to set prices centrally without the need to affix a label to every single can and carton. Consumers resisted being asked to put unpriced items into their shopping carts, so that particular savings opportunity was not realized. Nevertheless, the scanners paid for themselves with increased check-out speeds, more accurate pricing, and better inventory control.

Almost unnoticed at first, was another important consequence of the adoption of check-out scanners: they generate lots of data. Data by the gigabyte, data by the terabyte. More data than anyone knew what to do with. In this chapter we explore some of the ways that the industry is beginning to take advantage of this unexpected bounty. We start with a look at what the future may hold by envisioning a time when supermarkets see themselves as information brokers as well as sellers of groceries. We then review three case studies, each of which is a pilot or demonstration project designed to test the usefulness of data mining in the grocery industry. The first case shows how even summarized, anonymous transaction data can be combined with outside demographic information to study and compare the shopping habits of different ethnic groups. The second case shows how loyalty cards allow purchases to be linked with individual consumers, allowing targeted marketing based on customer behavior in an industry that has relied heavily on the mass distribution of identical circulars and coupons. The third case shows how a variety of directed and undirected data mining techniques including association rules, automatic cluster detection, and decision trees can be used to identify profitable customer segments.

Although these case studies involve supermarkets and groceries, many aspects of them can be generalized to the wider world of retail sales in general, not to mention cataloging and e-commerce.

An Industry in Transition

Retailers are only beginning to grasp the true value of the information they collect, but we can look to other industries to see how much can be accomplished. The credit card industry is similar to the retail industry in that it collects data about who is buying what products, although any one company only has the data for purchases made with their credit cards. This information can be resold, in one form or another, to companies that want to reach particular individuals. The sidebar has an excellent illustration of how a credit card company can use information gleaned from its customers' purchasing behavior to offer corporate marketers access to finely tuned market segments, while providing a valuable service to its cardholders.

The large increase in available data has so far brought incremental and evolutionary changes to supermarkets, but that is changing. The data they collect has handed retailers a rare opportunity to change the balance of power between themselves and their suppliers who control the brands. When used in conjunction with a frequent shopper program (or any other way of linking individual shoppers with their purchases) the point of sale data can answer a question that suppliers, such as Proctor & Gamble, Unilever, Coca Cola, Pepsi, Clorox, General Mills, Kellogg's and so on, would love to have answered: Who is actually buying all that stuff? Knowledge, it is often remarked, is power. Knowledge of *who* is buying *what* gives retailers the power to become information brokers as well as sellers of merchandise.

Supermarkets as Information Brokers

A supermarket chain stands in the same relationship to the packaged goods suppliers as the credit card company does to the airlines. Suppose you are the brand manager for a premium brand of "scoopable" kitty litter. Your target market is the small segment of cat owners willing to pay extra for whatever benefits your marketing efforts have been able to get them to associate with this advance in cat waste-removal technology. Since many cat owners have never tried any product in the category you manage, you would like to put a

Credit Card Companies as Information Brokers—A True Story

The credit card industry has led the way in turning data once used only for operational purposes (in their case, credit card transactions) into useful information that can itself be sold to third parties—very similar to what supermarkets are now beginning to contemplate.

Recently, we had a personal experience that illustrates the point. One of the authors flies a lot of miles on US Airways and is rewarded with a "preferred" membership in Dividend Miles, the US Airways frequent flier program. The dividend miles preferred membership was earned the hard way— with many trips to New York, Washington, Charlotte, and Pittsburgh (US Airways hubs). His preferred membership does not protect him from having his flight canceled, but it does mean that his name rises to the top of the stand-by list for the oversold next flight out. This and other privileges, such as free upgrades to first or business class and a choice of almonds or cashews in addition to peanuts, work just the way they are supposed to. He evinces an unnatural loyalty to US Airways, even preferring, when taking the red-eye back from the west coast, to ride up front in the big seats and stop in Pittsburgh rather than squeezing into coach seats and having to pay for drinks on a nonstop flight on another airline.

The frequent flier program is doing its job. Members tend to choose one particular airline, even when the schedule or routing is not necessarily the most convenient. But, this same author recently was offered equivalent status on Delta and Continental, two airlines that he flies infrequently. How did he acquire them?

To get Silver Medallion status on Delta, he had to fill out a short form that was included in his American Express credit card statement. The second one was even easier—it simply arrived unasked for in the same credit card statement a month or two later. These were clearly not mass mailings, but well-targeted efforts on the part of Delta and Continental to poach a highly profitable customer from a competitor. Certainly, the authors are just the sorts of customers that any airline would be pleased to have. We fly all over the world on short notice cheerfully paying the higher, last-minute fares since our clients often want us to move quickly and aren't willing to wait for us to find a 21-day advance ticket. So, although it would be foolhardy to hand out elite status to just anyone, it is a very sensible offer to make to people like us; people who, should they become hooked on the new service, will be very profitable. But how can an airline with which we don't currently do business possibly find us without also finding a lot of bargain-hunting leisure travelers or stay-at-homes?

How could an airline gain such information? First of all, it is important to note that the invitation to enjoy the privileges of an elite membership in one of the new programs was not mailed by the airlines themselves. That means that American Express did not have to reveal the names or addresses of any of its cardholders.

(Continues)

> ## Credit Card Companies as Information Brokers—A True Story (*Continued*)
>
> Indeed, American Express has a good reputation for protecting the privacy of its customers. Their privacy policy is a model and may be read online at www.americanexpress.com/corp/consumerinfo/principles.asp. Without revealing any names, American Express can still act as an information broker by selling access to people with certain characteristics.
>
> We imagined a pitch to the airlines something like this: "We can put your offer in the hands of people with billing addresses in the markets you serve who spent in excess of $2,000 on air fare in four of the last six months, *but who are not your frequent fliers.*" We can safely guess that airlines are willing to pay considerably more per contact to reach such a well-defined subset of the population than for a mass market promotion to be inserted in the statement of every cardholder.
>
> The one thing we couldn't figure out was why, if the solicitation was based on data mining, did it target one of us and not the other, since both of us are members of American Express's Membership Miles program?
>
> Before writing this aside, we did a little research. This particular marketing effort was only directed at members of the Membership Miles program. It turns out that one of us has used the Membership Miles, and in doing so, has registered his frequent flier numbers. American Express knows which programs he belongs to, and can offer him elite status on *other* airlines. The other relishes his time at home and doesn't feel the need to make additional trips, even for pleasure. He has not yet registered any frequent flyer numbers. For him, American Express cannot determine the "but who are not your frequent fliers" part of the query, so he never gets special offers from other airlines.

coupon for your product into their hands. Unfortunately, you don't know who the cat owners are, let alone the actual target audience of people with indoor cats and low sensitivity to price.

Because the store sees who buys what, it knows (or *could know*) who the best prospects are for this product. As the brand manager, you are no doubt ready to pay for this information. At the simplest level, something similar is already commonplace. A coupon printer at the checkout stand can be programmed to print out a coupon for your special kitty litter every time a shopper buys cat food, cat toys, or another brand of kitty litter. A company called Catalina Marketing supplies systems to do just this at the checkout aisle. Other companies, such as Net Perceptions, perform the same service for e-commerce sites on the Web. These services give you, the brand manager, a way to ensure that people who are currently buying products in your categories are offered an incentive to try your particular brand.

Note that in this scenario, the system does not need to know much about a customer in order to figure out which coupon to print. If you buy diet soda today, you will get coupons for other low-calorie soft drinks. If tomorrow you come back and buy diapers, you will get coupons for other baby products. The shopping transaction remains anonymous and no customer relationship management is involved. The level of customer focus achievable in any industry depends on what view of the customer is made possible by the available data. If all you know about a customer is what he or she has purchased in the current transaction, the coupon-in-category approach is about as far as you can go. The customer who buys a case of diet soda today is fairly likely to buy another one some day, but, unless she is very thirsty or has a large family, probably not for a while. Clearly, it would be better to offer her a product that she hadn't just stocked up on—one which, based on past shopping behavior, she is likely to want. That requires a way of identifying the customer and a way of analyzing her purchase history.

Shifting the Focus from Products to Customers

When all that is known about a customer is what he or she is buying at this very moment, it is hard to improve on a coupon-printing system at the checkout counter where the particular coupon is triggered by the contents of the shopping cart. And, as we will see in the first of this chapter's case studies, this anonymous point of sale data can yield important information and answer a number of interesting questions. The most basic form of market-basket analysis is the study of what products tend to sell together. This form of market-basket analysis is performed using association rules, which are explained later in this chapter. These rules, which indicate what things tend to be purchased together, do not require any information on the person pushing the cart because there is no attempt to link multiple trips by the same shopper. Nor is it necessary to identify individual shoppers in order to aggregate behavior patterns for entire groups of customers. There are, however, many questions that cannot be answered without somehow being able to observe individual shoppers over time:

- Do the people buying eggs and milk in the "8 items or fewer" lane on Thursday night come back on Saturday to do a complete stock up?

- Are people who use the express lanes profitable because they purchase high margin products or because they return to stock up on many goods?

- Is there a core set of products that drive the sales of high volume consumers?

- Do customers who purchase items on special (when the profit margin is zero or negative) exhibit profitable behavior over time?

- For each customer, which products not being purchased now could he or she be purchasing in the store?

- Which shoppers are most likely to be open to trying new, house-brand products?

- How profitable has this shopper been over the course of the last year?

Fortunately (at least from a data miner's point of view), anonymous transactions are being replaced by purchases linked to individual shoppers, because of the increased use of loyalty card programs in supermarkets. Loyalty card programs are not primarily designed to provide better sources of data to mine, but that is one of their side benefits. The primary purpose of a loyalty card is to reward the shopper for coming back frequently and spending lots of money. In that way, they are similar to the old S&H Green Stamps and to airline frequent flier programs. Up until the 1970s, many supermarkets offered S&H Green Stamps with purchases—something like ten stamps for every dollar. Housewives (for the most part) kept track of the stamps by pasting them into little books. And when the books were filled, they could be traded for useful items such as a toaster or blender. In the modern system, the store keeps track of your purchase points. A crucial difference is that the 1960s housewife kept track of her own stamps by pasting them into little books, but in the modern system, the store keeps track of your purchase points for you in its computer. Now, when the store is offering a new service, such as ready-to-eat, store-cooked meals, they can offer it just to people who have purchased frozen ready-to-eat meals in the past. Or, if the goal is simply to increase spending, they could offer shoppers a free dinner for spending more than $400 during a month. Throughout the month, they would let you know how close you are getting to the free dinner. Of course, the store cannot keep track of your points without knowing who you are so your purchase records are tied to your loyalty card number in a database.

Even with the most rudimentary data mining, the store can use the loyalty card data to better target its promotions. For example, Catalina Marketing helps supermarkets run loyalty programs, using each shopper's aggregate weekly spending (a figure not available without some way of linking purchases to shoppers) to tune rewards programs.

Let's revisit the free dinner for spending $400 promotion. It has the nice feature that the reward is to try a new product that the store is trying to promote, but it also has an important flaw. Some people don't spend anywhere near $400 per month and so do not even try for the reward; their behavior is not changed by the promotion. Other people routinely spend more than $400 a month and collect the free dinner without even trying; they too, are left unmoved by the promotion although they may develop a taste for the take-out dinners. Only the people for whom $400 per month is a small stretch exhibit the desired behavior—which is, of course, to spend more money than they otherwise would have. The solution is to give each customer (or, more likely, each of several bands of customers) a different spending target. That way, all customers are encouraged to spend more while no money is wasted on rewards for people who don't increase their spending. With more extensive data mining, the rewards themselves can be tailored to the customer both in price and content. Ultimately, each customer could be rewarded with a product that they have not bought in the past, but which, through data mining, we think they *ought* to like!

The cases presented in this chapter demonstrate that with the help of good visualization and analysis tools, even highly summarized, impersonal data collected from grocery store point-of-sale devices can be coaxed into revealing important information about the shopping habits of a particular population of interest. Before the advent of supermarket frequent shopper programs, the only personalized data on consumer buying habits was the so-called "panel data" collected by marketing organizations such as A. C. Nielson and IRI. Even today, the typical retail transaction is anonymous. If you make your purchase with cash, there is nothing to identify you. Even if you use a check, credit card, or debit card to make the purchase, the identifying information you supply is not usually stored for later analysis. Even if it were, it would be of limited value since people may have more than one credit card and make some of their purchases with cash. Under the circumstances, there is no reason to believe that the identifiable purchases are representative.

Check-out scanners record each item purchased, but without any identification of the buyer. With data of this kind, there is no way of knowing whether the shopper who just bought a box of cereal is male or female, old or young, rich or poor. Certainly, we do not know what language he or she speaks at home! And yet, that was essentially the goal of the project that is the subject of the first case study.

Three Case Studies

The case studies presented in this chapter must remain— like the majority of shopping transactions—anonymous. The clients for whom we performed this work requested that a few details be changed to make them harder to identify. We have therefore occasionally availed ourselves of the opportunity to take insights or findings from one case and graft them onto another where appropriate. The data analyzed in these case studies came from a large manufacturer of packaged goods sold in supermarkets and from several supermarket chains including a national chain, a regional chain in Texas, an association of independent supermarkets in the mid-Atlantic states, and a health food store in New England. The health food store and two of the supermarket chains had loyalty card data. The Texas chain did not. These projects employed a variety of data mining tools including MineSet from SGI and Enterprise Miner from SAS Institute.

Analyzing Ethnic Purchasing Patterns

Our client for this engagement was a manufacturer of packaged goods that was looking into starting an ethnic marketing campaign aimed at Spanish-speaking shoppers in South Texas. Using data supplied by a leading super-market chain in Texas, this case study describes how the manufacturer learned about ethnic purchasing patterns. This section starts with an introduction to the business problem followed by an examination of the store-level sales history data that was available for mining. Finally we chronicle our less than successful efforts to coax interesting association rules from the data and the success of visualization as a data mining tool in this situation.

Business Background

Before embarking on a program of ethnic marketing, the brand managers with the manufacturer needed to know whether there were any significant differences in the tastes and preferences that might differentiate the target population from the market as a whole.

In past studies of this kind, our client had been restricted to looking for patterns at high levels in the product hierarchy where variations in the popularity of individual products is masked by aggregation. This project was a pilot to determine whether the immense power of a data mining and visualization tool running on an SGI parallel processor would allow them to dispense with that restriction and perform analysis and visualization at the individual product level. This proved to be very fruitful. The pilot project demonstrated that even though there is not much variation in the performance of categories such as "ready-to-eat cereals" across ethnic groups, there is great variation in the performance of some of the category's constituent products.

The Data

The data set made available for this project consisted of sales data for our client's products together with competing products from other manufacturers. The data was collected from a supermarket chain in Texas, a state with a large enough Spanish-speaking population to justify a special marketing program.

In addition to weekly sales figures aggregated by store and item, we were provided with demographic data for the area surrounding each store (in industry parlance, the store's "catchment" area). Of particular interest for this study was the percentage of Hispanic shoppers. Our goal was to discover whether the data provided revealed any differences between the stores with a high percentage of Spanish-speaking customers and those having fewer.

The data consisted of weekly sales figures for the period of June 1996 through December 1997 for products from five basic categories:

- Ready-to-eat cereals
- Desserts
- Snacks
- Main meals
- Pancake and variety baking mixes

For each product within these categories, there was a variety of information including the category and subcategory to which the product was assigned, the actual units sold, the dollar volume, and the equivalent case sales—an industry measure of product quantity that counts two 8-ounce packages the same as one 16-ounce one. For each store, we had information on store size, the percentage of Hispanic shoppers, and the percentage of African-American shoppers.

Since the data was anonymous and already aggregated by week, there was no opportunity for market-basket analysis. Information detailing which products were purchased together had been collected at the point of sale, but later was lost through aggregation. There was no information to tie purchases to individual customers, nor any direct information on customers such as might be obtained through the application form for a store loyalty card.

While exploring the data, it became apparent that in some of the fields, useful information was obscured by complex coding schemes. The first step was to perform transformations to bring the information closer to the surface. One of the most important transformations for this data set was to decode variables that carried more than one piece of information.

Wily database designers frequently combine multiple, unrelated pieces of information inside a single variable, in effect camouflaging useful information so that data mining tools can't find it. This data provided some good examples of that practice. The database contained fields HISPLVL and AALEVEL to record the percentage of Hispanics and African-Americans, respectively, in the stores' catchment areas. Oddly, the two variables had different ranges. AALEVEL went from 1 to 10 with 1 indicating a neighborhood that was 90—100 percent African-American and 10 indicating a neighborhood that was 0—

10 percent African-American. HISPLVL(Hispanic Level), meanwhile, took on values from 1 to 15. It turned out that this field encoded information about both demographics and location. A value of 1 in the HISPLVL field indicated a store outside San Antonio with 90 percent or more Hispanic population. A 2 indicates a store outside San Antonio with 80–89 percent Hispanic population, and so on, up to the value of 10 for a store in a market with little or no Hispanic population. These values corresponded exactly with those of the AALEVEL variable. So far so good, but only for stores that were not in San Antonio. In San Antonio, a neighborhood with 90 percent or more Hispanic population is given the value 11. So in terms of Hispanic population, an 11 is equivalent to a 1, and a 15 is equivalent to a 5.

Presumably, the database designers wanted to treat San Antonio, with its historically high Mexican-American population differently from the rest of the state where the Hispanic influx was more recent. It makes sense to make use of whatever industry knowledge is available, so we have no quarrel with singling out one city for special treatment; we just want to do it in a different way. Encoding multiple pieces of information in a single variable in this manner is very likely to confuse data-mining algorithms, which often try to group numeric values into meaningful ranges. In this case, the solution was to use one field to represent the demographic information and another field, ALAMO, to flag San Antonio stores.

Another set of transformations was necessary to compare sales between stores of different sizes. To make these comparisons valid, we had to normalize values by taking the sales volume of the store into account. These derived variables divided the units, dollars, and equivalent cases by the total sales volume of the store so as to express all of these measures in relation to the size of the store.

Still more transformations were necessary to compare the sales performance of a product across different levels of Hispanic population. For this purpose, the stores were divided into three groups—low, medium, and high Hispanic; each group had weighted sums of sales, dollars, and equivalent cases. Finally, a set of "Hispanicity Scores" for each product was calculated by subtracting the average values for the least Hispanic stores from the average values for the most Hispanic stores. These final scores have the property that a large positive value indicates a product that sells much *better* in the heavily Hispanic stores, and a large negative value indicates a product that does significantly *worse* in heavily Hispanic stores.

As is usually the case, the most valuable part of the project was preparing the data and getting familiar with it, rather than in running fancy data mining algorithms.

A Triumph for Visualization

The makers of MineSet have a strong belief in the power of visualization as a data mining tool and in this case, we proved them right. Our client learned little of value from the various data mining algorithms we threw at the data, but as we will see, a single three-dimensional scatter plot gave them great insight into the problem at hand. Of course, on the way to that picture worth a thousand words and several tens of thousands of dollars, we looked at many less interesting graphical images.

A Visualization That Looked Interesting but Wasn't

One of the analytic tools in MineSet is the evidence visualizer. For a given target variable, the evidence model calculates the contribution that each input variable makes to the outcome. Using this tool, which displays the results from a statistical data mining technique known as naïve Bayesian modeling, the analyst can quickly determine which values or ranges of values for which variables are good evidence, either for or against a particular classification. The tool can be used interactively for "what if" analysis in a manner reminiscent of a graphical OLAP query tool. The user can pick a combination of variables and values that seems interesting and then see immediately the effect on the pie chart that represents the probabilities associated with various outcomes.

We ran the evidence visualizer with the Hispanic percentage quintile as the target variable in order to see if any shopping-related variables were strongly correlated with the demographics of the stores (see Figure 13.1). They were not. In fact, the variables that correlated most strongly with Hispanic percentage were

- The percentage of African-Americans
- Whether or not the store was in San Antonio
- The size of the store

The right side of this evidence chart shows the percentage of stores falling into each of five bins created from the percentage of Hispanic residents. On the left are the variables that contribute most to the classification. The most significant variable turns out to be the percent of African-Americans. At first, we hypothesized that perhaps African-Americans and Mexican-Americans would be found in the same neighborhoods because nationwide, both groups tend to be poorer than average. In fact, however, what MineSet discovered was that a *high* percentage of one group correlates with a *low* percentage of the other. The reason is that although in the wider world, Spanish speakers come in all colors and many black people have Spanish as their mother tongue, in this part of

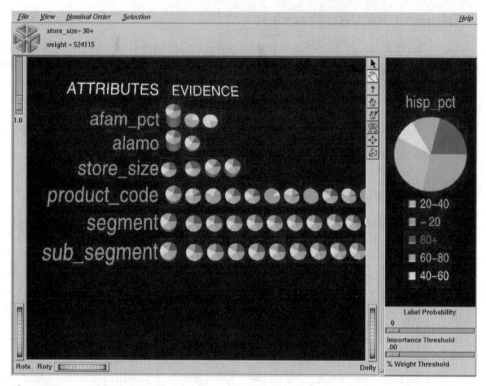

Figure 13.1 Evidence visualization for Hispanic percentage.

Texas, the Hispanic population is mostly Mexican and the black population is mostly non-Hispanic. A moment's thought shows that in a population where the two traits are pretty much mutually exclusive, if a particular neighborhood is more than 80 percent black, it can't possibly be more than 20 percent Hispanic. So much for what had at first appeared to be a data mining insight!

The San Antonio and store size variables that ranked next were similarly uninteresting for our marketing purpose. The former shows that different parts of the state have different demographics. We already knew that, and it doesn't help us decide what products to promote in Spanish. The latter shows that the chain has built larger stores in some kinds of neighborhoods than it has in others. That fact is interesting in its own right, but it too sheds little light on the problem at hand.

The next three variables, product code, segment, and subsegment, are a bit more interesting, because they do come from the grocery data. Product codes are integers assigned to the products to identify them in the database. MineSet bins these codes into product code ranges, and it was able to correlate particular groups of product codes with the target variable. That seemed very surprising until we learned that the product codes are not assigned randomly; similar products have similar codes. In fact, the product code ranges are expressing the same information as the segments and subsegments. A peanut butter segment might have subsegments creamy and chunky, and all items in the segment would have adjacent product codes.

A Failed Approach

Association rules are used for market basket analysis. The input data for market basket analysis consists of many records, each of which contains a list of products found in a single purchase. If the same combination of items turns up many times, it can become the basis for a rule such as "if peanut butter, then jelly."

The data we were working with was not suitable for ordinary market basket analysis because there is only one record for each product in each store and time period. However, we decided to create a market basket style analysis by using the amount of each product sold as a replication factor for each record. Each record also included a flag indicating whether it came from a store with high, medium, or low Hispanic population. Our hope was that we could then find some products in which high or low Hispanic level would show up together with certain products often enough to allow some association rules to be generated.

Unfortunately, at reasonable levels of prevalence and predictability (the usual measures of the significance for associations), no rules were found. Relaxing the standards for rule formation eventually produced the single rule illustrated in Figure 13.2. The chart says that sales of a particular brand of cereal in 10 oz. packages is an indicator for a store with low Hispanic level. The *predictability* of this rule is reasonably high, meaning that more than half the time if this product is purchased it is in a non-Hispanic store. However, the *prevalence* is low, meaning that there are not many examples of this combination in the data. Most likely, this particular product in this particular size is not stocked much anywhere, but happens to be stocked in some store that happens to be in a non-Hispanic area.

Just the Facts

The most exciting results came from visualizing derived hispanicity scores for every product. The hispanicity score of a product is the difference between its average normalized sales volume in the most Hispanic and least Hispanic stores. Thus, a product that sells better in Hispanic stores has positive hispanicity, whereas one that sells better in non-Hispanic stores has negative

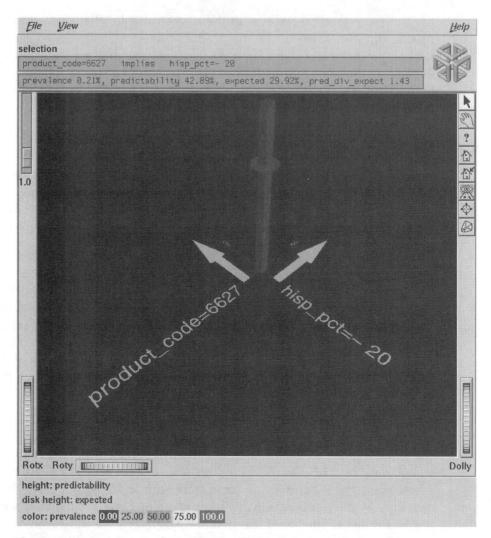

File   View   Help

selection

product_code=6627   implies   hisp_pct=- 20

prevalence 0.21%, predictability 42.89%, expected 29.92%, pred_div_expect 1.43

1.0

Rotx   Roty   Dolly

height: predictability
disk height: expected
color: prevalence 0.00 25.00 50.00 75.00 100.0

Figure 13.2   Association rule visualization for Hispanic percentage.

hispanicity. MineSet visualizations make heavy use of color, so the impact of this picture was much greater on the screen than on the pages of a black and white book.

Figure 13.3 is a scatterplot that shows the hispanicity scores. The color of each block is the hispanicity score, which represents the popularity of the product with Hispanic customers. It varies from red meaning "very popular" to blue meaning "very unpopular." The vertical bar represents units sold. The size of the box indicates dollar volume. Information about which products were favored and disfavored by shoppers in Spanish-speaking areas leapt right off the screen. This plot shows that

Figure 13.3   Scatterplot showing which products sell well in Hispanic neighborhoods.

a particular brand of corn flakes is a favorite among Hispanic consumers. Also of interest is the cluster of dark blue boxes in the lower right of the picture. These turn out to be various brands, shapes, and sizes of shredded wheat products that apparently do not appeal to the Spanish-speaking Texans who are the potential targets of an ethnic marketing campaign.

The client was very excited to be able to simply move the cursor over the big red boxes to discover the best selling products. In fact, in the eyes of the client, this picture justified the entire project.

WARNING

Although in this case it led to an interesting visualization, it does not normally make sense to treat inherently categorical data such a product IDs, customer codes, or telephone area codes as numeric variables even if they happen to be expressed as integers.

Previous attempts to find ethnic buying patterns at the category level had met with little success. At that level of summarization, there were only a few weak correlations such as slightly lower popularity of the microwave subcategory for most packaged food categories in the Hispanic stores. One scatterplot, shown in Figure 13.4, did reveal something interesting about the categories,

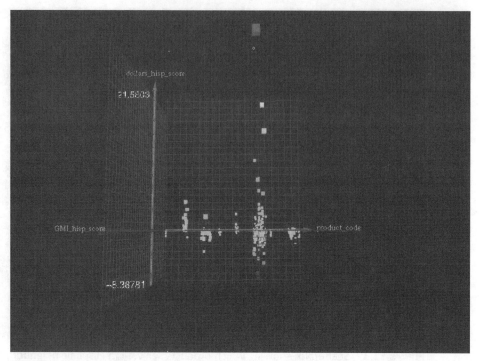

Figure 13.4   Scatterplot showing variability of Hispanic appeal by category.

however. In this plot, one of the axes is labeled with the item number of each product. Because the item numbers reflect the taxonomy of the product hierarchy, products in the same category are clustered together on the graph. This picture tells us that on average, all categories do about as well with both ethnic groups, but there is much greater *variation* in the hispanicity score within some categories than others.

Who Buys Yogurt at the Supermarket?

In this case study, we leave behind the old world of summarized, anonymous sales data and set sail for the El Dorado of detailed transaction histories for individual shoppers. The section starts with the business problem, how can loyalty cards be used to improve category management? Next, we take a closer look at the transaction detail data and explain what it takes to transform this low-level data about purchases into information on customer behavior. Finally, we suggest a way that this kind of analysis could be used to improve the targeting of coupons by spotting potential users of a product that have not yet revealed themselves by purchasing it.

Business Background

The second case was a collaboration between a packaged goods manufacturer and one of the retail chains where its goods are sold. Such collaborations are common in the grocery industry where many functions that would seem to belong to the retailer are actually performed by a supplier. In particular, a retail chain often names one vendor as the "category captain" for a particular category of products such as laundry products or salty snacks. The category captain manages the entire category on behalf of the store. If, for example, the Clorox company is the category captain for household cleaning products, they will get to decide how much of which products from Johnson & Johnson and other competitors get onto the shelves. This unlikely sounding arrangement is a result of two characteristics of the industry:

- Assuming the profit margins are the same, it makes no difference to the supermarket what brand of soap you buy.

- Supermarkets have very low margins and they are always looking for ways to get services for free from their suppliers.

Given this situation, it is not surprising that product manufacturers vie with one another for the job of managing the categories in which they compete. One way that a manufacturer can distinguish itself from its competitors is by showing that it can make effective use of sales data to make the category as a whole more profitable for the retailer. This is precisely what our client sought to demonstrate through data mining.

The Data

The data available for this study was composed of every single item scanned at the point of sale for a full year in each of seven supermarkets. For each item, we had the fields shown in Table 13.1.

Actually, the data arrived in two files. One file had all the fields listed in Table 13.1 except for the customer ID and tender type. The customer IDs were in a separate file, called the order file, which contained summary data for each market basket. Working with business people who understood the data, it was a simple matter to figure out that the common key for joining the files was date-store-lane-time. Joining the tables made it possible to apply customer IDs and tender types to the detailed transactions.

It was much harder to reconcile the *information* contained in the two files. The order file contained summary data such as the total number of items purchased, the number of distinct items purchased and the total dollar amount for the order, all ostensibly obtained by aggregating the detailed transactions. Our

Table 13.1 Transaction Detail Fields

FIELD	DESCRIPTION
Date	Date of transaction, YYYY-MM-DD
Store	Store of transaction, CCCSSSS, where CCC=chain, SSSS=store
Lane	Lane of transaction
Time	The time-stamp of the order start time
Customer ID	The loyalty card number presented by the customer; a customer ID of 0 means the customer did not present a card
Tender type	Payment type: 1=cash, 2=check, 3=American Express, 4=Visa, 5=MasterCard, 6=Discover, 7=debit card, 8=Diners Club, 9=food stamps
UPC	The universal product code for item purchased (see sidebar)
Quantity	The total quantity of this item (number of items or weight)
Dollar Amount	The total $ amount for the quantity of a particular UPC purchased

usual practice, when presented with one file that claims to summarize another, is to try to generate the summaries ourselves from the detail data. We are rarely successful. The problem is that whether it is telephone calls being rolled up into monthly usage reports, print signatures being rolled up into press runs, or scanner events being rolled up into market baskets, all sorts of hidden business rules come into play. In this case, we had no actual use for the order data since most of the useful information had been summarized away, but we did learn a lot about the data in the process of trying to recreate it:

TIP

When both summary and detailed or "drill through" data is available for the same time period, it is useful and educational to attempt to recreate the summaries from the detailed transactions. This often proves to be more difficult than expected and all sorts of data quality problems and hidden business rules can be revealed.

- Some UPCs are coupons, not products. These UPCs do not increment the total items field in the summary.

- For some items, such as potatoes, the quantity field is a weight, not a number of items. These items are recognizable by a 2 in the initial digit of the UPC (see sidebar). Anything sold by weight counts as one item.

- The dollar total in the summary data reflects taxes and discounts that apply to the whole order so the individual prices do not add up to the total.

- There are many ways to record the fact that a shopper purchased six cans of low-salt, reduced-fat, chicken broth—six individual scan events each with a quantity of one, one scan event with a quantity of six, one scan event with a quantity of one followed by another with a quantity of five, and so on.

Universal Product Codes

Universal product codes are the numbers, encoded as machine-readable bar codes, that identify nearly every product that might be sold in a grocery store. The codes actually are not all that universal. Although they may look similar, a product coded in France will not be recognized correctly by a scanner in the U.S. The codes used in the United States and Canada are controlled by an organization called the Uniform Code Council, which maintains a fascinating web site at www.uc-council.org. A similar organization, the European Article Numbering Association (EAN) administers product codes in Europe and much of the rest of the world. Their Web site is at www.ean.be. The two organizations are working together to develop worldwide standards.

In the meantime, our North American codes consist of 12 digits. The code itself fits in 11 digits; the twelfth is a checksum. The first digit identifies a particular encoding scheme. For example, an initial 2 indicates the coding scheme for items sold by weight. The next five digits are assigned by the Uniform Code Council to identify particular manufacturers. What they do with the remaining six digits is up to them. Some industry groups, such as the Turkey Growers Association, have developed standards for how their members should use the digits under their control. In other industries, it is left completely up to the discretion of the manufacturers.

To take advantage of UPCs, a store must maintain a continually updated database that maps UPCs into its own product codes or stock-keeping units (SKU) and thus into a product hierarchy of departments, categories, and subcategories.

WARNING

When working with summarized data, be sure you know the rules that govern the summarization. These rules may reveal important information about the underlying business process. We generally prefer to receive data at the most detailed level available and then perform our own aggregations as necessary. There are perils to this approach—an imperfect understanding of the field definitions (or a too trusting reading of the data dictionary) may lead to nonsensical aggregations such as mixing item counts with item weights—but at least the mistakes will be your own!

The snippet of data in Table 13.2 includes information about two market baskets. Both were purchased on 17 May 1998 at around 2:30 in the afternoon at store #405 belonging to supermarket chain #210. The first purchase, in lane 1, consists of three occurrences of item 87300233. First, one of these items was scanned at a cost of 98 cents. Then, a second was scanned and the cashier

Table 13.2 Sample Transaction Detail Data

DATE	CHAIN/ STORE	LANE	TIME	CUSTOMER ID	TENDER TYPE	UPC	QUANTITY	$ AMOUNT
5/17/98	210405	1	14:30:11	47045500611	1	87300233	1	0.99
5/17/98	210405	1	14:30:11	47045500611	1	87300233	2	1.98
5/17/98	210405	2	14:30:42	41196010012	1	87300309	1	0.99
5/17/98	210405	2	14:30:42	41196010012	1	812700021	2	1.33
5/17/98	210405	2	14:30:42	41196010012	1	834601635	1	6.29
5/17/98	210405	2	14:30:42	41196010012	1	834601695	2	1.98
5/17/98	210405	2	14:30:42	41196010012	1	834601695	4	3.96
5/17/98	210405	2	14:30:42	41196010012	1	834601695	3	2.97
5/17/98	210405	2	14:30:42	41196010012	1	834601695	1	0.99
5/17/98	210405	2	14:30:42	41196010012	1	834601696	4	3.96
5/17/98	210405	2	14:30:42	41196010012	1	834601696	12	11.88
5/17/98	210405	2	14:30:42	41196010012	1	834601696	2	1.98
5/17/98	210405	2	14:30:42	41196010012	1	834601749	2	1.98
5/17/98	210405	2	14:30:42	41196010012	4	834601749	1	0.99
5/17/98	210405	2	14:30:42	41196010012	1	834601749	2	1.98

Table 13.2 (Continued)

DATE	CHAIN/ STORE	LANE	TIME	CUSTOMER ID	TENDER TYPE	UPC	QUANTITY	$ AMOUNT
5/17/98	210405	2	14:30:42	41196010012	1	834601749	2	1.98
5/17/98	210405	2	14:30:42	41196010012	1	834601749	2	1.98
5/17/98	210405	2	14:30:42	41196010012	1	834601750	2	1.98
5/17/98	210405	2	14:30:42	41196010012	1	834601750	1	0.99
5/17/98	210405	2	14:30:42	41196010012	1	834602918	1	0.99
5/17/98	210405	2	14:30:42	41196010012	1	834602920	1	0.99
5/17/98	210405	2	14:30:42	41196010012	1	834663038	1	5.94
5/17/98	210405	2	14:30:42	41196010012	1	834663049	1	5.94
5/17/98	210405	2	14:30:42	41196010012	1	1600066610	2	6.58
5/17/98	210405	2	14:30:42	41196010012	1	920001475	1	1.85
5/17/98	210405	2	14:30:42	41196010012	1	920001475	1	1.85
5/17/98	210405	2	14:30:42	41196010012	1	920009301	1	2.99
5/17/98	210405	2	14:30:42	41196010012	1	980000003	1	0.5
5/17/98	210405	2	14:30:42	41196010012	1	1800070350	1	1.99
5/17/98	210405	2	14:30:42	41196010012	1	980000003	1	0.5

keyed in a quantity of two so that the dollar amount field of the second record contains $1.98. The third record starts a new market basket because although the date, store, and time are the same, this transaction happens in the next lane over. (Note that the customer ID cannot be used as a key because (1) customers who do not present a card will have ID 0 and (2) we may not want to roll up separate trips made by the same customers.)

From Groceries to Customers

Multiply these transactions by all the people in all the lanes in all the stores for every day for a year and the resulting database is vast and unwieldy. Somehow, all that scanner data about cans, cartons, pounds, and ounces had to be turned into derived data that could reveal something about customer behavior. Answering questions about who is buying what, when they are buying it, and what else they might like to buy in the future, requires many more variables and far fewer records. It also requires some auxiliary data describing the items purchased so we can tell the difference between beer and diapers in the shopping cart, and the similarity between butter and margarine.

The auxiliary data takes the form of a mapping from the universal product codes scanned into the item numbers or SKUs (stock-keeping units) used by the chain and a mapping of those item numbers into a product hierarchy. With the help of these additional tables, upon seeing UPC 002700048918, we can say that the category is popcorn, the subcategory is microwave, the segment is shelf-stable, the manufacturer is Hunt & Wesson, the brand is Orville Redenbacker, the flavor is "butter," and the product description printed on the shoppers register receipt reads "OR MW G BT B 6CT 21 OZ." We also know that the product is salted, not considered low-fat, and ships 36 to the case. Appending all of this information to each record in the transaction detail table might seem an odd way to reduce the data size, but it is a necessary first step in order to reduce the number of records by performing meaningful aggregations (see Table 13.3).

From transaction detail records of this form, it is possible to create hundreds of behavioral fields for each customer (see Table 13.4). For this project, the focus was on the time of day that people habitually shop and how they allocate their grocery dollars across the categories. For each shopper, we calculated the number of trips and the amount of money spent at each time of day (morning, lunch time, after lunch, evening, and late night) and on weekends, holidays, and week days. We also calculated the percentage of the items purchased that carried high, medium, and low profit margins for the store. For each of the categories of interest, we calculated the percent of each shopper's total spending that went to that category, the total number of trips and the total dollar amount spent for the year along with the total number of items purchased and the total number of distinct items purchased. These new variables, all of which were based on simple aggregations of the transaction detail, were used to create fur-

Table 13.3 The Expanded Transaction Detail Record

FIELD	DESCRIPTION
CKOUT_KEY	Unique key identifying checkout
STOR_KEY	Unique key identifying store and chain
CHN_CD	Chain code
STOR_CD	Store code
LANE_NBR	Lane number
EVNT_DT_KEY	Date (MMDDYYYY)
EVNT_TM_KEY	Time (HHMMSS)
PRD_UPC_KEY	Product UPC
PRD_UPC_QTY	Number of particular UPCs purchased
PRD_UPC_AMT	$ amount spent on particular UPC
CUST_CARD_CD	Frequent shopper ID
CKOUT_AMT	Total purchased $ amount
CKOUT_ITM_QTY	Total # of items purchased
UNIQUE_UPC_QTY	Total # of distinct UPCs purchased
PAYT_TY_NBR	Payment type code
UPC_DESC	Product UPC description
SIZE_DESC	Size description
SIZ	Size
UOM	Unit of measure
CASE_PACK	Case pack
MFG_DESC	Manufacturer's description
MFR_CD	Manufacturer ID
ITEM_NUM	Item number
MARGIN	High, medium, or low profitability
PRIV_LABEL	Private label flag
SEGMENT	Product grouping description
SEGMENT_CD	Product grouping code
CATEGORY	Category description
CATEGORY_CD	Category code
SUBCATEGORY	Subcategory description
SUBCATEGORY_CD	Subcategory code
HSHLD_CD	Frequent shopper household ID
TCARD_IN_HSHLD_QTY	Number of cards in household

Table 13.4   Partial Listing of Customer Fields Derived from Transaction Detail

FIELD
CUST_CARD_CD
TOT_DAYTIME_CKOUT_AMT
TOT_DAYTIME_CKOUT_CNT
TOT_EVENING_CKOUT_AMT
TOT_EVENING_CKOUT_CNT
TOT_LATENIT_CKOUT_AMT
TOT_LATENIT_CKOUT_CNT
TOT_HOLIDAY_AMT
TOT_HOLIDAY_CNT
TOT_WEEKEND_AMT
TOT_WEEKEND_CNT
TOT_WEEKDAY_AMT
TOT_WEEKDAY_CNT
TOT_CKOUTS
TOT_AMT
MAX_AMT
MIN_AMT
AVG_AMT
MAX_ITM_QTY
MIN_ITM_QTY
AVG_ITM_QTY
MAX_UNIQUE
AVG_UNIQUE
MIN_UNIQUE
OUR_BRAND_PKGD_ICE_CRM
TOT_PKGD_ICE_CRM
OUR_BRAND_ICE_CRM_NVLTIES
TOT_ICE_CRM_NVLTIES
OUR_BRAND_DAIRY_YOGURT
TOT_DAIRY_YOGURT

ther derived variables such as an adventurousness index defined as the ratio of a customer's distinct items to total items.

Finding Clusters of Customers

With hundreds of variables describing the customers, the next step was to run an automatic cluster detection program to find groups of customers with similar behavior. The clustering algorithm supported by MineSet is called *k*-means, and is described in Chapter 5. You will recall a certain number, *k*, of the records are selected as candidate cluster centers and every record is provisionally assigned to the cluster whose center it is nearest. Then the centers of the clusters are recalculated and the records are reassigned based on their proximity to the new cluster centers. This process goes on until the clusters settle down.

One problem with this algorithm is that there is no obvious way of choosing the value of *k*. MineSet provides the option of specifying a range of values for *k*. In this case, we asked MineSet to find from 5 to 10 clusters. When presented with a range of values for *k*, MineSet first finds the smaller number of clusters by the traditional *k*-means algorithm sketched previously. It then finds the most dispersed cluster and splits it into two more cohesive ones. This process continues until the upper bound of the range for *k* is reached. The algorithm then decides which set of clusters is best and keeps them. In this particular case, we ended up with eight clusters, some of which are visible in Figure 13.5.

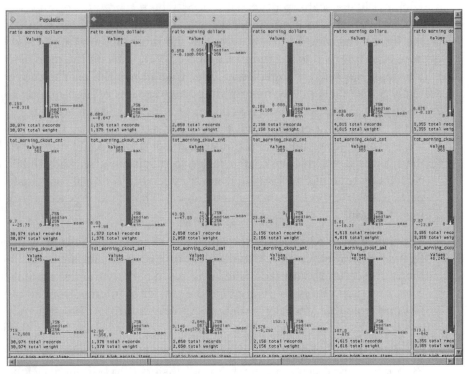

Figure 13.5 Clusters of shoppers.

The hardest thing about automatic cluster detection is making sense of the clusters once they have been automatically detected. The MineSet cluster visualizer consists of a set of small graphs showing statistics on each variable within the clusters. By default, the variables are sorted in decreasing order of their ability to differentiate the clusters from the general population. In Figure 13.6, we can see that the most important variables for distinguishing the clusters are the ratio of dollars spent in the morning to total dollars spent and the total number of morning checkouts. In the general population, people averaged around 10 morning checkouts over the course of the study period, accounting for about 15 percent of total spending. In cluster one, the average number of morning checkouts is less than one and morning checkouts account for only about 1 percent of total spending. Cluster two, on the other hand, is full of people who like to leap out of bed and head for the supermarket. In that cluster, the average shopper had around 44 morning checkouts accounting for nearly 86 percent of total spending.

At the very bottom of Figure 13.5, it is just possible to see that after three highly correlated variables having to do with morning shopping, the next most important variable for distinguishing the clusters is the ratio of high margin (that is to say, very profitable) items to total items. That suggested the visualization shown in Figure 13.6. This is output from the MineSet splat visualizer, which is like a scatterplot for situations where there are too many points to plot individually. Individual points get averaged into a sort of colored haze. In the figure, the ratio of dollars spent in the morning, afternoon, and evening have been mapped to the three axes of the splat plot, and the ratio of high margin items has been mapped to a slider that allows the user to move interactively from a view of low-margin shoppers to a view of high-margin shoppers. The figure captures the screen as it looked with the slider all the way to the left, so the colors represent clusters of low-margin customers by time of day. If this were an interactive book, and if it were in color, you could move the slider to the right and watch the colors change to display higher and higher margin clusters by time of day. Having done so, you would notice that cluster four is particularly rich in high-margin customers. That cluster is worthy of further investigation!

The statistical cluster viewer shown in Figure 13.5 provides one way of investigating the high margin cluster. By clicking on a cluster's colored bar at the top of the column, you tell MineSet to reorder the variables so that they are sorted by their ability to distinguish the cluster of interest from all other clusters and from the general population. Another approach, not shown here, is to use the MineSet evidence visualizer to see which variables play the greatest part in determining cluster membership.

Yet another approach to understanding clusters is to build a decision tree that classifies records by cluster membership. This gives approximate rules for

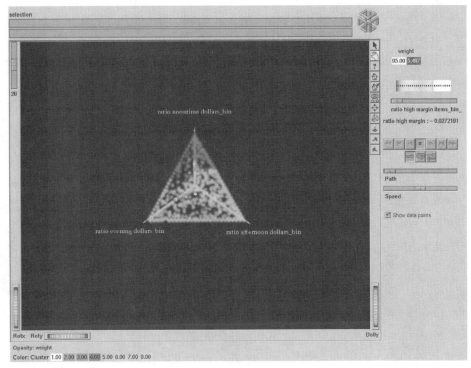

Figure 13.6   Visualizing clusters of shoppers.

cluster membership. When a leaf of the tree bears a certain cluster label, the path from the root node to that leaf can be read as a rule for inclusion in that cluster. Of course, there may be several leaves labeled with the same cluster and therefore, several rules describing its members. Figure 13.7 shows such a tree. The spotlight is on a leaf node where nearly every record is from the most populous cluster, which seems to consist of afternoon shoppers of medium profitability.

Putting the Clusters to Work

Finding clusters is rarely the final goal of a data mining project. Clusters are only useful when they can be put to some practical use. One way of using clusters is to identify customer segments that could benefit from some new product or service. If there is a cluster of customers who come into the store at lunch time to purchase ready-to-eat items from the deli counter, but also pick up a few groceries, perhaps they could be enticed to pick up a few more groceries by offering a delayed home delivery service. Another way to use clustering is to feed them back into the data as an aid to further analysis.

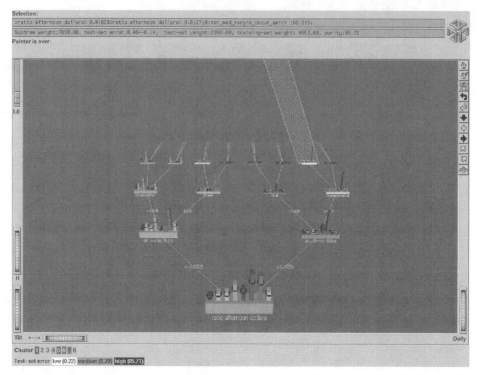

Figure 13.7 A decision tree to explain the clusters.

In an OLAP context, the clusters might become customer segments that become an additional dimension in a multidimensional database to enable reports of sales by category, by store, by time of day, by customer cluster, say. In a data mining context, there are three main ways to use clusters. The first, which we have already seen, is to gain insight into customer behavior by understanding what differentiates one cluster from another.

The second is to build further models *within* the clusters. It sometimes happens that when no patterns are observable in a large data set, it is not because there are no patterns to be found, but because there are too many competing patterns canceling each other out. If we want to build a best next offer model to determine what new product to offer each customer, we are likely to get better results by building a separate model for each customer cluster than by building a single model for the whole population.

The third use for clusters in data mining is as additional input variables to another model. In this case, we wanted to build models that would help identify a target audience for a promotion that would be of mutual benefit for the producer and the retailer. One product that generates high margins for both parties is yogurt, so we decided to identify big yogurt buyers and, even more importantly, *potential* big yogurt buyers.

We defined a yogurt lover as someone who is in the top third of the population for the total amount of yogurt purchased *and* in the top third of the population in terms of the percentage of their yearly grocery bill that goes to yogurt. Many other definitions could be made, but this one made sense to our client. Just having such a definition gives us the opportunity to put a yogurt lover flag on a customer's record in the customer database. One use of such a flag is to have a coupon for our client's brand of yogurt generated at the point of sale when a yogurt-lover checks out *even if they haven't bought any yogurt this trip.* Arguably, the worst time to offer someone a coupon for your brand is when they have just stocked up on your competitor's brand and won't need to shop for that product for some time. Only an empirical study will determine whether this use of the yogurt flag proves to be effective. We are hoping for such an experiment, but as of this writing, it has yet to be performed.

An even more untested idea, but one that appeals to us as data miners, is to use the identified yogurt lovers to identify people who *look like* yogurt buyers, but who, for some reason, are culturing their own yogurt at home, or buying it in some other store, or simply haven't yet recognized their inner yogurt-lover because they haven't yet received the free trial pack that will change their lives forever. Finding records that are similar to a known set of records cries out for some sort of nearest neighbor approach. Among the tools at our disposal, the simplest approach to the problem was to build a decision tree with yogurt lover as the target class. The idea is that if you end up in a leaf of the tree with lots of yogurt lovers, you look like one, too. The higher the proportion of known yogurt lovers in your node, the higher your score from our potential yogurt buyer model.

From our point of view, MineSet produced a very good model of the yogurt lover. The decision tree obtained excellent lift when used to find the known yogurt lovers in a test set of unseen data. Unfortunately, the tree that was lovely in our eyes because of the fruit it bore, seemed less lovely to our client because of its unruly tangle of branches. They were hoping that the model would paint an understandable picture of the yogurt lover—something like "women aged 20 to 25 who shop mainly in the evenings and weekends and buy a low proportion of meat and salty snacks." Alas, instead of finding one or two easy-to-describe groups of yogurt buyers like that, we found 20 or so little pockets of yogurt buyers each described by a different rule. All of these rules could easily be expressed in SQL and used to generate a database flag or a direct mail offer of some kind. We believe that such an offer might have yielded good results but, for better or worse, it was not our marketing budget, so we never got to find out.

Who Buys Meat at the Health Food Store?

You cannot have read this far without realizing that we believe strongly that data mining should not go on in a vacuum. Data mining belongs in a business context where it can serve well-articulated goals and answer important questions. Despite this, it sometimes happens that we are simply handed a data set and asked to show what data mining can do with it. In one such case, the data we were asked to investigate was transaction-level data from loyalty card holders at a New England health food supermarket. We loaded the data into SAS Enterprise Miner and together with Anne Milley of SAS Institute, we discovered a few interesting things.

Since there was no actual business problem to be solved, the search for interesting patterns in the data started by generating association rules, a common approach to market basket analysis. Then, because we are more interested in customer behavior than in learning which products sell well together, we used undirected data mining to look for naturally occurring customer segments and undirected data mining to learn more about one particular segment that seemed interesting to us—people who buy meat in a store frequented largely by vegetarians.

Association Rules for Market Basket Analysis

We don't often get much mileage out of association rules, but market basket analysis is what they were made for, so we put them to work on the health food data. Association rules are an undirected data mining technique for examining what sells well with what. The rules all have the form

```
Left-hand side implies right-hand side
```

Association rules go in only one direction. In a restaurant, we might discover that "caviar implies vodka" is a strong association, but that "vodka implies caviar" is much weaker. Both the left-hand side and the right-hand side may be combinations of more than one item as in the first rule in Table 13.5: "red peppers imply yellow peppers, bananas, and bakery." Of course, any market basket is full of potential rules since any one item in the basket may imply all of the others. How do we decide which associations have predictive power? As it turns out, there are three separate measures that must all be taken into consideration: support (also called prevalence), confidence (also called predictability), and lift.

Support is the percentage of baskets that contain both the left-hand side and the right-hand side of the association. That is, the percentage of baskets where the rule is true.

Confidence is the percentage of baskets having the left-hand side that also contain the right-hand side. In other words, confidence is the probability that the right-hand product is present given that we know the left-hand product is in the basket.

Lift compares the likelihood of finding the right-hand product in a basket known to contain the left-hand product, to the likelihood of finding the right-hand product in any random basket. This is the same measure we use for comparing other kinds of models. It measures how well the rule performs by comparing the performance of the rule to the "null" rule; that is, to the concentration of the right-hand side. Lift in this case is sometimes called *improvement*, because it measures the improvement of the prediction.

It is easy to come up with examples where any one of these numbers, used in isolation, is misleading. The rule that caviar implies vodka is likely to have high confidence, but if it has very little support because hardly anyone ever orders caviar, then it isn't much use. High confidence is also misleading when there is a popular item on the right-hand side of the association. The rules "peanut butter implies milk," "eggs imply milk," and "bread implies milk" have high confidence because it is hard to find a shopping basket that contains no milk. It is hard to think of anything useful to do with these high confidence, high prevalence associations.

Of the three measures, lift comes closest to being useful on its own because it measures the extent to which the rule improves our ability to predict the right-hand side. It, too, can be misleading when the support is low, however.

One of the difficulties with association rules is that there are just too many of them. Even after setting minimum thresholds for support, confidence, and lift, the miner must sort through thousands of rules looking for something interesting. Unfortunately, we are not yet able to teach a computer to distinguish between the intriguing and the deadly dull. To be interesting, a rule must be both unexpected and potentially useful. The association rule algorithms do not share our expectations, nor do they know what information might be useful, so they just spit out all the associations they find. Table 13.5 is a small excerpt from the list of association rules that Enterprise Miner found in the health food data. This happens to be all the rules involving red, yellow, and green peppers. We challenge you to spend some time staring at this list trying to spot what we found interesting about it before turning to the page following the table to read our answer.

Table 13.5 Association Rules for Market Basket Analysis

	RELATIONS	LIFT	SUPPORT	CONFIDENCE	RULE
1	4	2.47	3.23	33.72	RED PEPPERS → YELLOW PEPPERS & BANANAS & BAKERY
2	3	2.24	4.75	49.51	RED PEPPERS → YELLOW PEPPERS & BANANAS
3	2	2.22	3.23	33.72	RED PEPPERS → VINE TOMATOES
4	4	2.16	4.28	14.14	YELLOW PEPPERS → KITCHEN & BANANAS & BAKERY
5	3	2.15	3.46	36.06	RED PEPPERS → YELLOW PEPPERS & BAKERY
6	3	2.14	3.18	10.49	YELLOW PEPPERS → FLORAL & BANANA
7	4	2.11	3.66	12.10	YELLOW PEPPERS → BODY CARE & BANANAS & BAKERY
8	3	2.06	4.93	16.30	YELLOW PEPPERS → KITCHEN & BAKERY
9	3	2.01	5.21	17.22	YELLOW PEPPERS → BODY CARE & BANANAS
10	4	1.98	3.23	10.68	YELLOW PEPPERS → RED PEPPERS & BANANAS & BAKERY
11	3	1.97	5.98	19.75	YELLOW PEPPERS → KITCHEN & BANANAS
12	3	1.96	4.19	13.83	YELLOW PEPPERS → BODY CARE & BAKERY
13	3	1.95	3.46	11.42	YELLOW PEPPERS → RED PEPPERS & BAKERY
14	4	1.93	3.23	62.01	YELLOW PEPPERS & RED PEPPERS → BANANAS & BAKERY
15	4	1.87	3.14	10.37	YELLOW PEPPERS → PRODUCE & BANANAS & BAKERY
16	2	1.86	3.68	12.16	YELLOW PEPPERS → FLORAL
17	3	1.86	3.94	13.02	YELLOW PEPPERS → MED MUSHROOMS & BANANAS
18	3	1.83	4.75	15.68	YELLOW PEPPERS → RED PEPPERS & BANANAS
19	3	1.80	3.31	10.93	YELLOW PEPPERS → OG SALAD MIX & BANANAS
20	2	1.80	5.21	17.22	YELLOW PEPPERS → RED PEPPERS
21	2	1.80	5.21	54.39	RED PEPPERS → YELLOW PEPPERS
22	2	1.80	7.32	24.20	YELLOW PEPPERS → KITCHEN
23	3	1.79	3.40	11.23	YELLOW PEPPERS → PRODUCE & BAKERY
24	4	1.78	3.27	10.80	YELLOW PEPPERS → OG CANTALOUPE & BANANAS & BAKERY
25	2	1.78	6.28	20.74	YELLOW PEPPERS → BODY CARE
26	3	1.77	3.12	10.31	YELLOW PEPPERS → OG BARTLETT PEARS & BANANAS

Table 13.5   *(Continued)*

	RELATIONS	LIFT	SUPPORT	CONFIDENCE	RULE
27	3	1.76	5.40	56.34	RED PEPPERS → BANANAS & BAKERY
28	3	1.75	3.49	11.54	YELLOW PEPPERS → OG BANANAS & BANANAS
29	3	1.75	3.53	11.67	YELLOW PEPPERS → OG YELLOW ONIONS & BANANAS
30	4	1.74	4.30	14.20	YELLOW PEPPERS → BANANAS & BAKERY & 5 CENT DEPOSIT
31	3	1.74	3.36	11.11	YELLOW PEPPERS → OG RED LEAF & BANANAS
32	2	1.74	3.40	11.23	YELLOW PEPPERS → OG BROCCOLI
33	2	1.73	4.33	14.32	YELLOW PEPPERS → MED MUSHROOMS
34	3	1.71	3.61	11.91	YELLOW PEPPERS → OG RED FLAME GRAPES & BANANAS
35	4	1.71	3.14	10.37	YELLOW PEPPERS → PERISHABLE GROC. & BANANAS & BAKERY
36	2	1.71	3.33	10.99	YELLOW PEPPERS → OG PEACHES
37	3	1.70	3.51	11.60	YELLOW PEPPERS → OG CANTALOUPE & BAKERY
38	3	1.68	3.31	10.93	YELLOW PEPPERS → OG GALA APPLES & BANANAS
39	3	1.67	3.61	11.91	YELLOW PEPPERS → OG CUCUMBERS & BANANAS
40	2	1.66	3.66	12.10	YELLOW PEPPERS → OG SALAD MIX
41	4	1.66	3.96	13.09	YELLOW PEPPERS → VINE TOMATOES & BANANAS & BAKERY
42	2	1.66	3.96	13.09	YELLOW PEPPERS → OG RED FLAME GRAPES
43	3	1.64	4.24	14.01	YELLOW PEPPERS → PRODUCE & BANANAS
44	2	1.64	3.44	11.36	YELLOW PEPPERS → OG BARTLETT PEARS
45	2	1.64	3.70	12.22	YELLOW PEPPERS → OG RED LEAF
46	2	1.64	3.27	10.80	YELLOW PEPPERS → OG ZUCCHINI SQUASH
47	2	1.63	3.38	11.17	YELLOW PEPPERS → OG GREEN ONIONS
48	3	1.63	3.25	10.74	YELLOW PEPPERS → PERISHABLE GROC. & BAKERY
49	2	1.62	3.81	12.59	YELLOW PEPPERS → OG YELLOW ONIONS
50	3	1.62	3.14	10.37	YELLOW PEPPERS → BANANAS & 30 CENT DEPOSIT
51	2	1.61	3.61	11.91	YELLOW PEPPERS → OG GALA APPLES
52	2	1.61	3.79	12.53	YELLOW PEPPERS → OG BANANAS
53	3	1.60	4.39	14.51	YELLOW PEPPERS ' VINE TOMATOES & BAKERY

(Continues)

Table 13.5 Association Rules for Market Basket Analysis *(Continued)*

	RELATIONS	LIFT	SUPPORT	CONFIDENCE	RULE
54	3	1.60	4.32	14.26	YELLOW PEPPERS → OG CANTALOUPE & BANANAS
55	3	1.59	3.64	12.04	YELLOW PEPPERS → OG CARROTS LOOSE & BANANAS
56	3	1.59	4.60	15.19	YELLOW PEPPERS → BAKERY & 5 CENT DEPOSIT
57	3	1.59	4.19	13.83	YELLOW PEPPERS → PERISHABLE GROC. & BANANAS
58	3	1.57	3.53	11.67	YELLOW PEPPERS → GENERAL GROCERY & BANANAS
59	3	1.56	6.05	20.00	YELLOW PEPPERS → BANANAS & 5 CENT DEPOSIT
60	3	1.55	5.83	19.26	YELLOW PEPPERS → VINE TOMATOES & BANANAS
61	2	1.54	3.53	11.67	YELLOW PEPPERS → 30 CENT DEPOSIT
62	2	1.54	3.94	13.02	YELLOW PEPPERS → OG CUCUMBERS
63	3	1.53	3.46	11.42	YELLOW PEPPERS → OG VALENCIA ORANGES LGE & BANANAS
64	2	1.52	4.67	15.43	YELLOW PEPPERS → PRODUCE
65	2	1.51	4.75	15.68	YELLOW PEPPERS → OG CANTALOUPE
66	2	1.49	3.20	10.56	YELLOW PEPPERS → OG THOMPSON GRAPES
67	3	1.49	3.46	66.31	YELLOW PEPPERS & RED PEPPERS → BAKERY
68	2	1.47	3.85	12.72	YELLOW PEPPERS → GENERAL GROCERY
69	2	1.47	3.23	10.68	YELLOW PEPPERS → BAGELS
70	2	1.46	4.47	14.75	YELLOW PEPPERS → PERISHABLE GROC.
71	3	1.45	4.75	91.04	YELLOW PEPPERS & RED PEPPERS → BANANAS
72	2	1.44	6.63	21.91	YELLOW PEPPERS → VINE TOMATOES
73	2	1.44	3.94	13.02	YELLOW PEPPERS → OG CARROTS LOOSE
74	2	1.44	3.40	11.23	YELLOW PEPPERS → MISC. RANDOM MEAT
75	2	1.43	8.58	89.47	RED PEPPERS → BANANAS
76	3	1.41	13.68	45.19	YELLOW PEPPERS → BANANAS & BAKERY
77	2	1.39	3.76	12.41	YELLOW PEPPERS → OG VALENCIA ORANGES LGE
78	2	1.38	6.54	21.60	YELLOW PEPPERS → 5 CENT DEPOSIT
79	2	1.38	5.87	61.21	RED PEPPERS → BAKERY
80	2	1.37	3.77	85.96	GREEN PEPPERS → BANANAS
81	2	1.25	16.78	55.43	YELLOW PEPPERS → BAKERY
82	2	1.17	22.12	73.09	YELLOW PEPPERS → BANANAS

Give up? Well, we thought it was interesting that although there are many rules about red and yellow peppers, and a few even linking them, there is only one rule in this list of pepper rules for green peppers. In fact, in this list of pepper rules, which is sorted by lift, you have to go all the way down to rule number 80 to find the first rule that even mentions green peppers, and that turns out to be one of those high-confidence, high-support rules that simply means that nearly everyone buys bananas, and green pepper buyers are no exception. It isn't that no one is buying green peppers; at 1.37 percent of all baskets, the support for the rule "green peppers imply bananas" is between the 1.17 percent for "yellow peppers imply bananas" and the 1.43 percent for "red peppers imply bananas." Since bananas are universally popular, this means that green peppers sell in about the same quantities as red and yellow peppers—they just aren't as predictive.

Presumably, the reason for this finding is that both red and yellow peppers are flown in, like cut flowers, from hothouses in the Netherlands and so are quite expensive compared to the green peppers grown right here in the North American Free Trade Area. This suggests that red and yellow peppers go together not just because of their pretty colors (after all, a splash of green would also be nice in the stir-fry) but because of their snob appeal. If they have not already done so, the store should try putting the red and yellow peppers with the fresh morels and other exotica rather that with the common peppers. They might even try tripling the price of a few of the green peppers and displaying them with their high-priced cousins. Perhaps all three colors would sell together at the higher price!

People are More Interesting Than Groceries

Having exhausted our interest in the association rules, we then turned to another undirected data mining technique—clustering. Before building the clusters, we added a number of derived behavioral variables to the data. One that proved interesting was a flag showing whether the customer had ever purchased anything from the meat department. Only a small percentage of shoppers ever buy meat at the health food store, but those that do are an interesting segment.

The Enterprise Miner cluster visualizer allows us to display three variables at a time to explore the way they interact with the clusters. In Figure 13.8, we are looking at the way gender, meat buying, and total spending vary across the population and the three clusters found by the tool. The height of the pies corresponds to total spending; the shaded pie slice represents the percentage of people in the cluster who buy meat. The top row contains data on women and the bottom row contains data on men. Cluster three is interesting because nearly half the people—both men and women—are meat eaters. Cluster one is even more interesting—these people all spend more money than the people in the other clusters, and the women, but not the men, buy more meat than the

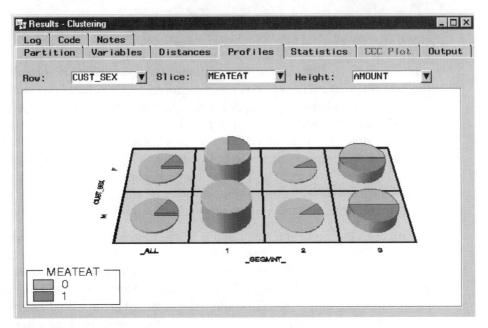

Figure 13.8 Customer clusters.

general population. We were not too sure what to make of these clusters, but it was certainly fun to make up stories about how the kind of man who does enough grocery shopping to have a loyalty card is a bit new-age to begin with, and if he does all his shopping at the health food store (as indicated by the high spending levels in cluster one) he must be even more so. Naturally, guys like him are vegetarians! Then again, maybe they come to this store because of the great produce, but buy all their meat at a favorite local butcher.

We decided to investigate meat buyers a little further by building a decision tree with the meat buyer flag as the target variable. Figure 13.9 shows Enterprise Miner's initial top view of a decision tree, which actually looks more like a stump. The rings signify levels in the tree. The lighter areas represent high concentrations of meat eaters.

Figure 13.10 shows a more conventional view of the tree. Here we can see that the most meat-buying branches of the tree are the people who spend the most money and buy the largest number of items. Although only about 5 percent of the shoppers buy meat, they are among the most valuable shoppers the store has. It seems likely that these people are doing all their shopping in this store rather than picking up a few specialty items after doing the bulk of their shopping at a regular supermarket.

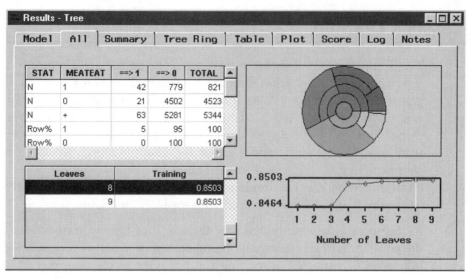

Figure 13.9   Top view of meat eaters tree.

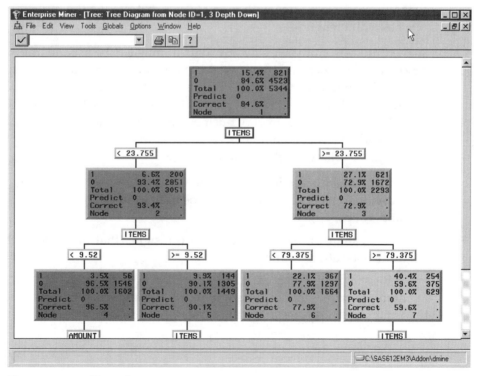

Figure 13.10   More about meat.

Lessons Learned

The first case study focused, out of necessity, on the grocery products themselves because that is what the data contained. Except for a couple of demographic variables about the neighborhood where the store was located, there was no information about customers and their behavior. Nevertheless, by using demographic data on the neighborhoods surrounding the stores we were able to make inferences about the shopping preferences of Hispanic shoppers. In this case, one of the strongest lessons is about the power of visualization. Sometimes, a simple scatterplot reveals more about what the data has to say than can be discovered with sophisticated tools.

In the second case study, we saw the value of having transactions that are linked to individual customers. Using customer IDs, it was possible to derive hundreds of variables describing the behavior of the shoppers themselves. These variables were used to feed predictive models capable of identifying good targets for a coupon or direct mail campaign. A secondary lesson was that even models that do a good job of predicting who is likely to respond to an offer may not paint a clear picture of that person. This is true even of models, such as decision trees, that can be translated into rules. The problem is that when there is a large tree with many leaves that predict the same thing, each one has a different rule.

In the third case study, we saw how data mining can be used to improve shelf placement decisions and to uncover a small, but very profitable group of customers that might leave entirely if one line of products were discontinued. Overall, this chapter has tried to convey the range of exciting possibilities that are set to transform the grocery business and other similar businesses including the wider world of retail sales, cataloging, and e-commerce. Along the way, we made the following observations:

- Anonymous transactions do not allow the data miner to learn much about individual customers, but they can be used to study the behavior of important groups.

- Visualization can sometimes provide insights that are difficult to glean from associations or models.

- Transaction level data must be aggregated in imaginative ways in order to derive variables that capture important aspects of customer behavior, such as favorite categories and habitual shopping days and times.

- Models with good predictive value may still fail to paint a recognizable portrait of the consumers whose behavior is being predicted. This is fine if the goal is targeting likely buyers, but disappointing if the goal is to understand who those buyers are and what makes them such good prospects.

- Association rules often discover trivial or uninteresting associations, but sometimes the absence of an expected association (as between green peppers and their more colorful cousins) can lead to insight.

- Automatically detected clusters can sometimes suggest market segments (like the meat buyers in the third case study) worthy of further study.

Waste Not, Want Not: Improving Manufacturing Processes

Customer relationship management is the "killer application" that spawned the dozens of data mining software packages and consultancies now competing in the marketplace. It is, however, by no means the only profitable area where data mining can be employed. Another fruitful application for data mining is cost reduction through industrial process improvement. This is especially true in environments where factory automation allows the relevant data to be collected automatically, but as the first case study demonstrates, data mining can be applied even in less automated facilities.

The efficiency of many manufacturing processes depends on hundreds or thousands of variables whose interactions are not well understood. Small variations in temperatures, pressures, amperage, weight, viscosity, speed, humidity, and air pressure can make the difference between profitable yields and unprofitable waste. Data mining has been applied successfully to manufacturing processes ranging from chip fabrication to coffee roasting. The case studies in this chapter come from the commercial printing industry where deadlines are often tight and a break in a roll of paper or a stripe of ink across the printed page can be very costly.

This chapter looks at two publishing companies—R. R. Donnelley & Sons and Time Inc.—that have both saved millions of dollars by mining production data to find ways to cut waste. The first case involves a technical problem known as *banding*, which can occur in the rotogravure printing process, causing costly delays and repair work. This technical problem is also a business problem because it increases the overall cost of production. We will see how

R. R. Donnelley used decision trees to come up with a set of operating procedures that greatly reduced the incidence of this problem. The second case shows how Time Inc. was able to mine a large database of print-run data to find causes for reducing paper waste in their web-fed offset presses by identifying the best practices that caused some of their plants to waste less paper than others.

Data Mining to Reduce Cost at R. R. Donnelley

R. R. Donnelley and Sons, a *Fortune*-500 company founded in 1864, is the largest printing company in the United States. It has sales of around $5 billion yearly from printing magazines, catalogs, telephone directories, text books, newspapers, direct mail pieces, and just about anything else that can be printed. The company has 49 manufacturing plants. One of these plants, in Gallatin, Tennessee, is the setting for this chapter's first case study.

According to a corporate information document from Donnelley, the company has three principal strategies for enhancing customer and shareholder value. The document describes the first of these strategies as "driving continuous cost reduction and productivity improvement by creating process improvements, optimizing our manufacturing operations and enhancing supply-chain management." One way that Donnelley can increase productivity is by isolating conditions that lead to presses being stopped in the middle of a run. One such problem is cylinder banding.

The Technical Problem

At the Donnelley printing plant in Gallatin, Tennessee, high-speed printing is done on rotogravure presses (see sidebar). Ever since the plant opened in 1975, it has experienced occasional outbreaks of a mysterious problem called "cylinder banding." A cylinder band is a series of grooves that appears in the chrome-plated, copper cylinder that has been engraved with the image to be printed. The symptom of cylinder banding is a streak of ink running across the printed image, ruining the print job. The rotogravure process has been in use for about a century, but cylinder bands only became a problem in the 1950s when presses began operating at over 1,000 feet per minute. Today, the fastest rotogravure presses turn out magazines and catalogs at rates of up to 3000 feet per minute (and you thought your laser printer was fast!). By 1989, cylinder banding had become common enough to warrant special study. Donnelley formed a task force to address the problem.

One of the task force members was Bob Evans, a software engineer at Donnelley who was then working on a Masters degree at Vanderbilt University. Bob's academic focus was on machine learning, including the use of decision trees for rule induction. He decided to apply this technique to the cylinder band problem in order to induce a set of rules that could be used prescriptively to avoid banding.

We first heard about the project by attending a talk that Bob Evans gave at a data mining conference called the "Data Mining Summit" sponsored by Miller-Freeman in March of 1998. Our account of what happened in Gallatin is based on what we heard there, on subsequent conversations with Bob, and on articles that he published in the February1994 issue of *IEEE Expert* and the April 1997 issue of *Database Programming & Design*.

Rotogravure Printing

In rotogravure printing, the image to be printed is engraved in a chrome plate that is wrapped around a copper cylinder. Gravure is an *intaglio* process, meaning that the nonprinting area is on a plane surface into which the printing areas are engraved. The image on the plate actually consists of tiny wells or depressions that hold the ink. The unetched parts of the plate are nonprinting areas. The electromechanical process that engraves the plate can vary the depth and area of the cells, so some hold more ink than others. The cylinder rotates in a bath of ink. After excess ink is removed from the nonprinting surface by a flexible steel *doctor blade*, a continuous band of paper known as the *web* is pressed against the printing cylinder by a rubber-coated impression cylinder. The ink in the wells is transferred to the paper where, since gravure ink is highly volatile, it dries almost instantly. Sometimes, electrostatic forces are used to help draw ink from the wells onto the paper. This is called electrostatic assist, or ESA.

The Business Problem

The business problem to be addressed by data mining was learning how to avoid costly interruptions to print runs by isolating the conditions under which certain defects appear. The rotogravure printing process is generally used only for long print runs because the process of etching the plate and fitting it to the cylinder is time-consuming and expensive. It takes a long print run to amortize this initial setup cost. When a cylinder band forms, it cuts the run short (and, with the web running through the press at two or three thousand feet per minute, ruins a lot of impressions, wasting ink and paper). When a band is spotted, at the very least, a technician must remove the cylinder from the press in order to polish the grooves out of the cylinder. In more severe cases, the cylinder must be transported to a plating station where the chrome surface is removed in order to polish the band out of the copper subsurface, after which the cylinder must be replated. In extreme cases, the costly printing cylinder must be entirely replaced.

On average, fixing the band takes an hour and a half. The minimum delay is half an hour and the worst case delay is six hours. During this time, a 3- to 10-member printing crew is idle and their wages are charged to a delay account. Print jobs are typically run on tight deadlines, so delays result in overtime and weekend pay. The technical problem is quickly translated into lost productivity, higher expense, potentially missed deadlines, and unhappy customers. In the year before the data mining effort, 800 hours were lost to cylinder bands.

The Data

As you are well aware, data mining depends on data. In particular, in order to build a decision tree capable of explaining anything, there must be a training set consisting of observations of relevant variables for both positive and negative outcomes.

At the start of the cylinder band investigation, no such data existed. It was not even clear what data ought to be gathered. The press operators had a general feeling that certain factors might have something to do with banding, and a few of these factors were being monitored for other reasons. Most, however, were not. In the past, when cylinder bands appeared, people had made note of the values of various variables that they believed to be important, but since there was no corresponding data for press runs in which no banding occurred, this was not suitable for data mining. Data collection became the project team's first priority.

Donnelley needed to choose a data mining approach that would help explore the data and identify a handful of the most important variables. Decision tree algorithms are good for this kind of data exploration because they are good at ignoring unimportant variables. In a decision tree, the most important variables are found near the root. The team set out to collect data on humidity, ink temperature, ink viscosity, acidity, voltage level, blade pressure, paper type, and many other inputs for both successful and unsuccessful runs. Although the presses were instrumented so that all of these things were measurable, there was no automatic reporting system. The measurements had to be recorded by hand on paper forms for later entry into a computer system. Convincing people who already had their hands full running the presses that this data collection was an important task was one of the chief obstacles that had to be overcome.

Because data collection was a laborious, manual process, only 500 job records were collected. That is a very small number compared to other databases described in this book, but it proved to be sufficient.

Deciding on the Right Attributes

The final list of input variables was compiled through an iterative process of consulting with experts on printing for ideas of what might be important, using them to build trees, and keeping the ones that proved to have predictive value. The final set of input variables (which, for our purposes we do not need to fully understand) included

- ESA anode distance in millimeters
- Chrome solution ratio
- ESA current density in amperes per square decimeter
- Plating tank
- Viscosity
- Humidity
- Ink temperature
- Doctor blade oscillation in inches
- Doctor blade pressure in pounds
- Basis weight of paper
- Paper type
- Solvent type
- Cylinder circumference in inches
- Press type
- Press speed in feet per second
- Electrostatic assist current in milliamps
- Electrostatic assist voltage in kilovolts

All of these variables take on values that either fall into clearly defined categories (paper type, solvent type) or can be measured in the specified units. Early on in the project, the team used some variables that were more subjective. For example, there was one variable called *chrome condition* that could take on the values "cloudy" and "clear." Unfortunately, these values turned out to depend more on the person making the observation than on the condition of the chrome.

The decision tree algorithm used in this early work could only split on categorical variables. Continuous variables such as temperature, humidity, and viscosity had to be binned. The printing experts felt that for most of the numeric variables there were naturally three ranges: favorable, neutral, and unfavorable. For example, they regarded high humidity as favorable and low humidity as unfavorable. The sense of the experts was that in some middle range, humidity would have no effect, so other input variables would control the outcome. Unfortunately, the experts could not agree on boundary values for the ranges.

Data Preparation for Continuous Inputs

Experiments showed that simply partitioning the continuous variables into three arbitrary ranges did not produce good results. What was needed was a way to pick splits that captured the notion that there is one range that affects the outcome in one direction, a second range that affects the outcome in the opposite direction, and a neutral range separating the first two. Bob Evans' approach was to use the median value for the runs with banding as one boundary and the median value for the runs without banding as the other. Once the continuous variables had been binned in this manner, the decision tree algorithm was able to make good use of them.

There are now automated approaches to binning continuous variables that might have helped even more. In his book, *Data Preparation for Data Mining* (1999, Morgan Kaufmann), Dorian Pyle describes a technique called "least information loss binning" for choosing the optimal number and size of the bins. This technique requires too much understanding of concepts from information theory such as *entropy* and *mutual information* to be described here, but it is nice to know that these kinds of transformations exist and are beginning to be incorporated into commercial data mining tools.

Defining the Target Classes

A data mining training set is not complete until the data has been preclassified so that the data mining algorithms know what they are looking for. Sometimes this is straightforward; a prospect either did or did not mail in a response card. Other times it is more subtle. In Chapter 11, we saw that in order to predict churn we first had to define it. In addition to distinguishing between voluntary churn and involuntary churn, this involved choosing a time frame. In the wireless customer churn case, if the question is "who will cancel their wireless phone contract within the next 100 years?" all customers will get high churn scores, but if the question is "who will churn tomorrow?" all customers will appear loyal. So, a model built to classify people as churners or loyal customers is really predicting which customers will cancel their subscription before a certain date. Clearly, the choice of date affects the outcome of the classification.

In manufacturing, there is a parallel notion. A product's reliability is often measured in terms of MTBF (mean time between failures)—the average time between breakdowns. The problem with classifying print runs is that they vary widely in length. Clearly any print run in which a band develops should be classified as banded and recorded along with the values of all its input variables. But what can we say about a short print run in which no banding occurs? Print runs vary enormously; many are shorter than the MTBF. Even when these short runs complete successfully without a band forming, we cannot feel confident that a band would not have formed later had the run been longer. Since the task was to identify the conditions that eventually lead to banding, short print runs that did not exhibit banding had to be excluded from the training set.

How long a run is long enough to be considered free of banding? Figure 14.1 shows that cylinder bands are not evenly distributed. If banding is going to take place, it usually shows up fairly early in the print run. More than half the banding events occurred before 50,000 impressions had been made, and nearly 90 percent occurred before a million impressions had been made. Based on this data, the team at Donnelley decided to use one million impressions as the cutoff. Any print run that went for at least one million impressions and finished without a cylinder band forming was classed as a nonbanding run and saved in the training set along with the values of the input variables as measured at the end of the run. So, the final composition of the training set was all print

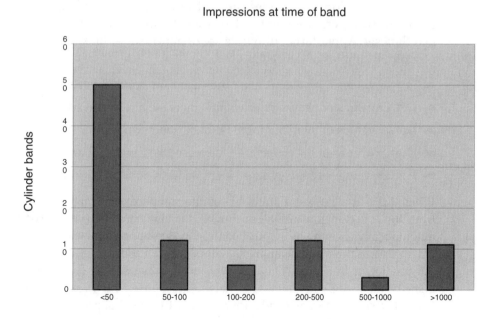

Figure 14.1 Cylinder bands by length of print run.

runs of any length that resulted in banding, and all print runs that ran longer than the cut-off and finished without banding.

While solving one problem, this solution introduces another. The sample skew with respect to print-run length means that a spurious rule will easily be discovered: *short print runs lead to cylinder bands.* However, the tree growing program used at Donnelley allowed users to interact with the tool by accepting or rejecting proposed splits.

Inducing Rules for Cylinder Bands

The goals for the cylinder band project were different from the goals of most of the data mining projects we have discussed. In this case, there was no plan to use the decision trees as predictive models. Instead, the trees were used to generate a set of practical, prescriptive rules that could be applied on the shop floor. In this situation, the best model is not the one that does the best job of predicting when a job will fail, it is the one that provides a set of *implementable* guidelines for preventing future failures. The word "implementable" is very important. It is of little use knowing that cylinders are less likely to band in humid conditions if there is no way of controlling the humidity in the plant.

R. R. Donnelley now uses commercial data mining software for its ongoing projects, but the work described here was done before commercial data mining software was widely available. The decision trees were developed in a home-grown software environment called Apos. In addition to the usual preclassified data set, Apos starts out with a set of heuristics—rules based on received wisdom. Examples of heuristics used are

- Lower values for *anode distance* increase likelihood of banding
- Lower values of *chrome solution ratio* increase likelihood of banding
- Lower values of *humidity* increase likelihood of banding
- Higher values of *ink temperature* increase likelihood of banding
- Higher values of *blade pressure* increase likelihood of banding

When Apos is choosing a split, it uses the standard information gain criterion from the ID3 decision tree algorithm, but it also consults the heuristics. If the automatically chosen split would contradict expert opinion, it looks for a different one. Apos presents the analysts with several proposed splits along with their information gain scores. This way, the experts can see where their beliefs are being challenged by the data. The analyst can choose which variable will be used to create a split and may decide not to choose the one that provides the best split.

Figure 14.2 shows a subtree from one of the decision trees developed at the Gallatin printing plant. There is one leaf in the tree with only one banding

Figure 14.2 Finding conditions that reduce banding.

event and 18 successful print runs with over a million impressions. This suggests a set of operating guidelines to try on the shop floor:

- Keep the chrome solution ratio high.
- Keep the ink temperature low.
- Keep the ink viscosity high.

Note that these rules do not in any way *explain* cylinder banding. They shed no light on the actual cause of the problem or the mechanism by which this combination of chrome solution ratio, ink temperature, and ink viscosity can somehow guard against grooves appearing in the etched plate. In that sense the results may seem intellectually unsatisfying, but, if they save the company millions of dollars, they are good rules just the same. No one had heard of vitamin C when the British navy started issuing limes to its sailors to ward off scurvy, but it was effective all the same.

Change on the Shop Floor

The proof of the pudding is in the eating, it is said; and the proof of the new guidelines is in the banding statistics. Figure 14.3 shows the incidence of banding over time. The bars represent the count of bands each month; the line is a moving average of the counts. It is not hard to pinpoint the time when the new guidelines came into effect. Before the decision tree rules were distributed in the form of guidelines, they were simplified by printing experts to eliminate dependencies on particular press types in use in the plant. For example, if for one press type it was important to keep blade pressure below 30 pounds and for another type the magic number was 20 pounds, the distributed guidelines would say to keep pressure below 20 pounds.

As might be expected, it took some time for confidence in the new guidelines to spread through the print crews. A few early adopters began using guidelines based on the decision tree rules in December of 1990, but it was not until May of 1991 that printing experts at the plant had enough confidence in the rules to distribute a table of conditions associated with banding and the avoidance of banding to all presses. From that time on, the frequency of banding began decreasing as more and more printers bought into the system.

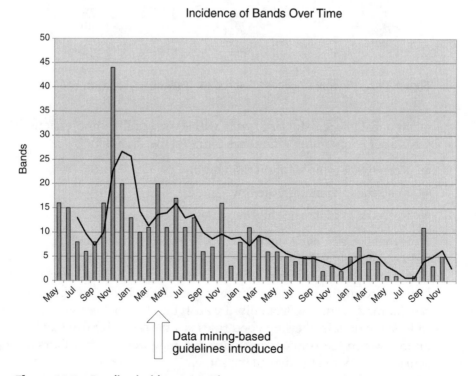

Figure 14.3 Banding incidence over time.

Although the principal use of the project was to come up with prescriptive rules, rather than to do predictive modeling, the fact is that any set of rules is also a model and therefore can be used to make predictions. One clear prediction coming out of the rules that were distributed was that banding increases in periods of low humidity. In Tennessee, the driest time of the year is late fall and early winter. Sure enough, banding increased when the drier whether started. Also, when a cylinder band appeared and the data about the operating conditions at the time of the event were compared to the guidelines, more often than not the press was found to be operating outside the suggested bounds. This, along with a program to give special recognition to the crew with the fewest cylinder bands for the year, resulted in steadily increasing acceptance of the computer-generated guidelines and steadily decreasing banding.

The success of the project depended on the ability of the analytical team to prove the worth of new ways of operating, some of which went against the received wisdom of both management and press operators, by demonstrating concrete results.

Long-Term Impact

The results of the banding study were dramatic. In 1989, before the data mining effort, 538 banding incidents caused more than 800 hours of downtime. In 1995, the plant experienced only 21 such incidents resulting in 30 hours of downtime.

The success of the anti-banding project in Gallatin helped speed the introduction of more automated monitoring and data acquisition devices around the company. The initial pilot project at Gallatin was replicated at other plants. It turned out that the guidelines developed in one location could not simply be transferred to another; too many factors were different at each new plant. Donnelley recognizes that data mining is not a one-time fix. Over the years they have continued to build on the success of this initial project in keeping with the stated corporate goal of continually improving performance and productivity.

Reducing Paper Wastage at Time Inc.

Time Inc., the magazine publishing arm of the giant media conglomerate, Time-Warner, is the world's largest magazine publisher. Its flagship *Time* magazine has been published for over three-quarters of a century. Its 30 or so other titles include *Life, People, Sports Illustrated, Entertainment Weekly, Teen People, In Style, Southern Living, Cooking Light, Sunset, Sports Illustrated for Women, This Old House, People en Español, Fortune,* and *Martha Stewart Living*. With 120 million readers worldwide, Time Inc. goes through huge quantities of paper.

The case study presented here is from the production division at Time Inc. From Time Inc.'s Manhattan headquarters, the production division looks after every aspect of printing and producing all those magazines. Many of the division's activities are centered around paper. Time Inc. buys paper from manufacturers around the world and prints its US magazines in printing plants across the country. A sophisticated database keeps track of each 1-ton roll of paper from the time it is ordered to the time it is mounted on the press at one of its plants.

As usual, the case study begins with a presentation of the business problem—in this case, the need to reduce paper waste. Next comes a discussion of the data and the technical approach, which consisted of OLAP-style analysis and reporting augmented by data mining techniques including visualization, decision trees, and association rules. Because you are likely to be less familiar with magazine production than with the marketing tasks discussed in other chapters, we spend a fair amount of time introducing the process and explaining the variables available for analysis. The section ends with a discussion of the opportunities for saving millions of dollars that were uncovered by the project.

The Business Problem

There are always two ways to increase profitability: Increase revenues or decrease expenses. At a magazine publisher like Time Inc., there are many departments working on the revenue side by increasing circulation and selling ad pages. The production division attacks the cost side. In magazine publishing, three costs dominate all others—paper, printing, and postage. Since the price of postage is not under Time Inc.'s control, the focus of cost-reduction efforts is on paper and printing. A single roll of paper for the big offset presses that Time Inc.'s printers use weighs about a ton and costs on the order of a thousand dollars. Since hundreds of thousands of rolls are used each year, the total cost is in the hundreds of millions.

One way to control paper cost is to buy when the price is right. As with all commodities, the price of paper is volatile. At Time Inc., a system called the Statistical Paper Ordering Tool (SPOT) uses 12 months of history to calculate the best time and place to order paper. Since the type of paper used for magazines has a useful life of about two years, cheap paper can be stockpiled against future price increases.

The other way to control paper costs is to use less paper. One approach to using less paper is printing magazines on smaller pages. This approach has, in fact, been tried although the original motivation was to reduce postage rather than to reduce the amount of paper consumed. Early in the 1990s, the standard magazine size was reduced slightly to lower mailing costs. At first, this did not reduce the amount of paper used since the presses were the same

From Forest to Recycle Bin: The Story of Paper

Paper—the focus of this case study—is a fascinating product. Since many of the variables in the data described aspects of paper (basis weight, runnability, etc.), we had to learn a fair amount about its manufacture, shipping, and use.

Paper is made from pulp. Pulp can come from many sources, but wood is by far the most common. There are several processes for turning wood into pulp. In the most straightforward, logs are simply ground up mechanically. This is the most economical method because it uses all the wood, but the resulting paper will have imperfections that make it unfit for many purposes. Pulp made by the purely mechanical process is used for newsprint and other inexpensive types of paper. Chemical pulping is used for higher grades of paper. In this process, wood chips are simmered in a broth of chemicals such as caustic soda and sodium sulfide. The resulting pulp is called kraft. Paper for grocery bags and some other applications is made directly from kraft. Most of Time Inc.'s magazines are printed on bleached groundwood paper (paper made from groundwood pulp and that has been treated with chemicals such as sodium peroxide or zinc hydrosulfite to make it brighter and whiter).

Pulp gets turned into paper by a huge machine that has a "wet end" where the pulp starts out and a "dry end" where paper emerges. The liquid pulp stock rides on a fine wire-mesh belt through the machine and water gets pressed out of it by a series of rollers and dryers. Finally, the paper is passed between a series of smooth-ground rollers called *calenders* that give the paper a smooth finish. Because one side of the paper goes through the machine on the wire mesh, while the other side gets pressed by felt-covered rollers, the two sides of a piece of paper have different characteristics. Printers speak of the "felt side" and the "wire side" of a sheet of paper.

Paper is made in many different thicknesses or *weights.* In most of the world paper weight is measured in grams per square meter so the same measure holds regardless of paper size. As often happens, we have a somewhat more convoluted system here in the United States. Paper is classified by *basis weight,* which is the weight of a *ream* (500 sheets) of that type of paper. What complicates things is that each type of paper has a different *basic size* so 500 sheets of one kind of paper are not the same size as 500 sheets of another. For example, *32-pound bond* means paper for which 500 17-inch by 22-inch sheets (the basic size for bond paper) weighs 32 pounds. That 32-pound paper may go into a publication whose cover is printed on 60-pound cover stock. The exact relationship between 60-pound cover stock and 32-pound bond is left as an exercise for the reader. To complete the exercise, you need to know that the basic size for cover stock is 20-inches by 26-inches.

Of course, the paper used in these case studies does not come in 500-sheet reams, but on large rolls cut from the even larger reels that come off the paper-making machine. The rolls are shipped to printing plants by specially designed rail car.

size. Less paper went into the magazines and more ended up as waste. Gradually, as the printers shift from 22-inch presses to 21-inch presses, the move is reducing paper costs as well.

This sort of waste, called *trim waste*, is only one of many ways that paper ends up in the recycling plant instead of in the magazine. The Time Inc. database contains records of this and all the other kinds of waste that can show up at the printing plants. In fact, Time Inc. keeps detailed performance data on every press run at every plant and on every roll of paper consumed in the process. This detailed tracking reflects the close relationship between the publisher and the printing plants.

Relationship of Time Inc. to the Printing Plants

Although Time Inc.'s goals for this project were very similar to those of R. R. Donnelley—cost reduction and productivity improvement—the focus of the study was somewhat different due to differences in the business arrangements of the two companies. Time Inc. does not own the printing plants where its magazines are printed. Instead, the publisher contracts with more than twenty printing plants around the country. Time Inc. purchases its own paper and has it shipped to the printing plants, so the printing plants have no direct incentive to be frugal with paper.

The interests of Time Inc. and of the printing plants are kept in alignment by contractual limits on the amount of waste allowed as a percentage of the total pounds of paper used; also many of the conditions that lead to paper waste can lead to printer down-time, which, as we saw in the R. R. Donnelley study, is very expensive. For these reasons, and because it is always a good idea to look out for the interests of your biggest customer, the printing plants work very closely with the production division at Time Inc. to find ways to improve the manufacturing process.

Performance Variation between Plants

One of the key reasons that Time Inc. was sure that overall paper waste could be reduced substantially was the wide range of performance among the printing plants. As we can see in Figure 14.4, which reports paper waste by plant and type of waste for selected locations over the study period, the best-performing plants waste only half as much paper as the worst-performing plant. Of course, some plant-to-plant differences reflect differences in machinery or workload that cannot easily be altered, but if even a small amount of variation is due to best practices that can be codified and disseminated to all plants, the savings potential is very large. Time Inc. estimates that for its New York titles (the ones of concern in this study), each one tenth of one percent improvement is worth

Paper Waste Percentages by Plant

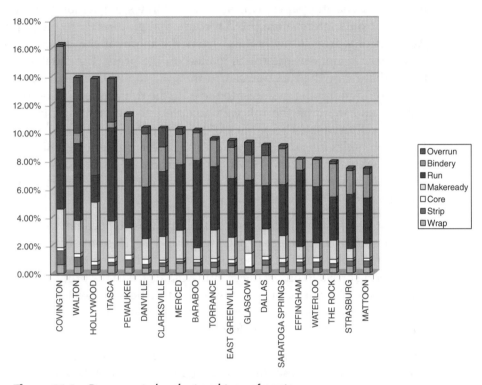

Figure 14.4 Paper waste by plant and type of waste.

$200,000 per year. Those are the kinds of numbers that data miners love to hear because even a small improvement in manufacturing efficiency will pay for a lot of data mining.

In 1998, a task force headed by Dave Trevorrow, the business manager of the production division at Time Inc., set out to sift through the press-run and mill-roll data from all the plants looking for ways to reduce waste. The team included Bill Walsh, a former production director for *Money* magazine and an expert in all phases of paper making and printing, and Alan and Geoff Parker, data analysis experts from Apower Solutions. The authors worked with Apower, using MineSet to look for predictors of addressable waste in the press-run and mill-roll detail data.

The Data

In sharp contrast to the situation at Donnelley where data from a few hundred press runs was laboriously collected by hand, the data at Time Inc. had already been collected in a relational database. This database is fed by several operational systems. We have already alluded to one of them, the SPOT system for purchasing paper. This system generates the actual paper orders as electronic data interchange (EDI) records that go directly to the paper mills. An electronic trail is maintained from the moment the purchase order is issued to the moment the roll is loaded on the press. The database contains tables that relate the P.O. number to the mill, the P.O. number to a shipping manifest, the shipping manifest to the time the roll was loaded onto a truck or rail car, and the time the roll was accepted at the printing plant's loading dock. Inventory tables keep track of how long the paper is stored before use. Press run tables keep track of which rolls were brought to which presses as part of which print jobs. Waste paper produced at various points in the process is weighed and recorded. In short, there was no shortage of ore for the miners.

The first task facing the outside consultants was to become familiar with all this data and the processes that lay behind it. This involved interviewing experts from finance as well as production, pouring over the data dictionaries, and making a visit to one of the printing plants to see the process in action and to interview plant personnel. Apower used ad hoc queries to profile the data in many different ways. This exercise resulted in an initial overview of the data that the team at Time Inc. found useful in its own right.

After the initial profiling, the analysis team understood the data well enough to create a mining data set that contained two years of relevant data on paper and press runs.

Useful Tables from the Relational Database

The Time Inc. data dictionary was over an inch thick. The outside consultants sat down with people at Time Inc. who were familiar with every table in it in order to understand their contents well enough to choose fields to extract for the mining data set.

Invoice

This table contains useful information for a shipment of paper such as the P.O. number, the shipment date, the paper company, the basis weight of the paper, the paper grade, the plant to which the paper was shipped. This data makes it possible to analyze waste by paper origin.

Stock Status

This table contains information on paper in inventory including transit damage and in-plant damage to paper rolls.

Transfer

Sometimes paper is transferred between printing plants. These transfers are performed by trucks that are not specially designed to transport paper, unlike the rail cars that usually carry the paper from mill to plant.

Usage

This very important table tracks the magazine or department that gets charged for a press run. This is important because different magazines have different characteristics that affect waste performance. Some, like *Time*, are very complicated with many different regional and demographic editions with different ads. *Sports Illustrated* uses more ink per pound of paper than the other magazines due to its emphasis on photography.

The usage table also allows waste to be tracked by form type. There are three types of forms:

- Cover—for the covers of magazines
- Advance—for material such as ads or horoscopes, that can be printed in advance
- Current—for late-breaking material that must be printed at the last minute

Press

This table contains information about the presses themselves—the number of webs, the greatest paper width the press can accommodate, the press manufacturer, the data the press was installed, and so on. This data is important because different presses have different operating characteristics that affect the amount and kinds of waste to which they are prone.

Press Run

This was the most important table for our work. It includes the press start time, the linear feet of paper used after makeready, the press stop time, the weight of paper on core when the final roll was removed from the press, the number of pages produced, the weight of wrapper removed (wrap waste), the weight of outer layers removed from the roll before mounting (strip waste), the weight of paper run through the press during makeready (preparing the presses to print), the number of times the press was stopped during the run, the number of rolls brought to the press during the run, the number of web breaks (an important component of running waste), the number of colors used, the basis weight of the paper, the number of impressions made, and the amount of downtime for mechanical reasons.

Spoilage Detail

This table contains more information about waste, including calculated allowances for blanket-wash waste and bindery waste and the weight of paper printed after the correct number of pages has been reached.

Shipment

This table records information about how the paper got to the plant, and the carriers that transported it down to which door of a two-door box car from which it was unloaded.

Summary of Mining Data Set

The summary statistics of the mining data set give a good first overview of what we had to work with:

- Number of press runs: 30,041
- Number of rolls: 523,893
- Rolls/Press Run statistics

  Average: 17 rolls/run

  Minimum: 1 roll/run

  Maximum: 293 rolls/run

- Press run length statistics

  Average: 6.68 hours

  Minimum: 0.03 hours

  Maximum: 759 hours

- Distribution of form types in press runs

  Advance: 14,806 runs

  Cover: 4,143 runs

  Current: 11,092 runs

Together, the press runs collected in the data mining data set accounted for 100,552,816 pounds of wasted paper with a dollar value of close to $50 million.

Approach to the Problem

The data analysts split into two teams. Apower, in Atlanta, began doing hypothesis testing—looking at various kinds of waste as a function of a long list of known or suspected causal factors. Meanwhile, we, at Data Miners in Cambridge, Massachusetts loaded the data into SGI MineSet and began trying to find predictive factors for high levels of avoidable waste.

Hypothesis Testing

The printing experts at Time Inc. had many insights into likely causes of waste that they wanted tested through single-variable regressions. Some examples are

- Waste as a function of press type
- Waste as a function of paper age
- Waste as a function of basis weight
- Waste as a function of time of day
- Waste as a function of presses equipped with automatic blanket washers
- Waste as a function of number of rolls in press run

As we shall see in the section entitled "Putting It All Together," many of these relationships did prove to be important.

Types of Waste

Although the goal of the project was to reduce overall waste, there are actually many different classes of waste. Each class has its own set of causes and some afford much greater opportunities for intervention than others. We cannot go any further into the data mining process without explaining the various types of paper waste that are tracked in the database. The Time Inc. database tracks eight categories of waste:

- Wrapper waste
- Strip waste
- Make-ready waste
- Running waste
- Core waste
- Bindery waste
- Trim waste
- Overrun

Paper is priced by weight; every pound that Time Inc. pays for that doesn't end up in a magazine is considered waste. Total waste is typically about 10 percent of the purchased weight of paper. The different categories of waste can be understood by analogy to another paper product familiar to all of us—toilet paper. Like toilet paper, the paper that this book is printed on arrives on a roll covered with a paper wrapper.

Wrapper Waste

The paper rolls arrive in a protective wrapper made of brown kraft paper. This paper contributes to the weight of the roll, but is not used for printing. It therefore counts as waste, but it is not of much analytical interest since there is nothing to be done about it.

Offset Printing

Offset printing is different from rotogravure printing. In offset printing, the image to be printed is not transferred directly from the plate to the paper, but first to an intermediate surface. Although this principle can be used with several printing methods, most offset presses are lithographic. In lithography, the plates are *planographic,* meaning that the printing areas and nonprinting areas are all at the same height, rather than depressed as in gravure printing or raised as in letterpress or flexographic printing. The main advantage of the offset method is that the flexible rubber blanket makes a smooth, sharp, clear image over a wide range of paper texture and smoothness.

Lithography works on the well-known principle that oil and water do not mix. The printing area of the plate are oil-receptive and water-repellent. The nonprinting areas are water-receptive and oil-repellent. As the plate cylinder rotates, it first comes in contact with dampening rollers. This ensures that the nonprinting areas are wet and will repel the oil-based ink. Next, the plate comes in contact with the ink roller. Thick, oil-based ink sticks to the printing surface.

The image is then transferred to a sheet of rubber known as the *blanket.* The blanket is wrapped around its own cylinder, called the *blanket cylinder.* The paper web runs between the blanket cylinder and an impression cylinder, which presses the paper against the rubber so that ink is transferred from the blanket to the paper. In some presses, there are two blanket cylinders, each serving as the impression cylinder for the other. In these machines, knows as *blanket-to-blanket* presses, the web is printed on both sides at once.

Strip Waste

Just as the first few squares of toilet paper often get damaged in the process of getting the roll started, a few layers of offset paper are often damaged. This is strip waste. Excess strip waste often occurs when the knife used to remove the wrapper cuts too deep and damages many layers of usable paper.

Makeready Waste

Makeready is the printing term for all the work that goes into getting the press ready to print. The details vary from press to press, but one way or another, plate pressure, ink flow, and alignments have to be adjusted. For the web offset presses used to print Time Inc.'s magazines, makeready takes about 5,000 impressions. Operator skill is a significant factor in reducing makeready time.

Running Waste

Running waste is waste that occurs during the actual printing process. Web breaks are a major cause of running waste. A web break is exactly what it sounds like—the paper breaks as it is flying through the press at 3,000 feet per minute. This makes a big mess and wastes many pounds of paper. Much of the data mining effort went into trying to isolate the conditions under which web breaks are most likely to occur. Another cause of running waste is blanket washing. From time to time, the rubber blanket that transfers the printed image to the paper (see sidebar on web offset printing) needs to be washed. This can be done by automatic blanket washers while the press is still in motion, but hundreds of impressions are wasted.

Core Waste

Just as the last square of toilet paper is glued to the toilet paper tube, the end of a roll of offset paper is glued to the core. The paper must be cut off and spliced to the start of the next roll before the last crinkled bit of paper comes off the core. The paper left on the core, and the core itself, become core waste.

Bindery Waste

After the printed pages come off the press as *signatures* (folded sections of paper containing 4 to 48 magazine pages), the signatures go to the bindery to be combined with other signatures and turned into magazines. Some get damaged in this process, so a few extra signatures are always printed. This bindery allowance is normally about 2 percent and those extra signatures are considered bindery waste whether or not they actually are needed at the bindery. It is paper that is used without ending up in a magazine.

Trim Waste

Trim waste is the paper that is trimmed off after printing to create pages of the desired size.

Overrun

Overrun occurs when more signatures are printed than were ordered. At the speed that these presses operate, letting a press run for a few extra minutes translates into a large overrun.

Addressable Waste

Some waste is inevitable. All of the wrapper waste and trim waste, most of the core waste and makeready waste, and even some of the running waste is simply unavoidable. Time Inc. makes a distinction, therefore, between addressable and nonaddressable waste. Addressable waste is avoidable waste that represents an opportunity for process improvement and potential savings. Addressable waste is the focus of this case study because something can be done about it.

Inducing Rules for Addressable Waste

The portion of the Time Inc. project that involved us was an effort to induce rules governing addressable waste from the bottom up using decision trees and association rules.

The data selected for the rule induction exercise combined data from tables describing the individual rolls of paper with data from tables describing the press runs in which those rolls were used. The resulting data set contained a large number of fields describing 30,041 press runs (including the printing plant, magazine, type of form, press used, press start time, number of impressions, and the minimum expected and actual pounds of waste in each of seven defined categories) along with a smaller number of fields describing each of the 523,893 individual rolls of paper that went into them. Data on the paper included such things as the mill where the paper was manufactured, the weight and dimensions of the roll, the basis weight of the paper, and the original position of each roll on the reel from which it was cut.

The effort to induce rules from the bottom up proved useful not only for rules discovered, but also because certain expected rules were not supported by the data. For instance, in line with expectation, the printing plant was a strong determinant of paper waste, but contrary to expectation, web breaks were less important than makeready and overrun. In fact, web breaks were recorded so infrequently that a separate investigation was launched to determine whether their apparent rarity was real or evidence of a reporting problem.

Data Transformation

Once the data arrived at the Data Miners office in Cambridge, two kinds of transformations were required. The first kind of transformation simply reflects differences between the formats supported by the source system and those supported by MineSet. For instance, a date that comes in as Jan 30 1996 1:12PM has to be transformed into 1/30/96 13:12:00 in order to be recognized as a date by the version of MineSet software we were using. Similarly, many fields that were stored as integers in the source system were translated into floating point numbers because of the role they needed to play in data mining calculations.

The more important transformations were geared to making more information accessible to the data mining algorithms. Here again, dates provide a good example. A date string can be exploded into many potentially useful variables such as the year, month, day of the week, and time of day. A rule or pattern based on any of these variables will be much easier to detect if each date feature is presented independently instead of being buried in a date string.

Transformations of both kinds were performed using scripts written in the pattern-matching language, Perl 5.

Before Import

The following is a listing of a few fields from the beginning and end of a typical record from the roll-run data before transformation. This record contains data on a single roll of paper and a press run in which it was used.

```
mill_roll_id contains 95WVL2359801H
manufacture_date: Nov 1 1995 12:00AM
mill_cd: 2W
gross_lb: 2050.0
invoice_lb: 2041.0
length_ft: 18276.0
is_length_calculated_flag: N
diameter_in: 40.0
basis_weight_lb: 120.0
basis_weight_actual_lb: 120.0
grade_cd: Z
   .
   .
   .
overrun_pct: 0.5
overrun_signature_cnt: 4265
actual_bindery_waste_lb: 919
requested_bindery_waste_pct: 2.7
bindery_waste_signature_cnt: 17281
actual_bindery_waste_pct: 2.3
press_run_signature_cnt: 661612
pr_order_signature_cnt: 640066
min_trim_pct: 0.0
min_trim_lb: 0
tot_trim_pct: 0.0
tot_trim_lb: 0
```

Convenience Fields

In addition to format conversions and type conversions, several convenience fields were added to the data. In the source data, a compound key consisting of the mill_roll_id, plant_cd, and press_run_start_time fields was required to identify a particular press run. Before being brought into MineSet, each unique press run was assigned an integer press_run_id and each roll-run record was assigned an integer record_id. The press run IDs are there to facilitate interactive analysis at the press run level. The record IDs are there to facilitate communication about suspected data problems.

It is sometimes convenient to add fields to a data set that will take no part in model building or rule induction, but which will make it easier for the data miner to define samples and subsets or to identify particular records without resorting to long compound keys.

After Import

Data transformation does not end with the importation of records into the data mining tool. Indeed, the mining process involves the continual creation of new fields on an exploratory basis. These new fields are derived from the original fields through binning or through transformation expressions created with the small equation editor that is part of the MineSet user interface.

Derived Fields

Two types of derived fields were created to aid in data mining. The first type of transformation was required in order to convert continuous variables into categorical variables (e.g., high, medium, low) so that they could be used with data mining techniques, such as association rules, that cannot handle continuous variables. Fortunately, MineSet supports a wide range of binning approaches.

The second type of transformation involved creating derived fields that contain information from two or more other fields. The data mining algorithms supported by MineSet all examine one field at a time. This means, for instance, that the date of manufacture and date of use of a roll of paper will be considered individually (and found to have no predictive value). To have the paper's *age* taken into account, it was necessary to create a new variable, paper_age_months, by subtracting the year of the press run from the year of manufacture, multiplying by 12, and then subtracting the difference of the months.

Classification Target

After much experimentation, we settled on a derived variable, total_ blame_waste_flag. This field contains a "W" for any press run where the percentage of addressable waste is in the 75th percentile or above. The definition is based on addressable waste rather than total waste because our goal is to find actionable information and, by definition, there is nothing that can be done about nonaddressable waste. Addressable waste is a derived field defined as the difference between total_waste_pct and min_total_waste_pct. min_ total_ waste_pct is the calculated minimum *expected* (nonaddressable) waste.

Data Characterization and Profiling

Once the data has been imported, the next step is to profile it. MineSet provides a "statviz" tool for this purpose. Statviz produces a small graph for each variable. For numeric variables, there is a panel showing the number of values, range, median, mean, and standard deviation along with the 25th and 75th percentiles. For categorical variables, there is an annotated bar chart showing the prevalence of each category label. These graphs will often reveal problems with the data. For example, although the profiles for press_run_start_time and manufacture_date look perfectly reasonable on their own, when the field derived from them to determine the age in months of a paper roll was profiled it became immediately apparent that there is a sprinkling of negative ages in the data, meaning that some rolls claim to have been used before being manufactured!

Decision Trees

The task we set ourselves at Time Inc. was very similar to the work at R. R. Donnelley in that we were more interested in generating rules to explain paper waste than in classifying particular runs as wasteful or predicting which future runs would be wasteful. As a consequence, the decision tree that made the best predictions was not the one most useful to us.

Classification versus Explanation

Taken as a whole, a decision tree is a classifier. Any previously unseen record can be fed into the tree. At each node it will be sent either left or right according to some test. Eventually, it will reach a leaf node and be given the label associated with that leaf.

Using MineSet, we used 5 percent of the data to build a decision tree which, when applied to the entire data set, was able to predict the correct value of the blame_total_waste_flag with better than 90 percent accuracy. This is an important result because it means that there really are patterns in the data that can be discovered and expressed as rules that determine whether a particular run is likely to produce excessive waste.

Classification, however, was not the goal of this data mining exercise. We did not wish to simply classify print runs as wasteful or not, we wanted to come to an understanding of the most important factors affecting waste so as to be able to do something about them! The decision tree in Figure 14.5 that does such a good job of classification is ill-suited to our purpose because it has 17 levels with many hundreds of leaves, many of which contain only a handful of cases. This is the display that results when we ask the tool to spotlight all leaf nodes having the label "W" for high waste and over 90 percent purity. Without even looking at any of the individual nodes, we can see that there are too many of them to produce the small, manageable set of rules we are looking for.

To extract more actionable information, we need to pare down the decision tree until it represents a manageable number of understandable rules, each of which accounts for a large number of press runs. As the tree gets smaller, it becomes less discriminating but more informative.

Extracting Rules for Addressable Waste

There are several ways to prune a decision tree. One way would be simply to set an upper limit on the number of levels to be created. Another would be to increase the minimum number of records allowed in a node so that as

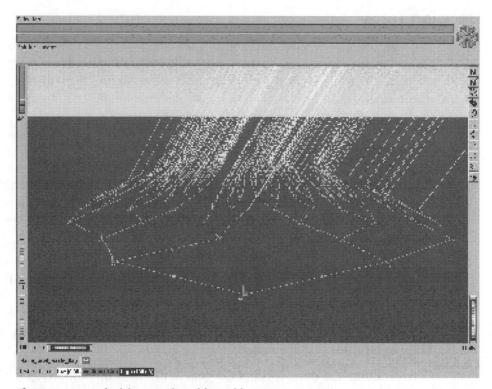

Figure 14.5   A decision tree for addressable waste.

nodes begin to handle fewer press runs, they are no longer split. We chose the latter course because it does a better job of ensuring the generality of the rules produced.

To further simplify the rule extraction task, we looked only at nodes classified as high waste (defined as being in the 75th percentile or above for total addressable waste) ignoring those which describe more usual runs.

Figure 14.6 is a screen shot of the MineSet tree visualizer. In the foreground, we see the root node. Each node has a gray base, the height of which corresponds to the "subtree weight" or, the number of records that passed through that node. On top of the base, the two bars represent the two values of the total addressable waste flag. The bar on the right represents the number of records classed as high waste; the blue bar represents the rest of the records. At the root, 25 percent of the records are classified as high waste by definition.

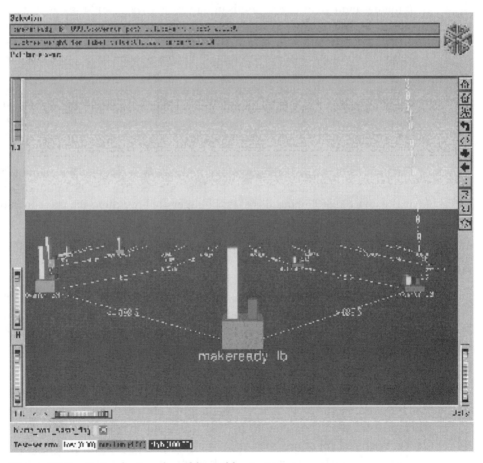

Figure 14.6 A simpler tree for addressable waste.

The white spotlight illuminating a node several levels down in the tree means that it is the selected node. Information for that node is displayed near the top of the window. In this case, the selected node has a high concentration of wasteful press runs. 98.24 percent of the 613 records that reached this leaf had high addressable waste. The path from the root to the selected node can be simplified to the following rule:

> If there is more than 899.5 lbs. of makeready waste and the overrun percentage is greater than 2.95 then this is a wasteful run.

Other rules extracted from this tree include

> If makeready waste is between 881.5 and 1284 pounds and the overrun percentage is less than or equal to 2.45% and the consumed roll weight is less than 329,914 pounds and there is more than 1,500 pounds of running waste then this is a wasteful run.

> If there is more than 1,284 pounds of makeready waste and the overrun percentage is less than or equal to 2.45% and actual bindery waste is less than or equal to 2,114.5 pounds and total waste is greater than 9,488.5 pounds but less than 100,369.5 pounds of paper is brought to the press then this is a wasteful run.

> If there is more than 881.5 pounds of makeready waste and the actual bindery waste is greater than 2,114.5 pounds and there is more than 7,483 pounds of running waste and 271,844 pounds or less of paper are brought to the press and there is less than 11,663.5 pounds of trim waste then this is a wasteful press run.

> If there is more than 1,284 pounds of makeready waste and the actual bindery waste is 2,114.5 pounds or less and there is more than 9,488.5 pounds of total waste and 100,369.5 pounds or less of paper are brought to the press then this is a wasteful press run.

Association Rules

Association rules are another way of generating rules from data. Here they did not prove to be as effective as decision trees because many of the rules discovered by the software were trivially obvious. For example, print runs with a lot of wrapper waste also have a lot of core waste.

Figure 14.7 highlights one of the more useful association rules produced. It ties high addressable waste to high overrun count. In the illustration, the height of the bars represents *predictability*, the height of the disk represents expected predictability. Color (not visible in this grayscale rendering) represents prevalence, with red meaning more prevalent and blue meaning less. So, a tall red bar with a low disk is a rule worth looking at.

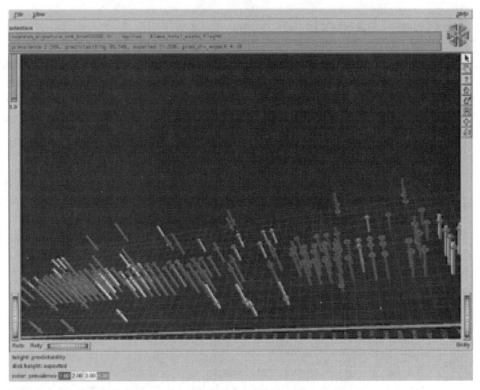

Figure 14.7   MineSet's visualization for association rules.

Putting It All Together

The rules induced by software became part of the larger picture that included the results of many exploratory queries and visualizations. When the dust cleared, Time Inc. was left with actionable information that they could use to decrease waste and potentially save millions of dollars. Recommendations coming out of the data mining project included the following:

- There is correlation between paper age and running waste. The project team estimated that using all paper within six months of manufacture would save over $75,000 a year.

- Print runs using paper from multiple mills had slightly higher running waste percentages. The project team recommended that each press run use paper from a single mill.

- A fifth color in addition to the usual four, something that happens fairly often with the cover of *Time* magazine, leads to increased running waste. The project team estimated that using four colors instead of five would save over $10,000 per year.

Lessons Learned

In this chapter we have seen that data mining can be profitably applied to the cost side as well as the revenue side of a business. The two examples of data mining for process improvement in the printing industry had many differences, but they shared key similarities:

- The projects used data mining to find prescriptive rules that could be used to improve the production process.

- The projects succeeded due to the constant involvement of subject matter experts who understood paper and printing inside out and were willing to provide guidance to the data miners.

- Implementation of the new policies suggested by data mining requires the active cooperation of the people on the plant floor.

- Data mining does not always require huge volumes of data—the Donnelley study used only a few hundred records.

- Where huge volumes of data are available, as at Time Inc., data mining can help make sense of it.

As we said in Chapter 1, data mining is useful wherever there are large quantities of data and something worth learning. Manufacturing process control certainly fits the bill.

CHAPTER 15

The Societal Context: Data Mining and Privacy

During the nineteenth century, photography was a new technology, and as with many new technologies, it inspired the fear that photographic images could steal the very souls of the people captured in the images. Eternal damnation was a greater preoccupation than mere intrusiveness. After all, not only did early photographs require several minutes of exposure to the subject, they also required hours of careful treatment with rank and dangerous chemicals. The mere fact of producing a photograph was a wonder and an art to some, and a threat to others.

Fast forward to the end of the twentieth century, and we have the travails of Princess Diana, caught in her dying moments for the world to see. The image of paparazzi chasing the Princess through tunnels in Paris, leading to her ultimate demise, is a striking image of one person's loss of privacy to the photographer's lens.

Today's technology has almost nothing in common with the technology of yesteryear. A "photograph" today may be made using digital technology, never developed in a darkroom, and published over the Web, to a potential audience of hundreds of millions, in a matter of minutes. Within hours, it can be on the front pages of millions of newspapers and magazines. Technology has conspired to make the world not only a smaller place, but potentially much more intimate. And, it is not only celebrities who are concerned about privacy.

The rise of the Web is propelling privacy as a major concern. The electronic world is, in many ways, a reflection of the more material world where data has been proliferating for decades. Ironically, although the Web seems frightening in its ability to monitor, it also offers some privacy protections. At the same time, data mining holds the promise of using all this data for more constructive ends, for customizing the Web experience.

In this final chapter, we are taking a look at data mining in the context of society, focusing primarily on privacy issues. Interspersed throughout the chapter are anecdotes and news stories about privacy—both with data mining and without. It is important to realize that any discussion of privacy must talk about the threats and invasions. Every day, though, there are literally billions of transactions that take place—both on the Web and in the rest of the world—that are not the subject of horror stories. Data mining is part of a technological, social, and economic revolution that is making the world smaller, more connected, more service-driven, and providing unprecedented levels of prosperity. At the same time, more information is known, stored, and transmitted about us, as individuals, than ever before.

The Privacy Prism

The world is changing fast, especially with regards to privacy and private spaces. Once upon a time, it was sufficient merely to build walls high enough to keep out peering eyes. Now there are satellites that peer down from above and can read the license plate on a car. One dictionary suggests that privacy is "being withdrawn from society or public interest; being alone and undisturbed." Another suggests that it is "being not open or controlled by the public; or for an individual person."

The dictionary definition provides little guidance for understanding threats to privacy. The idea is very subjective, with every person having his or her own limits and levels of tolerance. Every form of commerce leaves an electronic trail. Acts that were once private, or at least quickly forgotten, are now stored for future reference.

Privacy acts on new technologies the way a prism divides light. For each advance in technology, the privacy prism splits the technology into a multitude of issues, representing potential threats to privacy. It is possible to identify the exact location of a cell phone when it is turned on (and the approximate location is available through the tower routing the call). For motorists requiring assistance, this can save lives; most would agree that the greater good of saving lives is worth some intrusion into the privacy of the phone owner. On the other hand, being able to identify the location of phones brings up a range of issues. Who owns the location information, and who has rights to know it? Does the wireless phone company have a right to know my location? Does the government? Can Burger King send a message, saying "next restaurant at Exit 15"? Does the employer, if they own the cell phone? Do parents, who may have bought the cell phone for their teenage children? Can a person opt out of the location-identifying technology when they purchase a handset?

Just as high walls protect from peering eyes, high walls also protect from criminals. Society's need to maintain safety and security definitely places some limits on privacy. Willingly or unwillingly, we must accept the social contract and these types of infringements. The government already intrudes into our private lives. What about the private sector? Companies collect information about us, sometimes without our consent. They can then use then information directly, or sell it to others. What right do people, as individuals, have about their own data? Once, the only way to spread information about others was through gossip and idle chatter. Then more people became literate, and we invented printing, and newspapers and magazines. Then we invented photography, telecommunications, and Web sites. Personal data, even our images and voices, can be transmitted without our consent.

Some people are very sensitive about their private lives. In the United States, they use their Social Security Number only when they have to. They lie about their mother's maiden name. Even the occasional marketing letter offering a product or service is too much of an intrusion. They do not want to be a row in someone's database. But, for most people, it seems that one of the bargains we make in living in the modern world includes a certain lack of privacy. We must assume when using a credit card, for instance, that the credit card company might keep track of our purchases. Letting credit card companies have access to such information is, for most people, a worthwhile bargain for the convenience of making purchases using plastic. And, we still have the option of using cash or checks—at least in the brick-and-mortar world.

The seamier side of the Web shows another extreme on the privacy scale. Once, people could strive to "tell-all" in books, or by shouting on a street corner. A woman named Jenni taught the world about watching the humdrum lives of ordinary people, a lesson that has since been copied by others. These activities may be erotic, or may be as common as eating a snack and reading a book, or as uncommon as a woman giving birth on the Web. Jenni lived her home life in view of a bunch of cameras connected to a Web site—what are now called Webcams. Her example, although voluntary, shows the possibility of having every detail of one's life recorded and transmitted to a medium that can reach hundreds of millions of people. It shows just how far privacy can be sacrificed.

This extreme is not as far removed from the average person as it may seem. Many communities around the world monitor public streets with cameras to reduce crime. Security cameras watch us at ATMs, in elevators, and in parking garages. And, as celebrities have long known, these images belong to whomever takes them, so they may appear in a newspaper, on the nightly news, or on yet another Web site.

Privacy is a complex issue that, because of technology, is increasingly becoming a social issue.

- It is an issue that we must be concerned about, both as individuals and in work we do that may intrude on the privacy of others.

- The social contract already places limits on privacy; the issue is really how much and who is in control. Different societies will likely resolve these issues in different ways.

- Some people are very reluctant to have any information known about them. Others are willing to have the most intimate details of their lives revealed to the world.

- Technology plays a role in defining privacy, in protecting privacy, and in intruding on privacy.

Although privacy in general is a fascinating subject, a full treatment is beyond the scope of this book. Here we are most interested in the business world. And, of course, in data mining itself.

Is Data Mining a Threat?

Data mining, as described in this book, is a business process that enables companies to maximize the value of the data they have collected and purchased. Data mining is a competence that addresses the strategic need of businesses to manage their customer relationships and run more efficiently.

Many of the uses of data mining are in the area of marketing. And the result, from the individual's perspective, is yet another piece of unsolicited mail. Or yet another telemarketing call at an inconvenient time. Or yet another large banner ad that delays the downloading of more interesting information. Of course, the purpose of data mining is to direct the communication to people who are more interested; however, some people resent any exposure to marketing programs.

This aspect of data mining does not seem particularly threatening to the individual. However, if we move out of the realm of direct marketing and into other areas, the lines become more blurred. Consider the section "How Sick Is She?" where a letter sent out by health care providers caused a woman to panic and created a potential legal liability. This aside points out another aspect of privacy: *Privacy violations may incur legal liability.* Even when they don't, they can be the cause of bad press, which can do considerable harm to brand or corporate image.

How Sick Is She?

In the United States, health maintenance organizations (HMOs) are striving to deliver higher quality services for less money. One of their strategies is to focus on preventive medicine, where an ounce of prevention saves tens of thousands of dollars of cure.

Diabetes, the inability of the pancreas to produce insulin, is a chronic disease that leaves sufferers susceptible to many other conditions, even when properly controlled. One common side effect is damage to the eyes, which results in the patient losing all sight.

Fortunately, there is a simple test, the retinal eye exam, that can be performed by physicians in their office. If this test indicates that damage is occurring to the eyes, the physician can intervene early enough to save the patient's sight.

One large regional HMO decided to encourage diabetics to get retinal eye exams. It pored through its databases of medical records, and identified diabetics as people who had been prescribed insulin or who had a diagnosis of a particular type of diabetes. If they hadn't had a retinal eye exam in the past 12 months, then they were sent a "Dear Diabetic" letter.

Of course, any such delving into data will expose miscoded records, so without manual review there are bound to be problems. In this case, the people putting together the list were IT specialists, not medical specialists; they had to rely on doctors and nurses to define the list of diabetics.

More disturbing than a problem of miscoding, was the case of one woman who received such a letter, but who did not have active diabetes. Although diabetes is usually chronic and incurable, there is a form of temporary diabetes, called gestational diabetes, that occurs in pregnant women.

This particular patient panicked because she interpreted the letter as an indication that her diabetes had recurred. Of course, this was not the case—despite her panic, she was quite healthy. And, as is often the case in the United States, she threatened to sue.

This anecdote teaches us that, in some cases, a spurious modeling result can have a big impact on individuals' lives. It also shows the importance of communicating domain knowledge when analyzing data.

There are two important considerations concerning data mining and threats to privacy. First is whether consumers are likely to feel threatened. Second is whether it poses a legal liability. Depending on local laws, the first may "merely" cause bad press; the second may cost millions of dollars.

The data used for data mining is really the cause of most perceived threats to privacy. There are three general ways that this data is collected:

- From operational sources, where the data in question is needed to run the business. For example, telephone companies record when telephone calls take place, but they do not record the conversations themselves. Retailers record the purchases being made, but do not attempt to track identifying features of the person making the purchase.

- By tracking interactions, particularly over the Web. An e-commerce site can maintain clickstream information identifying all the pages a customer looked at and all the ads the customer was exposed to. A media site can keep track of which articles a customer downloaded.

- By purchasing information from outside vendors. This occurs in both the brick-and-mortar world and the e-commerce world. This information may include specifics about demographics, preferences, and so on.

We often stress that the first source of data provides a wealth of behavioral information about customers, and is, in some respects, one of the key competitive advantages that companies have with respect to their existing customers. The last two sources of data often bring up concerns about privacy. Later in the chapter, we will look at how personal data is handled, at least in the United States, and how much of that data is available over the Web.

The Expectation of Privacy

Most people generally take for granted that no one is watching over their shoulder to keep track of their activities. So no one knows what we watch on television although statistically certain demographic segments are targeted by specific television shows. No one knows what we read in the newspaper, but the auto advertisements are in the automobile section, and the travel ads are in the travel section, presumably because people targeted by the ads are attracted to those sections. No one knows what purchases we make, except for the retailers who have to keep track of inventory. No one knows when we are at home, although utilities may track our electricity usage. We may voluntarily divulge bits of information, whenever or to whomever we want. But, most people generally feel better believing that information about our private lives is under control. This is the expectation of privacy.

If the Y2K computer bug leaves any lasting legacy, then part of the legacy should definitely be the constant reminder of how many activities are tracked and processed electronically, and how much information really is available. Of course telephone calls and credit card transactions are recorded, as are bill payments and magazine subscriptions. Electronic door locks in hotel rooms keep track of comings and goings. Frequent shopper cards keep track of many items we purchase. Even cell phones are starting to be able to pinpoint the exact location of the telephone. There is an extraordinary amount of data collected in the course of our daily lives. And with the rise of the Web for e-mail, e-commerce, news, and entertainment, almost no aspect of daily life will be unrecorded.

Is this a danger? On balance, we believe that it is not. We do believe that the expectation of privacy is quite reasonable. And maintaining privacy is a concern and requires vigilance. The expectation is that only the individuals or organizations that *need* information will use it. Of course, with demographic and psychographic data readily available (at least in the United States), we, as a society, have violated this expectation long before the rise of e-commerce.

The expectation of privacy leads quite readily into government policy and regulations. The purpose of this chapter is not to delve into these in great detail. It is worth noting, though, that there are two policy extremes:

Consumer rights. The more laissez-faire approach is to educate the public and ensure that individuals have control over their own information. Companies may use the information, but only after obtaining permission. This is the prevalent philosophy in the United States. It manifests itself by allowing consumers to "opt out" of specific uses of information.

Consumer protection. The stricter approach is to protect all consumers by making it illegal for companies to collect certain types of information, or to use information in certain ways. This approach tends to be favored in Europe, which has a more recent societal memory of atrocities directed toward minorities. Even in the United States, banks avoid using race when making offers of credit, because of fair credit lending laws made necessary by recent history.

Each of these approaches has good points and bad points. Although we tend to lean more toward the consumer rights side, we recognize that "consent statements" are often obscured in legalese buried in the small print of standardized contracts. On the other hand, consumer protection often makes it difficult to target individuals with tailored marketing messages that would benefit them.

The Importance of Privacy

Is all the hoopla about privacy just the result of asocial, oversensitive individuals? Actually not. Most people would agree that the images of Big Brother, conjured up by George Orwell, truly are a nightmare. It is also worth considering that violating the expectation of privacy can have serious implications for individuals.

On the other hand, people are not perfect and society plays a protective role as well. To what extent do we allow law enforcement to investigate suspicious activities? To what extent do we need to sacrifice our own personal privacy to be fully involved, economically and socially?

Anonymity and Seclusion

An open society allows anonymity, at least some of the time. So, purchases made with cash generally cannot be traced (at least not easily), and telephone calls made from pay-phones do not reveal who is making the call.

Anonymity plays a special role. For instance, witnesses to a crime may be reluctant to provide information, unless they have some protections (although *habeus corpus* gives the accused the right to face the accuser). People calling a substance abuse hotline might be less likely to seek help if they must reveal their identities. Abused women and children need safe houses, where abusive partners cannot locate them. Parents who have given their children up for adoption may never want to be found. Even for such a mundane task as students evaluating a professor, anonymity encourages evaluations to be as honest as possible.

Often, people may simply be embarrassed or reluctant to reveal certain details—and there is no reason they should have to. Is there a reason to know that a job applicant has been divorced? Probably not, even though this information may be readily available. The section "Marketing Program Leads to Divorce" tells the story of how a marketing program led to the demise of one man's marriage. Is this a violation of privacy? Or, is BT no more culpable than a neighbor who happened to witness the indiscretions?

Legal Discrimination

A pernicious problem occurs when certain forms of discrimination are legal. For instance, in the United States, health insurance companies can legally charge higher premiums to people who smoke than they can to nonsmokers. Does this give the insurance companies the right to analyze the shopping habits of applicants to determine if they ever purchase cigarettes?

Maybe we think that health insurance is special, in some way. Consider life insurance companies that either refuse to insure, or charge much higher premiums for, sky divers. If a life insurance company purchases the mailing list for a sky diving magazine, and treated everyone on that list as uninsurable because of their propensity to engage in dangerous pastimes, does that give them the right to deny insurance? Note that their actuaries may have calculated that the subscribers of sky diving magazines (as opposed to the activity itself) do pose an uninsurable risk. Is this somehow different from asking people whether they

Marketing Program Leads to Divorce

Many years ago, MCI introduced the "Friends and Family" program to encourage their customers to encourage their friends and family to switch to MCI. MCI asked their customers to provide names for the marketing effort. Of course, MCI did not really *have* to ask, since they have the data about everyone their customers call.

Across the Atlantic (according to *Wired*, 29 Mar 1999), BT is locked in a fierce battle for telephone customers. In the United Kingdom, every telephone call has a toll charge, including local telephone calls. To inspire loyalty, BT introduced their own version of a "Friends and Family" program. In this version, customers would get discounts on calls to particular numbers that they identified to BT in advance.

As a courtesy to customers, BT notices which numbers should be on the list. That is, if a customer has a frequently called number, then the company will send out a letter suggesting the number be added to the customer's friends and family list.

One lucky household received such a letter. However, in this case, the wife opened the letter, but did not recognize the most-frequently-called number. After some investigation on her part, she uncovered her husband's infidelity, and threw him out of the house.

The risk here goes beyond wrecking one marriage. The customer has threatened to sue BT saying that the promotion "wrecked" his 40-year marriage. It is good to remember that violations of privacy can have high personal costs, as well as exposing companies to legal liability.

sky dive in the first place? Many people would say yes—they have lost control over information about themselves when a third party (the magazine) sells their name.

Insurance is inherently a difficult area. After all, the idea behind insurance is to pool people with similar risks and charge premiums based on the calculated risk. Assigning risk to a "market-of-one" contradicts the benefits of pooling. And, although it may be beneficial for the vast majority of people (who are low risk), it tends to cost the few a lot more money.

The section "Violation of Privacy = Loss of Career" tells the story of Timothy McVeigh, who was discharged from the Navy because an illegal violation of his privacy suggested that he might be gay. This is an example of someone's job being at risk due to privacy violations. This may seem to be a special case, because the American military has an expressed policy of discriminating against gay people—and few institutions have such explicit discriminatory policies. It does bring up the issue that in a world of Web pages and chat rooms, much more information is potentially available about individuals, and this information could be used to deny employment, credit, or insurance.

Violation of Privacy = Loss of Career

Many forms of discrimination are illegal in the United States; and most forms of discrimination, if not illegal, are frowned upon in recognition of the need for diversity in the workforce. However, discrimination against gay men and lesbians is institutionalized in the military forces in the United States. Suspicion of homosexuality (as opposed to evidence of sexual relations) is sufficient for discharging members.

The case of former-US Naval Officer Timothy McVeigh is an example of how a violation of one individual's privacy cost him his livelihood. He was a 17-year veteran when, in December 1997, a civilian naval employee received an e-mail from someone she thought might be him. Unsure of the sender, she checked the online profile, where she found someone described only as "Tim" of Honolulu who marital status was checked off as "gay." She forwarded the information to the Navy.

During the investigation, an official from the Navy called up AOL and talked to a customer service representative. The representative tracked the screen name back to McVeigh. Based only on this evidence, the Navy held a trial and discharged McVeigh, just three years before he was eligible for a pension.

There are two violations of privacy here:

- First, AOL violated its own privacy policy, which specified that no subscriber information would be released without authorization.
- Second, the Navy violated the Electronic Communications Privacy Act (ECPA) of 1986, which requires government agents to identify themselves and present a court order to get information, such as online subscriber names.

An open question about privacy is who enforces the policies and the laws. For the most part, the recourse provided by ECPA is to allow civil law suits for damages.

The case of Timothy McVeigh has a happier ending. On appeal, the courts ruled that, indeed, the Navy did illegally violate the privacy of McVeigh during the course of the investigation. The Navy gave him an honorable discharge with the pension. AOL also settled with McVeigh for an undisclosed amount of money, for violating his privacy.

Illegal Activities and Public Good

On the other hand, many activities are illegal. Anonymous cash transactions are well and good. However, if the purchased materials are for making a bomb, then we, as a society, want law enforcement to know. Uncensored corporate e-mail is nice, but sexual innuendo or racial jokes in e-mail can lead to a hostile work environment.

It is not permitted to sell some goods, such as pornography, alcohol, and tobacco, to children. In order to purchase these goods, we give up a little bit of privacy—by identifying our age—for the greater public good of protecting children. Anonymous e-mail may be a great benefit for some groups, such as battered women seeking information. However, the contents of anonymous email may also be threatening and conspiratorial.

Law in the United States (at least) has recognized that there is a balance between the public good and individual privacy. So, with a court order, it is possible to tap a phone line or to find the identity of an online user profile. Under other circumstances, individuals are protected from such intrusions.

It is illegal, of course, to sell credit card numbers, PIN numbers, telephone access codes, and similar information. However, since these numbers are valuable, such thefts still occur. And when they do occur, they can impose financial hardships on individuals. In the US, there is a limit of $50 liability for charges on stolen cards; in other places, such limits do not exist and many cardholders may have no insurance.

These types of incidents make companies very, very careful. For instance, when offering credit through the mail, it is critical to be sure that the right person is responding—and not "borrowing" someone else's identity. In the 1970s, the Federal government made it illegal to send credit cards through the mail, without the permission of the cardholder. In more recent years, we have faced the problem of "credit checks" being sent through the mail—and occasionally cashed by someone other than the intended recipient.

In some cases, there can be an actual public good at stake. Consider antibiotics: These drugs are used to cure certain bacterial diseases. The regimen for most oral antibiotics usually requires taking them over the course of several days, often longer than a week. Often, the patient starts feeling better after the first dose—because most of the disease-causing germs have been killed off—most, but not all. That is the problem. The surviving bacteria have withstood the first dose of the antibiotic, but the full dose would eventually kill them. However, the small number that survive the first doses are a little bit resistant to the antibiotic.

To avoid developing antibiotic resistant strains, it is critically important to take the full dose. Once a strain of bacteria has developed resistance to one particular medicine, that medicine is no longer useful. It is worth remembering that before the discovery of antibiotics, such diseases were the leading cause of death.

In the United States, oral antibiotics are available only by prescription. This is supposed to mean that a medical doctor instructs patients about the proper use of the medicine. Consider the implications of selling medicine over the Web. The Web site itself may be outside the United States, so the American government has no authority. There may be no doctor-patient interaction, and people may not be informed sufficiently to take the full dose of medicine—whether because of ignorance, limited finances, or other reasons. Where does the greater good take precedence over the right of individuals to make such purchases—especially where the consumer's government has no authority?

Information in the Material World

Once upon a time, if a car were illegally parked in front of your home, then you would have difficulty tracking down the car's owner. Of course you could, by trekking to the Department of Motor Vehicles and looking through the license plate number in a file, discover the owner. It would be unlikely, however since it would be time-consuming and inconvenient.

Now such information is readily available on the Web (although many states, including California and Michigan, have passed legislation restricting access to motor vehicle registration data). It is possible to type in a telephone number in the United States and not only get the owner and the address, but a convenient map showing the location with an option for driving directions! Curious about fathers who don't pay child support, or who is registered to vote (and what party)?—the information is available electronically.

That the government provides such information should not be surprising. The government has always regularly published many different types of information. Having open lists of voters, for instance, is part of the foundation of democracy, helping candidates for public office as well as deterring voter fraud. Having the information available with a few clicks of a mouse, though, introduces a new element. Access is orders of magnitude easier, resulting in a qualitative change as well as a quantitative change.

The private sector is also a prodigious collector of information. Probably one of the best known (and best protected) sources of information is the credit history record. This contains information on all loans and credit cards held by an individual, including monthly balances, late payments, defaults, and so on. Credit history is well-protected, and such information is available only to a company making an offer of credit to the individual—it cannot be purchased for other purposes. And further, customers have the right to see their credit report and a grievance procedure when there are problems.

Other data, though, is much less protected. For instance, Abacus maintains a database of purchases made through catalogs. This information is available to the hundreds of catalog companies in the consortium that forms Abacus. Most of you are probably not even aware that such a list exists.

Subscription lists are often freely sold. Want to reach Hispanics? Buy the mailing list to *People en Español*. Want to introduce an audience to the wonders of

Olestra? Buy the mailing list to *Cooking Light*. Want to reach IT managers implementing enterprise-wide solutions? Buy the mailing list to *Intelligent Enterprise*. And beyond magazines, some nonprofit groups and political organizations sell information about members. Some conferences sell attendee lists. Some retailers sell information about purchase patterns. In other words, information about individuals is a valuable commodity, and many companies, such as Acxiom, Polk, Experian, and First Data, provide such data.

This has an impact on data mining as well. These sorts of external information are often used for building models, as we have seen in several chapters.

Information in the Electronic World

The electronic world is introducing a whole new dimension to the problem of privacy. Prior to e-commerce, computers mimicked business practices in the material world. Magazines have existed for centuries and, with or without computers, they have always been able to sell their subscription lists. Computers make the process more efficient, but they do not radically change the business processes.

The Web, the world of interconnected commerce, information, and entertainment, has some new dimensions. For the first time, it is possible to track:

- Advertising messages that have been seen by a particular individual, over time

- Advertising messages that a particular individual is responding to

- The content an individual has been exposed to

- Especially, the advertising messages, content, and purchases made throughout the electronic world—as opposed to through a single vendor

The difference between the electronic world and the material world is significant. In the material world, the magazine publisher may know which magazines you subscribe to. In the electronic world, the content provider knows which ads you have seen, which articles you have read, and which sites you have visited.

E-commerce is still in its infancy. Content providers are still determining how they will work together and how they will share information among themselves. Governments have not yet fully addressed the privacy issues arising on the Web. Web sites are still busy getting up and running, attracting consumers, investment, and advertising dollars; they are not yet fully in the business of using the data that they collect. Consumers still make only a small portion of their purchases online, so they are not yet fully sensitized to the privacy issues.

This is all in the process of changing. Let us look at this from two perspectives: one, despite being a completely automated media, it is not that easy to spot the individual on the Web; and two, how is information is shared and what direction is e-privacy likely to take?

Identifying the Customer

Surprisingly, identifying the consumer on the Web is perhaps harder than identifying consumers in the material world. After all, there is no Web-equivalent of a social security number or street address. And consumers are reluctant to give such information online, unless they are in the midst of a purchase.

When talking about customers online, there are three different streams of data that are available to identify users: clickstream events, cookies, and registrations.

Clickstream Events

Every Web page is identified by a uniform record locator (URL), such as http://www.data-miners.com. This URL specifies that the computer protocol for accessing the page is http. The part following the double slashes is the name of the computer. And, this URL could have a file path at the end, although it does not in this case (it actually defaults to www.data-miners.com/index.shtml).

When a user clicks on a Web address, the browser passes on information to the server handling the desired page. Some of this information, such as browser type, CPU, operating system, and screen resolution, is quite harmless and can be used to optimize the page being returned. The most interesting information is the address of the referring page. This makes it possible to follow all the pages visited, when they stay within a single site (or on cooperating sites).

Using this information, it is possible to determine things like:

- When people visit an automobile site looking for information on vans, they also look for information on sports utility vehicles.
- When people visit Amazon and look for technical books, they almost never visit the music portion of the site.
- When people shop for insurance, the site with the cheapest quote gets twice as many clickthroughs as the site with the second cheapest quote.

Clickstreams do not track individuals over time, or even when they start bouncing among many different Web sites. They only connect Web pages together to describe a single visit. There is really no analogy in the brick-and-mortar world. It is as if someone followed each shopper around a shopping mall, and jotted down which stores each shopper visits, which departments the shopper goes in, and which items the shopper looks at—all without identifying the shopper or recognizing the shopper the next time he or she goes to the mall.

Cookies

A cookie is a small amount of information sent by a Web server to be stored by the Web browser. The site that sent the information—and only the site that sent the information—is authorized to retrieve it later or to update the information. Cookies allow Web sites to remember information about a user in between visits—a major advantage over raw clickstream information. (A good source of information on cookies is www.cookiecentral.com.)

Cookies themselves are stored in a text file that can readily be read. More recent versions of browsers give users the ability to control which, if any, cookies they want to store. The information itself is, more often than not, unintelligible, because the format is whatever that particular server wants to store, and may even be encoded. Happily, a Web server can only read cookies for its own site.

Cookies bring up privacy issues because some remote server is placing information on the user's own hard disk. The defaults for most browsers are to allow cookies, with no notification given to the user. However, browsers typically do have an option for notifying users about cookies and it is relatively easy to eliminate all cookies from your computer (or to selectively eliminate cookies for a few sites). It is not so much the cookies themselves that may tread on privacy; it is how Web sites use them.

A first observation about cookies is that they are rather limited. They do not identify an individual; they identify a browser/computer combination. This results in:

- The same person using two different browsers on the same computer has two different sets of cookies, one for each browser.
- Multiple people using the same computer (with the same login) and the same browser all share the same cookies.
- The same person using multiple computers has a different set of cookies on each computer.

And, of course, it is possible for users to "turn off" cookies; sites are unable to track these users over time. Despite these limitations, cookies are useful. For each cookie, the site can know:

- Which preferences have been set
- Which pages have been visited

- Which referring pages were visited prior to coming to this site
- Which ads have been displayed

This information is often used immediately to choose Web ads for display, as described in the sidebar.

One other interesting note about cookies is that many sites—including most e-commerce sites and sites that allow customization—do use cookies. This means that the cookie file also keeps track of which Web pages someone has been visiting—a warning to anyone who borrows a computer!

Registration

The third way that sites keep track of visitors is by having visitors register at the site, typically using a login name and password. Registration serves many purposes:

- The site can customize itself for the user.
- The site can offer additional services, such as e-mail, messaging, and stock quotes.
- The site can keep track of very confidential information, such as credit card numbers, for e-commerce.
- The site can identify the user, and differentiate among multiple users from the same machine.

Users that register at sites often use their registration regardless of the machine they use to access the Web. A cookie keeps information only on a single machine. A registration keeps the information on the server computer, so it is accessible regardless of where the user logs in from. The two capabilities are often used together. So, the login/password combination is often maintained in a cookie for the convenience of users who do not want to retype their name and password every time they access the site.

Registration offers all of the capabilities of cookies. One of their advantages, though, is that the user is fully aware of where he or she is registering. Users can also be encouraged to read privacy policies (as well as other relevant business practices) during the course of registration.

Putting It All Together

Clickstreams, cookies, and registrations are important tools for driving e-commerce. They are responsible for much of the popularity and potential that the Web offers as a new channel for reaching customers.

Directed Advertising on the Web

How does directed advertising work on the Web? In some ways, it is quite similar to how advertising works in the material world. Advertising agencies often purchase space in media—newspapers, magazines, television channels, radio ads. Because they purchase the space in bulk, they get good rates. The agencies then sell this space to their clients, trying to match client interests to the appropriate media. Ads for hip clothing are more likely to appear in *Teen People* than in *National Geographic*.

The Web offers the same facility, with one major advantage. The agencies can actually keep track of individual consumers (or at least of browser/computer pairs) by using cookies. The largest advertising agency on the Web, Doubleclick (www.doubleclick.com), is an example of how powerful this can be.

Many people who look at their cookie files will find a cookie for doubleclick.net, even though they have never knowingly visited the site. However, they have, even if inadvertently. Many sites display banner ads on their Web pages. They sell the space for the banner ad to Doubleclick, who in turn has a bunch of companies that want to purchase advertising space on the Web (and many sites both sell space and purchase space on other sites). Doubleclick determines which ad to put in front of a user looking at a Web page.

And cookies let them do this. The Doubleclick cookies help the agency keep track of which Doubleclick sites a user has visited, and which ads the user has already seen. This allows them to determine interests, at least broadly, and to choose the most appropriate ad for that user.

Many sites, but by no means all of them, are Doubleclick clients. The advertising agency knows when a person visits one of these sites. So they know if a person tends to visits sites directed toward news, or toward cars, or toward travel, or children's media, or whatever. Using this information, they can direct the appropriate ad to that user. Of course, for users who do not have a cookie, they will still get a banner ad—just one that is more generic and less likely to be of interest to them.

Doubleclick has no way of actually identifying individuals. They do not keep e-mail addresses, telephone numbers, names, or other identifying information. They are building profiles of Web behavior that they can use, within their network of clients, to direct advertising—in much the same way that advertising agencies purchase advertising space on certain television shows to reach target audiences.

Privacy has been an important issue since the founding of the Web. The underlying technology—from the network protocols to http—does not require that users identify themselves publicly. In addition, the Web was founded on a philosophy of self-regulation, with minimal governmental interference. The fact that a Web server could be anywhere and still accessible everywhere diminishes the regulatory power of any single government.

This philosophy has resulted in moves toward self-regulation. The TRUSTe initiative (www.etrust.org) has developed a "seal of approval" for privacy on the Internet. The basic proposition is that sites must post a privacy policy and adhere to that policy. TRUSTe also helps sites develop such a policy, corresponding to industry norms, and audits compliance to them. They are developing additional seals, for instance, to identify sites appropriate for children.

Major advertisers have always shied away from placing their ads in contexts, such as television documentaries dealing with controversial subjects, that might lead consumers to have a negative association with the company placing the ad. On the Web, companies are also demanding that sites where they advertise have posted privacy statements. These two initiatives will likely lead to almost every site that collects any sort of information having a posted privacy policy.

Such a policy is good. However, the example of Doubleclick shows that networks of companies also share information. Another example is Engage.com, which collects information about Web usage and sells the information. Engage has the ability to tie together all the cookies left by members of their consortium, allowing Engage to understand behavior across multiple sites. In addition, they also collect some registration information from sites that register users. However, like Doubleclick, they do not collect any identifying information such as name, address, e-mail address, or telephone number.

Their interest is in being able to rent profiles so subscribing companies can customize content, by targeting ads, personalizing Web sites, and so on. This idea of renting profiles is quite similar to what companies such as Acxiom, Experion, and Polk (among others) do in the nonelectronic world. Engage has a very detailed privacy policy (and was an early adopter of TRUSTe), and they refuse to collect information from a variety of controversial sites, including sexually explicit sites, medical sites, and "hate" sites.

The e-world has some very interesting traits. When users identify themselves, then a site can customize itself to meet the needs of that user. Companies such as Primary Knowledge (www.primaryknowledge.com) and Blue Martini (www.bluemartini.com) help companies analyze Web data for customization purposes, to understand their customers, and to understand investments made over the Web. This "customized experience" is one of the very important features of the Web as a new channel for reaching consumers.

For many purposes, though, it is not necessary to actually identify the person at the other end. You may want to know that they are in the 8–10 age group—and offer a banner ad for an age-specific site. Or know that they bought jeans three months ago on the Web, and offer them another pair. In the material world, making such direct offers requires actually having identifying information, such as name, address, telephone number, social security number. On the Web, cookies can be much more anonymous. The question is simply "what do I know about this stream of binary digits?" The answer is a customized Web experience.

The Promise of Data Mining

The issue of privacy points out that data mining exists in the context of a larger society. When we are using data mining for customer relationship management, we are bringing the weight of technology to bear on the challenge of understanding other people. We are trying to predict what their actions are likely to be in the future. We are learning from what people did in the past to predict what they need in the future.

In principle, this activity is no different from the personal relationships that once permeated a nostalgic past of corner stores, friendly banks, and helpful insurance agents. In that world, people learned from their own experience and applied the results to their line of work.

Data mining is about expanding this learning culture to companies that are also big enough to reap economies of scale. The Wal-Mart on the edge of town, the ATM machines outside the former bank branch, insurance on the Web—these all exist for a reason, because they offer more efficient distribution networks, lower prices, and greater convenience. The large impersonal corporation, despite advertising to the contrary, has in many cases lost sight of its customers. The customers are merely numbers. And disconnected numbers across incompatible databases, at that.

The promise of data mining is to return the focus of businesses to serving customers and to providing efficient business processes. This is true in the material world, where, we hope, more targeted marketing will lead to more satisfied, more profitable customers, as well as fewer items of wasted mail and fewer telephone interruptions during dinner. It is even more true in the world of electronic commerce, where the entire image of a corporation can potentially be personalized for every customer.

Throughout this book, we have shown how mastering data mining is more than mastering a bunch of advanced algorithms. Mastering data mining requires incorporating data analysis into the business and asking questions. Collecting data unobtrusively and with informed consent, recognizing important patterns, and acting on the results in a responsible way—this is truly "The Virtuous Cycle of Data Mining."